TRIAL PRACTICE SERIES

Impeachment of Witnesses

The Cross-Examiner's Art

Roberto Aron (LL.M.)
New York University

Kevin Thomas Duffy
United States District Judge, Southern District of New York

Jonathan L. Rosner
Member of the New York Bar

Shepard's/McGraw-Hill, Inc.
P.O. Box 35300
Colorado Springs, Colorado 80935-3530

McGRAW-HILL, INC.
New York • St. Louis • San Francisco • Auckland • Bogotá
Caracas • Colorado Springs • Hamburg • Lisbon • London
Madrid • Mexico • Milan • Montreal • New Delhi • Panama
Paris • San Juan • São Paulo • Singapore • Sydney • Tokyo • Toronto

12345678910 SHHI 909876543210

Library of Congress Cataloging-in-Publication Data

Aron, Roberto.
Impeachment of witnesses : the cross-examiner's art / Roberto Aron, Kevin Thomas Duffy, Jonathan L. Rosner.
p. cm. — (Trial practice series)
Includes index.
ISBN 0-07-172007-3
1. Witnesses—United States. 2. Impeachments—United States. I. Duffy, Kevin Thomas. II. Rosner, Jonathan L., 1932-. III. Title. IV. Series.
KF8950.A96 1990
347.73'66—dc20
[347.30766] 90.43882
CIP

ISBN 0-07-172007-3

The Sponsoring Editor for this book was Margaret Makar and the Legal Editor was Laurel Cohn.

Shepard's Trial Practice Series

Advocacy: The Art of Pleading a Cause
Attorney Fee Awards
Constitutional Limitations of Criminal Procedure
Cross-Examination of Witnesses: The Litigator's Puzzle
Defense of Equal Employment Claims
Engineering Evidence
Eyewitness Testimony: Strategies and Tactics
Federal Appeals: Jurisdiction and Practice
Guide to Multistate Litigation
Hearsay Handbook Second Edition
How to Prepare Witnesses for Trial
Jury Selection
Psychiatric and Psychological Evidence
Questioning Techniques and Tactics
Statistics in Litigation: Practical Applications for Lawyers
Testimonial Privileges
Toxic Torts: Litigation of Hazardous Substance Cases
Trial Communication Skills

Dedication

I dedicate this book to the Faculties of Law of three Universities: To the University of Chile where I received my Bachelor of Laws degree; to New York University where I received my Master's Degrees, and where I am still studying for a third. At both Universities I was taught to understand the law, to believe in justice and to love my profession. Finally, to Tel Aviv University for giving me the opportunity to teach trial advocacy, and to learn that to teach is to learn twice.

To all of them my gratitude and deepest thanks for making me a lawyer and a teacher, and for the ethics and human principles that they instilled in me.

Roberto Aron

Even though some have advised that dedications of each of one's books should be different, I believe that my wife and my family deserve much more than just having another book dedicated to them. Yet, mentioning here their patience and support is but one of the few ways available publicly to acknowledge that, without them, I would be unable to do even this. Thus, this book is dedicated to Judge Irene J. Duffy and Kevin, Irene Moira, Gavin, and Patrick.

Kevin Thomas Duffy

I dedicate this book to four persons whose love of and dedication to the law guided me to this point in my life: My beloved father, Oscar S. Rosner, practicing lawyer for fifty years, whose goodness, ethics, and wisdom have guided me from childhood; Robert B. McKay, teacher and friend, who taught me that law should be an instrument for good; Honorable Alexander Bicks, who showed me that the end result of litigation was extremely human and more than merely application of the law to a set of facts; and William M. Tendy, mentor and friend, whose example enabled me to develop the skills essential to bring the law to life in a courtroom; all are gone but with me forever.

Jonathan L. Rosner

Acknowledgments

Since one of the cornerstones of justice is to give each person what is due, the authors must recognize with sincere gratitude the collaboration of the trial lawyers who made possible the presentation of their works in Part Two of the book, and to the judges who so kindly answered our questionnaire included in Part Three of this volume.

Roberto Aron expresses his gratitude also to his colleagues James C. Gray, Jr. and Bruce Guitter, for their advice and review of parts of the manuscript.

Roberto Aron

Judge Kevin Thomas Duffy acknowledges the help that he has received over the years from all of his law clerks in the formulation and the articulation of the precepts laid out in this book. Particular mention must be made of Jacqueline LiCalzi and Robyn Stanton, who have given freely of themselves in assisting in the editing and the proofreading of the manuscript of his contributions to this volume.

Appreciation is also expressed to my many friends among the judiciary who took the time and effort to complete the questionnaire which is the focus of the third part of this book. The answers given by some of those surveyed were so thought-provoking as to cause changes in the text of the book and in this judge's thinking.

Kevin Thomas Duffy

There is little in a trial to exceed the excitement of an artistic cross-examination which culminates in the devastating impeachment of a witness. Few lawyers are sufficiently practiced to be able to attain that ultimate goal on a consistent basis. The exceptional litigating lawyers whose pieces illuminate Part Two of this work are among the elite few in that regard and we wish to acknowledge with deep appreciation their talents and generous contributions of time and wisdom. Indeed, sharing of experiences is what distinguished the litigating bar through the years and we are privileged and delighted to continue that tradition.

Jonathan L. Rosner is, as always, indebted to his partner, Andrew J. Goodman, whose warm friendship, pithy comments, continuing encouragement and generous indulgence allowed for completion of work. Jonathan L. Rosner is indebted, as well, to his friend and co-author, Kevin Thomas Duffy, whose continuous good humor when there was little to laugh at kept things in perspective.

Jonathan L. Rosner

Preface

Notwithstanding the importance of the impeachment of witnesses and decisive effects impeachment can have during a trial, most authors of legal texts refer to it in only one chapter of their book, sometimes combined with cross-examination.

The ability to persuade the trier of fact of the rightness of one's cause is significantly advanced by the discrediting of adverse witnesses. Indeed, a carefully conceived, painstakingly prepared and inspired impeachment can be pivotal to any trial.

The ability to satisfy the legal and dramatic requirements of an effective impeachment requires that the litigating lawyer have an instinctive knowledge of the law of evidence, an ability to communicate verbally on many levels, an intuitive sense of what moves persons and how they react and a burning desire to excel. Indeed, that is likely why no matter how long one is admitted to the bar it is still called practicing law.

Considering the essentiality of impeachment of witnesses in the judicial process, the authors decided to treat this theme from as many angles possible and to dedicate a full volume to it.

In this book, the trial lawyer's role in impeaching witnesses is considered as an art. As such, the subject is analyzed in depth: Beginning with an historical overview of Jewish and Anglo-Saxon Law and the history of American Law of Evidence relating to Impeachment; continuing with the basis for impeachment of witnesses; the problem if to impeach or not; the detailed examination of witnesses characteristics; strategies for impeachment; the impeachment of expert witnesses; and ending with an analysis of the influence of a witness's demeanor. We have tried to make a thorough study of the subject.

In addition, we were fortunate to have the gracious collaboration of outstanding expert trial lawyers. We have included in the Second Part of the book articles contributed by F. Lee Bailey, Norman L. Cousins, William E. Johnson, Kenneth M. Robinson, Karl F. Salzer, Patrick A. Tuite, and Dianne J. Weaver.

In order to have a complete picture of the subject of impeachment of witnesses, we also carried out a research study (Part Three of the book) asking judges for their opinions and reactions to the different aspects of a lawyer's performance during cross-examination and impeachment of witnesses. We hope that the judges' answers will be of great interest to the reader and a useful guide for trial lawyers.

It is hoped that within this modest volume on impeachment of witnesses the law student and the practicing lawyer may find some new way to approach an old problem or at least an impetus to ponder how to improve upon the impeachment that was assayed in the practicing lawyer's last few trials.

The Authors

Contents

Part Two Contributions by Other Authors

Part Two Contributions by Other Authors

Part Three Research Work

Tables

Part One
Contributions by the Authors

1 Introduction

§1.01 A Historical Overview of Jewish Law in Impeachment Matters

Cross-examination is the procedural framework for impeachment. In order to understand the basic principles which permitted a court in Talmudic times to prevent incompetent or disqualified persons from being trial witnesses, it is necessary to review the system of interrogation which existed in those times and the commandments relevant to witnesses.

The Talmud is zealous and precise when establishing the procedural rules for questioning witnesses. First of all, it prohibits any physical violence in the questioning. The objective of the inquiry is to find the truth without harming the witness's sense of human dignity.

During the witness's examination, the guiding objective is to persuade the witness to tell the truth and not to arouse his or her imagination.

As noted by Professor Aaron Kirshenbaum,

> The basic rule of rabbinic criminal jurisprudence is found in Deuteronomy 17:6: "At the mouth of two witnesses, or three witnesses, shall he

that is to die be put to death." The rabbis of the Talmud asked the obvious question: "If the evidence is established by two witnesses, why does Scripture specify 'three' as well?" Their answer is unusual:

> "In order to equate three with two. Just as three witnesses may establish the falseness of two other witnesses [since they outnumber them], so two witnesses may establish the falseness of three. And whence do we derive the rule that two may establish the falseness even of a hundred? Scripture teaches, 'Witnesses' (M. Makkot 1:7)."

The reasoning behind this rather odd passage would appear to be as follows. By prescribing capital convictions on the basis of the testimony of two eye-witnesses, Scripture has in effect stated that the testimony of two witnesses represents the ultimate in judicial truth—the thought being, "[i]f three witnesses could produce 'more truth' than two, how could the Torah regard the evidence of two as sufficient to put a man to death?" Once this fundamental notion is accepted, it follows that no group of witnesses contradicting another group of witnesses can render the latter group false, nor can they brand them as liars; for the court has no more reason to accept the testimony of the former as more valid than that of the latter. In other words, conflicting groups of witnesses, regardless of their quantitative components, can only create a stalemate; they cannot establish the falseness of their rivals' allegations.

Scripture, however, does proclaim that false witnesses shall be punished by the courts in the same manner as they had purposed to do to their intended victim (Deuteronomy 19:19). How can this commandment be fulfilled? The rabbis solved this problem by interpreting the verse as referring to a single type of false witnesses, whom they called "conspiring witnesses (edim zomemim)."[1]

The framework for interrogation of witnesses, including cross-examination, was established in rabbinical law by three basic procedures: *Hakirah, Derishah,* and *Bedikah.*

As explained by Justice Haim H. Cohn, of the Supreme Court of Israel,

> The Biblical injunction "thou shalt inquire and make search and ask diligently" (Deut. 13:15), was literally interpreted to require testifying witnesses to be subject to three different kinds of examination: inquiry (hakirah), investigation (derishah), and interrogation (bedikah) (Sanhedrin 40a). Originally, the rule was held to apply in all cases, both civil and criminal (Sanh. 4:1), but it was later limited to apply to criminal and possibly tort cases, so as not to render the recovery of debts too cumbersome and thus "shut the doors before borrowers" (Sanh. 3a, 32a; Yev. 122b; Yad, Edut 3:1; Sh. Ar. HM 30:1). It is the duty of the court, according to Maimonides, "to interrogate the witnesses and examine them and

[1] Kirshenbaum, *Prosecution and Defense in Jewish Criminal Law,* 5 (No 4) Dimension 5, 5-10 (Summer 1971). Reprinted by permission.

question them extensively and probe into their accuracy and refer them back to the previous questions so as to make them desist from or change their testimony if it was in any way faulty; but the court must be very careful lest, by such examination, 'the witness might learn to lie' " (Yad, Edut 1:4 based on Sanh. 32b). The purpose of the examination is, of course, to find out if the witnesses are being truthful and consistent; even though all potentially unreliable witnesses hopefully would have been excluded by disqualification, further precautionary rules were deemed necessary to ensure the witness's veracity.[2]

§1.02 Incompetent and Disqualified Witnesses

Hundreds of instructions were given to judges in Jewish courts so that impartiality would prevail and discrimination against one of the parties would not occur. Some examples of such instructions are: "Do not do evil in judgment; do not offend the poor, and don't be impressed by the face of the wealthy; with justice judge your fellows" (*Leviticus* 19:15); "The judge must not need to be benevolent with one of the parties and tough with the other; neither to invite one of them to sit down and let the other to be standing. Because if the judge is partial toward one of the parties the other will feel powerless and confused" (Sanhedrin, Fol 4).

The general principle regarding testimony was that "any person who knew or had any evidence on behalf of his fellow was under a duty to make it known" (*compare Leviticus* 5, 1).

There were two main exceptions to the general principle: (a) persons incompetent to be witnesses on account of personal status; and (b) persons disqualified to be witnesses because of questions regarding their veracity, interest in the case, or trustworthiness.

These exceptions are discussed in the next section.

§1.03 —Disqualification of Witnesses

Justice H. H. Cohn of the Supreme Court of Israel discusses witness disqualification at length:

> No witness may say that he is (or was) wicked so as to disqualify himself from attesting or testifying (Sanh. 9b; Yad, Edut 121:2; Sh. Ar. HM 34:25). A party who wishes to disqualify witnesses of the other party has to prove their incompetency by the evidence of at least two other competent witnesses (Sanh. 3:1; Yad, Edut 12:1; Sh. Ar. HM 34:25). Disqualification as a witness is not regarded as a penalty, and hence no previous warning is required; but in cases of improper or contemptible conduct and minor transgressions, it has been suggested that a person should not be disquali-

---

[2] H.H. Cohn, The Principles of Jewish Law 609, 610 (Justice Menachem Elon ed 1978). Reprinted by permission of Keter Publishing House Jerusalem Ltd.

> fied as a witness unless previously warned that this would happen if he persisted in his conduct (Yad, loc. cit.; Sh. Ar., HM 34:24).
>
> Where a witness attested an act or document, he cannot testify that he was incompetent to do so (Ket. 18b & 19b; Yad, Edut 3:7; Sh. Ar., HM 46:37). It might be otherwise if his signature could be identified only by his own testimony; if he could be heard to deny his signature, he ought also to be heard to say that his signature was worthless (Ket 2:3; Sh. Ar. HM loc. cit.) always provided he did not incriminate himself.
>
> Where the court has reason to suspect that a person offered as a witness is incompetent, it may decline to admit his testimony (Rema HM 34:25; Yad, To'en 2:3), and ought to turn him down as an attesting witness (Sh. Ar. HM 92:5 and Siftei Kohen and loc.).
>
> Where a witness has given evidence, and it subsequently transpires that he was incompetent, his evidence will be regarded as wrongly admitted and the case reopened only if the incompetence was derived from Scripture or had been announced by public proclamation (Sanh. 26b; Yad, Edut 11:6; Sh. Ar. HM 34:23). A person called to attest or testify together with another person whom he knows to be incompetent as a witness must decline to attest or testify, even though the incompetence of the other is not yet known or proved to the court (Yad, Edut 10:1; Sh. Ar. HM 34:1). The rationale of this rule appears to be that since the incompetence of any one witness invalidates the evidence of the whole group of witnesses to which he belongs (Mak. 1:8; Yad, Edut 5:3; Sh. Ar. HM 36:1), if the first man attested or testified notwithstanding the other's incompetence, the evidence would be nullified (cf. Siftei Kohen HM 34, n.3). In civil cases, parties may stipulate that, notwithstanding any incompetence, the evidence of witnesses named shall be accepted and acted upon by the court (Sanh. 3:2; Yad, Sanhedrin 7:2; Sh. Ar. HM 22:1).
>
> Disqualification no longer holds: in the case of criminals, after their punishment is completed (Yad, Edut 12:4; Sh. Ar. HM 34:29); in the case of wicked persons not liable to punishment, when it is proved to the satisfaction of the court that they have repented and that their conduct is now irreproachable (ibid) there are detailed provisions as to what acts constitute sufficient proof of repentance (Yad, Edut 12:5-10; Sh. Ar. HM 34:29-35); and in the case of relatives, after the relationship or affinity has come to an end (Yad, Edut 14:1; Sh. Ar. HM 33:12).[3]

In civil cases also, the disqualification to be a witness was not absolute; a party could waive any disqualification of a witness and agree to let him or her testify (Mordecai, Sanhedrin 686).

---

[3] H.H. Cohn, The Principles of Jewish Law 608, 609 (Justice Menachem Elon ed 1978). Reprinted by permission of Keter Publishing House Jerusalem Ltd.

§1.04 Roots of Testimony and Impeachment in Anglo-Saxon Law

"To say truth, although it is not necessary for counsel to know what the history of a point is, but to know how it now stands resolved, yet it is a wonderful accomplishment, and, without it, a lawyer cannot be accounted learned in the law."[4]

With these words of Roger North in mind, this chapter will summarize some basic points about the different kinds of trials in England, the sources of oral evidence, witnesses, and impeachment of witnesses, as a foreword to the remainder of this book.

Different Kinds of Trials

A court of justice is the forum in which trials are conducted. For our study of the history of English trials, we will refer to the works of Sir William Blackstone, the English jurist and writer on law (1723-80).

Blackstone wrote that the species of trials in civil cases are seven: by record, by inspection or examination, by certificate, by witnesses, by wager of battle, by wager of law, and by jury. We will quote Blackstone in reference to trial by witnesses and trial by jury.

> TRIAL BY WITNESSES. This is the only method of trial known to the civil law, in which the judge is left to form in his own breast his sentence upon the credit of the witnesses examined; but it is very rarely used in our law [in England] which prefers the trial by jury before it in almost every instance.
>
> TRIAL BY JURY. This is a trial that hath been used time out of mind in this nationa, and seems to have been coeval with the first civil government thereof.
>
> Trials by jury in civil cases are of two kinds: extraordinary and ordinary.
>
> The Grand Assize. The first species of extraordinary trial by jury is the Grand Assize, which was instituted by King Henry the Second in parliament, by way of alternative offered to the choice of the tenant or defendant in a writ of right, instead of the barbarous and unchristian custom of dueling.
>
> On Attaint. Another species of extraordinary juries, is the jury to try an attaint, which is a process commenced against a former jury, for bringing in a false verdict . . . . This jury is to consist of twenty-four of the best men in the county, who are called the "grand" jury in the attaint, to distinguish them from the first or "petit" jury; and these are to hear and try the goodness of the former verdict.[5]

---

[4] Quoted in 5 Sir W.S. Holdsworth, A History of English Law (1927) (mentioned in each front page of the nine volumes).

[5] 2 W. Blackstone, Commentaries of the Laws of England 1102-16 (1899). Reprinted with permission from *Commentaries of the Laws of England* (pp. 1102-1116, Vol II, 1899), published by Callaghan & Co., 155 Pfingsten Rd., Deerfield, IL. 60015.

With regard to the ordinary trial by jury in civil cases, it is important for the purpose of this book, to follow Blackstone's words about the participation of witnesses, omitting references to other parts of the ordinary trial.

> Blackstone wrote: Evidence in the trial by jury is of two kinds, either that which is given in proof, or that which the jury may receive by their own private knowledge. The former, or "proofs" (to which in common speech the name of evidence is usually confined), are either written, or "parol," that is by word of mouth.
>
> . . . With regard to "parol" evidence or "witnesses"; it must first be remembered, that there is a process to bring them in by writ of "subpoena ad testificandum": which commands them, laying aside all pretences and excuses, to appear at the trial on pain of economic sanctions . . . . This compulsory process, to bring in unwilling witnesses, and the additional terrors of an attachment in case of disobedience, are of excellent use in the thorough investigation of truth: and, upon the same principle.
>
> . . . All witnesses, of whatever religion or county, that have the use of their reason, are to be received and examined, except such as are "infamous," or such as are "interested" in the event of the cause. All others are "competent" witnesses; though secrets of the cause by the party himself, shall be compelled, or perhaps allowed, to give evidence of such conversation or matters of privacy, as came to his knowledge by virtue of such trust and confidence: but he may be examined as to mere matters of fact, as the execution of a deed or the like, which might have come to his knowledge without being intrusted in the cause.
>
> . . . The oath administered to the witness is not only that what he deposes shall be true, but that he shall also depose the "whole" truth; so that he is not to conceal any part of what he knows, whether interrogated particularly to that point or not. And all this evidence is to be given in open court, in the presence of the parties, their attorneys, the counsel, and all bystanders, and before the judge and the jury; each party having the liberty to except to its competency, which exceptions are publicly stated, and by the judge are openly and publicly allowed or disallowed, in the face of the country; which must curb any secret bias or partiality that might arise in his own breast.[6]

Having refreshed our basic knowledge about the history of the different kinds of common law trials and some characteristics of witness participation, we will now examine how the use of oral evidence came to be accepted in courts of justice.

Oral Evidence

W. S. Holdsworth states:

---

[6] 2 (Books 3 & 4) W. Blackstone, Commentaries of the Laws of England 243-59 (1893).

> [D]uring the whole of the mediaeval period, the view which the law took of the oral evidence offered by witnesses, was affected, as many other legal rules and institutions were affected, both by the theories which underlay the rules of the canon law, and by survivals of some very primitive ideas as to the functions of witnesses. In this, as in other branches of the law, these theories and these ideas diverged widely from one another, because they represented two different periods of legal development. But in one respect they tended, for very different reasons, to coincide. Both laid down the rule that a certain number of witnesses was requisite for proof. Of this rule, therefore, and its causes and effects I must speak, in the first place. In the second place, I must say something of the effects which it has had upon English law. We shall see that some of the reasons for the smallness of its direct effects upon English law, will help to explain why the most important branch of this part of the law of evidence has taken the form of certain rules, which definitely refuse to admit certain kinds of testimony. In the third place, therefore, I shall deal with these excluding rules.[7]

From Holdsworth's words we can learn that, in the medieval period, the institution of oral evidence offered by witnesses was influenced by the rules of the canon law and by the survival of some primitive ideas; and that, even with wide differences in the two systems, in one point they coincided: the rule that a certain number of witnesses were required for proof.

Holdsworth continues his treatise analyzing three different situations: (1) the rule that a certain number of witnesses is requisite for proof; (2) the effect of this rule upon the development of English law; and (3) the rules which exclude certain classes of oral evidence.

> <u>(1) THE RULE THAT A CERTAIN NUMBER OF WITNESSES IS REQUISITE FOR PROOF.</u> The rule that at least two witnesses were needed for proof is found in the classical Roman law; but it gained its great authority in mediaeval Europe from the fact that it became a rule of the canon law, justified, not only by the civil law, but by the authority of the Old and New Testaments . . . .
>
> This rule that more than one witness was needed to prove the truth of a matter in issue, also assorted well with some primitive notions as to the nature of the probative force of the testimony of witnesses. That probative force was attached, not so much to the matter to which they testified under the sanction of an oath, as to the act of swearing to the truth of a fact under the prescribed forms . . . . A greater degree of certainty is thought to be attained, not by analyzing the significance of each oath in itself and relatively to the person, but by increasing the number of oaths.
>
> It is true that the older modes of trials, in which this conception was prominent, decayed during the mediaeval period, and gave place to trial by

[7] 9 Sir W.S. Holdsworth, A History of English Law 203-11 (Methuen & Co 1927). Reprinted with permission.

> jury. But this by no means destroyed the primitive idea that an oath "per se" has a formal value, and that therefore a multiplication of oaths will produce greater certainty. The jury themselves were witnesses; and their verdict amounted to an assertion backed by the oaths of twelve men. This idea comes out clearly in the answer made by Fortescue to the Prince's objection. He points out that, though the law of God forbids proof by less than two witnesses, it does not forbid the law to exact a proof by more than two; and that, in effect, the law which requires the verdict of twelve men exacts a proof by twelve witnesses. He adds, moreover, that if for any reason the proof by twelve jurors is not available, e.g., if the matter alleged be done upon the high seas or abroad, the law of England provides that proof must be made by more than one witness.
>
> Thus both lines of thought led to the rule that a certain number of witnesses were necessary for proof.[8]

At this point it is opportune to remember the rule, mentioned in **§1.01,** established in *Deuteronomy* 17:6: "At the mouth of two witnesses, or three witnesses, shall he that is to die be put to death." Comparing Holdsworth and *Deuteronomy* provides an excellent example of how the rules of evidence were developed through different times and countries, arriving at the modern concept of need for and use of witnesses.

Holdsworth's treatise made reference to a concept that, in contemporary procedure law, is considered unacceptable: the fact that "the jury themselves were witnesses." The concept of the "witness-juror" was accepted due to the jury's verdict being considered an assertion backed by the oaths of the 12 members of the jury.

Holdsworth continues:

> Let us now examine the effect of this rule (that a certain number of witnesses were necessary for proof) upon the development of the modern law.
>
> <u>(2) THE EFFECT OF THIS RULE UPON THE DEVELOPMENT OF ENGLISH LAW.</u> It was inevitable that a rule, backed by such authority as this, would leave its marks upon the law. What is remarkable is not the fact that its influence can be traced, but the fact that its direct influence has been so small. We shall see that, subject to two important exceptions, English law has rejected the rule that there can be no proof without more than one witness. At the same time we can trace its indirect effects in different directions. I shall consider, firstly, the direct influence of the rule; secondly, its indirect influence; and thirdly, the reasons why it was a general rule of the law of evidence, rejected by English law.
>
> (i) The idea that the evidence of one witness is not enough to prove the fact in issue emerges, during the sixteenth and seventeenth centuries, sometimes in the provisions of statutes, and sometimes in arguments and judicial dicta. Various statutes of the sixteenth and seventeenth centuries,

---

[8] *Id.*

which required the evidence of two witnesses for a conviction of the offenses created by them, show that the Legislature was convinced of the danger of allowing a conviction on the unsupported testimony of one person. But it is in the arguments and judicial dicta of these centuries that we get the clearest evidence of the survival of the old idea. In 1551, in the case of *Reniger v. Fogossa,* the attorney-general argued that the testimony of one witness "was not sufficient in any law," because it was contrary to the law of God; and he was answered by Brooke on exactly the same lines as Fortescue answered the Prince. In the proceedings on Bacon's impeachment in 1620, Coke thought necessary to combat the idea that more than one witness was necessary; and in 1632, in *Sherfield's Case,* Heath, C.J., commented on the fact that there was only one witness to prove one part of the charge. Indeed, it would seem from the two cases of *Adams v. Canon* and *R. v. Newton,* that it was almost an accepted rule of the court of Star Chamber that a charge must be proved by two witnesses; though, from what was said by Lord Cottington in the Bishop of Lincoln's case, it would seem that it was not an invariable rule. It was stated in the widest terms by Strafford on his impeachment. He is reported as saying "that the testimonies brought against him were all of them single, not two one way; and therefore could not make faith in matter of debt, much less in matter of life and death." . . .

The most beneficial effect of the rejection of the rule requiring more than one witness was that it led the court to lay more stress upon the character of the evidence offered than upon the number of the witnesses produced. Just as the abandonment of artificial rules as to the competency of witnesses forced to the front the question of weight of the evidence, so the refusal to require more than a single witness made it necessary, as Hale pointed out, to consider more carefully the character, the means of knowledge, and the demeanour of the witness, in order to estimate the value of his evidence. The result was that the witness's character was always a fact relevant to the issue; and, in the latter part of the seventeenth century, witnesses were called to speak for or against credibility. But it was not 'till quite the end of the seventeenth century that we hear of the rule that evidence of specific acts of misconduct must be excluded, and that only evidence of general reputation can be given.

(ii) Though the direct influence of the rule requiring more than a single witness has been small, the ideas which underlay it have had a certain amount of indirect influence in different directions. Firstly, though the rejection of the rule caused the court to pay more attention to the weight of a witness's evidence, we shall see that juries still continued for a long period to attach much weight to an oath merely as an oath. Even the judges in the latter part of the seventeenth century made very few attempts in criminal cases to weigh the evidence; and, according to Stephen, this is still the prevailing habit of juries. Secondly, the influence of the same set of ideas can be seen in certain outlying branches of the law of evidence. If evidence given on oath must be believed because it is so given, the witness who has sworn to it cannot be allowed to retract

> it. This gave rise to the unsuccessful attempt to establish a rule that an attesting witness cannot be allowed to repudiate his attestation; and to the rule, which prevailed down to the end of the eighteenth century, that a person who by his signature has acknowledged an instrument to be valid, cannot be allowed to give evidence to show that it is invalid—"allegans suam turpitudinem non est audiendus." It also seems to be answerable for the rule that a person cannot impeach the competence or credit of his own witness. So long as the only witnesses known to the law were literally "oath helpers," "it was inconceivable that a party should gainsay his own witness." This tradition survived, perhaps because it had been recognized in a modified form by the civil canon law; and it was applied very illogically to the modern witness. It was stated as a general rule of law in the later part of the seventeenth century; it was accepted as an established rule in the eighteenth century; and it was not modified till 1854, though by the end of the eighteenth century, it had been admitted that other evidence could be produced by a party to contradict his own witness. Rationalistic reasons were found for it; but its historical origin seems to have been the result of the survival of these primitive ideas as to the functions of a witness, and the probative effect of his testimony . . . .
>
> The rule "testis unus testis nullus" permeated the continental procedure, and tended to preserve those primitive ideas which led men to count witnesses, rather than to weigh their testimony. The abandonment of this rule by the common law, which was due in part to the small influence of the civil canon law, in part to the peculiar character of the jury, and in part to the late arrival of the modern witness, helped English law to a far more rational treatment of the law of evidence than was possible in most continental states. Stress could be and was laid far more exclusively upon the character of the evidence.[9]

It is interesting to note, for the theme of this book about impeachment of witnesses, the process mentioned by the English author of how the importance of the number of witnesses was replaced by the importance given to the "character, the means of knowledge, and the demeanour of the witness, in order to estimate the value of his evidence."

The influence this evolution has had on other aspects of the law of evidence is also worthy of remark; for example, the principle—accepted until 1854—that a person cannot impeach the competence or credit of his own witness, a consequence of the idea that "[i]f evidence given on oath must be believed because it is so given, the witness who has sworn to it cannot be allowed to retract it."

Holdsworth continues his analysis:

> We shall now see that the need to guide the jury to a right judgment upon

---

[9] *Id.*

> the character of this oral evidence, has led to the formation of those excluding rules, which are the most salient and peculiar characteristics of the common law.[10]
>
> (3) THE RULES WHICH EXCLUDE CERTAIN CLASSES OF ORAL EVIDENCE. The three leading rules which were beginning to emerge during this period, were the rules that the contents of a written document cannot be varied by oral evidence, that mere opinion is not generally admissible, and that "hearsay" is not evidence.[11]

Thus, Holdsworth's treatise reveals the origin of three principles which are fundamental in the modern law of evidence.

Since the process of impeaching a witness is based on the capacity, quality, and credibility of the witness, it is necessary to refer to the history of the use of witness testimony more extensively.

Professor Theodore F. T. Plucknett has written:

> [F]rom the earliest days of the jury, witnesses were used, although by differing procedures. At first the jurors themselves might have first-hand knowledge of the facts, or they might obtain that knowledge by private inquiry. It was later possible to bring witnesses to give testimony before the jury, but they did so at some risk. As late as 1450 it was considered normal for the jurors to go to a man's home and ask him what he knows about a matter, but if he goes to the jury, it is maintenance. [Note: In criminal law, *maintenance* is the act of interfering unlawfully in a suit between others by helping either party, as by giving money, etc., to carry it on.] Honest witnesses were therefore reluctant, although in Chancery proceedings a useful method was devised by summoning them by "subpoena," which enabled them to testify without fear. At common law witnesses were not compellable, and no process issued against them. In civil proceedings counsel were so closely identified with their principals, and so great an obligation rested on them to tell the truth, that the allegations of counsel seem to have been treated as evidence. Even Coke was moved to say that the evidence of witnesses to the jury is no part of a criminal trial, for trial is by jury, not by witnesses. The jury was indeed inscrutable, and trial by witnesses had been distrusted for some five hundred years in Coke's day.
>
> Nevertheless, the importance of witnesses steadily grew in spite of this tendency to what must have been already mere archaism. A great landmark is Elizabeth's Statute which established a process to compel the attendance of witnesses and made perjury by them a crime. This act seems only to touch civil proceedings, but as we have already noted, witnesses could be bound over to appear under the second act of Philip and Mary, to testify against the prisoner, and so the Crown could compel its own witnesses.

---

[10] *Id.*

[11] *Id.*

A curious sign of the new spirit appears when courts began to allow prisoners to produce witnesses, although refusing to let them be sworn. A greater advance is to be found in an Act of Elizabeth creating a new offense of "embezzling" arms from royal arsenals. This Act concludes by allowing a person charged under it "to make any lawful proof that he can, by lawful witness or otherwise" for his defence. So too under an Act of 1606 making certain felonies done by Englishmen in Scotland triable in England, prisoners are allowed to produce witnesses, who shall be sworn, for their defence. The same privilege was allowed on trials for treason in 1696, and in 1702 the legislature finally extended the principle generally by enacting that in treason and felony the defence may bring witnesses and have them sworn.[12]

§1.05 Roots of the Rules of Evidence in American Law

This chapter relating impeachment to the history of the rules of evidence, in which we discuss primarily Jewish and Anglo-Saxon Law, would not be complete without a reference to the history of the American law of evidence.

In this section we will draw upon part of the work of Professors Carlson, Imwinkelried, and Kionka.

In the history of American evidence law, there are five fundamental cornerstones:

> [I.] Dean Wigmore's Treatise. In 1904, . . . American evidence law . . . was synthesized in . . . Northwestern law professor John Henry Wigmore's monumental treatise. . . . [H]is work has remained the dominant authority in [this] . . . field. . . .
>
> [II.] The Commonwealth Fund Report. In 1920, a charitable foundation, the Commonwealth Fund, appropriated funds to encourage legal research, . . . [and appointed] an evidence law committee chaired by Professor Edmund M. Morgan of the Harvard Law School. The committee's report, published in 1927, recommended five reforms. Four of its proposals had little or no effect on American evidence law, but the fifth—a modernized rule governing the foundation required for the admission of business records—became the basis for a federal statute and statutes or court rules in many states.
>
> The Fund's report was resurrected in the late 1930s. A Committee on Improvements in the Law of Evidence of the American Bar Association's Section of Judicial Administration, chaired by Professor Wigmore, issued its report in 1938. It endorsed the Commonwealth Fund report and proposed a wide-ranging array of changes in evidence law. . . .

---

[12] T. Pluckett, A Concise History of the Common Law 435-36 (5th ed 1956). Reprinted with permission of Little, Brown and Company.

[III.] The Model Code. In 1939, the American Law Institute . . . began work on the Model Code of Evidence. Professor Morgan was the project's reporter. . . .

The Model Code, published in 1942, was not merely a codification of the existing law of evidence; it contained many radical changes. While many of these reforms would be accepted in subsequent codifications, they were apparently too many too soon at the time. . . . Wigmore himself led the opposition to the Model Code and promoted instead a new edition of his own code, published in 1942.

[IV.] The Uniform Rules. [Since] . . . the Model Code . . . was not adopted in any jurisdiction, . . . the codification banner was taken up by the National Conference of Commissioners on Uniform State Laws. The Conference undertook an alternative code. . . . [I]n 1953 the Conference unanimously approved the proposed Uniform Rules of Evidence. Several days later, they were endorsed by the American Bar Association.

The 1953 Uniform Rules differed significantly from the Model Code. The Code had sought to drastically reform evidence law; the Uniform Rules were designed to modestly restate existing law to promote uniformity. The seventy-two Uniform Rules . . . were simpler and much less controversial than the Model Code.

. . . [T]he 1953 Uniform Rules met with only slightly greater success than their predecessors. . . .

[V.] The Federal Rules. By far the most important event in the history of American evidence law was the advent of the Federal Rules of Evidence. . . .

In 1961, Chief Justice Earl Warren, in response to action by the Judicial Conference of the United States, appointed a Special Committee on Evidence. . . . One of the perennial questions addressed was whether the Supreme Court's rulemaking power extends to the promulgation of rules of evidence. The committee concluded that it does. . . . [T]he committee noted that the 1953 Uniform Rules of Evidence could serve as a suitable model for reform. . . .

One reason that federal practitioners and judges favored codification was that there was no common body of federal evidence law. . . . [T]he existing federal law was of little help in making evidence rulings. In civil cases, the applicable provision was Rule 43(a) of the Federal Rules of Civil Procedure, . . . [while in] . . . criminal cases, . . . Rule 26 of the Federal Rules of Criminal Procedure [applied]. . . .

The Preliminary Report of the Special Committee on Evidence was published in February 1962, and distributed to the bench and bar for comments. The response was largely favorable. In 1963 the Special Committee's final report . . . was submitted to the Judicial Conference's Standing Committee on Rules of Practice and Procedure.

After receiving informal approval from the Supreme Court, the Standing Committee recommended the appointment of an advisory committee to prepare the rules of evidence. In March 1965, Chief Justice Warren announced the appointment of the committee, with Albert E. Jenner, Jr., of Chicago as its chairperson and Professor Edward W. Cleary . . . as reporter.

The Advisory Committee's Preliminary Draft of the Federal Rules of Evidence was published and circulated to the legal profession for comment in March 1969. The Committee reviewed the large number of suggestions for changes it received and produced what is known as the Revised Draft. That draft was approved by the Judicial Conference in October 1970 and forwarded to the Supreme Court.

The Court elected not to promulgate the Rules immediately, but instead returned the Revised Draft to the Judicial Conference to be published again to the profession. The Rules in this form were widely circulated in March 1971. . . . [O]rganized opposition surfaced, notably from the United States Justice Department. Conservative members of Congress were also upset, probably as much by the Court's exercise of what they saw as a legislative power as by the Rules' substance that they perceived as too favorable to criminal defendants. . . .

Following . . . [various discussions], . . . a third version of the Rules was sent to the Court, which included many of the Justice Department's suggested changes. However, the Justice Department still was not satisfied, and the Attorney General wrote to the Chief Justice to request further revisions. The Advisory Committee rejected most of these requests. After making a few further changes agreed to by the committee, the Supreme Court approved the Rules on November 20, 1972, and authorized the Chief Justice to transmit them to Congress in accordance with the Rules Enabling Act procedures. . . .

If Congress had done nothing, the Rules would have become effective in ninety days. But that was not to be . . .

. . . After a number of significant revisions, the Rules (in the form of H.R. 5463) were reported out on November 15. On February 6, 1974, . . . the House passed the bill.

. . . The Senate debated and passed the bill on November 21-22. The Senate's version differed substantially from the House-passed bill; it was closer to the Rules originally promulgated by the Court. . . . [A] conference committee resolved the differences in short order, usually in favor of the House version. The Conference Report passed both houses in December, and the Federal Rules of Evidence became law when the bill was signed by President Ford on January 2, 1975. The Rules took effect on July 1, 1975.[13]

---

[13] R.L. Carlson, E.J. Imwinkelried, & E.J. Kionka, Materials for the Study of Evidence: Cases and Materials 19-24 (2d ed 1986). Copyright 1983, 1986 The Michie Company. Reprinted from *Materials for the Study of Evidence: Cases and Materials, Second Edition* by Ronald L. Carlson, Edward J. Imwinkelried, and Edward J. Kionka with permission from The Michie Company, Charlottesville, Virginia.

§1.06 History of Rules of Evidence Relating to Impeachment

This chapter has traced the rise and progress of the laws of evidence in different cultures and in American law. But because this book is about impeachment, it is necessary to refer, if not to all the rules governing impeachment proposed by the numerous commissions and committees, at least to the different proposals made by the Supreme Court,[14] the Judiciary Committee of the House of Representatives,[15] and the Conference Report recommending to the houses of Congress a solution to their disagreeing votes.[16]

It should be noted that after the Report of the Judiciary Committee, the text suffered significant revisions, with the Senate's version and, finally, the Conference Report version.

The preceding section mentioned that on November 20, 1972, the Supreme Court approved a final draft of Rules of Evidence and authorized the Chief Justice to transmit it to Congress. When the Judiciary Committee of the House of Representatives submitted its Report (Nov 15, 1973), it said: "In some instances, the Committee has deleted entire rules or parts of rules proposed by the Supreme Court; in other instances, rules have been retained but significantly amended."[17]

This section will deal with three different steps in the approval process for some of the rules on impeachment that were included in the Federal Rules of Evidence: (a) the text sent by the Supreme Court to Congress; (b) modifications made by the Judiciary Committee to the text; and (c) the influence of both of these on the final text approved by Congress.

Proposed Rule 608(a)

The Committee amended the text submitted by the Court, which permitted impeachment of a witness by attacking the character for truthfulness or untruthfulness by either reputation or opinion testimony. The reference to "opinion testimony" was deleted by the Committee.

The reference to "opinion testimony" was restored in the final text approved by Congress. Also, the final text allows evidence not only for attacking credibility, but also for supporting credibility.

Proposed Rule 608(b)

In the text submitted by the Court to the Committee, there was a section permitting cross-examination of a witness regarding specific instances of conduct for the purpose of attacking credibility, if probative of truthfulness or untruthfulness "and not remote in time."

---

[14] See **app 1-1** for text of the Supreme Court's proposed Rules of Evidence.

[15] See **app 1-2** for text of House Comm on Judiciary, Federal Rules of Evidence HR Rep No 650, 93d Cong, 1st Sess (1973).

[16] See **app 1-3** for final text approved in HR Conf Rep No 1597, 93d Cong, 2d Sess (1974), of the rules involving impeachment.

[17] See **app 1-2,** HR Rep No 650, 93 Cong, 1st Sess (1973).

The Committee deleted the reference to remoteness in time, emphasizing instead the discretionary power of the court to permit such testimony.

The current text of the rule establishes that "specific instances of the conduct of a witness, for the purpose of attacking or supporting his credibility, other than conviction of crime as provided in rule 609, may not be proved by extrinsic evidence." Notwithstanding this provision, some leave to do so is left "to the discretion of the court" under certain circumstances mentioned in the law.

Proposed Rule 609(a)

The text proposed by the Court provided for the admissibility of evidence of a witness's conviction of a crime for the purpose of attacking credibility, "only if the crime (1) was punishable by death or imprisonment in excess of one year under the law under which he was convicted. . . ."

The Committee changed the text, eliminating the phrase "under the law under which he was convicted" and replacing it with "unless the court determines that the danger of unfair prejudice outweighs the probative value of the evidence of the conviction . . . ."

The final text approved on this matter reads ". . . only if the crime (1) was punishable by death or imprisonment in excess of one year under the law under which he was convicted, and the court determines that the probative value of admitting this evidence outweighs its prejudicial effect to the defendant, or . . . ."

Proposed Rule 609(b)

The text proposed by the Court established:

> Evidence of a conviction under this rule is not admissible if a period of more than 10 years has elapsed since the date of the release of the witness from confinement imposed for his most recent conviction, or the expiration of the period of his parole, probation, or sentence granted or imposed with respect to his most recent conviction, whichever is the later date.

The Committee amended the rule to read that "upon the expiration of ten years from the date of a conviction of a witness, or of his release from confinement for that offense, that conviction may no longer be used for impeachment." The Committee was of the view that "after ten years following a person's release from confinement (or from the date of his conviction) the probative value of the conviction with respect to that person's credibility diminished to a point where it should no longer be admissible."[18]

In the final text approved by Congress on this matter, it was established that evidence of a conviction older than 10 years was inadmissible

---

[18] See **app 1-2,** HR Rep No 650, 93d Cong, 1st Sess (1973).

> unless the court determines, in the interests of justice, that the probative value of the conviction, supported by specific facts and circumstances, substantially outweighs its prejudicial effect.
>
> However, evidence of a conviction more than 10 years old as calculated herein, is not admissible unless the proponent gives to the adverse party sufficient advance written notice of intent to use such evidence to provide the adverse party with a fair opportunity to contest the use of such evidence.

Proposed Rule 609(c)

The rule proposed by the Court establishes in part that evidence of a witness's prior conviction is not admissible to attack his credibility if "the conviction has been the subject of a pardon, annulment, certificate of rehabilitation, or other equivalent procedure based on a substantial showing of rehabilitation and the witness has not been convicted of a subsequent crime. . . ."

The Committee amended the proposed rule to provide that the "subsequent crime" must have been "punishable by death or imprisonment in excess of one year," on the ground that "a subsequent conviction of an offense not a felony is insufficient to rebut the finding that the witness has been rehabilitated."[19] The Committee also stated that the words "based on a finding of the rehabilitation of the person convicted" applied not only to "certificate of rehabilitation, or other equivalent procedure," but also to "pardon" and "annulment."

The final text approved by Congress on this matter establishes:

> Evidence of a conviction is not admissible under this rule if (1) the conviction has been the subject of a pardon, annulment, certificate of rehabilitation, or other equivalent procedure based on a finding of the rehabilitation of the person convicted, and that person has not been convicted of a subsequent crime which was punishable by death or imprisonment in excess of one year, or (2) the conviction has been the subject of a pardon, annulment, or other equivalent procedure based on a finding of innocence.

Proposed Rule 801(d)(1)

As proposed by the Court, prior inconsistent statements of a witness used for impeachment would have been admissible as substantive evidence, too, as long as they were not hearsay.

The Committee decided to draw a distinction between types of prior inconsistent statements, and allowed only those made in proceedings in which the declarant was subject to cross-examination, such as trials, hearings, and depositions, to be admissible as substantive evidence.

The Committee supported its position by saying that "(1) unlike in most other situations involving unsworn or oral statements, there can be no dispute

---

[19] See **app 1-2,** HR Rep No 650, 93d Cong, 1st Sess (1973).

as to whether the prior statement was made; and (2) the context of a formal proceeding, an oath, and the opportunity for cross-examination provide firm additional assurances of the reliability of the prior statement."[20]

The final text approved by Congress establishes two different requirements for admissibility as substantive evidence, each of them with some conditions: (1) The witness must be subject to cross-examination concerning the statement, and the statement is

> (A) inconsistent with his testimony and was given under oath subject to the penalty of perjury at a trial, hearing, or other proceeding, or in a deposition, or (B) consistent with his testimony and is offered to rebut an express or implied charge against him of recent fabrication or improper influence or motive, or (C) one of identification of a person made after perceiving him; or (2) The statement is offered against a party and is (A) his own statement, in either his individual or a representative capacity, or (B) a statement of which he has manifested his adoption or belief in its truth, or (C) a statement by a person authorized by him to make a statement concerning the subject, or (D) a statement by his agent or servant concerning a matter within the scope of his agency or employment, made during the existence of the relationship, or (E) a statement by a coconspirator of a party during the course and in furtherance of the conspiracy.

We hope that by having briefly discussed the process by which Rules 608(a) and (b), 609(a), (b), and (c), and 801(d)(1), which are some of the basic rules regarding impeachment, came into being, we have given the reader a general idea of how the matter of evidence for impeachment purposes was discussed and analyzed by the Supreme Court and by Congress, leading to the final text that was enacted into law.

§1.07 General Guidelines for Impeachment

Procedurally, impeachment is a special kind of cross-examination; consequently, all the rules and tactics of cross-examination in general are applicable to this particular type of cross-examination. Thus, *impeachment of a witness* is an attack on the witness's credibility or capability made through cross-examination with the intent to discredit or neutralize the witness's testimony.

One of the essential "don'ts" in cross-examination is *not* to cross-examine a witness if the lawyer is not certain of achieving at least one of the main objectives of cross-examination. Before deciding to impeach a witness, this rule must be carefully considered. The lawyer must be sure, not 99 per cent, but 100 per cent sure, that he or she has the elements to succeed in impeaching the witness. In other words, if the lawyer is not sure that he or she has all the tools to succeed in the impeachment process, it is better not to attempt impeachment.

---

[20] See **app 1-2,** HR Rep No 650, 93d Cong, 1st Sess (1973).

There are many possible questions to ask when cross-examining a witness. Anytime a question does not receive the expected answer, there is the possibility that perhaps another inquiry about a different fact will be more successful.

When a lawyer decides to attempt impeachment, however, based, for example, on contradictory statements by the witness, the lawyer will not be able to counter an undesired response by shifting the line of questioning to other facts; there are no alternative questions.

After an unsuccessful impeachment attempt, if the lawyer goes on to cross-examine the same witness regarding other matters, he or she will be facing a totally hostile person on the stand. Furthermore, in the eyes of the jury, the witness's image will improve (since the witness survived the impeachment attempt). This fact will certainly not swing the jury's sympathy toward the cross-examiner.

The following provisions of the Federal Rules of Evidence serve as a list of legal guidelines for impeachment of witnesses. The next few chapters will refer to and expand upon these provisions.

The main rules are:

Rule 607. Who may impeach

Rule 608. Evidence of character and conduct of witness, with its two subdivisions: (a) opinion and reputation evidence of character, and (b) specific instances of conduct, (1) concerning the witness's character for truthfulness or untruthfulness, or (2) concerning the character for truthfulness or untruthfulness of another witness as to which character the witness being cross-examined has testified

Rule 609. Impeachment by evidence of conviction of a crime, with its five subdivisions: (a) general rule; (b) time limit; (c) effect of pardon, annulment, or certificate of rehabilitation; (d) juvenile adjudications; (e) pendency of appeal

Rule 610. Religious beliefs or opinions

Rule 613. Prior statements of witnesses, with its two subdivisions: (a) examining witness concerning prior statement, and (b) extrinsic evidence of prior inconsistent statement of witness

Rule 801(d). Statements which are not hearsay: (1) prior statement by witness

Other Federal Rules of Evidence which can have application during a witness's impeachment are:

Rule 105. Limited admissibility

Rule 403. Exclusion of relevant evidence on grounds of prejudice, confusion, or waste of time

One of the fundamental requirements for a successful impeachment is proper foundation. The lawyer's first task is to obtain the witness's acknowledgment that he or she made a statement or signed a given document. The next step is to confront the witness with another statement or document, made or written by the witness, contradicting the previous one.

Imagine the following example: Defendant, Mr. Williams said, in his declaration after the crime at the police station, that when the crime occurred he was walking in the park with Peter, a friend. During the trial, the defendant said that the other person walking with him was his sister, Andrea.

The following cross-examination might occur for the purpose of laying the impeachment's foundation:

> Q. Isn't it true that on July 3, 1988, around midnight, you were arrested at Sunset Park, and taken to the police station?
>
> A. Yes, sir.
>
> Q. Isn't it true that when the officer asked you what you were doing in the park, your answer was, "I was taking a walk with my friend Peter?"
>
> A. I don't remember saying "with my friend Peter." I think that I said "with my sister Andrea," because she was walking with me.
>
> Q. I will show you the statement that you signed at the police station. Is this your signature?
>
> A. Yes, it is.
>
> Q. In this report that you just acknowledged signing, it says, "I was taking a walk with my friend Peter."
>
> A. Yes, you are right. Now I remember . . . .

As shown in this example, after the witness acknowledges having said "my friend Peter," he should be confronted with the testimony he has given during the trial saying "with my sister Andrea." The foundation for impeachment is then set.

Sometimes there are more than two documents or statements of the same witness regarding the same fact, which, in the lawyer's opinion, are not true and contradict a prior statement or document. It could also happen that all of the documents or statements, without contradicting a prior statement or document, are simply false. In order not to confuse the jury in such a situation, the best technique is to impeach the witness about each fact which is a basis for the impeachment. In this manner, by way of elimination, the lawyer can prove the inconsistency of the witness's testimony.

John Henry Wigmore wrote:

> [T]he term "impeachment," however, is by some courts and practitioners limited to a discrediting of CHARACTER for veracity; e.g. Lenz v. Public Service Ry. Co. 98 N.J.L. 849, 121 Atl. 741 (1923); but this usage is incorrect.
>
> A person must have given testimony if the impeachment process is to become operative as to him. Taylor v. Klahm, 8 Mich. App. 516, 519, 154 N.W. 2d 529, 531 (1967) ("The proper time for impeaching the credit of a witness is after he has been examined, and evidence is not admissible to impeach a person who has not yet been introduced, sworn, or examined as a witness"); Crowder v. Carroll, 251 S. C. 192, 161 S. E. 2d 235 (1968)

(accord); Reitano v. Dobbs, 31 App. Div. 2d 104, 295 N.Y.S. 2d 573 (1968) (accord, semble).

The two cases which follow involve the question whether a witness had so far testified that he became subject to impeachment. In each case the court neglects to take account of the possibility of dissembling by the witness. Pellegrini v. Chicago Great Western Ry., 319 F. 2d 447, 454 (1963) (Plaintiff contends that the court erroneously permitted introduction of proof that he had been arrested on a felony in 1944, for the purpose of impeachment. The contention rests on the premise that plaintiff had testified to no material fact, which is a prerequisite to the right to impeach by the introduction of a felony conviction. He was called as a witness in his own behalf, for what purpose we do not know, and testified only as follows:

Q. Would you tell us your name?

A. Willie Pellegrini.

Q. Where do you live, Willie?

A. 5044-31st Street, Melrose Park. I have a headache now. Noise.

Q. All right.

A. Where is Edie? Where is Edie? Where is my sister? I am going to find Edie now. There's some noise out here . . .

Defendant recognizes that impeachment in the manner under discussion is proper only where the witness has testified under oath to facts material to the issues in the case but makes the strained and untenable contention that plaintiff's testimony and his actions on the stand, characterized as 'demonstrative' evidence, justify the admission of the impeaching testimony. No case is cited and we know of none which supports the admission of this testimony . . ." Duffy, C.J.: "I think defendant should have been entitled to place in evidence, proof of plaintiff's felony conviction on the question of whether plaintiff's actions were genuine"); People v. MacIntosh, 14 Mich. App. 755, 756, 165 N.W. 2d 895, 896 (1968) ("At trial defendant took the stand and testified but only to establish a speech defect. He gave no testimony on direct examination relating to the crime. During cross-examination of defendant, the prosecuting attorney was permitted, over objection, to question defendant with respect to prior convictions. Defendant concedes that the statute, M.C.L.A. S. 600.2158 (Stat. Ann. 1962 Rev. S. 27A. 2158) permits such cross-examination to draw in question the credibility of defendant, but defendant contends such was not the purpose here. A review of the trial transcript convinces this Court that the cross-examination of defendant with respect to his past convictions was not for the purpose of attacking his credibility. It was done to attack his character, which had not been put in issue by defendant. This practice is reversibly erroneous. People v. Boske (1922) 221 Mich. 129, 190 N.W. 656").

When a witness has been impeached the effect of the process "is a matter to be determined by the trier of facts." Denver Decorators, Inc. v. Twin Teepee Lodge Inc., 163 Colo. 343, 347, 431 P.2d 8, 10 (1967). Thus "[w]hether impeachment, once attempted, is successful is essentially a question for the jury." Myers v. Gaither, 232 A. 2d 577, 581 (D.C.App. 1967), aff'd, 404 F 2d 216.[21]

---

[21] 3A Wigmore, Evidence in Trials at Common Law 636, 637 (Chadbourn rev ed 1970). Reprinted with permission of Little, Brown and Company.

Appendix 1-1

Rules of Evidence
Submitted by Supreme Court

Rules of Evidence
for
United States Courts and Magistrates

Amendments
to the
Federal Rules of Civil Procedure

Amendments
to the
Federal Rules of Criminal Procedure

NOVEMBER 20, 1972

Letter of Submittal

SUPREME COURT OF THE UNITED STATES,
Washington, D.C., February 5, 1973.

To the Senate and House of Representatives of the United States of America in Congress assembled:

By direction of the Supreme Court, I have the honor to submit to the Congress the Rules of Evidence of the United States Courts and Magistrates, amendments and further amendments to the Federal Rules of Civil Procedure and amendments to the Federal Rules of Criminal Procedure which have been adopted by the Supreme Court, pursuant to Title 28, United States Code, Sections 2072 and 2075 and Title 18, United States Code, Sections 3402, 3771 and 3772. Mr. Justice Douglas dissents from the adoption of these rules and amendments.

Accompanying these amendments is the report of the Judicial Conference of the United States submitted to the Court for its consideration, pursuant to Title 28, United States Code, Section 331.

Respectfully,

WARREN E. BURGER,
Chief Justice of the United States.

• • • •

Rule 607. Who May Impeach

The credibility of a witness may be attacked by any party, including the party calling him.

Rule 608. Evidence of Character and Conduct of Witness

(a) Opinion and reputation evidence of character.—The credibility of a witness may be attacked or supported by evidence in the form of reputation or opinion, but subject to these limitations: (1) the evidence may refer only to character for truthfulness or untruthfulness, and (2) evidence of truthful character is admissible only after the character of the witness for truthfulness has been attacked by opinion or reputation evidence or otherwise.

(b) Specific instances of conduct.—Specific instances of the conduct of a witness, for the purpose of attacking or supporting his credibility, other than conviction of crime as provided in Rule 609, may not be proved by extrinsic evidence. They may, however, if probative of truthfulness or untruthfulness and not remote in time, be inquired into on cross-examination of the witness himself or on cross-examination of a witness who testifies to his character for truthfulness or untruthfulness.

The giving of testimony, whether by an accused or by any other witness, does not operate as a waiver of his privilege against self-incrimination when examined with respect to matters which relate only to credibility.

Rule 609. Impeachment by Evidence of Conviction of Crime

(a) General rule.—For the purpose of attacking the credibility of a witness, evidence that he has been convicted of a crime is admissible but only if the crime (1) was punishable by death or imprisonment in excess of one year under the law under which he was convicted or (2) involved dishonesty or false statement regardless of the punishment.

(b) Time limit.—Evidence of a conviction under this rule is not admissible if a period of more than 10 years has elapsed since the date of the release of the witness from confinement imposed for his most recent conviction, or the expiration of the period of his parole, probation, or sentence granted or imposed with respect to his most recent conviction, whichever is the later date.

(c) Effect of pardon, annulment, or certificate of rehabilitation.—Evidence of a conviction is not admissible under this rule if (1) the conviction has been the subject of a pardon, annulment, certificate of rehabilitation, or other equivalent procedure based on a substantial showing of rehabilitation and the witness has not been convicted of a subsequent crime, or (2) the conviction has been the subject of a pardon, annulment, or other equivalent procedure based on innocence.

(d) Juvenile adjudications.—Evidence of juvenile adjudications is generally not admissible under this rule. The judge may, however, allow evidence of a juvenile adjudication of a witness other than the accused if conviction of the offense would be admissible to attack the credibility of an adult and the judge is satisfied that admission in evidence is necessary for a fair determination of the issue of guilt or innocence.

(e) Pendency of appeal.—The pendency of an appeal therefrom does not render evidence of a conviction inadmissible. Evidence of the pendency of an appeal is admissible.

Rule 610. Religious Beliefs or Opinions

Evidence of the beliefs or opinions of a witness on matters of religion is not admissible for the purpose of showing that by reason of their nature his credibility is impaired or enhanced.

* * *

ARTICLE VIII. HEARSAY

Rule 801. Definitions

The following definitions apply under this Article:

(a) Statement.—A "statement" is (1) an oral or written assertion or (2) nonverbal conduct of a person, if it is intended by him as an assertion.

(b) Declarant.—A "declarant" is a person who makes a statement.

(c) Hearsay.—"Hearsay" is a statement, other than one made by the declarant while testifying at the trial or hearing, offered in evidence to prove the truth of the matter asserted.

(d) Statements which are not hearsay.—A statement is not hearsay if—

(1) Prior statement by witness.—The declarant testifies at the trial or hearing and is subject to cross-examination concerning the statement, and the statement is (A) inconsistent with his testimony, or (B) consistent with his testimony and is offered to rebut an express or implied charge against him of recent fabrication or improper influence or motive, or (C) one of identification of a person made after perceiving him; or

(2) Admission by party-opponent.—The statement is offered against a party and is (A) his own statement, in either his individual or a representative capacity or (B) a statement of which he has manifested his adoption or belief in its truth, or (C) a statement by a person authorized by him to make a statement concerning the subject, or (D) a statement by his agent or servant concerning a matter within the scope of his agency or employment, made during the existence of the relationship, or (E) a statement by a co-conspirator of a party during the course and in furtherance of the conspiracy.

Rule 802. Hearsay Rule

Hearsay is not admissible except as provided by these rules or by other rules adopted by the Supreme Court or by Act of Congress.

Appendix 1-2

Report of the Committee on the Judiciary

93D CONGRESS *1st Session*	HOUSE OF REPRESENTATIVES	REPORT No. 93–650

FEDERAL RULES OF EVIDENCE

* * *

NOVEMBER 15, 1973.—Committed to the Committee of the Whole House on the State of the Union and ordered to be printed

* * *

Mr. HUNGATE, from the Committee on the Judiciary, submitted the following

REPORT

together with

ADDITIONAL AND SEPARATE VIEWS

[To accompany H.R. 5463]

The Committee on Judiciary, to whom was referred the bill (H.R. 5463) to establish rules of evidence for certain courts and proceedings, having considered the same, report favorably thereon with an amendment, and recommend that the bill as amended do pass.

The amendment strikes out all after the enacting clause and inserts in lieu thereof a substitute text which appears in italic type in the reported bill.

PURPOSE

The purpose of this legislation is to provide a uniform code of evidence for use in the Federal courts, and to make conforming amendments to the Federal Rules of Civil Procedure and the Federal Rules of Criminal Procedure.

STATEMENT

Judge Albert B. Maris, then Chairman of the Standing Committee on Rules of Practice and Procedure of the Judicial Conference of the United States, testified on February 7, 1973. He said: "[T]he adoption of the Federal Rules of Evidence represents, and in the future will be regarded as, a significant milestone on the road to the better administration of justice in the Federal courts, by providing clear, precise, and readily available rules for trial judges and trial lawyers to follow, which will be uniformly applicable throughout the Federal judicial system."

This view was echoed by Mr. Albert E. Jenner, Jr., Chairman of the Advisory Committee on Rules of Evidence, Judicial Conference of the United States. In his words: "I point to my own experience as a trial lawyer throughout the Nation in the trial of cases, that really this is what brought about the demand of the American Bar Association, its Special Committee on Rules of Evidence that we must have, in order to administer justice in the Federal Courts, uniform rules of evidence that are applicable to all district courts." Mr. Jenner also suggested that the uniform rules would be of particular assistance to judges who are assigned to districts or circuits other than their own to assist with congested calendars, and to the younger members of the bar. As he said, we will for the first time in the history of the nation have a pamphlet of rules in the "hands of the gladiators trying the case in the courtroom" and on the judge's bench.

The case against an evidence code was ably stated by a number of witnesses, including former Supreme Court Justice Arthur J. Goldberg and Chief Judge Henry J. Friendly of the United States Court of Appeals for the Second Circuit. Judge Friendly voiced three major objections—there is no need for the proposed rules, evidence is a subject which does not lend itself to codification but is peculiarly apt for case-by-case development, and uniform rules in the Federal courts which may overturn State social policies with respect to inter-personal relationships may well render equal protection of the law impossible.

After six days of hearings, the Subcommittee on Criminal Justice concluded that, on balance, there should be an evidence code.

However, recognizing that rules of evidence are in large measure substantive in their nature or impact, the Subcommittee and the Full Committee concluded they were not within the scope of the enabling acts which authorize the Supreme Court to promulgate rules of "practice and procedure" (18 USC 3771, 3772, 3402; 28 USC 2072, 2075).

H.R. 5463 constitutes the Committee's demonstration of these two conclusions, as well as its view as to what should be the content and scope of a uniform code of evidence.

Within the Subcommittee and the Full Committee there was no dispute with respect to many of the Rules. As a matter of fact, 27 of the Rules were not amended at all. Non-substantive changes were made to another 14. Thus, more than 50% of the Rules are substantively unchanged from those submitted by the Supreme Court.

HISTORICAL BACKGROUND

H.R. 5463 is the culmination of almost thirteen years of study by distinguished judges, Members of Congress, lawyers and others interested in and affected by the administration of justice in the Federal courts.

In 1961, the Judicial Conference of the United States authorized Earl Warren, then Chief Justice of the United States, to appoint an advisory committee to study the advisability and feasibility of uniform rules of evidence for use in the Federal courts. The Conference expressed the view that if uniform rules were found to be advisable and feasible, they should be promulgated.

The Chief Justice decided to move first toward a determination of whether uniform rules were advisable and feasible. He appointed a Special Committee on Evidence to make this initial exploration.

Because of the importance of the project and the fact that matters of evidence and proof cross the jurisdictional and interest lines of all of the Judicial Conference Advisory Committee, Chief Justice Warren designated the chairmen of the Civil, Criminal, Bankruptcy, Admiralty and Appellate Advisory Committees to serve on the Special Committee on Evidence.

By December 11, 1961, the Special Committee on Evidence submitted its preliminary report to the Judicial Conference Standing Committee on Rules of Practice and Procedure. In that report the Special Committee on Evidence concluded that uniform rules of evidence were advisable and feasible, and recommended that such rules should be promulgated promptly.

This preliminary report of the Special Committee was circulated for approximately one year with an invitation to the "bench and bar for consideration and suggestions." Thereafter, at its March, 1963 meeting, the Judicial Conference approved the final report of the Special Committee and recommended the appointment of an Advisory Committee on Rules of Evidence to prepare uniform rules of evidence for adoption and promulgation by the Supreme Court of the United States.

A distinguished Advisory Committee composed of judges, lawyers and teachers was appointed on March 8, 1965, and assigned the monumental task of developing a uniform code of evidence for use in the Federal courts.

Approximately four years later, in March, 1969, the Judicial Conference Standing Committee on Rules of Practice and Procedure printed and circulated widely for comment a preliminary draft of proposed rules of evidence which had been developed by the Advisory Committee. The draft was accompanied by detailed Advisory Committee notes.

After reviewing the numerous comments, suggests, and proposals received on the preliminary draft, the Advisory Committee and, in turn, the Judicial Conference, approved a revised draft which it submitted to the Supreme Court for promulgation in October, 1970.

The Court, however, returned the draft to the Judicial Conference for further public circulation and opportunity to comment, and in March, 1971, that draft was printed and widely circulated. The final work product of the Advisory Committee of the Judicial Conference and the Standing Committee on Rules of Practice and Procedure, was forwarded to the Supreme Court in October, 1971.

On November 20, 1972, the Supreme Court promulgated the Federal Rules of Evidence pursuant to the various enabling acts in title 18 and 28 of the United States Code, to take effect on July 1, 1973.

On February 5, 1973, Chief Justice Warren Burger, acting pursuant to the Supreme Court order of November 20, 1972, transmitted the proposed rules to the Congress. As transmitted, the proposed rules and accompanying Advisory Committee notes occupied 168 closely printed pages.

CONGRESSIONAL CONSIDERATION

Recognizing the importance and the enormity of the task before it, and in light of the serious question raised by Mr. Justice Douglas, in dissenting to the Supreme Court Order, as to the authority of the Supreme Court to promulgate rules of evidence, the Congress promptly enacted Public Law 93-12. This

Public Law (which passed the House 399 to 1) deferred the effectiveness of the rules until expressly approved by the Congress.

Two days after receipt of the proposed rules, on February 7, 1973, the Subcommittee on Criminal Justice opened hearings and began to take testimony on the desirability of a uniform code of evidence and the merits of each individual rule. H.R. 5463 was introduced by the Chairman of the Subcommittee, Congressman William L. Hungate, and other Members, so that the proposed rules would be before the Committee in legislative form.

The Subcommittee held six days of hearings, heard twenty-eight witnesses, received numerous written communications, and developed a hearing record of approximately 600 pages. By March 21, the Subcommittee was ready to begin its markup sessions with a view to developing a Subcommittee draft. Between March 21 and June 22, the Subcommittee held 17 markup sessions which culminated in a Committee Print of H.R. 5463 dated June 28, 1973. The Committee Print was circulated nationwide for comment and printed in the Congressional Record to assure the widest distribution. Over the course of the next six weeks, approximately 90 comments were received by the Subcommittee. By and large, the Committee Print was well received, even by those individuals and organizations objecting to the Subcommittee treatment of specific rules and those who objected to having uniform rules of any kind. The American Bar Association House of Delegates, for example, endorsed most of the provisions generally and "concurs in the Hungate Subcommittee's Report . . . insofar as it omits Rules 803 (24), 804(b)(6); all of the rules pertaining to privilege . . .; and the rule on summing up and comment by judges (105)". The American College of Trial Lawyers "approves thoroughly". From the Association of the Bar of the City of New York, "The Committee is to be commended for a most thorough, scholarly revision of the Federal Rules of Evidence". Chief Judge Friendly wrote ". . . if there are to be Federal rules of evidence, I do not see how there could be much better ones than your Subcommittee has proposed". Assistant Attorney General Robert Repasky of Wisconsin advised that "the balance the Committee has arrived at is a most reasonable balance between the rather clear interest of the individual States and the interest of the Federal courts in having some formalized Rules of Evidence to guide their decisions." Similar comments were received from numerous other individuals and organizations in the legal field. Laudatory comments were also received from non-legal groups, for example, the communications media, the American Hospital Association, the National Association of Social Workers, Inc., and others.

All comments were thoroughly considered and the Subcommittee developed a revised Committee Print in the course of five additional markup sessions. This Print, dated October 10, 1973, was approved by the Subcommittee and reported to the full Judiciary Committee for its consideration.

On October 16 and 18 and on November 6, 1973, the full Committee thoroughly debated H.R. 5463, amended it in several respects, and ordered it favorably reported.

COMMITTEE AMENDMENTS

In some instances, the Committee has deleted entire rules or parts of rules proposed by the Supreme Court; in other instances, rules have been retained but significantly amended. The following explanatory information reflects the Committee views in taking each individual action.

PROPOSED RULES DELETED BY COMMITTEE

Proposed Rule 105

Rule 105 as submitted by the Supreme Court concerned the issue of summing up and comment by the judge. It provided that after the close of the evidence and the arguments of counsel, the presiding judge could fairly and impartially sum up the evidence and comment to the jury upon its weight and the credibility of the witnesses, if he also instructed the jury that it was not bound thereby and must make its own determination of those matters. The Committee recognized that the Rule as submitted is consistent with long standing and current federal practice. However, the aspect of the Rule dealing with the authority of a judge to comment on the weight of the evidence and the credibility of witnesses—an authority not granted to judges in most State courts—was highly controversial. After much debate the Committee determined to delete the entire Rule, intending that its action be understood as reflecting no conclusion as to the merits of the proposed Rule and that the subject should be left for separate consideration at another time.

Proposed Rule 303

Rule 303, as submitted by the Supreme Court was directed to the issues of when, in criminal cases, a court may submit a presumption to a jury and the type of instruction it should give. The Committee deleted this Rule since the subject of presumptions in criminal cases is addressed in detail in bills now pending before the Committee to revise the federal criminal code. The Committee determined to consider this question in the course of its study of these proposals.

Proposed Rule 406(b)

Rule 406 as submitted to Congress contained a subdivision (b) providing that the method of proof of habit or routine practice could be "in the form of an opinion or by specific instances of conduct sufficient in number to warrant a finding that the habit existed or that the practice was routine." The Committee deleted this subdivision believing that the method of proof of habit and routine practice should be left to the courts to deal with on a case-by-case basis. At the same time, the Committee does not intend that its action be construed as sanctioning a general authorization of opinion evidence in this area.

Proposed Rules 803(24) and 804(b)(6)

The proposed Rules of Evidence submitted to Congress contained identical provisions in Rules 803 and 804 (which set forth the various hearsay exceptions), to the effect that the federal courts could admit any hearsay statement not specifically covered by any of the stated exceptions, if the hearsay statement was found to have "comparable circumstantial guarantees of trustworthiness."

* * *

Rule 608(a)

Rule 608(a) as submitted by the Court permitted attack to be made upon the character for truthfulness or untruthfulness of a witness either by reputation or opinion testimony. For the same reasons underlying its decision to eliminate the admissibility of opinion testimony in Rule 405(a), the Committee amended Rule 608(a) to delete the reference to opinion testimony.

Rule 608(b)

The second sentence of Rule 608(b) as submitted by the Court permitted specific instances of misconduct of a witness to be inquired into on cross-examination for the purpose of attacking his credibility, if probative of truthfulness or untruthfulness, "and not remote in time". Such cross-examination could be of the witness himself or of another witness who testifies as to "his" character for truthfulness or untruthfulness.

The Committee amended the Rule to emphasize the discretionary power of the court in permitting such testimony and deleted the reference to remoteness in time as being unnecessary and confusing (remoteness from time of trial or remoteness from the incident involved?). As recast, the Committee amendment also makes clear the antecedent of "his" in the original Court proposal.

Rule 609(a)

Rule 609(a) as submitted by the Court was modeled after Section 133(a) of Public Law 91-358. 14 D.C. Code 305(b)(1), enacted in 1970. The Rule provided that:

> For the purpose of attacking the credibility of a witness, evidence that he has been convicted of a crime is admissible but only if the crime (1) was punishable by death or imprisonment in excess of one year under the law under which he was convicted or (2) involved dishonesty or false statement regardless of the punishment.

As reported to the Committee by the Subcommittee, Rule 609(a) was amended to read as follows:

> For the purpose of attacking the credibility of a witness, evidence that he has been convicted of a crime is admissible only if the crime (1) was punishable by death or imprisonment in excess of one year, unless the court determines that the danger of unfair prejudice outweighs the probative value of the evidence of the conviction, or (2) involved dishonesty or false statement.

In full committee, the provision was amended to permit attack upon the credibility of a witness by prior conviction only if the prior crime involved dishonesty or false statement. While recognizing that the prevailing doctrine in the federal courts and in most States allows a witness to be impeached by evidence of prior felony convictions without restriction as to type, the Committee was of the view that, because of the danger of unfair prejudice in such practice and the deterrent effect upon an accused who might wish to testify, and even upon a witness who was not the accused, cross-examination by evidence of prior conviction should be limited to those kinds of convictions bearing directly on credibility, *i.e.*, crimes involving dishonesty or false statement.

Rule 609(b)

Rule 609(b) as submitted by the Court was modeled after Section 133(a) of Public Law 91-358, 14 D.C. Code 305(b)(2)(B), enacted in 1970. The Rule provided:

> Evidence of a conviction under this rule is not admissible if a period of more than ten years has elapsed since the date of the release of the witness from confinement imposed for his most recent conviction, or the expiration of the period of his parole, probation, or sentence granted or imposed with respect to his most recent conviction, whichever is the later date.

Under this formulation, a witness' entire past record of criminal convictions could be used for impeachment (provided the conviction met the standard of subdivision (a), if the witness had been most recently released from confinement, or the period of his parole or probation had expired, within ten years of the conviction.

The Committee amended the Rule to read in the text of the 1971 Advisory Committee version to provide that upon the expiration of ten years from the date of a conviction of a witness, or of his release from confinement for that offense, that conviction may no longer be used for impeachment. The Committee was of the view that after ten years following a person's release from confinement (or from the date of his conviction) the probative value of the conviction with respect to that person's credibility diminished to a point where it should no longer be admissible.

Rule 609(c)

Rule 609(c) as submitted by the Court provided in part that evidence of a witness' prior conviction is not admissible to attack his credibility if the conviction was the subject of a pardon, annulment, or other equivalent procedure, based on a showing of rehabilitation, and the witness has not been convicted of a subsequent crime. The Committee amended the Rule to provide that the "subsequent crime" must have been "punishable by death or imprisonment in excess of one year", on the ground that a subsequent conviction of an offense not a felony is insufficient to rebut the finding that the witness has been rehabilitated. The Committee also intends that the words "based on a finding of the rehabilitation of the person convicted" apply not only to "certificate of rehabilitation, or other equivalent procedure", but also to "pardon" and "annulment."

Rule 611(b)

As submitted by the Court, Rule 611(b) provided:

> A witness may be cross-examined on any matter relevant to any issue in the case, including credibility. In the interests of justice, the judge may limit cross-examination with respect to matters not testified to on direct examination.

The Committee amended this provision to return to the rule which prevails in the federal courts and thirty-nine State jurisdictions. As amended, the Rule is in the text of the 1969 Advisory Committee draft. It limits cross-examination to credibility and to matters testified to on direct examination, unless the judge permits more, in which event the cross-examiner must proceed as if on direct examination. This traditional rule facilitates orderly presentation by each party at trial. Further, in light of existing discovery procedures, there appears to be no need to abandon the traditional rule.

Rule 611(c)

The third sentence of Rule 611(c) as submitted by the Court provided that:

> In civil cases, a party is entitled to call an adverse party or witness identified with him and interrogate by leading questions.

The Committee amended this Rule to permit leading questions to be used with respect to any hostile witness, not only an adverse party or person identified with such adverse party. The Committee also substituted the word "When" for the phrase "In civil cases" to reflect the possibility that in criminal cases a defendant may be entitled to call witnesses identified with the government, in which event the Committee believed the defendant should be permitted to inquire with leading questions.

Rule 612

As submitted to Congress, Rule 612 provided that except as set forth in 18 U.S.C. 3500, if a witness uses a writing to refresh his memory for the purpose of testifying, "either before or while testifying," an adverse party is entitled to have the writing produced at the hearing, to inspect it, to cross-examine the witness on it, and to introduce in evidence those portions relating to the witness' testimony. The Committee amended the Rule so as still to require the production of writings used by a witness while testifying, but to render the production of writings used by a witness to refresh his memory before testifying discretionary with the court in the interests of justice, as is the case under existing federal law. See *Goldman* v. *United States,* 316 U.S. 129 (1942). The Committee considered that permitting an adverse party to require the production of writings used before testifying could result in fishing expeditions among a multitude of papers which a witness may have used in preparing for trial.

The Committee intends that nothing in the Rule be construed as barring the assertion of a privilege with respect to writings used by a witness to refresh his memory.

Rule 801(d)(1)

Present federal law, except in the Second Circuit, permits the use of prior inconsistent statements of a witness for impeachment only. Rule 801(d)(1) as proposed by the Court would have permitted all such statements to be admissible as substantive evidence, an approach followed by a small but growing number of State jurisdictions and recently held constitutional in *California* v. *Green,* 399 U.S. 149 (1970). Although there was some support expressed for the Court Rule, based largely on the need to counteract the effect of witness intimidation in criminal cases, the Committee decided to adopt a compromise version of the Rule similar to the position of the Second Circuit. The Rule as amended draws a distinction between types of prior inconsistent statements (other than statements of identification of a person made after perceiving him which are currently admissible, see *United States* v. *Anderson,* 406 F.2d 719, 720 (4th Cir.), cert. denied, 395 U.S. 967 (1969)) and allows only those made while the declarant was subject to cross-examination at a trial or hearing or in a deposition, to be admissible for their truth. Compare *United States* v. *DeSisto,* 329 F.2d 929 (2nd Cir.), cert. denied, 377 U.S. 979 (1964); *United States* v. *Cunningham,* 446 F.2d 194 (2nd Cir. 1971) (restricting the admissibility of prior inconsistent statements as substantive evidence to those made under oath in a formal proceeding, but not requiring that there have been an opportunity for cross-examination). The rationale for the Committee's decision is that (1) unlike in most other situations involving unsworn or oral statements, there can be no dispute as to whether the prior statement was made; and (2) the context of a formal proceeding, an oath, and the opportunity for cross-examination provide firm additional assurances of the reliability of the prior statement.

Rule 803(3)

Rule 803(3) was approved in the form submitted by the Court to Congress. However, the Committee intends that the Rule be construed to limit the doctrine of *Mutual Life Insurance Co.* v. *Hillmon,* 145 U.S. 285, 295-300 (1892), so as to render statements of intent by a declarant admissible only to prove his future conduct, not the future conduct of another person.

Rule 803(4)

After giving particular attention to the question of physical examination made solely to enable a physician to testify, the Committee approved Rule 803(4) as submitted to Congress, with the understanding that it is not intended in any way to adversely affect present privilege rules or those subsequently adopted.

Rule 803(5)

Rule 803(5) as submitted by the Court permitted the reading into evidence of a memorandum or record concerning a matter about which a witness once had knowledge but now has insufficient recollection to enable him to testify accurately and fully, "shown to have been made when the matter was fresh in his memory and to reflect that knowledge correctly." The Committee amended this Rule to add the words "or adopted by the witness" after the phrase "shown to have been made", a treatment consistent with the definition of "statement" in the Jencks Act, 18 U.S.C. 3500. Moreover, it is the Committee's understanding that a memorandum or report, although barred under this

Rule, would nonetheless be admissible if it came within another hearsay exception. This last stated principle is deemed applicable to all the hearsay rules.

Rule 803(6)

Rule 803(6) as submitted by the Court permitted a record made "in the course of a regularly conducted activity" to be admissible in certain circumstances. The Committee believed there were insufficient guarantees of reliability in records made in the course of activities falling outside the scope of "business" activities as that term is broadly defined in 28 U.S.C. 1732. Moreover, the Committee concluded that the additional requirement of Section 1732 that it must have been the regular practice of a business to make the record is a necessary further assurance of its trustworthiness. The Committee accordingly amended the Rule to incorporate these limitations.

Rule 803(7)

Rule 803(7) as submitted by the Court concerned the *absence* of entry in the records of a "regularly conducted activity." The Committee amended this Rule to conform with its action with respect to Rule 803(6).

Rule 803(8)

The Committee approved Rule 803(8) without substantive change from the form in which it was submitted by the Court. The Committee intends that the phrase "factual findings" be strictly construed and that evaluations or opinions contained in public reports shall not be admissible under this Rule.

ADDITIONAL VIEWS OF HON. LAWRENCE J. HOGAN

While I consider codification of the Proposed Federal Rules of Evidence of highest importance, I nonetheless feel compelled to set forth in these dissenting views my strenuous objection to the majority of the Judiciary Committee's reformulation of Rule 609.

There are, of course, some other proposed rules which, in my opinion, might have been improved upon but I want to focus in these dissenting views on my objection to Rule 609—Impeachment by Evidence of Conviction of Crime. My objection extends not only to the fact that the rule as drafted by the Judiciary Committee not only rejects the version of the Rule recommended by the Advisory Committee on Rules of Evidence of the Judicial Conference of the United States, but also abrogates the prevailing view in the Federal and State courts, but I object even more to the Judiciary Committee's clear disavowal of the Congressional mandate expressed as recently as 1970 on the principle underlying this rule.

I offered an amendment before the Subcommittee and full Committee to restore the version of the rule recommended by the Advisory Committee on the Rules of Evidence of the Judicial Conference of the United States. I believe it important to look at the policy behind the formulations and reformulations which this impeachment rule has undergone throughout the course of consideration of these Proposed Federal Rules. There is set forth below the precise language of each of these formulations:

March 1969 Draft: Rule 609(a) General Rule. For the purpose of attacking the credibility of a witness, evidence that he has been convicted of a crime is admissible but only if the crime, (1) was punishable by death or imprisonment in excess of one year under the law under which he was convicted, or (2) involved dishonesty or false statement regardless of the punishment.

March 1971 Draft: Rule 609(a) General Rule. For the purpose of attacking the credibility of a witness, evidence that he has been convicted of a crime, except on a plea of *nolo contendere,* is admissible but only if the crime (1) was punishable by death or imprisonment in excess of one year under the law under which he was convicted or (2) involved dishonesty or false statement regardless of the punishment, unless (3), in either case, the judge determines that the probative value of the evidence of the crime is substantially outweighed by the danger of unfair prejudice.

December 1972 Draft: Identical with March 1969 Draft.

Subcommittee Draft: Rule 609(a) General Rule. For the purpose of attacking the credibility of a witness, evidence that he has been convicted of a crime is admissible only if the crime (1) was punishable by death or imprisonment in excess of one year, unless the court determines that the danger of unfair prejudice outweighs the probative value of the evidence of the conviction, or (2) involved dishonesty or false statement.

Judiciary Committee Draft: Rule 609(a) General Rule. For the purpose of attacking the credibility of a witness, evidence that he has been convicted of a crime is admissible only if the crime involved dishonesty or false statement.

The conventional and majority judicial view of the impeachment rule has been that an accused who elects to take the stand is subject to impeachment as any other witnesses, including impeachment by proof of conviction. The raging debate over impeachment of the accused's credibility by conviction of crime exemplifies the continual attempt by all involved with the judicial system to balance the scales of justice between the rights of the individual and the rights of society.

It is for this very reason that the draftsmen of the March 1969 draft of the Proposed Rules specifically undertook to study and evaluate every formulation of the impeachment rule brought to their attention. Reduced to their essentials, these included the following six alternatives:

(1) Allow *no* impeachment by conviction when the witness is the accused.

(2) Allow only *crimen falsi.*

(3) Exclude if the crime is similar.

(4) Allow conviction evidence only if the accused first introduces evidence of character for truthfulness.

(5) Leave the matter to the discretion of the trial judge.

(6) Allow impeachment by conviction when the witness is the accused—the traditional and majority rule among the State and Federal Courts.

After giving consideration to each of these six proposals, and concluding that each was only a partial solution or, at the least, no clear improvement, the Advisory Committee chose to promulgate the sixth possibility, thereby retaining the rule of the overwhelming majority of Federal and State courts as well as the views unhesitatingly exposued by Dean Wigmore, renowned expert on evidence (See 3 Wigmore, § 889-891). This formulation adopts the prevailing prosecutorial view that it would be misleading to permit the accused to appear as a witness of blameless life on those occasions when the accused chooses to take the stand.

The first alternative above, that of excluding all convictions of the accused for impeachment purposes, has been given short shrift because there is little dissent from the proposition that at least some crimes are relevant to credibility. (See McCormick § 43 (2nd ed. (1972); 2 Wright, *Federal Practice and Procedure:* Criminal § 416 (1969).

In the second draft disseminated in March 1971, the Advisory Committee on the Rules of Evidence, totally without explanation, reversed its earlier position adopting the majority rule of Courts throughout the country and instead adopted the fifth alternative above. In effect, this was a particularized application of the *Luck* rule, expounded by the United States Court of Appeals for the District of Columbia in *Luck* v. *U.S.,* (121 U.S. App. D.C. 151, 348 F.2d 763) in 1965. The most significant feature of the rule is the requirement that the evidence of conviction be excluded if the judge determines that its probative value is outweighed by the danger of unfair prejudice. In July, 1969, the Congress specifically repudiated the *Luck* rule when it enacted the traditional rule as the impeachment rule to be followed in all criminal trials in the District of Columbia. The D.C. Court Reorganization and Criminal Procedure Act of 1970, incorporating the traditional impeachment rule, was approved by the House by a vote of 294-47.

The Advisory Committee took note of the 1969 Congressional pronouncement on the impeachment question and returned to its original position in endorsing the traditional rule in the third and final version which was submitted to this Congress for our consideration and enactment in December 1972.

In spite of the fact that the eminent members of the Bench and Bar who made up the Advisory Committee on the Rules of Evidence made their position clear, the majority of the House Committee on the Judiciary rejected the majority rule in the State and Federal courts and have changed the rule once again. But with this change the dimensions of the rule are totally immeasurable either from a prosecutorial or from a defense viewpoint. The Judiciary Committee has seen fit not only to renounce the traditional rule which is that under which their fellow members of the Bar labor in the majority of their Federal courts and in 90% of their State courts but the majority of the full Judiciary Committee has also defeated the compromise effected by the Subcommittee on Criminal Justice after many hours of arguing the merits and demerits of the various alternative formulations.

The rule which the majority has now settled upon is, of all the alternatives set out above, the most unsettling. Allowing only evidence of the *crimen falsi* to impeach the credibility of the accused adopts only the worst feature of the

Luck rule, i.e., unpredictability, without bestowing upon the Bench and Bar any useful new tool for coping with the evidentiary problem which is at the heart of this debate.

When the draftsmen of the Advisory Committee on the Rules of Evidence originally rejected the *crimen falsi* alternative for Rule 609, they did so because most of the crimes regarded as having a substantial impeaching effect would be excluded, resulting in virtually the same effect as if the alternative allowing no prior convictions for impeachment purposes were adopted.

In the commentaries to the first draft, the Advisory Committee on the Rules of Evidence noted:

"While it may be argued that considerations of relevancy should limit provable convictions to those of crimes of untruthfulness, acts are constituted major crimes because they entail substantial injury to and disregard of the rights of other persons or the public. A demonstrated instance of willingness to engage in conduct in disregard of accepted patterns is translatable into willingness to give false testimony.

A further argument against adoption of the *crimen falsi* alternative, as noted above, is that of its unpredictability and its uneven application to criminal defendants across the board. One of the major objections to the *Luck* rule in the District of Columbia, and one of the major reasons that it has failed to be adopted in most of the other Federal circuit courts, is that the discretionary authority which *Luck* vests in the trial judge imposes another discriminatory element into an already overly-criticized criminal justice system in this country.

Even more so is this true of the *crimen falsi* alternative. What, really, is dishonesty or false statement in judicial or legal terms? Unless one practices in a jurisdiction which has statutorily defined *crimen falsi,* the common law definition of "any crime which may injuriously affect the administration of justice, by the introduction of falsehood and fraud" is applicable. This definition has been held to include forgery, perjury, subornation of perjury, suppression of testimony by bribery, conspiracy to procure the absence of a witness or to accuse of crime, obtaining money under false pretenses, stealing, moral turpitude, shoplifting, intoxication, petit larceny, jury tampering, embezzlement and filing a false estate tax return. In other jurisdictions, some of these same offenses have been found not to fit the *crimen falsi* definition.

From the foregoing analyses undertaken by the eminent professors, jurists and lawyers of the Advisory Committee, as well as by my colleagues on the Committee on the Judiciary, I am convinced that the only viable alternative is that which has stood the test of time. If for no other reason than that the other considered alternatives are no improvement over the shortcomings of the traditional, I shall offer an amendment on the floor to reinstate the traditional, majority rule as promulgated by the Advisory Committee on the Rules of Evidence of the Judicial Conferences of the United States, and as it is known in the majority of our American courts. I am hopeful that this amendment will receive the support of the House as it did in 1970 when the *crimen falsi* alternative was specifically voted down in the D.C. Court Reorganization and Criminal Procedure Act of 1970.

LAWRENCE J. HOGAN.

Appendix 1-3

Conference Report on the Federal Rules of Evidence

93D CONGRESS
2d Session

HOUSE OF REPRESENTATIVES

REPORT
No. 93-1597

FEDERAL RULES OF EVIDENCE

* * *

DECEMBER 14, 1974.—Ordered to be printed

* * *

Mr. HUNGATE, from the committee of conference, submitted the following

CONFERENCE REPORT

[To accompany H.R. 5463]

The committee of conference on the disagreeing votes of the two Houses on the amendments of the Senate to the bill (H.R. 5463) to establish rules of evidence for certain courts and proceedings, having met, after full and free conference, have agreed to recommend and do recommend to their respective Houses as follows:

That the Senate recede from its amendments numbered 2, 15, 16, 17, 18, 19, 20, 30, 31, 33, 35, 39, 42, 44.

That the House recede from its disagreement to the amendments of the Senate numbered 1, 4, 5, 6, 7, 8, 9, 10, 11, 12, 13, 21, 22, 23, 24, 25, 36, 37, 38, 41, 43, and agree to the same.

Amendment numbered 3:

That the House recede from its disagreement to the amendment of the Senate numbered 3, and agree to the same with an amendment as follows:

In lieu of the matter proposed to be inserted by the Senate amendment, insert the following: *(5) Other exceptions.*

And the Senate agree to the same.

Amendment numbered 14:

That the House recede from its disagreement to the amendment of the Senate numbered 14, and agree to the same with an amendment as follows:

At the end of the matter proposed to be inserted by the Senate amendment insert the following:

This rule shall not take effect until August 1, 1975, and shall be superseded by any amendment to the Federal Rules of Criminal Procedure which is inconsistent with this rule, and which takes effect after the date of the enactment of the Act establishing these Federal Rules of Evidence.

And the Senate agree to the same.

* * *

JOINT EXPLANATORY STATEMENT OF THE COMMITTEE OF CONFERENCE

The managers on the part of the House and the Senate at the conference on the disagreeing votes of the two houses on the amendments of the Senate to the bill (H.R. 5463) to establish rules of evidence for certain courts and proceedings, submit the following joint statement to the House and the Senate in explanation of the effect of the action agreed upon by the managers and recommended in the accompanying conference report:

The House and Senate conferees met twice to discuss the differences in the Senate and House versions of H.R. 5463. The first meeting took place in the afternoon of Wednesday, December 11, 1974, and the second took place in the afternoon of Thursday, December 12, 1974.

The Senate made 44 amendments to the House bill, seven of which are of a technical or conforming nature. Of these seven, the Conference adopts 5, the Senate recedes from 1, and the Conference adopts one of the technical amendments with an amendment.

The more significant differences in the House and Senate versions of the bill were resolved as follows:

RULE 601. GENERAL RULE OF COMPETENCY

Rule 601 deals with competency of witnesses. Both the House and Senate bills provide that federal competency law applies in criminal cases. In civil actions and proceedings, the House bill provides that state competency law applies "to an element of a claim or defense as to which State law supplies the rule of decision." The Senate bill provides that "in civil actions and proceedings arising under 28 U.S.C. § 1332 or 28 U.S.C. § 1335, or between citizens of different States and removed under 28 U.S.C. § 1441(b) the competency of a witness, person, government, State or political subdivision thereof is determined in accordance with State law, unless with respect to the particular claim or defense, Federal law supplies the rule of decision."

The wording of the House and Senate bills differs in the treatment of civil actions and proceedings. The rule in the House bill applies to evidence that relates to "an element of a claim or defense." If an item of proof tends to support or defeat a claim or defense, or an element of a claim or defense, and if state law supplies the rule of decision for that claim or defense, then state competency law applies to that item of proof.

For reasons similar to those underlying its action on Rule 501, the Conference adopts the House provision.

RULE 606. COMPETENCY OF JUROR AS WITNESS

Rule 606(b) deals with juror testimony in an inquiry into the validity of a verdict or indictment. The House bill provides that a juror cannot testify about his mental processes or about the effect of anything upon his or another juror's mind as influencing him to assent to or dissent from a verdict or indictment. Thus, the House bill allows a juror to testify about objective matters occurring during the jury's deliberation, such as the misconduct of another juror or the reaching of a quotient verdict. The Senate bill does not permit juror testimony about any matter or statement occurring during the course of the jury's deliberations. The Senate bill does provide, however, that a juror may testify on the question whether extraneous prejudicial information was improperly brought to the jury's attention and on the question whether any outside influence was improperly brought to bear on any juror.

The Conference adopts the Senate amendment. The Conferees believe that jurors should be encouraged to be conscientious in promptly reporting to the court misconduct that occurs during jury deliberations.

RULE 608. EVIDENCE OF CHARACTER AND CONDUCT OF WITNESS

The Senate amendment adds the words "opinion or" to conform the first sentence of the rule with the remainder of the rule.

The Conference adopts the Senate amendment.

RULE 609. IMPEACHMENT BY EVIDENCE OF CONVICTION OF CRIME

Rule 609 defines when a party may use evidence of a prior conviction in order to impeach a witness. The Senate amendments make changes in two subsections of Rule 609.

A. Rule 609(a)—General Rule

The House bill provides that the credibility of a witness can be attacked by proof of prior conviction of a crime only if the crime involves dishonesty or false statement. The Senate amendment provides that a witness' credibility may be attacked if the crime (1) was punishable by death or imprisonment in excess of one year under the law under which he was convicted or (2) involves dishonesty or false statement, regardless of the punishment.

The Conference adopts the Senate amendment with an amendment. The Conference amendment provides that the credibility of a witness, whether a defendant or someone else, may be attacked by proof of a prior conviction but only if the crime: (1) was punishable by death or imprisonment in excess of one year under the law under which he was convicted and the court determines that the probative value of the conviction outweighs its prejudicial effect to the defendant; or (2) involved dishonesty or false statement regardless of the punishment.

By the phrase "dishonesty and false statement" the Conference means crimes such as perjury or subornation of perjury, false statement, criminal fraud, embezzlement, or false pretense, or any other offense in the nature of crimen falsi, the commission of which involves some element of deceit, untruthfulness, or falsification bearing on the accused's propensity to testify truthfully.

The admission of prior convictions involving dishonesty and false statement is not within the discretion of the Court. Such convictions are peculiarly probative of credibility and, under this rule, are always to be admitted. Thus, judicial discretion granted with respect to the admissibility of other prior convictions is not applicable to those involving dishonesty or false statement.

With regard to the discretionary standard established by paragraph (1) of rule 609(a), the Conference determined that the prejudicial effect to be weighed against the probative value of the conviction is specifically the prejudicial effect *to the defendant.* The danger of prejudice to a witness other than the defendant (such as injury to the witness' reputation in his community) was considered and rejected by the Conference as an element to be weighed in determining admissibility. It was the judgment of the Conference that the danger of prejudice to a nondefendant witness is outweighed by the need for the trier of fact to have as much relevant evidence on the issue of credibility as possible. Such evidence should only be excluded where it presents a danger of improperly influencing the outcome of the trial by persuading the trier of fact to convict the defendant on the basis of his prior criminal record.

B. Rule 609(b)—Time Limit

The House bill provides in subsection (b) that evidence of conviction of a crime may not be used for impeachment purposes under subsection (a) if more than ten years have elapsed since the date of the conviction or the date the witness was released from confinement imposed for the conviction, whichever is later. The Senate amendment permits the use of convictions older than ten years, if the court determines, in the interests of justice, that the probative value of the conviction, supported by specific facts and circumstances, substantially outweighs its prejudicial effect.

The Conference adopts the Senate amendment with an amendment requiring notice by a party that he intends to request that the court allow him to use a conviction older than ten years. The Conferees anticipate that a written notice, in order to give the adversary a fair opportunity to contest the use of the evidence, will ordinarily include such information as the date of the conviction, the jurisdiction, and the offense or statute involved. In order to eliminate the possibility that the flexibility of this provision may impair the ability of a party-opponent to prepare for trial, the Conferees intend that the notice provision operate to avoid surprise.

RULE 801. DEFINITIONS

Rule 801 supplies some basic definitions for the rules of evidence that deal with hearsay. Rule 801(d)(1) defines certain statements as not hearsay. The Senate amendments make two changes in it.

A. Rule 801(d)(1)(A)

The House bill provides that a statement is not hearsay if the declarant testifies and is subject to cross-examination concerning the statement and if the statement is inconsistent with his testimony and was given under oath subject to cross-examination and subject to the penalty of perjury at a trial or hearing or in a deposition. The Senate amendment drops the requirement that the prior statement be given under oath subject to cross-examination and subject to the penalty of perjury at a trial or hearing or in a deposition.

The Conference adopts the Senate amendment with an amendment, so that the rule now requires that the prior inconsistent statement be given under oath subject to the penalty of perjury at a trial, hearing, or other proceeding, or in a deposition. The rule as adopted covers statements before a grand jury. Prior inconsistent statements may, of course, be used for impeaching the credibility of a witness. When the prior inconsistent statement is one made by a defendant in a criminal case, it is covered by Rule 801(d)(2).

B. Rule 801(d)(1)(C)

The House bill provides that a statement is not hearsay if the declarant testifies and is subject to cross-examination concerning the statement and the statement is one of identification of a person made after perceiving him. The Senate amendment eliminated this provision.

The Conference adopts the Senate amendment.

RULE 803. HEARSAY EXCEPTIONS; AVAILABILITY OF DECLARANT IMMATERIAL

Rule 803 defines when hearsay statements are admissible in evidence even though the declarant is available as a witness. The Senate amendments make three changes in this rule.

A. Rule 803(6)—Records of Regularly Conducted Activity

The House bill provides in subsection (6) that records of a regularly conducted "business" activity qualify for admission into evidence as an exception to the hearsay rule. "Business" is defined as including "business, profession, occupation and calling of every kind." The Senate amendment drops the requirement that the records be those of a "business" activity and eliminates the definition of "business." The Senate amendment provides that records are admissible if they are records of a regularly conducted "activity."

The Conference adopts the House provision that the records must be those of a regularly conducted "business" activity. The Conferees changed the definition of "business" contained in the House provision in order to make it clear that the records of institutions and associations like schools, churches and hospitals are admissible under this provision. The records of public schools and hospitals are also covered by Rule 803(8), which deals with public records and reports.

B. Rule 803(8)—Public Records and Reports

The Senate amendment adds language, not contained in the House bill, that refers to another rule that was added by the Senate in another amendment (Rule 804(b)(5)—Criminal law enforcement records and reports).

In view of its action on Rule 804(b)(5) (Criminal law enforcement records and reports), the Conference does not adopt the Senate amendment and restores the bill to the House version.

C. Rule 803(24)—Other exceptions

The Senate amendment adds a new subsection, (24), which makes admissible a hearsay statement not specifically covered by any of the previous twenty-three subsections, if the statement has equivalent circumstantial guarantees of trustworthiness and if the court determines that (A) the statement is offered as evidence of a material fact; (B) the statement is more probative on the point for which it is offered than any other evidence the proponent can procure through reasonable efforts; and (C) the general purposes of these rules and the interests of justice will best be served by admission of the statement into evidence.

The House bill eliminated a similar, but broader, provision because of the conviction that such a provision injected too much uncertainty into the law of evidence regarding hearsay and impaired the ability of a litigant to prepare adequately for trial.

The Conference adopts the Senate amendment with an amendment that provides that a party intending to request the court to use a statement under this provision must notify any adverse party of this intention as well as of the particulars of the statement, including the name and address of the declarant. This notice must be given sufficiently in advance of the trial or hearing to provide any adverse party with a fair opportunity to prepare to contest the use of the statement.

RULE 804. HEARSAY EXCEPTIONS: DECLARANT UNAVAILABLE

Rule 804 defines what hearsay statements are admissible in evidence if the declarant is unavailable as a witness. The Senate amendments make four changes in the rule.

A. Rule 804(a)(5)—Definition of Unavailability

Subsection (a) defines the term "unavailability as a witness". The House bill provides in subsection (a)(5) that the party who desires to use the statement must be unable to procure the declarant's attendance by process or other reasonable means. In the case of dying declarations, statements against interest and statements of personal or family history, the House bill requires that the proponent must also be unable to procure the declarant's *testimony* (such as by deposition or interrogatories) by process or other reasonable means. The Senate amendment eliminates this latter provision.

The Conference adopts the provision contained in the House bill.

B. Rule 804(b)(3)—Statement against Interest

The Senate amendment to subsection (b)(3) provides that a statement is against interest and not excluded by the hearsay rule when the declarant is unavailable as a witness, if the statement tends to subject a person to civil or criminal liability or renders invalid a claim by him against another. The House bill did not refer specifically to civil liability and to rendering invalid a claim against another. The Senate amendment also deletes from the House bill the provision that subsection (b)(3) does not apply to a statement or confession, made by a codefendant or another, which implicates the accused and the person who made the statement, when that statement or confession is offered against the accused in a criminal case.

The Conference adopts the Senate amendment. The Conferees intend to include within the purview of this rule, statements subjecting a person to civil liability and statements rendering claims invalid. The Conferees agree to delete the provision regarding statements by a codefendant, thereby reflecting the general approach in the Rules of Evidence to avoid attempting to codify constitutional evidentiary principles.

C. Rule 804(b)(5)—Criminal Law Enforcement Records and Reports

The Senate amendment adds a new hearsay exception, not contained in the House bill, which provides that certain law enforcement records are admissible if the officer-declarant is unavailable to testify or be present because of (1) death or physical or mental illness or infirmity or (2) absence from the proceeding and the proponent of the statement has been unable to procure his attendance by process or other reasonable means.

The Conference does not adopt the Senate amendment, preferring instead to leave the bill in the House version, which contained no such provision.

D. Rule 804(b)(6)—Other Exceptions

The Senate amendment adds a new subsection, (b)(6), which makes admissible a hearsay statement not specifically covered by any of the five previous subsections, if the statement has equivalent circumstantial guarantees of trustworthiness and if the court determines that (A) the statement is offered as evidence of a material fact; (B) the statement is more probative on the point for which it is offered than any other evidence the proponent can procure through reasonable efforts; and (C) the general purposes of these rules and the interests of justice will best be served by admission of the statement into evidence.

The House bill eliminated a similar, but broader, provision because of the conviction that such a provision injected too much uncertainty into the law of evidence regarding hearsay and impaired the ability of a litigant to prepare adequately for trial.

The Conference adopts the Senate amendment with an amendment that renumbers this subsection and provides that a party intending to request the court to use a statement under this provision must notify any adverse party of this intention as well as of the particulars of the statement, including the name and address of the declarant. This notice must be given sufficiently in advance of the trial or hearing to provide any adverse party with a fair opportunity to prepare to contest the use of the statement.

RULE 806. ATTACKING AND SUPPORTING CREDIBILITY OF DECLARANT

The Senate amendment permits an attack upon the credibility of the declarant of a statement if the statement is one by a person authorized by a party-opponent to make a statement concerning the subject, one by an agent of a party-opponent, or one by a coconspirator of the party-opponent, as these statements are defined in Rules 801(d)(2)(C), (D) and (E). The House bill has no such provision.

The Conference adopts the Senate amendment. The Senate amendment conforms the rule to present practice.

SECTION 2. ENABLING ACT

Section 2 of the bill adds a new section to title 28 of the United States Code that establishes a procedure for amending the rules of evidence in the future. The House bill provides that the Supreme Court may promulgate amendments, and these amendments become effective 180 days after being reported to Congress, However, any amendment that creates, abolishes or modifies a rule of privilege does not become effective until approved by Act of Congress. The Senate amendments changed the length of time that must elapse before an amendment becomes effective to 365 days. The Senate amendments also added language, not contained in the House provision, that (1) either House can defer the effective date of a proposed amendment to a later date or until approved by Act of Congress and (2) an Act of Congress can amend any rule of evidence, whether proposed or in effect. Finally, the Senate amendments struck the provision requiring that amendments creating, abolishing or modifying a privilege be approved by Act of Congress.

The Conference adopts the House provision on the time period (180 days) and the House provision requiring that an amendment creating, abolishing or modifying a rule of privilege cannot become effective until approved by Act of Congress. The Conference adopts the Senate amendment providing that either House can defer the effective date of an amendment to the rules of evidence and that any rule, either proposed or in effect, can be amended by Act of Congress. In making these changes in the enabling Act, Conference recognizes the continuing role of the Supreme Court in promulgating rules of evidence.

William L. Hungate,
Bob Kastenmeier,
Don Edwards,
Henry P. Smith III,
David W. Dennis,
Managers on the part of the House.

JAMES O. EASTLAND,
JOHN L. MCCLELLAN,
P. A. HART,
SAM J. ERVIN, Jr.,
QUENTIN N. BURDICK,
ROMAN L. HRUSKA,
STROM THURMOND,
HUGH SCOTT,
Managers on the part of the Senate.

Appendix 1-4 Guide to Terms and Abbreviations*

BEDIKAH: Interrogation

BEITH JOSEPH: (1) Comment. on Tur by Joseph B. Ephraim Caro; (2) Responsa by the same name.

BER.: Berakhot (Talmudic tractate).

B.M.: Babba Metzia (Talmudic tractate).

DERISHAH: Investigation

DEUTERONOMY: The Fifth Book of the Pentateuch in the Old Testament, in which the Law of Moses is set down in full for the second time

DIN MERUMMEH: An attempt to mislead the court

EDUY or Edut: Eduyot (Witnesses, Tractate in the Mishna order of Nezikin consisting mostly of the testimony of scholars in the Yavneh Court regarding doubtful cases.

EVIDENCE: In Biblical Law, the existence and availability of human witnesses and other modes of proof seem to have been part of judicial proceedings from the earliest times (cf. Ex. 22:9, 12)

EXIGENCY CASES: Cases in which it was necessary to establish a strong principle of conduct or require special jurisdiction (e.g., a war situation; cases of idolatry)

EXODUS: (called in Hebrew SHEMOT, "names") Second book of the Pentateuch

GEMARA: Second part of the Talmud; consists of discussions and commentaries on its first and basic part, the Mishna. The Gemara, compiled (third to sixth centuries C.E.) after the completion of the Mishna, consists of the teaching of the Amoraim. The Gemara was written in Aramaic instead of in Hebrew. Two distinct versions are in existence, the Palestinian and the Babylonian Gemara. The Gemara was developed by Rabbi Arrika and Rabbi Samuel, disciples of Rabbi Judah and Rabbi Ezequiel. The Mishna and the Gemara together make up the Talmud.

GENESIS: The first book of the Pentateuch, known in Hebrew by its first word, Bereshit ("In the beginning")

GIT.: Gittin (Talmudic tractate).

HAKIRAH: Inquiry

HATAM SOFER: Moses Sofer.

---

* Reprinted from R. Aron, K.T. Duffy, & J.L. Rosner, Cross-Examination of Witnesses: The Litigator's Puzzle 3-6 (Shepard's/McGraw-Hill 1989) copyright 1989 by Shepard's/McGraw-Hill, Inc. Reprinted by permission of Shepard's/McGraw-Hill, Inc. Further reproduction is strictly prohibited.

H.M.: Hoshen Ha-Mishpat, one of the four parts of Tur, a code of Jewish law.

KET.: Ketubbot (Talmudic tractate).

KETUBBAH: A contract dealing with marriage.

KID.: Kiddushin (Talmudic tractate).

KOHEN: Priest. The Priests were the principal functionaries in divine services, their special task being to engage in religious ceremonies, which the conducted mainly in the Temple.

LEVITICUS: Third book of the Pentateuch, dealing primarily with ritual and legal subjects

MAIMONIDES: Greatest Jewish philosopher and codifier of medieval times, often called Rambam from his title of rabbi and the initial of his name (Rabbi Moses ben Maimon). One of the leaders of the Jewish communities of his day, eminent physician to the Sultan of Egypt. Born in Cordoba, Spain (1135); died in Fostat (Old Cairo), Egypt (1204); buried in Tiberias, Israel. His great works are *two major works:* (1) Codification of Jewish Law (Mishne Torah) and (2) Guide for the Perplexed (More Nevuchim) (where he introduced the "heretical" idea that the Jewish religion was a rational religion); and two minor works: (1) "The Book of Commandments" consisting of a methodological preface to, and an enumeration of the 613 Precepts and (2) Commentaries of the Mishna which contains his well-known 13 Articles of Faith. Maimonides was the first Jewish leader who saw Christian and Islamic religions as an historic continuation of Judaism.

MAK.: Makkot (Talmudic tractate).

MALVE ve LOVEH: Lender (creditor) and borrower (debtor.

MISHNA: The first written compilation of the Oral Law. It consists of laws and commentaries passed on for generations by word of mouth. They were collected by Judah Hanasi (Rabbi Judah the Patriarch). The teachers and scholars whose decisions and discussions are recorded in the Mishna are called Tannaim. The Mishna has six grand divisions:

- I. ZERAIM = SEEDS (Law of agriculture)
- II. MOED = SEASONS (Laws of the shabath, new moon, new year, and all the seasonal and occasional feasts and fasts)
- III. NASHIM = WOMEN (Laws dealing with marriage and divorce; the Levirate, adultery, etc.)
- IV. NEZIKIN = HARMS OR DAMAGES (civil and criminal laws)
- V. KODASHIM = HOLY MATTERS (Laws regarding sacrifices and offerings; ritual, etc.)
- VI. TOHAROT = PURITIES (Laws of clean and unclean persons and things; purifications, etc.)

MISHNE TORAH: (The Second Torah). A treatise written by Maimonides, where he restored Prophetic Judaism as a spiritual life line to the Jews. This treatise is considered the most orderly and logical classification of the Halakah (a corpus of duties).

NASI: According to the Talmud, the presiding officer of Great Sanhedrin

NOV., NOVELLAE: (Hebrew: Hiddushim) Customary designation of a certain type of Talmudic commentary

PENTATEUCH: Greek name for the Hebrew name "Humash", referring to the 5 books of Moses in the Bible

PISKEI: Precepts

PISKEI HA-ROSH: Fundamental precedents

PROVERBS: The second book in the Hagiographa section of the Bible. The third and final part of the Jewish Scriptures.

RAB.: Rabbi. The meaning in English is "My Master," "My Teacher." The spiritual leader of a congregation ordained by a theological seminary or Yeshiva. The rabbi is expected to be devoted to the principles of Judaism, to be a scholar, and to lead an exemplary life. In the past, a rabbi was ordained by another rabbi of great repute.

RASHBA: Rabbi Shelomo ibn Adret (1235-1310).

REMA: Rabbi Moses Isserles (1530-1572).

RESPONSA: Replies to questions. Babylon was (c. 500-1000 A.D.) the center of the Jewish world and the prestige of its schools at Sura and Pumpedita, institutions centuries old, extended far beyond its borders. The heads of those two great schools bore the title of Gaon (Eminence, Excellency). After the close of the Talmudic Period the Geonim were recognized as the spiritual heads of Judaism and were consulted by Jewish communities everywhere concerning all manner of questions. This system was extended to places where famous rabbis lived. The name of the answers was "Responsa." The messengers of the Responsa brought "the Law" to the Jews in Egypt, Greece, Italy, Spain, France, Germany, wherever Jews lived. This was the Talmudic Age of Judaism.

RIBASH: Rabbi Isaac B. Sheshet (1326-1408).

SANHEDRIN: (Assembly). (1) It was the name of the High Court of Jerusalem, and was the main source of Oral Law. It was composed of 71 members. The Sanhedrin served as a council advising the government on matters laid before it. It acted as a legislative and administrative body, making rules and regulations for the Jewish nation. It sat as a supreme court of Jewish law, both as a court of first instance and as an appellate tribunal. (2) A tractate. (3) A section of Maimonides' Code; deals with criminal law and criminal procedure.

SCRIPTURE: THE Bible

SH.AR.: Shulhan Aruch. Famous Code of Jewish law written by Joseph Caro (1488-1575).

SHEVU.: Shevu'ot. (Talmudic tractate dealing with oath).

SIFREI: Corresponding to Hebrew "Sefarim", books

SIFTEIN KOHEN: Comment. to Sh.Ar. and H.M. by Shabbetai b. Meir ha-Kohen; usual abbreviation: Shakh.

SIMON BEN SHETAH: Scholar and Nasi of Sanhedrin. He was renowned for his courageous integrity

SMA.: Comment. to Sh.Ar. by Joshua B. Alexander ha-Kohen Falk; the full title is: Sefer Mei'rat Einaim.

TALMUD: Great book of post-Biblical writings on Jewish law and studies based on Oral Torah which in turn is based on the Torah. The Talmud consists of the Mishna and Gemara. There are two different versions of the Talmud, the Palestinian (also known as the Jerusalem Talmud) and the Babylonian; each is based on the same Mishna but has its own Gemara. The text of the Talmud consists of some 2.5 million words, on 5,894 folio pages.

T.B.: Babylonian Talmud.

T.J.: Palestinian or Jerushalmi Talmud.

TOS.: Tosafot. A collection of teaching, using the method of the Talmud on the Talmud itself.

TUR.: Or Arba'a Turim. Code of Jewish law by Rabbi Yaakov ben Asher (1268-1340).

URIM VE-TUVIM: Comment. to Sh.Ar. and H.M. by Jonathan Eybeschuetz; subdivided in places into Urim and Tummim.

YAD: Yad Hahazakah (in English: Strong Hand). Another name for the Code of Maimonides.

YEV.: Yevamoth (Talmudic tractate).[1]

---

[1] Sources: M.L. Dimont, Jews, God and History; M.L. Dimont, The Indestructible Jews; H.H. Cohn, The Principles of Jewish Law (Justice Menachem Elon ed); Justice Menachem Elon, Talmudic Civic Law; Encyclopedia of the Jewish Religion (R.J. Zwi Werblowsky & Geoffrey Wigoder eds); Encyclopedia Judaica (Keter House Jerusalem Ltd) reprinted by permission; G. Horowitz, The Spirit of Jewish Law reprinted by permission; A. Kirshenbaum, Classes' explanations (NYU 1988); Rabbi Ralph de Koven, Sidur Meforash; Rabbi Adin Shtainzlatz, Guide to Talmud (Madrich Letalmud); Moshe Silberg, *Law and Moral in Jewish Jurisprudence,* 75 Harv L Rev 306 (1961).

2 Bases for Impeaching Witnesses

§2.01 Introduction

Neither trial judge, jury, nor litigating lawyer need yet fear being replaced by a computer. No matter how much information a computer can assimilate, process, and analyze, science has not yet developed a computer sufficiently sophisticated to be able to assess the credibility of the source of the information it receives. Thus, like appellate judges, the computer assumes the credibility of the source of, and accepts as accurate and complete, the information it receives and assimilates, processes, and analyzes.

Unlike computers, every human being is required daily to determine whether acts or events not perceived with one's own senses are more likely than not to have occurred, determinations most people make almost reflexively without expending a great deal of time or conscious cerebrative effort on the task. Indeed, most of the time, the human brain, that most sophisticated computer, automatically segregates, processes, and analyzes from all the data it has that information and knowledge required to assess, *inter alia,* the credibility of the source of the information concerning the act or event which was not perceived, and makes the decision almost instinctively.

Similarly, in any proceeding where a fact-finder must decide what occurred without having personally observed the relevant events or audited the material communications, the fact-finder must assess the credibility of the information received upon which the decision must be made. In an adversary proceeding, the fact-finder is given conflicting information as to events and communications, and a significant function, indeed, responsibility, of each adversary is to offer the fact-finder all permissible evidence and information which is relevant to the credibility of the source of the evidence or the evidence itself. While the proponent of the information seeks to support the credibility of the source or the information, the adversary seeks to cast doubt upon one or the other or both.

The process by which the trustworthiness or credibility of the source of evidence or the evidence itself is illuminated and challenged is *cross-examination,* and its component purposed to discredit is *impeachment.*

In seeking to persuade the fact-finder that certain evidence is not trustworthy, the impeachment process may involve a direct attack on the evidence. For example, proof of a prior statement by the witness which is inconsistent with the witness's testimony on direct examination is a direct attack on the evidence; so is proof that the witness was not in a position to perceive what the witness testified to on direct examination.

On the other hand, impeachment may challenge the evidence generally. For example, absent sufficient basis to attack the evidence directly, the litigating lawyer may utilize the impeachment process to seek to persuade the fact-finder of the general unreliability of the evidence. One method by which the general unreliability of the evidence may well be suggested to the fact-finder is establishing that the source of the information, the witness, was convicted of perjury, though the perjury was in a proceeding unrelated to the trial or the subject matter of the witness's testimony on direct examination.

In short, impeachment seeks to persuade the fact-finder that evidence which is legally admissible and has been received is not sufficiently trustworthy and should either be utterly disregarded or given little weight in reaching a verdict, predicated on the unreliability of the evidence or its source.

§2.02 Impediments or Imperfections in Witnesses: Disqualification or Impeachment

In the early years of the common law's evolution, several classes of people were held incompetent to testify. These included, for example, women, persons convicted of treason, felonies, or crimes involving fraud or deceit, persons who did not acknowledge belief in a deity that would punish false swearing in this or another life and, astoundingly, the parties and all persons with a pecuniary or proprietary interest in the trial's outcome. Most common law jurisdictions have abolished those categories of disqualification and anyone having personal knowledge of relevant events may be called to testify as a witness.

For example, Federal Rules of Evidence Rule 601 assures that "[e]very person is competent to be a witness except as otherwise provided in these rules" and Rule 602 admonishes that "[a] witness may not testify to a matter unless evidence is introduced sufficient to support a finding that the witness has personal knowledge of the matter." However, since Rule 104(a) authorizes the trial court to determine the admissibility of evidence, in practice witnesses usually testify without being required to demonstrate preliminarily that personal knowledge which is a prerequisite.

Of course, the requirement of personal knowledge assumes that a person who is called to testify has (1) the sensory ability to have perceived the events which will be the subject of the witness's testimony, (2) the capacity to remember and recall those events, (3) the ability to relate those events, and (4) an understanding of the significance of an oath and the duty to tell the truth.

There are, of course, other impediments or imperfections that offer bases for disqualifying a witness, including, for example, privileges (e.g., spousal or marital, attorney-client, physician-patient) and lack of or insufficient foundation (e.g., for an expert's opinion).

On occasion, prior to or during direct examination a witness reveals an impediment or imperfection which may offer the basis for challenging competency and disqualifying the witness. What should the litigating lawyer do when such an impediment or imperfection appears? The answer depends on whether the impediment or imperfection is sufficient to render the witness incompetent, requiring that the trial court disqualify the witness and strike the testimony already in the record, or simply furnishes impeachment material for cross-examination to discredit the witness's testimony on direct examination. Since there is not always a bright line distinction between disqualifying and impeaching impediments or imperfections, the answer is not always crystal clear.

As earlier noted, preliminary questions, including the competency of witnesses and the admissibility of evidence, are determined by the trial court. These rulings will be disturbed only if clearly erroneous. Thus, whether an impediment or imperfection will disqualify a witness or merely provide material for impeaching the witness during cross-examination is determined by the trial judge's exercise of judicial discretion.

How does the litigating lawyer determine what to do if a witness reveals an impediment or imperfection in one or more of those abilities or capacities which are prerequisites to competency? There are three variables that should be considered in determining what to do: the significance of the witness's testimony; the strength of an objection to the witness's competency; and the attitude of the trial judge toward the rules of evidence and competency.

If the witness who revealed the impediment or imperfection is insignificant—the witness's testimony, while relevant, is neither crucial to the party calling the witness nor destructive of the adversary's case—it is at best unproductive and possibly counterproductive to challenge the witness's competency. The impediment or imperfection in such a witness's abilities should be utilized for impeachment on cross-examination. If, on the other hand, the witness is significant, the litigating lawyer should consider the strength of an objection to the witness's competency together with the attitude of the trial judge regarding witness competency.

The strength of an objection to witness competency and the approach of the trial judge toward the rules of evidence and witness competency are obviously interactive variables. A judge whose approach to the rules of evidence is literal is likely to sustain an objection to witness competency more readily than one whose approach is liberal. Thus, as in everything else in the litigating process, whether to pursue an objection to the competency of a witness requires the informed and sensitive exercise of judgment.

Assessing the strength of an objection to witness competency necessarily assumes familiarity with the evidentiary requirements for competency and is significantly enhanced by a sensitivity to the nuances of language and the specifics of the testimony on which the objection is predicated. For example, assume that a witness testified that he was not wearing eyeglasses at the time he observed the matters to which he testified; if his testimony suggests a total inability to see without glasses, there exists a stronger basis for objecting to competency than if his testimony indicates a marked impediment to sight without glasses.

A conscientious and sensitive litigating lawyer seeks to understand the nature and philosophy of the trial judge from the moment the case is assigned. If it appears that the trial judge applies the rules of evidence, and thus of witness competency, literally, anything other than clear and convincing proof of incompetency may well evoke, in addition to denial of the disqualification motion, a comment which will reflect on the litigating lawyer's lack of competence and which will not be lost on a jury. Thus, intelligent assessment of the approach of the trial judge toward the rules of evidence is essential and requires pretrial consideration of and conclusions concerning the predilections and foibles of the trial judge.

Of course, as in virtually all aspects of litigation, there is not sufficient time for reflection or real analysis of the three variables before determining whether to challenge a witness's competency. Indeed, the objection to competency must be made as soon as a basis for it appears. Failing to object timely to competency when a basis is apparent will usually be deemed a waiver of the objection. With that in mind and the knowledge that there is not always a bright line test for witness competency, the decision of whether to challenge must be made almost instinctively, requiring a continuing awareness of the variables and their respective components and interaction, and the willingness of the lawyer to exercise an informed judgment. That judgment should not be a hasty one, however, since the failed voir dire will very likely deprive the litigating lawyer of the opportunity of utilizing the impediment or imperfection in an effective way to impeach the witness during cross-examination.

Procedure for Challenging Competency

Assuming that the decision is made to challenge the competency of a witness, what procedure does the litigating lawyer utilize?

In most common law jurisdictions, the process involves interrogating the witness under oath outside the presence of the jury as to matters which may offer a basis for challenging competency. This process is called *voir dire.* The philosophy of the trial judge may have a significant bearing on the scope of the voir dire. A trial judge whose approach to the rules of evidence is literal may well interrupt the voir dire if the interrogation deviates from questions of competency and inquires into matters that touch on credibility. On occasion, as when a witness's mental capacity or sanity is challenged, the voir dire may include interrogation of persons other than the witness.

The process is initiated by the lawyer standing and stating, "Your Honor, I respectfully request a voir dire," or "Your Honor, I would like to question the witness to determine competency." With the invocation of the process the trial court will usually excuse the jury and the voir dire examination will follow.

Should competency be challenged when the witness first takes the stand or deferred until the witness is about to testify to the crucial event? If it is the trial court's practice to excuse the jury during the voir dire, the challenge should be made when the witness is sworn. If, as sometimes happens, the trial court permits the *voir dire* to be conducted in the jury's presence, deferring the challenge may have a substantial impact on the jury.

Assuming that the challenge to competency precedes the testimony concerning the crucial event, the voir dire must cover both the anticipated testimony and the impediment.

For example, assume that the lawyer learned prior to trial that an alleged eyewitness to a crucial event, whom the adversary will call, cannot see without glasses, and at the time of the event was not wearing glasses. The voir dire might develop along the following lines.

Q: Mr. Jones, you were at the intersection of Main Street and North Avenue on June 23, weren't you?

A: Yes, sir, I was.

Q: And I understand you are prepared to testify that you saw my client standing across the street, is that right?

A: Yes, that's right.

Q: And you are going to tell the jury that from across the street you saw my client hand a small envelope to another man, aren't you?

A: Yes, I am.

Q: Mr. Jones, how old are you?

A: I'm 78.

Q: Do you wear glasses, Mr. Jones?

A: Yes, I do.

Q: Do you wear glasses all of the time or only when you're reading?

A: Well, I have one pair I wear all of the time and another pair for reading.

Q: The pair you wear all the time; do you wear them because without them you can't see things that are far away?

A: That's right.

Q: And, Mr. Jones, you left your glasses home when you went out for a walk on June 23, didn't you?

A: I don't remember.

Q: In any event, you weren't wearing your glasses when you were at the intersection of Main Street and North Avenue on June 23, were you?

A: No sir, I don't believe I was.

As earlier noted, there is not always a bright line between questions concerning competency and those concerning credibility. Thus, in the example of voir dire just given, a trial judge whose approach to the rules of evidence is literal may apply a rigorous standard and conclude that voir dire exceeded the permissible limits of inquiry into competency and involved matters bearing on credibility.

At the conclusion of the voir dire, the litigating lawyer must immediately assess the results of the interrogation to decide whether there is sufficient in the record on which to move to disqualify the witness and to strike any testimony which the jury heard.

If by any reasonable standard at the conclusion of the voir dire there is sufficient in the record to make a respectable and plausible argument that the witness is not competent and should be disqualified, the motion should be made and, if the trial court permits it, argued on the record. On the other hand, if it seems clear that the record will not sustain a reasonable argument for disqualification, the litigating lawyer's candid acknowledgment of that fact with a simple statement, outside the jury's presence, withdrawing any objection to the witness's competency will convey confident professionalism and enhance the lawyer's credibility with the trial court.

If, when first disclosed, the litigating lawyer's evaluation of the witness's impediment or imperfection in light of the three variables leads to the conclusion that voir dire is unlikely to establish sufficient to have the trial court disqualify the witness, the lawyer should abjure requesting a voir dire. Indeed, while noting the impediment or imperfection and pondering the most effective way to utilize it for impeachment during cross-examination, the lawyer should avoid calling attention to it in order to minimize the likelihood that opposing counsel will prepare the witness to blunt its use as impeaching material on cross-examination.

§2.03 Impaired or Diminished Sensory Ability or Perception

As the preceding section notes, the difference between the absence of and impaired or diminished sensory ability or perception is not always clear and is subject to the discretion and judgment of the trial court. Indeed, in offering, as an example of a voir dire to disqualify a witness for absence of perception, the interrogation of a person who is virtually blind without glasses and who was not wearing glasses at the time of the events about which the witness would testify, it was suggested that some trial courts would consider the inquiry as bearing on competency while others would curtail the voir dire, holding the impediment or imperfection as impaired or diminished, rather than as the absence of, perception.

If the witness suffers from impaired or diminished, rather than the absence of, sensory ability or perception, most common law jurisdictions will permit impeachment for impaired or diminished sensory ability or perception by cross-examination of the witness or extrinsic evidence of the impaired or diminished ability or perception, or both.

Assume that in a personal injury action involving an intersection collision between two vehicles the plaintiff calls Mr. Smith, whose testimony on direct examination is that he was at the scene and saw the defendant's vehicle run into the plaintiff's vehicle. Assume further that the defendant's lawyer has an affidavit in which Mr. Owen asserts that on the day of the collision he was tending bar within a block of the intersection, that he knows Mr. Smith, and that Mr. Smith had three boilermakers in the hour preceding the accident and left the bar inebriated. Impeachment on cross-examination should first call the witness's attention to that portion of direct examination which is going to be impeached and then seek acknowledgment of the impaired or diminished sensory ability or perception. It should, if possible, conceal the ultimate impeaching question until the witness is fully committed to the testimony to be impeached, and should also inject some drama or suspense into the process.

Q: Mr. Smith, you testified on direct examination that on the evening of September 4, 1987 at about 8:30 you were at the intersection of Main Street and North Avenue, didn't you?

A: That's right.

Q: Was anyone with you there?

A: No, sir.

Q: You also testified on direct examination that you saw one car enter the intersection and run into another car, didn't you?

A: Yes.

Q: And you testified that you saw my client behind the wheel of the car that hit the other car?

A: Yes, I did.

Q: And you were about 50 to 100 feet away from the two vehicles?

A: Yes.

Q: It was early evening and getting dark?

A: Well, it was early September so it was not that dark.

Q: By the way, Mr. Smith, where were you just before you came to the intersection?

A: With some friends.

Q: Where?

A: In the neighborhood.

Q: Doing what?

A: Just talking.

Q: Do you remember the names of any of the friends you say you were with before getting to the intersection?

A: No, I don't.

Q: Do you remember where you were "just talking" with some friends before getting to the intersection?

A: No.

Q: Mr. Smith, do you know a Bob Owen?

A: The name rings a bell.

Q: Are you familiar with the Shamrock Bar at North Avenue and Huguenot Street?

A: I believe so.

Q: In fact, sir, you've been in the Shamrock Bar, haven't you?

A: I believe I have on occasion.

Q: Frequently?

A: On occasion.

Q: Mr. Smith, you know a Bob Owen who tends bar at the Shamrock Bar, don't you?

A: I think I do, yes.

Q: In fact, Mr. Smith, wasn't Bob Owen one of the friends with whom you were talking just before you went to the intersection of Main Street and North Avenue at about 8:30 on the evening of September 4, 1987?

A: Yes, now that you mention it, I think we were talking.

Q: How long were you at the Shamrock Bar that evening?

A: Oh, I guess about an hour or so.

Q: And did you have anything to drink?

A: Sure.

Q: What did you drink?

A: I was drinking beer.

Q: That's all?

A: Oh, maybe I had some rye.

Q: Mr. Smith, you know what a boilermaker is, don't you?

A: Of course.

Q: Isn't it a fact that during the hour you were in the Shamrock Bar before you say you saw the collision you had three boilermakers?

A: Maybe that's right.

Q: If Mr. Owen says that during the hour you were in the Shamrock Bar before you say you saw the collision you had three boilermakers, you wouldn't dispute that, would you?

A: Nope.

If, however, the witness denies the fact or the conduct which necessarily caused impairment or diminution of sensory ability or perception, that fact or conduct may be established by extrinsic evidence such as a witness or documents. Thus, in the preceding example, if Mr. Smith denied having imbibed sufficient intoxicants from which a trier of fact could infer impaired or diminished sensory ability or perception, evidence from which the trier of fact could draw that inference can be established by calling Mr. Owen, the bartender.

The following discussion involves impeachment based on the impairment or diminution of the ability to recall. A witness who had knowledge of relevant facts but is unable to testify to them during direct examination may refer to a document or writing to refresh recollection about those facts and then testify with a recollection refreshed. Of course, the assumption underlying the permissible use of this procedure is that the witness can testify after refreshing his or her recollection without referring to the document or writing. Thus, in theory, once the witness's recollection is refreshed, he or she should testify from that refreshed recollection, rather than from the document or writing used to refresh. Indeed, some trial judges insist that the examining attorney withdraw the document or writing from the witness before the witness resumes testifying; that, however, is rare. In practice, it is not unusual for the witness to continue to refer to the document or writing while testifying after "refreshing" recollection, particularly if the facts involved are complex or confusing.

If the lawyer who is to cross-examine concludes that the witness was testifying from the document or writing rather than from a refreshed recollection, a carefully prepared impeachment may be an exception to the rule that cross-examination should not allow the witness to repeat direct examination. Thus, posing the identical questions as on direct examination without permitting the witness to "refresh" recollection may well impeach the witness by establishing an impaired or diminished ability to recall.

Impairment or diminution of any sensory ability or other requisite for testifying—such as sight, sound, smell, touch, recall, and ability to explain or to narrate—is fit subject for impeachment. The opportunities to impeach such abilities and other requisites for testifying are as limitless as the law of evidence and the ingenuity of the litigating lawyer.

§2.04 —Witness Substance Abuse or Addiction: Lack of Competency or a Basis to Impeach

Historically, the need for a litigating lawyer to focus on, consider the implications of, and prepare to cross-examine a witness who abused, or is or was addicted to, alcohol or drugs was virtually limited to criminal prosecutions.

However, the relatively recent proliferation of alcohol and substance abuse and addiction and awareness that such abuse and addiction now transcend age and socio-economic categories substantially increase the likelihood that lawyers litigating civil as well as criminal cases will have to confront a witness who abuses or is addicted to alcohol or some other dangerous substance. As with all cross-examination that involves an attack on witness credibility, professional ethics and the need to avoid evoking sympathy for a witness who the jury feels is being abused by the cross-examiner require that the litigating lawyer have a well-founded, good faith basis to believe that the witness is or was addicted to or an abuser of alcohol or other substances, before embarking on cross-examination of the witness concerning that addiction or abuse.

While it is extremely rare, on occasion a witness will take the stand quite obviously under the influence of alcohol or some dangerous substance. As earlier noted, witness competency is determinable by the trial court. Thus, in that rare circumstance when such a witness takes the stand, the litigating lawyer who would otherwise be attentive to the witness's direct examination preparatory to cross-examination should consider a challenge to the witness's competency before direct examination commences. The challenge to the witness's competency may be pursued in one of several ways, depending on how obvious the defect in the witness's sensory perception, ability, or responsiveness is and the known propensities of the trial judge.

If it is decided to challenge witness competency, the litigating lawyer should first stand and simply ask the trial judge for leave to voir dire the witness—that is, initially test the witness's competency by examination out of the presence of the jury. The extent and thrust of the voir dire examination of a witness who is evidently under the influence of alcohol or some other substance necessarily depends on how obvious the witness's sensory defects are, or appear to be, during the initial interrogation. That initial examination should probably be, and appear to be, rather superficial—asking the witness his or her name, residence address, family circumstances, occupation, and the like—purposed to disclose the extent to which the witness is under the influence of alcohol or other substance.

If it is apparent from the manner in which the witness responds, or the substance of the witness's response, to that somewhat superficial interrogation that the witness's sensory abilities are impaired to the point where the witness is unresponsive or his or her responses are inappropriate or obviously halting, the lawyer should simply ask the court to exclude the witness on the basis of lack of competency.

If, on the other hand, it is evident that the witness's sensory perceptions are affected by recent abuse of alcohol or drugs but not so markedly as to make his or her answers wholly inappropriate or totally unresponsive, the litigating lawyer should consider expanding the scope and thrust of voir dire beyond the superficial. Indeed, the voir dire interrogation might include questions which the witness is likely to be asked on direct examination or cross-examination to test the witness's responsiveness, recall, or ability to testify. More rigorous voir dire interrogation is pursued with the expectation that more probing questions which require concentration, thought, and memory will disclose an absence of competency and will also afford the litigating lawyer a bit of discovery and the opportunity to assess the nature of the witness even in advance of direct examination.

An alternative, when it is evident that the witness's sensory perceptions are affected by recent abuse of alcohol or drugs but not so markedly as to make his or her answers wholly inappropriate or totally unresponsive, is for the litigating lawyer to ask the trial court to remand the witness to a public health facility for examination by a physician who can then advise the trial court as to the witness's ability to testify. While the decision of whether to have a witness examined to determine whether his or her sensory perceptions are presently so impaired as to disqualify the witness from testifying is within the trial court's discretion, the very request by the lawyer in the witness's presence, even if denied, has the potential for unnerving the witness before direct examination commences.

If, however, the witness's appearance when taking the stand does not permit a challenge to competency, the litigating lawyer's well-founded, good faith belief that the witness is, or has been, addicted to or abuses, or has abused, alcohol or other dangerous substances is a basis for, and offers an opportunity for, impeaching the witness's credibility.

However, as earlier emphasized, before attacking a witness's credibility, the litigating lawyer should assess whether the witness caused the kind of damage on direct examination that requires an assault on credibility. That decision is all the more sensitive when considering impeachment based on the witness's addiction or abuse of alcohol or other dangerous substance. What makes impeachment by evidence of addiction or abuse of alcohol or other dangerous substance different is that some persons regard addiction or abuse a disease and have sympathy for the afflicted person. Even if the witness acknowledges the addiction or abuse, or it is established by extrinsic evidence, its effect on the witness's credibility will require explanation in summation.

The witness's addiction to or abuse of alcohol or drugs at or about the time of the incidents which the witness is expected to recount may well have damaged or destroyed the ability of the witness to accurately perceive or store the incidents in the witness's memory. On the other hand, addiction to or abuse of alcohol or drugs at the time the witness is testifying may impact the ability of the witness to recall or narrate those events for which he or she is called to the stand. And, prolonged addiction or abuse of alcohol or drugs may damage or destroy the ability of the witness to perceive, remember, recall, and relate the events for which he or she is called as a witness.

To avoid evoking the sympathy of the jury, confirm the information on which impeachment for substance abuse or addiction is predicated, and determine the extent to which impeachment on that matter should be pursued, the initial inquiry on cross-examination concerning substance abuse or addiction should be informational and, thus, rather relaxed and nonconfrontational.

Q: Mr. Jones, have you ever used a dangerous substance?

A: What do you mean by "dangerous substance"?

Q: Marijuana, "downers," "uppers," cocaine—any so-called recreational drug?

A: Yes, I have.

Having obtained from the witness an admission of the fact of substance abuse or addiction, how the litigating lawyer employs the fact of abuse or addiction to impeach the witness depends on myriad factors, including, for example:

1. The specific substance which the witness is abusing or to which the witness is addicted and its characteristics, e.g., alcohol, prescription drugs, or illicit drugs, and the kind of drug and its characteristics
2. The origin of the abuse or addiction, e.g., medically through prolonged use under a physician's care, in the military through treatment for wounds or the like, or simply by personal choice
3. The temporal nature of the abuse or addiction, e.g., the length of time of the abuse or addiction, and whether the witness presently abuses or is addicted to substances
4. Criminal activity resulting from the abuse or addiction, e.g., involvement in transporting, selling, or distributing illicit substances, or criminal conduct to obtain the substance
5. The availability, nature, and quality of extrinsic evidence of the witness's abuse or addiction, e.g., prior statements by the witness in trial transcripts, hospital records, etc., testimony of physicians, law enforcement officers, or others, certified copies of criminal convictions, etc.

Knowing as much about the origin, nature, and temporal aspect of the witness's addiction or abuse and any resulting experiences will enable the lawyer to use the witness's addiction or abuse to impeach in the most persuasive manner possible.

Thus, for example, the most persuasive way to use addiction or abuse to impeach a witness who has no criminal record and whose addiction or abuse resulted from treatment of severe wounds during military service would appear to be substantially different from the way to use addiction or abuse to impeach a witness with an extensive criminal record for selling drugs or for economic crimes to satisfy an addiction that began with the witness's own choice to use a dangerous substance. Indeed, in the first example, the witness may acknowledge the fact of addiction or abuse, particularly if the approach of the cross-examiner is understanding and sympathetic, affording the cross-examiner the opportunity to argue its effect on credibility in summation. On the other hand, in the second example, it is likely that the witness will try to deny, minimize, or explain the addiction or abuse and will probably evoke little if any sympathy from a jury or judge. Thus, in the first example, it would seem a better tactic to establish the origin and extent of addiction sympathetically and quickly, laying a foundation to argue its impact on the witness's sensory perceptions in summation.

Q: Mr. Jones, you were in the Army in the Viet Nam conflict, weren't you?

A: That's right.

Q: And you were severely wounded while serving our country?

A: Yes, I got shot up pretty bad.

Q: Your wounds were extremely painful, weren't they?

A: That's right.

Q: And you still feel the pain now, 20 years later, don't you?

A: I do.

Q: And your addiction to morphine resulted from the wounds you sustained in Viet Nam?

A: Yes.

Q: And your addiction to morphine has continued for more than 20 years?

A: It has.

On the other hand, in the second example, the witness may try to deny, minimize, or explain the extent and origin of his addiction or abuse, even possibly offering an opportunity for subsequent impeachment by inconsistent statement or conviction of a crime, and, since there is little likelihood that the witness will evoke any sympathy from the jury, the cross-examination could be approached as follows.

Q: Mr. Smith, do you use drugs?

A: Sometimes, I guess.

Q: When you say "sometimes," could you be a bit more specific? How often have you used drugs in the past two months?

A: I don't know; I don't count those things, Counselor.

Q: What drugs do you use when you use drugs?

A: Mostly what I can get.

Q: Isn't it a fact that you're addicted to heroin?

A: Whaddya mean, addicted?

Q: Mr. Smith, weren't you sent to the medical facility in Lexington, Kentucky, for treatment for heroin addiction within the past two years?

A: Yes, I went to Lexington.

Q: And that was involuntary treatment for heroin addiction, wasn't it?

A: Okay, yes it was. What difference does it make?

Q: How long have you been addicted to heroin?

A: I don't know.

Q: When did you start using heroin?

A: A few years ago.

Q: How did you start to use heroin?
A: A pusher made me try some.
Q: How much did it cost you?
A: I got a nickel bag.
Q: You paid five dollars for your first fix?
A: I guess so.
Q: And you've been addicted for more than two years, haven't you?
A: I suppose so.
Q: How much does your habit cost you each day?
A: I dunno. It depends.
Q: Do you work to get money to get a fix?
A: Sometimes.
Q: And you sell heroin to feed your habit, don't you?
A: Yes.
Q: And steal money and jewelry, too.
A: Yes.
Q: Have you been convicted for selling heroin or stealing money and jewelry?
A: What does that have to do with it?
Q: Have you been convicted for selling heroin or stealing money and jewelry?
A: No!
Q: Are you certain you've never been convicted for selling heroin or stealing money and jewelry?
A: That's what I said!

In this example, the lawyer may use extrinsic evidence to establish the fact of conviction as it bears on the general credibility of the witness, regardless of the witness's addiction to or abuse of dangerous substances.

If the witness denies being addicted to or abusing a dangerous substance, is extrinsic evidence admissible to establish the fact of addiction or abuse? Clearly, if admissible, extrinsic evidence would deprive the witness of the ability to deny the fact of addiction or abuse or to divert the avenue of inquiry. Since the fact of addiction or abuse is not purposed to impeach a witness's general credibility but, rather, the witness's testimonial capacity or ability to have perceived or to recall or recount the conduct or events as to which the witness's testimony is sought, most jurisdictions admit extrinsic evidence to establish the fact of addiction or abuse, including, for example, certified records of a hospital or public health facility or the testimony of other individuals.

Some members of the jury may consider cross-examination of a witness as to addiction to or abuse of a dangerous substance a form of harassment and others may consider addiction or abuse as a sickness and harbor some sympathy for the witness. Thus, while perhaps it is not required, if a witness denies addiction to or abuse of a dangerous substance, the better course would seem to be to give the witness an opportunity to admit it by sharply focused questions and, if denials persist, to confront the witness with the extrinsic evidence of the addiction or abuse.

Q: Mr. Smith, you say that you've never been addicted to or abused any dangerous substance, that is, any drugs?

A: That's right!

Q: Have you ever used any drugs?

A: No, why would I?

Q: Please, Mr. Smith; just listen to my question and simply say "Yes" or "No." Have you ever used drugs?

A: No.

Q: Have you ever undergone treatment in a hospital or other health facility for using drugs?

A: No.

Q: Mr. Smith, where were you from, say, July 1983 to December 1984?

A: I don't remember.

Q: Your Honor, could this be marked as Plaintiff's Exhibit 23 for identification?

THE COURT:

Deemed marked.

Q: I show you what is marked Plaintiff's Exhibit 23 and ask you if that refreshes your recollection as to where you were from July 1983 to December 1984?

A: Do you want me to read it?

Q: Only to yourself, please.

A: Okay, I've read it. Now, what do you want to know?

Q: Does that refresh your recollection as to where you were from July 1983 to December 1984?

Here, of course, the witness can acknowledge that the document refreshes his recollection or deny it. If the witness acknowledges that the document refreshes his recollection, the witness should be asked where he was.

A: Yes, it does.

Q: Where were you?

A: I was at the public health institution in Lexington, Kentucky.

Q: And did you undergo treatment for addiction to heroin while you were there?

A: Yes, I did.

Q: And, Mr. Smith, were you sent there as a result of being convicted of conspiring to import and sell heroin?

A: Yes.

Q: And, Mr. Smith, was the treatment you received successful in that you have not used heroin since you were discharged?

A: No.

Q: "No," what, Mr. Smith. That the treatment was not successful or that you have not stopped using heroin?

A: The treatment was not successful.

Q: You mean you are still addicted to heroin?

A: Yes.

If the witness denies that the document refreshes his recollection and the document is self-authenticating the document should be offered into evidence immediately and, if received, read immediately to, or by, the jury.

A: No, sir, it does not refresh my recollection.

Q: Your Honor, Plaintiff's Exhibit 23 for identification is self-authenticating and I offer it into evidence.

THE COURT:

Show it to your adversary. (Pause) Is there an objection? Hearing none, Plaintiff's 23 is received. Please proceed, Counselor.

Q: Your Honor, might I read Plaintiff's Exhibit 23 in evidence to the jury?

THE COURT:

No, Counselor, but you may pass it to the jury so they might read it to themselves.

Q: Thank you, Your Honor.

Thus, extrinsic evidence is generally admissible to establish that a witness who denies being addicted to or abusing dangerous substances is an addict or abuser, as it is admissible to establish that a witness who admits to being addicted to or abusing dangerous substances, but denies having been convicted for selling heroin or stealing money and jewelry, has been convicted of such crimes; authenticated copies of judgments of conviction would be admissible to impeach, as would authenticated copies of records of hospitals or of other institutions to evidence diagnosis of and treatment for addiction or abuse.

Confirmation that addiction or abuse of alcohol or another dangerous substance is a basis for impeaching a witness's credibility is found in decisions under *Brady v Maryland*[1] and its progeny which require that evidence or information as to a prosecution witness's addiction or abuse be disclosed pretrial.

---

[1] 373 US 83 (1963).

Addiction to or abuse of a dangerous substance by a prosecution witness in a criminal case offers opportunity for impeachment in addition to that which suggests a defect in the witness's ability to perceive, recall, or relate. It is more than likely that a prosecution witness who is an addict or abuser is either subject to pending criminal charges or a paid informer. Evidence that a prosecution witness has criminal charges pending or is a paid informer is admissible as some evidence that the witness has a motive to fabricate evidence favorable to the prosecution. That motive to fabricate testimony favorable to the prosecution is substantially stronger if, in addition to having criminal charges pending or being a paid informer, the prosecution witness is an addict or abuser. Of course, extrinsic evidence is admissible to establish a witness's motive to testify as he did.

Q: Mr. Jones, you are addicted to heroin, aren't you?
A: Yes, I am.

Presumably, the prosecutor provided evidence or information pretrial that the witness is addicted to heroin. Thus, if the witness denied the fact of addiction and the prosecutor did not rise to correct that false testimony, the lawyer conducting cross-examination could ask the prosecutor for a stipulation in open court that the witness is addicted to heroin.

Q: And you are an informer for the Narcotics Squad of the Blackstone Police Department?
A: Yes, I am.
Q: Did you become an informer after you were arrested for a crime?
A: Yes.
Q: How long ago was that?
A: Two to three years ago.
Q: For what were you arrested?
A: Selling heroin.
Q: Are there criminal charges pending against you at this time?
A: Yes.
Q: For what?
A: Selling heroin.
Q: Have the same charges been pending against you all the time you've been an informer?
A: Yes.
Q: And do you have an understanding as to what will happen to those charges as a result of your being an informer?
A: Yes.
Q: What is that understanding?
A: My cooperation will be told to the Judge when I am sentenced.

Q: Have you been paid anything for being an informer?
A: Yes.
Q: What have you been paid?
A: From time to time I get $50.
Q: Do you use that money to buy heroin?
A: No, sir.
Q: Have you been selling heroin while you've been an informer?
A: No, sir.
Q: How, then, have you been feeding your habit?
A: Different ways.

The credibility of the witness has been substantially damaged not only by the fact of addiction and his status as an informer, but also by the implication that monies received or his privileged status as an informer has afforded him an opportunity to satisfy his habit—a strong evidentiary basis from which to argue in summation his motive to fabricate evidence favorable to his masters, the narcotics squad of the police department.

Success in impeaching witnesses requires not only thorough pretrial preparation, a working knowledge of the relevant rules of evidence, and sensitivity to what will impact a judge or jury positively and negatively, but also a bit of a sense for the dramatic. All of these are essential to impeaching a witness on the basis of addiction to or abuse of alcohol or other dangerous substances; but, in this area of impeachment perhaps more than in any other, sensitivity to what will impact a judge or jury positively and negatively is critical.

§2.05 Impeachment by Prior Inconsistent Statements

An experienced litigating lawyer will tingle with excitement confronting an adverse witness with a prior inconsistent statement on a material matter. Indeed, in the hands of a skilled and prepared advocate, a prior inconsistent statement on a material matter is uniquely devastating and has the potential of altering the course of a trial. On the other hand, few things are as frustrating to the knowledgeable observer as watching an inept, unprepared lawyer try to impeach a witness with a prior inconsistent statement.

As with any lethal weapon, the ability to use a prior inconsistent statement with at least modest success and effect requires knowledge of the nature and quality of the ammunition—the prior inconsistent statement. Thus, it is essential to be familiar with and understand the applicable evidentiary rules. Indeed, absent familiarity and understanding of the requisites to impeaching a witness with a prior inconsistent statement, the effort is almost certain to fail and, indeed, may incur a derogatory comment from the trial court which the jury will immediately grasp.

Familiarity with the rules of evidence is essential to understand how to and to prepare the most effective use of a prior inconsistent statement to impeach.

Indeed, lack of familiarity with the rules can sap the strength of or abort impeachment with a prior inconsistent statement. Thus, a brief review of evidentiary rules that significantly affect use of a witness's prior inconsistent statement for impeachment is appropriate.

Definition of Prior Inconsistent Statement

A prior inconsistent statement is any communication by a witness, oral or written, informal or formal, under oath or not under oath, made prior to the witness's testimonial appearance which is inconsistent with testimony the witness gave from the witness stand.

An oral prior inconsistent statement may be as informal as small talk by the witness at a cocktail party or around a dinner table. At the other end of the spectrum, an oral prior inconsistent statement may be a statement under oath at a deposition, trial, or executive or legislative hearing.

A written prior inconsistent statement may be nothing more formal than a postcard, note, or letter, or it may be a statement under oath in an affidavit, certificate, verified pleading, or other formal document.

As will be discussed later, any prior inconsistent statement may be utilized to impeach a witness. Most significantly, Rule 801(d)(1) of the Federal Rules of Evidence permits the trier of fact to consider the prior inconsistent statement as substantive evidence if it "was given under oath subject to the penalty of perjury at a trial, hearing or other proceeding, or in a deposition."

Use of Extrinsic Evidence to Impeach on Collateral Matters

In stating earlier that, if properly used, an adverse witness's prior inconsistent statement *on a material matter* can be devastating and alter the course of a trial, we did not intend to suggest that impeachment by prior inconsistent statement is limited to material matters only and that impeachment may not be predicated on a witness's prior inconsistent statement on any matter. Indeed it may be.

However, the rule that some mistakenly believe prohibits impeaching a witness on a collateral matter has a significant impact on the decision whether and how to use a witness's prior inconsistent statement to impeach. Properly put, the rule prohibits use of *extrinsic* evidence to impeach a witness on collateral matters. That means that one may not contradict a witness on a collateral matter by testimony from another witness.

In the context of impeaching a witness with a prior inconsistent statement, the rule simply means that if the prior inconsistent statement which is used to impeach is on a collateral rather than material matter and the witness denies making it, that is the end of the inquiry; the prior inconsistent statement cannot be put into evidence through another witness.

On the other hand, if the prior inconsistent statement is oral and on a material matter, and the witness denies making it, it may be introduced by the testimony of another witness; if the prior inconsistent statement is written and on a material matter, and the witness denies making it, the foundation for its admissibility may be furnished by the testimony of another witness.

Thus, when deciding if and how to use a witness's prior inconsistent statement, whether or not the statement can be established by extrinsic evidence is of substantial importance. If the inconsistency is on a collateral, rather than material, matter, it cannot be established by extrinsic evidence. In that case, the risk of damage if the witness denies making the statement may be greater than the benefit to be derived from the witness's acknowledgment of having made the statement, and the lawyer may decide to forego the opportunity to impeach. Moreover, seeking to impeach a witness by a prior inconsistent statement on a collateral and, thus, a relatively minor matter, may evoke a feeling of sympathy from the jury who understand that memories are fallible—particularly on seemingly irrelevant matters. Thus, here again the litigating lawyer must exercise the most informed judgment possible and, of course, be familiar with the rules and prepared adequately for the task.

Confronting Witness with Prior Statement

Historically, and in many jurisdictions today, to impeach a nonparty witness with a prior inconsistent statement, the witness must first be confronted with the statement, that is, the attention of the witness must be directed to the time, place, circumstance, and content of the statement and asked if the statement was made.

The requirement of confrontation was abolished by Rule 613, if "on request, the [statement is] shown or disclosed to opposing counsel." By rule or judicial decision, abolition of the confrontation rule is gaining broad acceptance.

Nonetheless, while some jurisdictions no longer require that a witness's attention be directed to the time when, place where, circumstance under which made, and the content of the statement to be used to impeach in most circumstances the process of confrontation enhances the significance of the prior inconsistent statement to the jury. As it is important in all impeachment that the witness be firmly committed to the testimony which is to be impeached, it is important for the witness to acknowledge to the jury making the prior statement (which is going to be used for impeachment). Then, the witness should be asked to recall a specific event or his or her presence at a particular location at a given time in the presence of identified persons (including the witness who will provide the extrinsic evidence if the witness denies making the prior inconsistent statement). Only then should the witness be confronted with the content of the prior inconsistent statement and asked to recall and acknowledge making it. The preliminaries and confrontation put the witness in the position either of having to acknowledge making the statement or of appearing to have purposefully forgotten it. It also gives credence to the witness who will offer the extrinsic evidence to put the inconsistent statement before the jury.

And, when confronting the witness with the prior inconsistent statement, the questioner should utilize the sparse and simple language that is custom and practice for experienced litigating lawyers. Indeed, there are time-worn sparse and simple ways of concluding the process of impeachment by prior inconsistent statements. For instance, when confronting the witness with prior testimony, the experienced lawyer will simply ask:

Q: Do you remember being asked this (these) question(s) and giving this (these) answer(s)?

There are several substantial advantages to concluding the process of impeaching by prior inconsistent statements with sparse and simple language and, where possible, with the precise question so familiar to experienced litigators and judges. Doing so compels the witness to respond simply "yes" or "no," minimizing the opportunity for the witness to offer a narrative response in an effort to harmonize the prior inconsistent statement with the impeached testimony. As well, its simplicity and sparseness rivets the attention of the jury on the prior inconsistent statement, the coup de grace in the process. And, significantly, it indicates to those familiar with the litigating process that the interrogator is an experienced professional.

Thus, assume that in the trial of an action for personal injuries, John Smith, the plaintiff, testified on direct examination, *inter alia,* that he was driving 35 miles an hour as he approached the intersection where the accident in which his car and one driven by Walter Jones collided. Assume that in Smith's deposition he testified that he was going more than 50 miles an hour as he approached the intersection. That portion of cross-examination involving Smith's prior inconsistent statement in the form of deposition testimony might be along the following lines.

First, of course, the witness should be committed to the testimony on direct examination to be impeached. If possible, as will be done here, the cross-examining lawyer should confirm to the jury that the testimony on direct examination responded to questions posed by the lawyer who called Smith as a witness.

Q: Mr. Smith, you testified in response to questions by your attorney that you were going approximately 35 miles an hour as you approached the intersection, didn't you?

A: Yes, I did.

The cross-examining lawyer might try to lure the witness into deeper water while trying to have the witness fully committed to the testimony to be impeached.

Q: Having driven that road many times, you were familiar with the intersection, right?

A: That's right.

Q: Knowing you were coming to the intersection, you slowed to 35 miles an hour?

A: Yes, I suppose so.

Q: Indeed, you said "I suppose so" because you slowed down automatically knowing that the intersection was coming up?

A: I guess that's right.

With the witness committed to the testimony on direct examination, and having reinforced it by having the witness state that speed was related to the witness's knowledge of the danger of approaching the intersection at great speed, the confrontation process begins. Here, as earlier noted, if possible, the witness should be quietly lured into recalling the circumstances under which the prior inconsistent statement was made.

Q: Mr. Smith, do you recall coming to my office with your lawyer about two years ago?

A: I think so.

Q: We met in a room lined with bookshelves and books?

A: Yes.

Q: Do you recall who was there?

A: My lawyer, you, myself, and another person with a machine of some sort. Am I right?

Q: That's right, and I asked you questions and you answered my questions, do you remember that?

A: Yes, I do.

Having recalled the circumstance of the deposition, if the witness now denies making the prior inconsistent statement the jury may well conclude that the denial is contrived. However, where the prior inconsistent statement is testimony, the cross-examining lawyer, before completing the impeachment, might try to have the witness acknowledge to the jury that the prior statement was under oath.

Q: You recall the deposition some two years ago where you answered my questions?

A: Yes.

Q: You testified under oath then, didn't you?

A: I guess so.

Q: Don't you recall taking an oath to tell the truth before I started asking questions?

A: I think so, yes.

Q: Then, Mr. Smith, do you remember being asked these questions and giving these answers:

> "Q: How fast were you going when you approached the intersection?
>
> A: About 55 miles an hour.
>
> Q: You were going 55 miles an hour as you approached the intersection?
>
> A: That's right, 55."

Q: Do you recall being asked those questions and giving those answers?

A: Yes, I do.

Some lawyers habitually conclude this kind of impeachment with one final question, either:

Q: Your recollection was better two years ago than it is today, isn't that right?

or:

Q: Were you telling the truth two years ago at your deposition or today when you testified on direct examination?

Generally, it is best to conclude impeachment by a prior inconsistent statement with the witness's acknowledgment of having made the statement. That last question may evoke a response that will detract from the effectiveness of the acknowledgment or elicit an objection from the opposing lawyer: Save the argument for summation.

There are, of course, myriad situations which do not fall within such an easy pattern. For example, what if the testimony the witness gave on direct examination that is to be impeached seemed a bit shaky and uncertain? The direct effort to commit the witness to that testimony may well push the witness into an unnecessary and unwanted certainty. Thus, a gentler initial approach may afford the witness the opportunity to back away from the testimony on direct examination and thus more readily acknowledge and reinforce the prior inconsistent statement.

Q: Mr. Smith, I think I heard you tell Lawyer Line earlier today that when you approached the intersection you were going 35 miles an hour?

A: Yes.

Q: I recall that about two years ago you discussed that with Lawyer Line and me, didn't you?

A: Yes, I believe I did.

Q: Do you remember telling us that you were going 55 miles an hour?

A: Yes, I do.

Q: You were under oath then, like you are today?

A: Yes.

And what of inconsistency by omission? May it be used to impeach a witness? Generally, if a witness's testimony omits a material fact included in a prior statement or adds a material fact not mentioned in a prior statement, the omission may be considered an inconsistency for impeachment purposes. Clearly, the witness may be cross-examined to impeach using the prior statement's apparent inconsistency.

However, where the inconsistency involves omission of a material matter on direct examination and the prior statement containing the material matter has not been memorialized, it is likely that the cross-examiner will be bound by the witness's denial of the prior inconsistency and be precluded from offering extrinsic evidence to establish the prior inconsistent statement.

If the prior statement with the material matter omitted during direct examination was memorialized in a document or prior testimony, the witness may be confronted with the document or transcript and asked to acknowledge the making of the statement or the authenticity of the document or transcript. If authenticated by the witness, it may be offered into evidence. On the other hand, since extrinsic evidence of a prior statement may be used to impeach testimony, the trial court may well hold that there is no testimony to impeach since the omission established nothing. However, though inadmissible through extrinsic evidence as a prior inconsistent statement, it may be offered as the admission of a party, prior testimony, or some other exception to the hearsay rule.

§2.06 Silence as a Basis for Impeachment

Contrary to age-old wisdom, silence is not always golden. Indeed, while almost everyone knows that "what you say may be used against you," few people appreciate the fact that there are instances when what you do *not* say may be used against you.

Simply put, depending upon the circumstances, the forum, and the issues determinable by the trier of fact, a witness's silence may offer an opportunity for impeachment during cross-examination. However, to utilize silence as a basis for impeaching a witness without risking a mistrial, it is essential to understand when and under what circumstances silence may provide a basis for impeachment.

Obviously, the witness's silence or failure to utter words or respond to a stimulus may have occurred on a prior occasion or during the examination itself.

Consider the witness's silence on a prior occasion. As a general rule, when someone says something in the presence of a party to the litigation, which is evidently heard by the party and consists of or includes statements of fact which, if untrue, one would expect the party to deny, the party's failure to deny or contravene the statement is deemed to be an admission which is receivable against the party.

As an admission, of course, silence in the face of a statement one would usually expect a party to deny is an exception to the hearsay rule, and may be established by the testimony of a person who heard the statement and can testify that the party heard the statement and said nothing.

Q: Mr. Jones, were you a passenger in the car Mr. Smith was driving on January 6, 1990?

A: Yes, I was.

Q: And were you in the car at the time of the accident?

A: Yes.

Q: And where were you seated at that time?

A: In the front seat on the passenger's side immediately next to Mr. Smith.

Q: And was the radio on at any time?

A: No, it wasn't.

Q: Did you say anything to Mr. Smith right after the accident?

A: I did.

Q: What did you say?

A: I said, "Jim, we were going too fast."

Q: Did Mr. Smith say anything in response?

A: No.

It would seem clear that Mr. Smith's silence—his failure to respond to the statement of fact—may be considered by the jury as an admission. However, the jury does not know the significance of Mr. Smith's silence until it is argued in summation and explained in the court's instructions. Thus, establishing the party's admission to the jury through the testimony of an observer seems rather bland and does not take advantage of the opportunity to etch it in the minds of the jurors by increasing the drama and thus maximizing its importance.

On the other hand, using cross-examination's impeachment process may offer an opportunity to pique the curiosity of the jury, maximizing the significance of the witness's silence and etching it in their minds to be extrapolated and argued in summation as an admission.

Q: Mr. Smith, was anyone in the car with you on January 6, 1990?

A: Yes.

Q: More than one person?

A: No, sir, just one person.

Q: Who was the one person with you in the car on January 6, 1990?

A: Mr. Jones.

Q: Where was he sitting?

A: In front in the passenger seat.

Q: Right next to you?

A: Yes, that's right.

Q: Was the radio on at any time?

A: No, I don't think it was.

Q: Did Mr. Jones say anything to you immediately after the accident?

The witness's response may be "Yes," "No," or "I don't recall." If the response is "Yes," the witness is, of course, acknowledging that Mr. Jones made a statement. If the response is "No," it may indicate that Mr. Jones made no statement, Mr. Smith did not hear the statement, or Mr. Smith does not recall the statement. If Mr. Smith says "I don't recall," it suggests that he heard a statement but cannot recall it. Since, as noted, a prerequisite to using silence as an admission is some evidence the person against whom silence is to be offered, the last question might better be phrased:

Q: Did you hear Mr. Jones say anything immediately after the accident?

With the question thus phrased, if the response is "Yes," the foundation for the impeaching evidence has been established.

Q: Please tell the jury what Mr. Jones said immediately after the accident?
A: He said, "Jim, you were going too fast."
Q: And what did you say in response, Mr. Smith?
A: Nothing.
Q: Did you deny that you were going too fast?
A: I just told you I said nothing.
Q: So you did not deny that you were going too fast?
A: I said nothing.

If the response is "No," further cross-examination may persuade the jury that Mr. Smith is not telling the truth and will probably not foreclose calling Mr. Jones to establish the making of the statement and the fact that Mr. Smith heard it.

Q: Well, did you hear Mr. Jones make any noise of any kind after the accident?
A: I don't recall.
Q: But you *do* recall Mr. Jones said nothing?
A: I don't know if he said something or not.
Q: Perhaps I can refresh your recollection, Mr. Smith. Do you recall Mr. Jones saying in words or substance, "Jim, you were going too fast"?

The question lets the witness know that Mr. Jones told the cross-examiner that Mr. Jones had made that statement and is probably willing to testify, and also lays the foundation to call Mr. Jones in rebuttal. Mr. Smith's acknowledgment that Mr. Jones made the statement calls the jury's attention to the statement, emphasizing its importance for subsequent explanation in summation. Mr. Smith's denial or failure to recall that Mr. Jones made the statement fixes the statement in the jurors' minds and maintains their interest and focus when Mr. Jones is subsequently called to testify that he made the statement and that Mr. Smith heard it and did not respond.

Of course, the general rule that silence by someone who would be expected to deny a statement of fact if it was false is an adoptive or tacit admission is applicable to criminal prosecutions and to civil actions. Thus, assume that one of the accused in a prosecution for armed robbery of a bank and murder committed by several persons testifies in his own defense. If there is a good faith basis for the line of questioning, the cross-examiner may impeach the accused by questioning his failure to respond to a statement by one of the other participants which other persons in the bank observed.

Q: Mr. Chuter, you testified on direct examination that you were in the bank with a friend of yours but did nothing, didn't you?

A: Yep.

Q: And you told the jury that your friend Mr. Bouch was in the bank with you?

A: That's right.

Q: And you said that you recalled hearing what you thought was a gun shot?

A: Yeah.

Q: Do you recall immediately after the gun shot hearing Mr. Bouch say to you, in words or in substance, "Jake, you shouldn't have pulled the trigger"?

A: Nah, I don't recall anything like that.

Q: You're not saying that it didn't happen, but only that you don't recall it?

A: That's right.

The jury's interest is piqued and the stage is thus set for the prosecution to call someone who was in the bank to testify that he heard Mr. Bouch make the statement and that Mr. Chuter did not respond, conveying the implication that Mr. Chuter was, indeed, the person who pulled the trigger.

In both civil and criminal litigation, a witness's prior silence may be used to impeach the witness's testimony on the basis that the testimony is a recent fabrication. For example, if a defendant in a murder prosecution was not apprehended for several months, during which time he knew he was wanted, testifies at his trial that he acted in self-defense, he may be impeached by inquiring whether, during the months before his arrest, he asserted that he acted in self-defense.

As with all general rules, there are exceptions to this rule deeming such silences admissions. The most significant exception to the use of an adoptive or tacit admission in a criminal case has a constitutional foundation.

In the previous section we considered and furnished examples of the impeachment of witnesses by prior inconsistent statements, while this section considers and gives examples of impeachment of witnesses predicated upon their prior silence. The distinction between prior inconsistent statements and prior silence is critical in comprehending the constitutionally based exception in criminal prosecutions to the general rule that silence by one who would be expected to deny a statement of fact if it was false is an adoptive or tacit admission. Stated most broadly, a person's silence in response to a statement that one would be expected to deny if false is *not* an adoptive or tacit admission *if* that silence was induced by explicit or implicit governmental assurance that the person has a right to remain silent without being penalized for that silence.

The rationale for that exception is evident: If one who knows that he is the target of a criminal investigation or who is under indictment is told that he has an absolute right to remain silent and that anything he does say may be used against him, his silence in the face of a false statement of fact is at least as likely to be founded on his right to remain silent as on an implication that the statement is true; thus, his silence may not be used to impeach him.

On the other hand, if one who knows that he is the target of a criminal investigation or who is under indictment responds to a statement or a question notwithstanding the assurance that he has a right to remain silent and the admonition that anything he says may be used against him, he waives the constitutionally based right to remain silent and his statement, if inconsistent with his later testimony, may be utilized to impeach him.

Thus, while the post-arrest silence of one who *is* advised of his right to remain silent may not be used to impeach his trial testimony, like the post-arrest inconsistent statement of one who is advised of his right to remain silent, the post-arrest silence of one who *is not* advised of his right to remain silent may be used to impeach his trial testimony.

Under some circumstances, silence in a judicial proceeding may be used subsequently to impeach. Thus, for example, while there is a general constitutional proscription against using the invocation of the privilege against self-incrimination against a defendant in a criminal prosecution, if a trial in which a defendant did not testify ended in a mistrial and the defendant does testify at the second trial, impeachment by cross-examination which compels the defendant to admit silence—failure to testify at the first trial—is not barred by any absolute constitutional proscription.

In a *civil* action, the prior silence of a party predicated on invocation of the privilege against self-incrimination at an examination before trial may be used to impeach the party at the trial and, indeed, entitles the adversary to a judicial instruction that the jury may draw an unfavorable inference by reason of that silence. In the trial of a civil action or criminal prosecution, the silence of a party or witness during cross-examination by refusing to respond to a proper question permits the trial court to strike all of the testimony of the party or witness and instruct the jury to disregard totally the direct and cross-examination of the party or witness.

Thus, as earlier observed, silence is not always golden and the litigating lawyer must understand precisely when and under what circumstances the silence of a party or witness may be used against the party or witness.

Of course, when a witness refuses to answer questions during cross-examination though directed to by the court, the witness' entire testimony may, in the exercise of discretion, be stricken.

§2.07 Prior Misconduct to Impeach

As earlier noted, impeachment may be purposed to persuade the trier of fact of the unreliability of the evidence itself or of the untrustworthiness of its source, the witness.

If evidence establishes that a witness has previously engaged in conduct reflecting adversely on the witness's honesty and integrity, it is altogether reasonable for the trier of fact to question the trustworthiness of that witness's testimony. Indeed, each of us makes judgments daily about the truth or falsity of information furnished by others predicated on knowledge or information we have concerning the integrity or reliability of the source.

Thus, if evidence establishes that a witness has previously prevaricated, the trier of fact may find the witness to be untrustworthy. Of course, the damage to credibility is in direct proportion to the seriousness of the subject matter of the untruth.

Similarly, if the evidence demonstrates that a witness is a thief or has engaged in violent conduct, the trier of fact may be persuaded that the witness lacks credibility. The impact on credibility depends in part on the proximity of the misconduct to the witness's testimonial appearance.

Consequently, to impeach the witness's credibility, most jurisdictions permit a witness to be cross-examined concerning prior acts of misconduct which adversely affect the witness's integrity or reliability. To pursue such impeachment, the witness must be confronted with the specific act or acts to be used to impeach and asked to admit or deny the conduct.

A trier of fact may reasonably conclude that if a witness will falsify an application to a bank for a loan, such a witness will falsify testimony.

> Q: Mr. Jones, didn't you apply to the First National Bank for a loan on January 6, 1982?
>
> A: Yes.
>
> Q: And you completed a written application for that loan, didn't you?
>
> A: Yes.
>
> Q: And in that written application you represented to the Bank that your annual income was $150,000?
>
> A: Yes, I believe I did.
>
> Q: Mr. Jones, your representation to the First National Bank that your income was $150,000 was not true, was it?

Mr. Jones will respond "Yes," "No," or "I don't recall."

If Mr. Jones admits falsifying the application, the impeaching evidence is before the trier of fact and may be urged in closing argument or summation as a reason to discredit the witness's testimony. What if Mr. Jones denies falsifying the application or does not recall making the application or its content? Clearly, putting the application into evidence would establish the existence of the application and its content for the trier of fact. It would not prove the falsity of the representation, however; proving such falsity would require one or more witnesses or documents and cause a proliferation of subsidiary issues to be determined by the trier of fact and a prolongation of the trial.

Use of Extrinsic Evidence

Thus, while most jurisdictions permit impeachment of a witness by cross-examination as to prior acts of misconduct which adversely affect the witness's integrity or reliability, to avoid the proliferation of subsidiary issues and prolongation of the trial where the misconduct did not result in a criminal conviction, the interrogating lawyer is bound by the witness's answer and may not establish the misconduct by extrinsic evidence.

Federal Rules of Evidence (Fed R Evid) Rule 608(b)(1) adopts this view:

> Specific instances of the conduct of a witness, for the purpose of attacking . . . credibility other than conviction of a crime . . . may not be proved by extrinsic evidence. They may, however, in the discretion of the court, if probative of . . . untruthfulness, be inquired into on cross-examination of the witness . . . concerning his character for . . . untruthfulness.

Here, as with virtually all evidence, the rule gives the trial court discretion to limit or preclude inquiry or proof if the prejudicial effect outweighs the probative value. It should be understood that, unlike judgments that persons make daily, the general rule is that evidence of a prior act of misconduct, whether resulting in criminal conviction or not, may not be utilized to establish by inference that the person commited the act in question; such evidence may be used only to impeach the witness's credibility.

Criminal Conviction

On the other hand, if the misconduct resulted in a criminal conviction, cross-examination as to the misconduct and conviction are generally permissible to impeach and, in most jurisdictions, as Rule 608(b)(1) implies, the conviction may be established by extrinsic evidence. Whereas establishing acts of misconduct not resulting in a conviction by extrinsic evidence leads to a proliferation of subsidiary issues to be determined by the trier of fact and a prolongation of the trial, establishing the fact of conviction by extrinsic evidence is relatively easy (and a trier of fact has already determined the act of misconduct).

Thus, assume that in the earlier effort to impeach Mr. Jones by cross-examination concerning falsification of a loan application, Mr. Jones denied misconduct but was convicted of the crime of submitting a false loan application to a bank.

A: No, sir, I never gave the Bank a false application to obtain a loan.

Q: But you did apply to the First National Bank for a loan on January 6, 1982?

A: Yes.

Q: And you completed a written application for that loan, didn't you?

A: Yes.

Q: But you deny stating in the application that your annual income was $150,000?A: Yes.

Q: Mr. Jones, I show you what has been marked as Exhibit 4 for identification and ask you if that is the loan application you submitted to the First National Bank on January 6, 1982?

A: No.

Recall, now, that the application cannot be established by extrinsic evidence.

Q: Mr. Jones, were you convicted on May 23, 1983 of filing a false application with the First National Bank on January 6, 1982?

As with the fact of misconduct, Mr. Jones may admit, deny, or fail to recall the fact of conviction. If he admits it, it is before the trier of fact to impeach credibility. If he denies or fails to recall it, cross-examination may continue and should be purposed and delivered to maximize the dramatic impact of two demonstrable falsehoods. As well, since extrinsic evidence is admissible to establish the fact of a criminal conviction for misconduct adversely affecting credibility, the lawyer seeking to impeach should have a certified copy of the judgment of conviction to offer in the event that the witness denies or does not recall the conviction; the certified copy is self-authenticating and thus admissible.

A: No, sir, I was not!

Q: Mr. Jones, you deny filing a false loan application with First National Bank on January 6, 1982?

A: That's right.

Q: And you deny that you were convicted on May 23, 1983 of filing a false loan application with First National Bank on January 6, 1982?

A: Yes.

Q: Mr. Jones, I show you what has been marked Exhibit 5 for identification and ask you to look at that and read it to yourself.

A: Yes.

Q: Have you read that to yourself?

A: I have.

Q: Have you ever seen that before? [Or, does that refresh your recollection?]

A: I don't recall. [Or, No.]

Q: Would you please read it aloud?

Since it is certified and thus self-authenticating, it is admissible without the need to call a foundation witness. Asking the witness to read from the document before it is in evidence will likely evoke an objection from the lawyer who called the witness, adding to the drama and emphasizing the fact that the witness did not tell the truth about the falsification and conviction.

MR. SMITH'S ATTORNEY:

Objection, Your Honor. The document is not in evidence.

THE COURT:

Objection sustained.

MR. JONES'S ATTORNEY:

I offer Exhibit 5 in evidence, Your Honor.

THE COURT:

Let me see it. Received. Exhibit 5 appears to be a certified copy of an official court record.

Q: Please read that to the jury, Mr. Smith?

A: "In the Second District Court for the State of Washington, on this 23d day of May, 1983, John Smith, the Defendant, was convicted on a jury verdict of 'Guilty' of the crime of falsifying a loan application to a bank, to wit, a loan application to First National Bank on January 6, 1982."

Virtually all jurisdictions permit impeachment of witnesses by proof of criminal conviction, and most authorize the use of any felony conviction. Many, however, limit such impeachment to convictions which bear on the witness's integrity or honesty, such as crimes involving false swearing, fraud, deceit, embezzlement, and the like.[2] As well, temporal limitations and the effect of a pardon restrict the use of criminal convictions for impeachment purposes.[3]

§2.08 Impeachment by Testimony Inconsistent with That of Other Witnesses

It is most unusual for the testimony on direct examination of two witnesses to coincide in all of the details. Indeed, if two witnesses give virtually identical testimony, it is likely that the lawyer who called them prepared them together to ensure that there would be no inconsistencies between them. It might be useful when cross-examining the second witness, whose testimony on direct examination seemingly parrots that of an earlier witness, to ask the second witness whether that witness discussed his or her testimony with the lawyer who called him or her and, if the witness responds in the affirmative, to ask whether anyone else was present!

Thus, when two witnesses testify on the same subject, it is likely that there will be inconsistencies between them as to details. Is impeachment of one witness by confrontation with testimony that another witness has given, or is expected to give, that is inconsistent with the one witness's testimony, appropriate? When witnesses testifying to the same event or on the same subject matter disagree on a material matter, the trier of fact must determine which

---

[2] *See, e.g.,* Fed R Evid 609(a).

[3] *Id* 609(c).

of them, if either, is telling the truth. The inconsistency, if significant, should be called to the attention of the trier of fact in closing argument.

Whether to impeach a witness on cross-examination by confronting the witness with testimony of another witness which is inconsistent with the other witness's testimony requires the exercise of litigating judgment and depends on many factors. Is the other witness whose testimony is inconsistent with that of the witness being cross-examined also an adverse witness? Is the inconsistency on a matter of substance and importance or on an insignificant detail? Has the witness impressed the jury favorably? Does the testimony of one of the witnesses favor the position of the cross-examining lawyer and, if so, which witness is more credible? Is it likely that the witness will utilize cross-examination on the inconsistency to reinforce his or her testimony? These and other factors all interact and must be considered before confronting one witness with inconsistent testimony from another.

For example, a well-prepared witness confronted on cross-examination with inconsistent testimony from a witness friendly to the cross-examining lawyer's cause is likely simply to say that the other witness is wrong. If we add the fact that the testimony given by the witness friendly to the cross-examining lawyer is corroborated by documents, confrontation to impeach by a witness's statement which is inconsistent with the other witness's statement may reap some benefit.

Generally, experienced litigating lawyers abjure confronting one witness with the inconsistent testimony of another, unless both witnesses were adverse or hostile, the inconsistencies glaring and involving a matter going to the heart of the litigation, and the witness whose testimony is most favorable is the more credible. Even then, some art and ethical deception should be used to snare the witness who is being confronted with significant inconsistent testimony from another witness.

For example, assume that in the hypothetical case used for illustrative purposes in **§2.05,** two witnesses are called by John Smith, the plaintiff. Assume that the first witness—Reverend Duncan, a local minister—testified that he believed that Smith's car was going more than 50 miles an hour as it approached the intersection, while the second witness, Jim Ager, a retired plumber, believed that Smith was driving no more than 35 miles an hour. Simply to confront Mr. Ager with Reverend Duncan's testimony does not make the most of the situation.

Q: Sir, do you know Reverend Duncan?

A: Of course.

Q: How well do you know him?

A: Well, I've known him about 20 years; I go to his church.

Q: Well, then, you must think highly of him.

A: Sure do.

Q: I guess you have no doubt about his intelligence and his honesty.

A: Of course not.

Q: By the way, Mr. Ager, is Reverend Duncan older or younger than you?

A: I'd say about 12 years younger.

Q: You testified earlier that you believed that Mr. Smith was going 35 miles an hour as he approached the intersection?

A: Yes, I did.

Q: Could he have been going 50 miles an hour as he approached the intersection?

A: No, sir; impossible.

Q: What if someone said he believed that Mr. Smith was going 50?

A: I'd say that he didn't know what he was talking about!

Q: What would you say if I told you that, sitting in the very witness chair you are in, Reverend Duncan testified under oath that he believed that Mr. Smith was going 50 miles an hour as he approached the intersection?

A: Well, sir, er, I don't know. Maybe Mr. Smith was going a bit faster than I thought.

By taking the time to use the available information and a little imagination to lay a trap for the witness, the impeachment is made significantly more effective.

§2.09 Interest in or Bias as to Party, Litigation, or Issues to Impeach

Few persons who take the stand to testify are totally devoid of bias for or against one or another of the parties, or totally disinterested in the outcome of or the issues involved in the litigation. Consciously or not, bias or interest tends to influence the testimony of the witness.

Virtually anything that furnishes a basis for a reasonable person to conclude that someone is biased for or against a party, consciously or otherwise, may be the predicate for impeaching a witness for bias or interest. Thus, it is altogether appropriate for a person to conclude that a witness who is related to, who is a friend or acquaintance of, or who is employed by or associated with a party has a bias favoring that party. Conversely, it is rational for someone to believe that a witness with an interest or relationship which is emotionally, financially, or in any other way antagonistic or adverse to a party is biased against that party. Further, it is logical to conclude that a witness who is compensated by a party will testify favorably for that party.

A personal, financial, tangible, emotional, philosophical, or ideological interest in the result of the resolution of or a preference for a particular outcome of, the issues involved in a litigation may form the basis for an inference that the testimony of the witness is influenced by that interest; of course, it is rational to believe that the stronger the interest the greater the influence, conscious or otherwise. It is similarly reasonable to conclude that the strength of a relationship with, or antagonism against, a party has a bearing on the extent of the bias of the witness and, thus, on the extent to which the witness's testimony is influenced.

Indeed, even absent a relationship with, or interest in, a party, or an interest in the issues, or in the result of the resolution of the issues, involved in a matter, one may reasonably expect that a witness called to testify for a party subconsciously favors that party. It is likely that, long before being called to testify, the witness was interviewed by the lawyer for the party on whose behalf the witness is called and, consciously or subconsciously, through the interview and preparation process, has come to believe in the rightness of the cause on whose behalf the witness is called. Obviously, it is unlikely that the witness would be asked to testify if his or her testimony was adverse.

Nonetheless, most witnesses, even those with some kind of interest in or bias for or against a party or some aspect of the litigation, will try to answer questions fairly and honestly; some will consciously or subconsciously shade their testimony, while making every effort to appear to answer questions fairly and honestly.

The challenge for the cross-examining lawyer is to detect the difference!

With broad discovery and the advent of pretrial orders listing the witnesses whom each party intends to call and the anticipated testimony of each, the litigating lawyer should be able to obtain knowledge or information concerning relationship with or interest in a party or some aspect of the litigation for every important witness before the witness begins testifying. Reviewing the witness list, depositions, and document discovery with the client and friendly witnesses and, if necessary, discreet inquiry by an investigator should furnish useful information concerning every important witness.

If the lawyer has neither knowledge nor information concerning the relationship or interest of the witness before the witness testifies, detection of any bias or interest while the witness is testifying on direct examination is not always easy. Indeed, an encyclopedic knowledge of the relevant facts, a thorough awareness and understanding of relevant physical phenomena, and a keen sensitivity to human behavior will be great assets.

For example, if physical phenomena are of significance, a visit to the location under circumstances as similar to those that the evidence establishes as extant at the relevant time may assist the lawyer in detecting a biased witness who, consciously or subconsciously, is shading testimony. Similarly, detailed knowledge and understanding of the relevant facts may enable the lawyer to seize on a witness who answers the most inconsequential or neutral questions in a manner purposed to aid the party on whose behalf he or she was called. Sensitivity to the demeanor of the witness in such circumstances may well afford the basis for concluding that the witness is uncomfortable with and, thus, consciously or subconsciously, torturing the testimony.

Impeaching a witness by establishing the witness's bias or interest may be elicited by cross-examination or by extrinsic evidence. As a prerequisite to admissibility of extrinsic evidence to establish bias or interest, most jurisdictions require, as with impeachment by prior inconsistent statement, that the witness be confronted on cross-examination with the impeaching material. Indeed, it seems fair, and likely to seem so to the jury, that the witness be confronted with the evidence from which an inference of bias or interest may be drawn and afforded an opportunity to admit or deny the bias or interest, or to try to explain the evidence before extrinsic evidence is admitted for such purposes.

Thus, assume that in a civil action in which Mr. Hurt is suing Mr. Hitt for assault, Mr. Ayer testified that he witnessed the assault and is being cross-examined by Hitt's lawyer.

Q: Mr. Ayer, you are acquainted with Mr. Hurt and Mr. Hitt, aren't you?

A: Yes.

Q: How long have you known them?

A: Ten to twenty years.

Q: Have you known both of them the same length of time?

A: Just about.

Q: Do you know one of them better than the other?

A: I wouldn't say so.

Q: Do you like one of them better than the other?

A: I guess so.

Q: And of the two gentlemen, sir, who do you like better?

A: Mr. Hurt.

Q: In fact, sir, you and Mr. Hurt are fraternal lodge brothers, aren't you?

A: Yes.

Having elicited a clear admission of friendship toward the party on whose behalf the witness testified through membership in a fraternal organization, the trial court would likely exclude extrinsic evidence to establish the fact that Ayer has a bias or preference for Hurt.

Q: As a matter of fact, Mr. Ayer, you don't like Mr. Hitt at all, do you?

A: I wouldn't say that.

Q: Didn't you say to Mr. Jim Jones a few weeks ago while waiting for a bus that you didn't like Hitt at all?

A: I said no such thing!

Q: And, sir, didn't Mr. Hitt sue you for backing into his car while it was parked near your house?

A: I don't recall.

It seems clear that Hurt's lawyer can put Mr. Jones on the stand to testify to the conversation with Mr. Ayer.

Q: Mr. Jones, do you know U.R. Ayer?

A: Yes, I do.

Q: Did you have a conversation with him within the past few weeks concerning Y.U. Hitt?

A: Yes, while waiting for a bus.

Q: Please tell the jury the substance of what Mr. Ayer said concerning Mr. Hitt.

A: Well, Ayer said he never did care much for Hitt and since Hitt sued him awhile back for backing into his car, he didn't like him at all.

Jones's testimony that Ayer expressed dislike for Hitt and acknowledged Hitt's lawsuit against Ayer is received as an exception to the hearsay rule. Will the trial court admit other extrinsic evidence to establish the fact of the lawsuit? For the prepared and experienced litigating lawyer, the possibility is worth the effort.

ATTORNEY:

Your Honor, I appreciate that Mr. Jones testified that Mr. Ayer referred to Defendant Hitt's lawsuit against Mr. Ayer, but the jury may consider that simply Mr. Jones's interpretation, and it is hearsay although received merely to establish the making of the statement. I would like to offer to lay the requisite foundation to introduce a copy of the Complaint in that action to establish the record fact for the jury.

THE COURT:

Very well; in the exercise of discretion I'll allow it.

The complaint or, perhaps, the docket entries may be offered by certified copy or by the custodian of the record laying the foundation. The latter approach is more dramatic and perhaps the better course if there had been no other evidence of the fact—i.e., if Jones had not testified.

Q: What is your occupation?

A: I am Clerk of the District Court of Berkshire County.

Q: And as Clerk are you custodian of the Court's records?

A: Yes, I am.

Q: I show you what is marked as Exhibit 7 and ask you to identify it.

A: It is a copy of a Complaint filed in my Court.

Q: How do you recognize it?

A: By the stamp receipt on it and by having compared it with the original filed with the Court.

Trial courts and juries react negatively to needless embarrassment of a witness. Thus, before pursuing the impeachment of a witness for bias or interest on cross-examination with the prospect of offering extrinsic evidence to complete the task, the experienced lawyer will make the litigating judgment that the witness or his or her testimony is important enough to require the effort.

§2.10 Using Inadmissible Evidence to Impeach

A first-year law student who has passed constitutional law will state the rule: Illegally obtained evidence is subject to suppression and, if suppressed, is inadmissible against a criminal accused. Actually, that statement of the rule is too broad, and the limitation has particular significance when considering cross-examination to impeach. Properly phrased, the rule should be stated thus: Illegally obtained evidence which is suppressed is inadmissible against a criminal accused in the prosecution's case-in-chief.

Suppression is not intended to benefit an accused but to deter official lawlessness in seizing evidence and securing incriminating statements, and to permit an accused to testify at a suppression hearing without concern that his or her testimony will be used against him or her at trial. Thus, as the courts put it, suppression is intended as a shield and not a sword. However, while illegally obtained evidence, if suppressed, is inadmissible against an accused during the prosecution's case-in-chief, it is available for use to impeach the accused on cross-examination.

For example, if heroin was illegally seized from the residence of a criminal accused and subsequently suppressed and, during his trial for bribing a federal agent, the accused testified on direct examination that he was never involved in illicit drugs, he may be cross-examined concerning the illegally seized heroin and, if he denies that it was found in his residence, extrinsic evidence may be offered to establish the fact. Similarly, if a suspect, during interrogation without having been advised of her rights, acknowledged the commission of crimes other than those for which she is being tried and, while testifying on direct examination, denies ever having engaged in illegal activity, she may be cross-examined about her admission of having committed those crimes. If she denies the admission, the interrogating officer may testify to the same.

This limitation on the inadmissibility of suppressed, illegally seized evidence is significant not only to the prosecutor but also to the lawyer representing the criminal accused. The prosecutor, of course, plans his or her case-in-chief without relying on the suppressed evidence, all the while waiting for the accused to testify and open the door to its use on cross-examination. The lawyer representing the accused must know the full extent of all evidence which has been suppressed and, if the accused exercises his or her right to testify, carefully plan direct examination to avoid opening the door to use of the suppressed evidence on cross-examination.

§2.11 Conclusion

The opportunities available to a litigating lawyer to impeach a witness are limited only by the lawyer's imagination and knowledge of the rules of evidence, and by the information, knowledge, and evidence acquired during pretrial preparation. Save for that which is excluded because it is thought to have prejudicial effect outweighing probative value, its admission may unduly prolong the trial or confuse the issues, or its receipt would be unfair to a party or the witness, almost any evidence from which the trier of fact may infer or conclude that a witness is not utterly disinterested and objective may be the subject of cross-examination to impeach.

3 To Impeach or Not to Impeach

§3.01 Introduction

Just as, sometimes, the best cross-examination is the one that is never carried out, so the best impeachment is often the one that never takes place.

It is natural for a lawyer, upon hearing direct testimony that hurts his or her theory of the case, to look for ways to impeach the witness. But, generally, following one's natural reactions is not the best way to find solutions. Advice such as "think it over" or "take your time before deciding" is most appropriate when a person wants to act in an impulsive way.

Before deciding to impeach a witness, the lawyer must remember that he or she is only the representative of the client; an impulsive decision to impeach as a result of what a witness said (perhaps hurting the lawyer's ego) can sometimes harm the lawyer's party more than the witness's testimony.

What must a lawyer consider before deciding whether to impeach a witness?

1. Was the witness's testimony as a whole harmful to the cross-examiner's party, or were only parts of the testimony harmful to his or her case? If the damage is only partial, which are more important to the lawyer's theory of the case: the positive or the negative facts brought out by the witness?
2. Did the lawyer make an exhaustive investigation of the facts that he or she intends to use as the basis for impeachment?
3. Why does the lawyer believe that, with the material in his or her possession or knowledge, the impeachment will be a success?

4. Did the lawyer analyze the potential situations which could change the effects of the impeachment planned?
5. Does the lawyer have the necessary witness or witnesses to support the impeachment, in case something goes wrong in the cross-examination?

If, after the foregoing self-examination, the lawyer reaches the conclusion that the impeachment material in his or her possession can be the basis for success, then, without any more hesitation or doubt, *impeach.* But, if there are facts that could be interpreted in more than one way, or the possibility exists that the witness will have a good explanation for what the cross-examiner uses in his or her attempt to impeach (for example, a good explanation for why there are contradictions in two statements given by the witness under oath), then the lawyer must think twice about whether to impeach the witness.

§3.02 The Don'ts of Impeachment

First of all, don't waste the court's time or the jury's emotions trying to impeach a witness by asking questions about trivial discrepancies. For example, if the witness, said on direct examination that the accident occurred at 5:30 p.m., and then said on cross-examination that it occurred at 5:45 p.m., and the exact time of the accident is not a crucial issue in the trial, forget it. Further, impeaching on secondary, unimportant facts might give the jury the impression that you don't have anything valuable in your arsenal with which to impeach the witness and are trying to do so without a real basis.

Second, don't forget one of the basic rules of cross-examination: Don't ask "Why," or "How," or "Can you explain the contradiction." If this rule is important during cross-examinationgenerally, it is a *must* during the impeachment process. At this stage, erase these kinds of questions from your "practitioner's dictionary."

Third, don't answer witnesses' questions, except for inquiries by qualified witnesses or requests for clarification of a question. Some witnesses, by instinct or as a tactic, try to invert the process, asking questions of the lawyer. At the first sign of such intent, put the witness back in his or her place by saying, for example, "You are here to answer questions, not to ask them." Remember that one of the ways to lose control of a witness is to answer the witness's questions. However, in your closing argument, if you think that the witness's questions may have planted doubts in jurors' minds, refer to and answer them.

Fourth, don't try to pull the noose too tight. If you received the admission that you were looking for, don't try to fill in all the details.

Fifth, don't try to impeach unless the inconsistency between two statements or declarations is clear, relevant, and material. For example, during depositions the witness might have said that a contract was signed in the plaintiff's office, but then on direct examination the witness says that the contract was signed at the defendant's office. If the place where the contract was signed is material to the controversy, you have reason to try to impeach the witness. But if the important point is whether the person signed the contract, where the contract was signed is a secondary question that may or may not affect the witness's credibility; trying to impeach on such a basis is taking an unnecessary risk.

Sixth, don't try to avoid the reading of a witness's prior statement by summarizing the witness's complete contradictory statement or declaration. If you summarize what the witness said or wrote, it could give the impression that you are stating the matter out of context. The law and fairness to the witness require the reading of the entire statement and relevant paragraph.

Finally, don't try to give the jury, during the impeachment process, material to analyze or facts to interpret. Lead the jury to conclusions, not to interpretations.

§3.03 When to Confront the Witness

Sometimes, when eating a good meal, it is pleasant to savor the taste little by little; in the same way, there are lawyers who enjoy playing with a witness before confronting him or her with the impeachment material. This is a dangerous game because, in the course of it, the witness may bring up some unexpected matter, take the opportunity to repeat and emphasize what he or she said on direct examination, or take the opportunity to ask questions of the lawyer.

If the lawyer has decided to impeach a witness, it is because he or she is sure that it can be done successfully. Do not play games; after a few introductory questions, confront the witness with what he or she has said or written.

There are many reasons why the use of this tactic is urged. At the beginning of the cross-examination, witnesses tend to be under great nervous tension (they are unsure about what questions will be asked; they are not used to the lawyer's style of cross-examination; consequently, they are not in the best condition to explain calmly their contradictions). Another reason for this tactic is that the jury, the most important audience for the questions and answers, is more attentive at the beginning of the impeachment process.

The decision when to confront the witness with impeachment material is a matter of tactics. There are litigators who prefer not to confront the witness immediately with available impeachment material, as mentioned before; they prefer to build up some suspense and then to pin down the witness as part of their impeachment strategy.

There are lawyers who use another tactic: not to confront the witness with the impeachment material during cross-examination, but to reserve it for their closing arguments.

This tactic was used in the case *Martinez v Del Valle*[1] by the Honorable Joseph H. Choate, considered to have been one of the greatest luminaries among all American trial lawyers. The case was analyzed and criticized by Francis L. Wellman in his classic book *The Art of Cross-Examination.* We present here some excerpts from Wellman's book dealing with Choate's tactic of reserving for summation a damaging letter by the plaintiff.

---

[1] Supreme Court, New York County, before Justice Donohue, in January 1877.

The plaintiff [Miss Eugenie Martinez] and defendant [Mr. Juan del Valle] were strangers until the day when she had slipped on the ice, and had fallen in front of the Gilsey House on the corner of 29th Street and Broadway. Mr. del Valle had rushed to her assistance, had lifted her to her feet, conducted her to her room, received the permission of her mother to become her friend, and six months later had become the defendant in this notorious suit which he had tried to avoid by offering the plaintiff $20,000 not to bring it into court. . . .

. . . Mr. Choate had in his possession a letter written by the plaintiff to Mr. del Valle during the first few weeks of their acquaintance. In this letter Miss Martinez had complained of the wretchedness of her home life in consequence of the amorous advances made to her by her stepfather. Mr. Choate was evidently of the opinion that this letter was a hoax and had been written by Miss Martinez for the sole purpose of eliciting Mr. del Valle's sympathy, and of inducing him to allow her to come and live in his family as the governess of his children with the idea that a proposal of marriage would naturally result from such propinquity. Suspecting that the contents of this letter were false, and judging from statements made in the plaintiff's testimony-in-chief that she had either forgotten all about this letter or concluded that it had been destroyed, Mr. Choate set the first trap for the plaintiff in the following simple and extremely clever manner.

MR. CHOATE:

By what name did you pass after you returned home from boarding school and found your mother married to Mr. Henriquez?

MISS MARTINEZ:

Eugenie Henriquez, invariably.

MR. CHOATE:

And when did you first resume the name of Martinez?

MISS MARTINEZ:

When I left the roof of Mr. Henriquez.

MR. CHOATE:

Always until that time were you called by his name?

MISS MARTINEZ:

Always.

MR. CHOATE:

Did your father exercise any very rigid discipline over yourself and your sister that you remember?

MISS MARTINEZ:

He did.

MR. CHOATE:

When did that rigid discipline begin?

MISS MARTINEZ:

It commenced when I first knew him.

MR. CHOATE:

And it was very rigid, wasn't it?

MISS MARTINEZ:

It was, very.

MR. CHOATE:

Both over yourself and over your younger sister?

MISS MARTINEZ:

Yes.

MR. CHOATE:

Taking very strict observation and care as to your morals and your manners?

MISS MARTINEZ:

Exceedingly so.

MR. CHOATE:

How did this manifest itself?

MISS MARTINEZ:

Well, in preventing my having any other associates. He thought there was no one good enough to associate with us.

MR. CHOATE:

Then he was always very strict in keeping you in the path of duty, was he not?

MISS MARTINEZ:

Most undeniably so.

MR. CHOATE:

Was this a united family of which you were a member? Were they united in feeling?

MISS MARTINEZ:

Very much so indeed. There are very few families that are more united than we were.

MR. CHOATE:

All fond of each other?

MISS MARTINEZ:

Always.

MR. CHOATE:

As to your stepfather, you were all fond of him and he of you?

MISS MARTINEZ:

Very fond of him indeed, and he very fond of us.

MR. CHOATE:

And except this matter of his rigid discipline, was he kind to you?

MISS MARTINEZ:

Very.

MR. CHOATE:

And gentle?

MISS MARTINEZ:

Very gentle and very kind.

MR. CHOATE:

Considerate?

MISS MARTINEZ:

Very considerate always of our happiness, but he did not wish us to associate with the people by whom we were surrounded, as we were not in circumstances to live amongst our class.

MR. CHOATE:

When was it that he first introduced the subject of marriage, or forbidding you to marry, or thinking of marrying?

MISS MARTINEZ:

Well, when I was about sixteen or seventeen.

MR. CHOATE:

And was it then that he said that if you married, he would shoot you and shoot any man that you married?

MISS MARTINEZ:

He did.

MR. CHOATE:

That was the one exception to his ordinary gentleness and kindness, wasn't it?

MISS MARTINEZ:

Yes.

MR. CHOATE:

And the only one?

MISS MARTINEZ:

And the only one.

MR. CHOATE:

Your stepfather is no longer living, is he?

MISS MARTINEZ:

He is not. He died last October.[2]

Here Mr. Wellman comments as follows:

It will be observed that Mr. Choate did not confront the witness at this point with the letter that she had written complaining of her father's brutal advances to her, and implying the necessity of her leaving her home in consequence. Many cross-examiners would have produced the letter and would have confronted the witness on the spot with the contradiction it contained, instead of saving it for the summing up. It is interesting to study the effect of such a procedure. By a production of this letter, the witness would have been immediately discredited in the eyes of the jury; the full force of the contradictory letter would have been borne in upon the jury as perhaps it could not have been at any other time in the proceeding, and the Sun reporter could not have said the plaintiff had not been "shaken."

On the other hand, it would have put the witness upon her guard at the very start of her cross-examination and she would have avoided many of the pitfalls which she confidingly stepped into later in her testimony. All through the examination Mr. Choate had frequent opportunities to put the witness on her guard, but at the same time "off her balance." It is a mooted question which method is the better one to employ. It all depends upon the nature of the case and the personality of the witness. . . .

. . . It is perhaps the safer course of the two in cases of this kind, but I doubt very much if, in the great majority of cases, it is the wiser one; for it must be remembered that there are few lawyers at the Bar who can make such use of their "points" in their summations as did Mr. Choate.

Had Miss Martinez been confronted with her own letter . . . it would be difficult to imagine any way in which she could reconcile her letter and her sworn testimony, and Mr. Choate would have had the upper hand of his witness from that time on.

Furthermore, during the examination of a witness the jury invariably form their opinion of the witness's integrity, and if that opinion is in favor of the witness it is often too late to try to shake it in the summing up. It is usually, therefore, the wiser course to expose the witness to the jury in his true colors during the examination, and, if possible, prejudice them against him at the outset. In such cases, oftentimes, no summing up at all is necessary, and the closing speech becomes a mere matter of form. Many lawyers save their points in order to make a brilliant summing up, but an opinion once formed by a juror is not easily changed by a speech, however eloquent. This is the experience of every trial lawyer.

---

[2] F. L. Wellman, The Art of Cross-Examination 311-26 (4th ed 1979). Reprinted with permission of Macmillan Publishing Company from The Art of Cross-Examination by F.L. Wellman. Copyright 1936 Macmillan Publishing Company; copyright renewed © 1964 by Ethel Wellman.

> As evidence of how completely this part of Mr. Choate's case flattened out because it was left until the final argument, it is only necessary to call the reader's attention to all that was said on the subject in the summing up, viz.: "Her letter was read to the jury, which she had delivered to the defendant on the fifteenth of March, revealing her stepfather's barbarous treatment of her. When I was cross-examining her, I did it with that letter in my hand, with a view to what was written in it; so I asked her about the relations existing between herself and her stepfather, and she said he was always kind and loving and considerate, tender and gentle."
>
> Instead of nailing this point in the cross-examination as Sir Charles Russell, for instance, would have done [the reference is to Lord Russell of Killowen, considered one of the most successful cross-examiners of modern times], Mr. Choate turns quietly to the next subject of his examination, which is one of vital importance to his client, and to the theory of his defense.[3]

During the same cross-examination Mr. Choate had the opportunity to confront Miss Martinez with another letter that she wrote; but rather than doing so, he reserved the letter to put it in evidence while the defendant himself was on the witness stand. Mr. Wellman criticizes the referred tactic, saying:

> Here Mr. Choate again treads upon the toes of the witness's veracity, but it is difficult to see why he did not confront her then and there with her own letter. By adopting such a course he took no chances whatever. He would have dealt her a serious blow in the eyes of the jury. Instead, Mr. Choate contented himself by putting this letter in evidence, while the defendant himself was on the witness stand, and the jury never really saw the point of it until the summing up, when their heads were so full of other things that this serious prevarication of the plaintiff probably went almost unnoticed.[4]

The tactic used by Mr. Choate was unsuccessful, and "[a]fter deliberating for twenty-six hours the jury returned a verdict in favor of the plaintiff, and assessed the damages at fifty dollars."[5]

Note that *Martinez v Del Valle* took place in 1877, and Mr. Wellman's commentary favorable to an immediate confrontation with the witness was written around 1902 or 1903. Some critics would say that today's tactics are different.

However, in our times, too, the option of confronting the witness with impeachment material without delay is accepted and recommended. For example, we quote the opinion of advocate Scott Baldwin:

> If you have truly devastating impeachment material, it is sometimes effective to cover this at the very beginning of the cross-examination. Wit-

---

[3] *Id* 335.

[4] *Id* 335.

[5] *Id* 365.

nesses are generally more uneasy when you first start asking cross-examination questions and they are therefore less able to explain away problems. Also, the jurors will typically be more attentive at the beginning of the cross.[6]

§3.04 Controversial Aspects of Impeachment

There are many grounds for impeachment which are subjects of controversy, one of which is the use of character evidence to prove conduct.

Rule 404(a) of the Federal Rules of Evidence establishes the general principle that "[e]vidence of a person's character or a trait of his character is not admissible for the purpose of proving that he acted in conformity therewith on a particular occasion."

If this rule did not have exceptions, the subject would be very simple, and would not be a controversial matter and the subject of numerous court decisions. Federal Rule of Evidence 404 establishes three main exceptions:

(1) *Character of accused.* Evidence of a pertinent trait of his character offered by an accused, or by the prosecution to rebut the same;

(2) *Character of a victim.* Evidence of a pertinent trait of character of the victim of the crime offered by an accused or by the prosecution to rebut the same, or evidence of a character trait of peacefulness of the victim offered by the prosecution in a homicide case to rebut evidence that the victim was the first aggressor;

(3) *Character of witness.* Evidence of the character of a witness, as provided in rules 607, 608, and 609.

But this is not all; the same Rule 404, in part (b), establishes another general rule, this one regarding other crimes, wrongs, or acts of a person that are not admissible to prove the character of a person. The rule, of course, also has exceptions under which the same crimes, wrongs, or acts may be admissible for other purposes. The provision is as follows:

> Rule 404 (b) Other crimes, wrongs or acts. Evidence of other crimes, wrongs, or acts is not admissible to prove character of a person in order to show that he acted in conformity therewith. It may, however, be admissible for other purposes, such as proof of motive, opportunity, intent, preparation, plan, knowledge, identity, or absence of mistake or accident.

As noted above, in the case of the character of a witness, it is necessary to take into consideration the provisions of Federal Rules of Evidence numbers 607, 608, and 609. Rule 607 establishes who may impeach, Rule 608 deals with when the credibility of a witness can be attacked or supported by evidence of

---

[6] S. Baldwin, Master Advocate's Handbook 115 (L.D. Rumsey ed 1986). Reproduced with the permission of the National Institute for Trial Advocacy, Notre Dame Law School, Notre Dame, IN 46556.

the person's character and conduct, and Rule 609 establishes when the credibility of a witness can be attacked by evidence that the witness has been convicted of a crime.

Usually the law establishes a general rule and then gives the exceptions. Sometimes, though, the exceptions are so numerous that one might say that the general rule is the exception and the exceptions are the general rule. The hearsay rule is a good example of this. The general principle in Federal Rule of Evidence 802 is that "hearsay is not admissible . . . except as provided by these rules or by other rules prescribed by the Supreme Court pursuant to statutory authority or by Act of Congress." Then, in Rule 803, there are 24 exceptions, the last one being a key for new exceptions.

A similar situation exists with the general principle established in Rule 404. The exceptions are so numerous that, as with hearsay, it sometimes seems as though the general rule is the exception and the exceptions are the general rule.

Suppose that the admissibility of character evidence has been allowed in a trial under the provisions of Rule 404. Then, to determine the appropriate method of proof, one must refer to Rule 405. This rule refers to two different situations:

(a) *Reputation or opinion.* In all cases in which evidence of character or a trait of character of a person is admissible, proof may be made by testimony as to reputation or by testimony in the form of an opinion. On cross-examination, inquiry is allowable into relevant specific instances of conduct.

(b) *Specific instances of conduct.* In cases in which character or a trait of character of a person is an essential element of a charge, claim, or defense, proof may also be made of specific instances of his conduct.

In order to understand the purposes and the application of Rules 404 and 405 (and in the case of witnesses' character, Rule 608), it is first necessary to have a clear concept of what character is.

We understand as *character* the mental or moral qualities that make one person different from another. If this is the accepted definition of character, a new question arises: What are the prescribed methods and standards for measuring "mental or moral qualities" in order to arrive at a conclusion as to the character of a person? For example, is it enough, in order to prove a person's good character, to present the testimony of the manager of a supermarket, of which the person has been a customer for many years, saying that the person is honorable, has paid his or her bills punctually, and has never had an argument with anybody in the supermarket, or is it necessary to present the opinion of a psychologist based on his or her examination of the person in question? It is difficult to establish a precise rule for impeachment; the solution must be left to the courts and trial lawyers to deal with on a case-by-case basis.

There is a paradox in all this legal construction. In order to prove character or conduct of a person (the witness), one must rely on the character and conduct of another person (the judge), or on the conduct of a third person (the trial lawyer) to select and argue in a persuasive manner the appropriate method of proof. . . .

§3.05 Impeachment: A Field for Applied Psychology

What is impeachment? It is a cross-examination technique, the goal of which is to discredit the witness's testimony. It is an assault on the credibility of a person who participates in a trial as a witness, an attack on his or her reliability based on a prior declaration or action, a charge against the character of the person.

There are no concrete rules indicating that if a person does so and so, he or she may or may not be believable. Credibility is a subjective concept, not an objective one, a decision about which depends on circumstances, feelings, and ideas. It is a concept at odds with concrete precepts. In other words, the determination whether a person is telling the truth is a matter of interpretation of behavior and circumstances.

Sometimes the significance of a fact, and its bearing on credibility, is relative to one's particular circumstances. For example, suppose that in an alimony case, a woman asked for a large monthly allowance, arguing that her former husband was a millionaire. During cross-examination of the husband, the woman's lawyer asked:

L. Isn't it true that you are a millionaire?

W. Yes, I am, but I am not a rich person and I cannot pay the astronomical figure being sought by my exwife.

L. What are you talking about? If you are a millionaire, you are a rich person, aren't you?

W. I am a citizen of a South American country where I have all my assets. The currency of my country, in comparison with the American dollar, has little value; if I want to buy an American dollar I need to pay 5,000 units of the local currency. This means that if I have the equivalent of 200 American dollars in my country, I am a millionaire.

In this example was the witness telling the truth or lying? The person told the truth. He is a millionaire in his country, but is he rich? Absolutely not.

Analyzing the basics of impeachment, the same principle could be applied to many circumstances regarding witnesses' testimony, such as sight, time, hearing, etc. A witness says, "I saw the killer"; this is not enough to show that the witness really saw the killer. In the witness's mind there is certainty that what he said was true, but before accepting the witness's testimony it is necessary to inquire into other circumstances, such as distance, lighting, whether the witness might have been under the influence of drugs or alcohol, etc.

There are other elements which, as bases for impeachment, raise difficult determination problems, such as character and its relation to credibility. In order to be able to judge the conduct of a person, it is necessary to consider behavioral patterns which can be focused with the help of psychology.

Consequently, one may arrive at the conclusion that in the impeachment process, where *credibility, character, reputation,* etc. are basic elements, the application of fundamental principles of psychology is indispensable. These concepts are subjective and, in order to arrive at a judgment, there is in each case a mental process which must be studied.

In any trial, the main task of the lawyer is to persuade the fact-finder that his or her theory of the case is the correct one. To do so, the lawyer must analyze the facts and the applicable law, and must present evidence and precedent.

Generally, as part of the evidence, counsel calls witnesses to the stand, whose message must also be persuasive. The authors Michael J. Saks and Reid Hastie, in their book *Social Psychology in Court,* discussed this matter as follows:

> Kelman (1961) has pointed out that the persuasiveness of a message depends on three aspects of its source: the source's credibility, the source's attractiveness, and the source's power over the listener. In the courtroom the witness's credibility is of primary concern.
>
> McGuire (1968) has argued that credibility can be analyzed into two underlying components—expertise and objectivity. A related analysis by the renowned legal scholar Wigmore (1935) has listed five grounds on which a witness may be impeached or discredited:
>
> 1. The witness exhibits a defect in the capacity to observe, remember, or recount the events being reported. . . .
> 2. The witness is motivated to have a bias or interest in the outcome of the case . . . . Human nature being as it is, there is virtually an infinite variety of ways in which testimony can be biased. Some common sources of bias in legal matters are friendship or kinship with parties in the case, hostility toward a defendant, plaintiff, or prosecutor, monetary interest in one side of a case (expert witnesses paid by one side to testify), or other self-interest (the government witness who testifies to avoid prosecution). Research by Carl Hovland and his associates at Yale University has confirmed the importance of perceived source objectivity or bias in determining the impact of a persuasive message (Hovland, Janis and Kelley, 1953; Hovland and Weiss, 1951). Furthermore, it seems that it is important for a witness to admit the existence of a potentially biasing factor. In fact, under some circumstances, warning the audience (judge and jury) of persuasive intent may even enhance persuasive impact.
> 3. The character of a witness may be regarded as relevant to his or her credibility. . . . We are in hearty agreement with an appellate court opinion that reversed a trial court's decision to allow a twelve-year-old pandering charge to be introduced as circumstantial evidence to evaluate a witness's credibility:
>
> > The logical connection between pandering and not testifying truthfully in auto accident litigation twelve years later completely escapes us. It would be surprising if any statistical correlation at all could be found between panderers of twelve years ago and witness stand liars today. Indeed it is difficult to see why someone who was convicted of pander-

> ing twelve days ago necessarily would be more likely to lie on the witness stand than any other randomly chosen citizen. If there is any connection at all, its probative value is so slight as to be clearly outweighed by the prejudice created (cited in Schum, 1977).

Furthermore, cross-examination of a witness which takes the form of character assassination is rarely an effective tactic (Keeton, 1973). . . .

4. One effective technique to impeach a witness's credibility is to show that the witness has made previous statements which conflict with current testimony. There has been almost no research relevant to the issue of self-consistency and persuasibility.
5. It is clear that when evidence from one side of a case conflicts with or contradicts another witness's testimony, the credibility of one or both witnesses is undermined. Again, there is little psychological research on this topic. We should cite the path-breaking research and theoretical analyses of Schum (1975, 1977), which apply probability theory to the courtroom situation. He has developed "cascade inference models" from mathematical decision theory and applied them to judicial proceedings. "Cascade inference" (Wigmore called it "concatenated inference") refers to the situation where evidence is related probabilistically to a verdict, *and* the veracity of the evidence itself is uncertain. Obviously, these conditional uncertainties are common in the courtroom, and it is possible that modern decision theory can simplify some judicial problems.[7]

When analyzing witnesses' credibility as a factor for impeachment, it is necessary to remember the elements that can affect witness credibility:

1. The person's testimony is affected not only by what he or she says, but also by *how* the words are said
2. The witness's body language must be coordinated with the words; the voice must vary in its inflections and not sound monotonous
3. Physical appearance must reflect socio-economic background
4. Personal mannerisms or bad habits may distract the jury from the substance of the testimony
5. Affectation, or the appearance that the witness is not being natural, damages credibility
6. Answering the lawyer's question before the question has been completed indicates that the witness has memorized a script; this person will appear to be a parrot, not a witness
7. Behavior during testimony (anything from a certain way of sitting or answering to trying to seem smarter than the lawyer) can damage credibility

---

[7] M.J. Saks & R. Hastie, Social Psychology in Court 165-67 (1978). Reprinted with permission of Van Nostrand Reinhold.

8. Giving the impression of impartiality is the best key to success for a witness[8]

In order to complete the general picture on this subject, it is necessary to discuss one of the most controversial matters affecting witnesses' reliability, that is, eyewitnesses' credibility and how juries react to eyewitness testimony.

Regarding this matter, Fredric D. Woocher observed in a law journal note:

> Although improper suggestive procedures used by law enforcement officials in procuring identification evidence account for many mistaken identifications, the great majority probably are attributable both to the inherent unreliability of human perception and memory and to human susceptibility to unintentional and often quite subtle, suggestive influences. That most juries, and even some judges, are unaware of the sources of error in eyewitness testimony and consequently place undue faith in its veracity seriously aggravates this problem. For the lay person, visual identification of the defendant by the victim or witness often provides the most persuasive evidence, which cannot be overcome by contrary evidence supporting the accused. Therefore, unless some steps are taken to ensure that the unreliability of eyewitness evidence is brought to the attention of the trier of fact, mistaken identifications will continue to be a major source of wrongful convictions.[9]

There have been numerous Supreme Court decisions on this matter. For example, in *United States v Wade,* the Court observed that "[a] major factor contributing to the high incidence of miscarriage of justice from mistaken identification has been the degree of suggestion inherent in the manner in which the prosecution presents the suspect to witnesses for pretrial identification."[10]

To a nonscientist, common sense seems like one of the best keys to understanding and resolving human problems, but scientists have a different idea on this topic. For example, the authors Saks and Hastie arrived at the following conclusion:

> The gap between the psychologist's understanding of human memory and the layman's is surprisingly large, given the role memory plays in individual experience and human affairs. There are several senses in which the scientific approach can be superior to common sense. First, common sense may simply be incorrect. For example, most lawyers, judges or jurors would guess that an observer can best detect lies in a verbal conversation if he is able to view the faces and bodies of the conversationalists. This is simply wrong. Lie detection is most acute if the observer has verbal

---

[8] R. Aron, J. Fast, & R. Klein, Trial Communication Skills 259, 260 (Shepard's/McGraw-Hill 1986) copyright 1986 by Shepard's/McGraw-Hill, Inc. Reprinted by permission of Shepard's/McGraw-Hill, Inc. Further reproduction is strictly prohibited.

[9] Woocher, *Did Your Eyes Deceive You? Expert Testimony on the Unreliability of Eyewitness Indentification,* 29 Stan L Rev 969, 969-1030 (1977). Reprinted with permission.

[10] United States v Wade, 388 US 218, 228 (1967).

> but not visual access to the liar. . . . Second, common sense may be correct but imprecise. Everyone would agree that estimates of time duration and vehicle speeds are inaccurate. However, the critical question is what are the direction and magnitude of error in these judgments? Third, the common-sense analysis may be partially correct but incomplete compared to the scientific analysis. The nonscientist may correctly note the effects of lighting, interposed objects, color, shape, and movement on subjective judgments but then fail to consider all of the relevant factors together in estimating bias in a particular setting.[11]

The theme of witness credibility is so broad that it far exceeds what can be covered in one chapter of a book. Our purpose in mentioning this subject is to give a general idea of its importance, its relationship to the impeachment process, and the necessity of applying psychological knowledge to this matter.

---

[11] M.J. Saks & R. Hastie, *supra* note 7, at 167, 168. Reprinted with permission of Van Nostrand Reinhold.

4 Witness Characteristics to Be Taken Into Consideration Before Deciding To Impeach

§4.01 Overview

The cross-examiner must recognize that catching a witness in a situation where it may be possible to impeach him or her does not necessarily mean that it is always wise to do so. If the witness to be cross-examined has made important concessions, it may be foolhardy to then attack that witness's credibility. The cross-examiner should also consider whether the witness is the type who would be particularly vulnerable to impeachment, or whether it would be better instead to impeach by bringing out contradictory information from other witnesses—the latter method avoiding the confrontation of impeachment, with its concomitant chance that the witness may be particularly apt at explaining away the potentially damaging impeachment material.

It is also worth noting that certain witnesses are not the type against whom confrontational impeachment is of much help. Thus, it generally is not advantageous to overtly attack, by impeachment or otherwise, a witness who appears to have engendered the sympathy of the jury, such as a "sweet little old lady" type. Often the testimony of such a witness must be discredited in a different fashion.

§4.02 Witness Personality

Impeachment can be a very harsh tool against a witness, particularly one with a weak personality. In rare instances, adroit impeachment has caused a witness to break down, to faint, or even to have a heart attack. Although such effects may make some cross-examiners' clients happy, they should not be so. Lawyers too often sight of the fact that the advocate's job during a trial is to convince the finder of the facts. This does not mean that the advocate should go easy on every witness for fear of causing a heart attack, but it does mean that the cross-examiner must recognize that the jurors may view certain types of witnesses as particularly vulnerable. The examiner must therefore take care to conduct the cross-examination in such a way as not to give offense.

In **§§4.03-4.07,** we will consider a few of the more common situations where such care must be taken.

§4.03 —Cross-Examination and Impeachment of Children

Children can make dynamite witnesses; but they must be handled with caution on both direct and cross, as if the stick of dynamite were attached to a lighted fuse.

A child, even of tender age, may be permitted to testify in court, provided that the child fulfills the basic requirements for giving testimony. Thus, the trial judge must be satisfied that the child:

1. Has personal knowledge of the facts (Federal Rules of Evidence (Fed R Evid) 602)
2. Understands the meaning of, and makes, an oath or affirmation that he or she will testify truthfully (Fed R Evid 603)
3. Demonstrates the ability to understand the questions
4. Demonstrates the ability to give rational and understandable answers

Before calling a child as a witness, every attorney should recognize the possible traumatic effect that testifying may have on the child—particularly one of younger years. This possibility should be in the forefront of the cross-examiner's mind before beginning cross-examination and impeachment. During the direct examination of the child, the cross-examiner must pay very close attention to the child's reactions to detect whether the child is undergoing any psychological trauma. If the cross-examiner believes that the jury has also recognized a deleterious psychological impact on the child, it is possible that the best cross-examination is no cross-examination. This tactic could well leave the finder of fact with the impression that the opponent who called the child is unfeeling and willing to go to any lengths to win the case.

Once a decision is made to cross-examine the child witness, the examiner should be aware of numerous possible distortions that may occur in the child's testimony. One common, and unintentional, distortion occurs when children mix elements from real life with matters remembered from a movie, a television program, or even conversation. Children are easily influenced by such outside forces. If the child's testimony parallels something which occurred on television or in a recent movie, the examiner should be prepared to ask whether the child may have seen such television program or movie. Of course, a child witness may also be manipulated by the party calling him or her as a witness. In addition to the ordinary means of rewards and punishment that can influence a child to testify in a particular way, various aspects of a child's psyche also may distort his or her testimony. Children often believe that they are responsible for things over which they have absolutely no control. For example, the child of an alcoholic often feels responsible for the alcoholic's aberrations. And who has not seen, at least dramatized, a child's guilt at the divorce of his or her parents?

Any discussion of impeachment of child testimony cannot avoid raising issues of such testimony in sexual abuse cases. The recent California case of *State v McMartin,*[1] in which the defendants were accused of sexually abusing children in their day-care center, was based in great part on the testimony of children, and highlights many of the problems involved in child testimony in child abuse cases. After the longest criminal trial in United States history (lasting from March, 1987 to January, 1990), the jury returned a verdict of acquittal on all counts, save 13 on which the jury hung. It is clear that the major problem the jurors had with the testimony of the children was their sense that much of it was more the result of the suggestive, leading, almost coercive questioning by the social workers and psychologists to whom the children had been referred, than of the children's own thoughts and experiences. Indeed, the most helpful evidence for the defense was the videotapes of these interviews. Such evidence, however, is rarely available to impeach a child. Apparently the videotapes were originally made in the *McMartin* case because it was felt that they might be admissible as evidence in the prosecution's case-in-chief. At least 29 states have now enacted various laws that protect a child from testifying in the same room as the accused molester. However, serious constitutional challenge has been made to such laws as being violation of the "confrontation" clause of the United States Constitution.[2]

The problems inherent to the cross-examination of a child witness are heightened because of the very fact that the witness is a child. On the one hand, jurors often feel sorry for a confused or intellectually disabled child witness and look upon the lawyer who is cross-examining or impeaching such a witness as a mere bully. On the other hand, jurors normally feel good about a child who is bright and clever and who outsmarts the lawyer on cross-examination.

The cross-examiner should also recognize that the normal fear a witness might have at the outset of cross-examination is greatly heightened in the case of a child witness. Children are generally reluctant to deal with strangers; particularly with the cross-examiner, who, the child has most likely been told, is dangerous and wants to damage the side which called the child as a witness.

---

[1] *See Two Acquitted of Child Molestation in Nation's Longest Trial,* NY Times, Jan 19, 1990, at A1, col 2.

[2] *See* Coy v Iowa, 487 US 1012 (1988).

The standard approach to cross-examining a child suggests that the cross-examiner should attempt to gain the child's confidence at the outset of the cross-examination. This may be achieved by talking to the child about the child's good points and building up his or her confidence in the examiner. The attorney forced to cross-examine a child can also ask the child for help, explaining that the examiner really doesn't know what happened during the incident in question, but is sorely in need of the child's help to find out what, in fact, went on. Normally, this latter tactic will thereafter permit impeachment better than the former. In contrast, if the examiner gains a child's confidence merely to set up impeachment of the child, the jury may well think the worst of the cross-examiner. With this admonition, the following is suggested as one way in which a lawyer may start a cross-examination, including impeachment, of a child witness:

Q: Now, John Wilson, my name is Joseph Smith and I am the lawyer who represents the defendant here. May I call you Johnny?

A: Sure, everybody calls me Johnny.

Q: Mr. Jones, the lawyer with whom you were just speaking, told you that I would be asking you some questions. Isn't that right, Johnny?

A: Yes.

Q: I don't know if he explained it to you, but I could not be a lawyer in this case if I had been a witness, like you, to all the events you testified about.

A: No, he didn't say that.

Q: He didn't tell you that the law would require the removal of a judge or juror who had been a witness to those events. We don't really know anything about the matter and we look to you and the other witnesses to tell us everything that happened. In effect, we need your help, Johnny, and we can count on you to help us, can't we?

A: Yes, sir.

Using the above as the opening gambit in the cross-examination of a child can accomplish a number of things for counsel. First, it tends to put the child at ease and more likely of a mind to answer questions without hesitation; second, it reminds the jurors that they are depending on the testimony of a child to find against the cross-examiner's client; and third, it leaves the cross-examiner free to later attack the answers given by, and the credibility of, the child, without running the risk of appearing to be a villain.

In any event, impeachment of a child witness should never be undertaken in a rude, rough, or hostile manner. Examination of a child witness done in such a way may result in the child's breaking down, and may leave the jury with memories of only the examiner's hostility and the child's tears. Where possible, by getting proof in through another witness or other means, the best tactic in dealing with a child witness is to avoid any cross-examination.

As usual, every rule is made to be broken. The cross-examiner may be presented with a situation where a young witness comes across to the jury as a delinquent or "wise guy." Such witnesses can generally be treated as adults. Note that the opening suggested above may be adapted as follows to take this situation into account:

Q: Now, John Wilson, my name is Joseph Smith and I am the lawyer who represents the defendant here. May I call you Johnny?

A: Sure, if I can call you Joey.

Q: Mr. Jones, the lawyer with whom you were just speaking, told you that I would be asking you some questions. Isn't that right, Johnny?

A: Yes, he said that you would try to make me look foolish.

Q: How could I make you look foolish? You were there and I wasn't. I don't know if the other lawyer explained it to you, but I could not be a lawyer in this case if I had been a witness like you to all the events you testified about.

A: No, he didn't say that, but I gathered you don't know what you're talking about.

Q: He didn't tell you that the law would require the removal of a judge or juror who had been a witness to those events. We don't really know anything about the matter and we look to you and the other witnesses to tell us everything that occurred there. In effect, we need your help, Johnny, and we can count on you to help us, can't we?

A: I will just answer your questions.

Using this tactic brings before the jury, at the very outset of cross-examination, both the hostility that the witness feels toward the examiner's client and the witness's reluctance to help the jury in their search for the truth. This is impeachment of the witness's testimony in and of itself.

§4.04 —Cross-Examination and Impeachment of Some Women

Although the notion that women are the "weaker sex" has been properly discredited, there are still some people who put women into a special category. That the authors of this work and many attorneys do not agree with that viewpoint is of little consolation to attorneys called upon to cross-examine female witnesses in front of a jury of persons who continue to hold that and related opinions. While we do not suggest that examiners seek to cater to the perceived prejudices of some jurors, we do point out that it is unwise to ignore the possibility that some jurors may view women as persons who must be "protected," perhaps identifying female witnesses with their mothers, sisters, daughters, or other significant persons in their lives. The interaction between the female witness and the jury depends in part on the type of testimony which the witness is giving on direct examination. A juror with a stereotypic view of women may react much more sympathetically to the testimony of a woman who suffered at the hands of a wife-beater than to a woman testifying to the physical injuries to a husband or a member of the family on the question of damages. Another problem is presented when the examiner senses that particular jurors will discount the testimony of female experts in areas typically considered to be "male professions," such as engineering or ballistics. While there now are few, if any, areas of activity or endeavors which are "male," to the person who perceives some area as such, that is reality.

The reality is the subtle prejudice which comes about because of how some jurors view women generally. This prejudice makes it more difficult for cross-examiners to impeach women who fit into the category of "being in need of protection." Cross-examiners should at least be aware of the possibilities of such prejudice and comport themselves accordingly.

§4.05 —Cross-Examination and Impeachment of the Handicapped

The fact that a person has some type of handicap does not disqualify that person from being a lawyer, juror, or witness. For example, the courts of New York have allowed deaf persons to serve as jurors, supplying sign language interpreters to assist deaf jurors in jury deliberations. When an attorney knows that a handicapped person will appear as a witness and that the attorney may have to cross-examine and possibly impeach that witness, it may be well for the attorney to bring up the matter in the voir dire of the jury in order to gain a "feel" for the reaction of the jury to such a situation. The proponent of the witness should also want to put the same type of questions to the jury on voir dire, since it would be helpful for that attorney to ascertain whether any of the jurors has a prejudice against handicapped people.

Even assuming that the jurors all truthfully have said that they have no prejudices against nor biases for a handicapped witness, the lawyer rising to cross-examine such a witness should be aware that the jury does not necessarily view the cross-examination as a fair contest and may unconsciously root for the witness against the lawyer. When possible, avoid cross-examination of the handicapped witness altogether; but when that is not possible, be aware of the possible unconscious bias of the jury and go about the cross-examination carefully. Such a situation requires a complete and thorough preparation of the cross-examination.

One of the first things that the examiner in this situation must know is how the handicap or disability came about. It is one thing to cross-examine a witness who is disabled as a result of wartime service, and an entirely different matter to cross-examine a witness who is disabled as the result of a gunshot wound suffered while involved in a robbery attempt. Except in a criminal case, this information generally can be obtained through discovery. In a criminal case, counsel for the defense generally can count on asking the court to obtain such information before the end of the direct examination, if the matter is not disclosed in the §3500 material (i.e., "any statement in the possession of the Government which relates to the subject matter as to which the witness has testified")[3]

Generally, it is not advisable to spend time questioning witnesses about their handicaps unless the handicaps are directly involved in the impeachment. Often the direct examiners have so prepared the witnesses that such questions are expected and answered in a way that redounds to the detriment of the cross-examiners. For example, although many lawyers and jurors are aware that blind people often have a heightened sense of hearing, they might not recognize that the blind often also have an extremely sensitive tactile sense and are able to tell much by their sense of touch. Cross-examiners who are not aware of such heightened senses could find themselves and their cases harmed by their uninformed questioning.

When cross-examining disabled witnesses, counsel should be very aware of the fact that certain words may be used by the witnesses with connotations different than those to which the attorneys are accustomed. For example, blind persons will talk about having "seen" someone to mean that they were in the company of some person and had some communication with that person. Finally, it should be noted that the fact that a witness has a disability or handicap is something that the jury can see and that can be commented on in summation, even though it appears nowhere else in the cold typed record.

§4.06 —Cross-Examination and Impeachment of the Aged

A greater percentage of the population of this country is of retirement age now than ever before. Within the next 20 years, reportedly 40 percent of the population will be age 65 or older. The fact that people may have garnered several birthdays over 65 obviously does not mean that they are no longer mentally fit and able to take care of themselves. But old age can bring its debilities and problems, and the litigating lawyer must recognize these problems when confronted by a jury made up in part of older people or when finding it necessary to cross-examine and possibly impeach an elderly adult.

Three problems come to mind almost immediately when discussing the elderly: loss of acuteness in vision; loss of acuteness in hearing; and the inability to readily find the word to express some idea or concept. The first two problems are physical in nature and affect not only the elderly but also, in more limited numbers, other segments of the community. The latter appears to have a basis in both the physical and mental aspects of the older person. It can be appropriate to impeach an older witness on each of these possible problems. However, the lawyer planning to conduct such a cross-examination should consider that many jurors have an ingrained respect for their elders, such that they might object to confronting an older person with his or her debilities. The lawyer who finds it necessary to conduct such an examination must recognize that it must be done gently and in such a way as to convey to the jury that the lawyer still respects the aged. More objectionable is the lawyer who, on cross-

---

[3] 18 USC §3500(b).

examination of an elderly and forgetful witness, suggests words to the witness that are obviously inappropriate to the situation. While some fledgling lawyers may find this to be an easy way to impeach the witness, they are doing a disservice to their client by following such a tactic. Instead of advancing the client's cause, the lawyer who abuses an elderly person loses credibility with the jury. Rather than making any suggestions as to word or concept that the elderly witness seeks to express, silence is by far the best tactic to use in such a situation.

§4.07 —Cross-Examination and Impeachment of the Terminally Ill

Every lawyer who has ever tried a negligence case for the defendant has had the opportunity and the challenge of cross-examining a person who claims to be infirm. And everyone should recognize that there are different types and stages of infirmity. The discussion in this section is restricted to nonparty witnesses who are suffering from terminal illnesses, such as AIDS or advanced asbestosis.

The law provides for an exception to the hearsay rule for the dying declarations of potential witnesses, on the basis that most people who are *in extremis* would not even consider lying about something as mundane as damages to be awarded to a party in a civil lawsuit. Yet, common sense tells us that some persons who are close to death may seek to provide for their loved ones after death. At times it becomes necessary to point out to a jury that there does exist this latter motive to exaggerate or to shade the truth; doing so is proper impeachment. The problem generally lies with the inexperienced attorney who wants not only to spell out the motive but also to accuse the witness of some type of perjury, either explicitly or implicitly. Generally, this is not the best approach to the problem; it can rub the sensibilities of the jury the wrong way with little or no gain to the attorney's client. Attorneys should recognize that most jurors are blessed with common sense; laying the foundation on cross-examination for the argument in summation of a possible motive to lie is generally sufficient for the jury to ascertain the truth.

Counsel should always be aware of the needs of the terminally ill witness. Taking a break to permit the witness to take medication or to rest does not really break the rhythm of cross-examination. Furthermore, such an offer by the cross-examiner is often taken by the jury as a positive sign of the attorney's good will toward the ends of justice. The record will provide sufficient connection so that the points being made in cross-examination can be driven home in summation.

§4.08 Examine the Witness's Knowledge

Each fact witness is expected to testify only from his or her own knowledge. But in every situation, with every witness, that knowledge is necessarily flawed. Each person experiences an incident from a different point of view, bringing to the experience a different background and life experience. The perception of each potential witness is colored by his or her prejudices and biases. For example, in Western civilization we think nothing of seeing two men shake hands; yet in other societies, such a gesture is used only to start physical combat. In Japan, when one person encounters another, it is common for each to bow to the other; yet such behavior is quite uncommon in Western society. When a witness not only testifies as to what happened but also suggests the meaning of what happened, the cross-examiner might have to show that the meaning has been distorted by the witness's interpretation.

The advocate must start not only cross-examination but also impeachment by determining exactly what the witness knows and what the witness thinks he or she knows. Proper preparation through discovery and investigation should have disclosed what the witness knows and what is merely the result of the witness's speculation and mental filtration.

A witness generally should not be impeached concerning testimony as to a fact which is conceded, but prior statements which are contradictory of the conceded fact may be proven to show that what the witness thinks, or reported, to be actual knowledge may be contrary to the fact. Sometimes an examiner encounters a witness who claims to have seen an entire incident; but, an examination of the scene where the incident took place, and of the place from which the witness allegedly saw the incident, discloses that it was physically impossible for the witness to have seen the entire event. This most commonly occurs with regard to automobile accidents, where the witness can view only the actual impact and what happened thereafter. Because of the witness's prior experience, the witness tends to surmise what happened before he or she actually saw the accident. In effect, the witness, based on his or her general experience as a driver or a passenger, fills in the facts which were not really experienced. The more that the witness reviews the surmise in his or her mind, the more the surmise turns into what the witness believes is actual perception.

An example may make this a little clearer. Assume that John Jones is walking down Main Street near the corner of First Avenue. From where he is located, Jones can see only that part of First Avenue which forms the intersection and that part which is immediately adjacent to the intersection. On his walk, Jones has been window shopping and thinking about his Christmas list. Jones hears the squeal of tires and, looking towards First Avenue, sees the defendant's car skid through the crosswalk and knock down the plaintiff. Jones knows that there is little traffic on First Avenue at that hour of the day. Because Jones heard the squeal of tires, he surmises that the defendant was speeding when the defendant's car approached the intersection. At trial, Jones will be willing to testify that he saw the defendant speeding down First Avenue before entering the intersection. However, the careful cross-examiner knows that the buildings in that neighborhood shield First Avenue from view.

To impeach such a witness, it is necessary to have the witness identify exactly where he was at the time of the incident. The cross-examiner could next produce a photograph taken from about the place where the witness says that he was and have the witness identify the photograph. It is not necessary to go much further with the witness, since the jury can inspect the photograph and see that the witness could not have seen what he claimed to have seen.

5 Strategies for Impeachment

§5.01 Overview

Impeachment is but one part of cross-examination. Before attempting to impeach a witness, the lawyer must consider the particular risks associated with impeachment in addition to the risks inherent in cross-examination. It should not be forgotten that the object of a trial is to attain a favorable result for the client by persuading the jury to view the facts from the client's perspective. Not only should an advocate seek to convince the fact-finder that the client's position is right and proper, but also should focus on the axiom that our legal system is fact-driven. At trial it is therefore the advocate's most important function to convince the fact-finders of the correctness of the client's position.

Except in the most unusual circumstances, do not cross-examine or impeach a witness where such tactics will turn the jury against you and your client's position. Remember that the sympathy of the jury is generally with the witness being cross-examined. Jurors may view cross-examination as an unfair battle between mismatched combatants. If that is the case, the witness becomes the underdog for whom the jurors root, rather than for the lawyer. Also consider the common suspicions that jurors have about lawyers and their motives; it becomes quite clear that the impeachment of a witness on cross-examination can be a risky business.

Cross-examination of a witness can have many purposes, some of which may not be furthered by an attempt to attack the witness by impeachment. For example, cross-examination can be used to elicit facts helpful to the examiner's client. In addition, cross-examination can reveal how other witnesses expected to be produced by the opposing side could not have been in a position to observe the incident about which they will testify. There are many other situations where the cross-examiner need not resort to the dramatic position of direct confrontation with the witness that is generally brought about by impeachment. As with cross-examination, the first question that the advocate presented with the opportunity to impeach a witness should consider is whether impeachment will advance the client's cause.

An oft-told example of the perils of impeachment involves a prosecutor faced with the possibility of impeaching the credibility of a defendant's aged, infirm mother who testified on behalf of her son. In that situation, the wiser course is for the prosecutor to restrain the urge to demolish the mother, even if there is a myriad of impeachment material available. To do otherwise may well evoke the jury's sympathy for the witness and also for the defendant. It is often more effective to restrict cross-examination to something like the following:

> PROSECUTOR: Mrs. Jones, you are the defendant's mother?
>
> WITNESS: Yes.
>
> PROSECUTOR: And you love your son, don't you?
>
> WITNESS: Yes, indeed.
>
> PROSECUTOR: And you want to help him as much as possible, now; don't you?
>
> WITNESS: Yes, I do.
>
> PROSECUTOR: No further questions.

Such an approach, carried off with the appropriate body language, can easily convince a jury to give little consideration to the witness's testimony and avoids a confrontation between lawyer and witness. Technically, this is "impeachment by showing bias," but we use it here not to point up that technical matter; rather, it should serve to remind the advocate to ask himself or herself whether the proposed impeachment will advance the cause of the client.

If the lawyer believes that impeachment of a particular witness will advance the client's cause, the next question to be asked is whether such impeachment can be done successfully. A failed attempt at impeachment can generally serve only to diminish the lawyer in the eyes of the jury.

To impeach a witness successfully the lawyer must take accurate measure of two personalities—that of the witness and that of himself or herself. Too many lawyers seek to emulate Clarence Darrow or Perry Mason, and thus attempt to fit their style into one that they have seen on television or even in a class on trial advocacy. An effective advocate, however, cannot change his or her personality and become someone else in the courtroom. Even the most skilled actor fails as an advocate when the jury recognizes that the personality being projected is merely a facade. Thus, it is incumbent on the lawyer to take true measure of himself or herself before undertaking the impeachment of a witness. Indeed, this self-evaluation should be done prior to the trial, as well as immediately prior to a confrontation with a witness.

The other personality to be measured is that of the witness to be impeached. It must be remembered that the witness at the outset of cross-examination is under a great amount of pressure. It is a rare person who is totally at ease and confident on the witness stand during direct examination, even when fully prepared and rehearsed. Nervousness and anxiety naturally increase when the witness faces cross-examination. A witness may fear the unknown or being made to look stupid in public. Moreover, the witness may dread the unexpected or unwanted disclosure of the witness's imperfections, lack of reputation for veracity, prior convictions or bad acts, as well as any bias, prejudice, interest, or corruption. Such disclosures come about by skillful impeachment of the witness and each type of impeachment will be considered in this section.

Bias, Prejudice, Interest, or Corruption of the Witness

Bias has been defined as an irrational predisposition *in favor* of one side in a dispute. Prejudice, in contrast, has been defined as an irrational predisposition *against* one side in a dispute. Both are marked by a certain hostility.

It is generally expected that a witness who is about to be cross-examined will be uncooperative and perhaps even overtly hostile. Even a "neutral" witness may have a certain degree of sympathy for the party who called the witness. Indeed, totally objective witnesses may be on the defensive and feel somewhat fearful of the lawyer who is to cross-examine them.

The advocate must be mindful of a more subtle hostility engendered by a dislike of the examiner's client or a blind bias toward the other party. It is difficult to prove such prejudice or bias, and the impeachment of a witness by such a showing is relatively rare. But if the lawyer is armed with the facts necessary to make that showing and believes that it can be done successfully, strategically it is often best to hold such impeachment for the end of cross-examination, after drawing from the witness whatever helpful testimony possible. As a result, practically every answer given by the witness can be turned to the use of the cross-examiner during summation. One must remember, however, not to waste time or to appear to be toying with the witness; either will cheapen the impact of the confrontation with the witness and damage the effectiveness of the advocate.

If the witness has an interest in the outcome of the case, such as a financial interest, that information is proper material for impeachment. However, confrontational impeachment regarding the witness's interest in the case rarely occurs. Generally, if a witness has a financial or other interest in the case, that matter is brought out on the direct testimony of the witness. Of course, a *party's* interest in the outcome of the case is readily apparent. But that does not preclude the cross-examiner from reviewing that interest on cross-examination as impeachment of the witness.

Showing interest on the part of the witness is far different from revealing true corruption where the witness, in effect, has been bribed by the party calling the witness. It should be hoped that the latter situation is extremely rare, for it would rock the entire foundation of the justice system if it became a common occurrence. It is even more unusual for the cross-examiner to have proof of such corruption prior to the completion of cross-examination.

Where such proof is available, however, it is incumbent on the advocate to elicit that information fairly early in the cross-examination. This will encourage the jury to focus on the corruption to the exclusion of the witness's direct testimony. Bringing out this information early in the cross-examination also enables the examiner to enlist the aid of the judge, who, as the symbol of the justice system, has the opportunity to take his or her own corrective action.

Prior Convictions and Prior Bad Acts of the Witness

At one time in the development of the common law, a person who had been convicted of a felony could not be a witness in court. Certain disqualifications still apply, but no longer is a felon prohibited from testifying at trial. The fact remains, however, that such a witness can be impeached by the prior conviction as to his or her veracity. Such impeachment is accomplished by simply asking the witness to admit the conviction, and, in the face of a denial, by producing a certified copy of the conviction. Although it is not crystal clear how, for example, a manslaughter conviction is related to veracity, impeachment of veracity by the conviction is permitted in some form in almost all jurisdictions. Such impeachment is accepted not only by the courts but also by juries. Several variations of the rule exist. For example, the Federal Rules of Evidence prohibit use of a conviction that is more than 10 years old.[1] Some jurisdictions require the conviction to be of a felony relating to truthfulness,[2] while others vest the trial judge with broad discretion to permit or reject such impeachment.[3]

Prior bad acts for which there have been no convictions may also be used as a tool to impeach credibility. It should be noted that the cross-examiner must have a good faith basis for a question regarding prior bad acts, and that such acts must be relevant to the testimony of the witness. If the witness denies the "bad act," the cross-examiner may be permitted to prove it by extrinsic evidence, provided that the material is not "collateral" to the issues on trial. Thus, if simple proof were offered to show that the witness had previously lied under oath, that evidence would most likely be received as not being collateral.

---

[1] Fed R Evid 609(b).

[2] *See* Model Code Rule 106; Uniform R Evid 21.

[3] *See* New Jersey v Sands & Sheldrick, 76 NJ 127, 386 A2d 378 (1978) and cases cited therein.

As the extrinsic evidence becomes either more complicated or time-consuming, however, the probability is greater that the court will sustain objection to this "impeachment" as collateral. The cross-examiner is then left with the denial by the witness standing alone. It is worth reiterating that impeachment of a witness by evidence of prior "bad acts" must pass two hurdles: (1) relevance; and (2) not collateral. Remember that each of these determinations is to be made by a busy trial judge whose ruling on such matters is rarely overturned. The ordinary trial judge, mindful of an overcrowded docket, will generally favor excluding the evidence.

As a final note, "bad act" impeachment is highly dangerous. If the witness denies the accusation, counsel cannot even comment on it. Many jurors may then jump to the conclusion that counsel has stooped to vile smear tactics to win the case. Further, the possibilities of being permitted to introduce extrinsic evidence to prove the prior bad act are scant. Before attempting such a tactic, it is best to ask for a side-bar conference where counsel can make an offer of proof and obtain an advance ruling, thus preventing any difficulties in front of the jury.

The Witness's Reputation for Veracity

Even if a person has the reputation for untruthfulness or is subject to a personality disorder that impairs the ability to tell the truth, he or she will be permitted to take the witness stand on the assumption that at least this one time the truth will be told. To what extent the cross-examiner can use extrinsic evidence to impeach that witness's testimony by showing a predisposition to lie or a poor reputation for veracity depends on the nature of the evidence and how "collateral" it is to the issues on trial.

Of course, if the plaintiff's case is built solely on the plaintiff's own testimony, and the defendant can produce the plaintiff's long-time psychiatrist who testifies that the plaintiff is a psychopathic liar, that testimony will not be collateral. However, in less obvious cases, it is well to remember that the penchant of a trial judge is to rule such matters collateral.

Disclosure of the Witness's Imperfections

In order for a witness to be competent to testify, he or she not only must have the disposition to tell the truth, but also must have had the ability to perceive the incident in question, the ability to remember what was perceived, and the ability to communicate that perception to the finders of the fact. All of these abilities are presumed to exist in the witness by the very fact of being called as a witness. But human experience teaches that no one person can perceive all aspects of every incident. Nor can a person remember every detail of everything he or she has perceived. Indeed, the ability to communicate accurately at all times is not even bestowed on scientists, engineers, and mathematicians, who spend their lives seeking certainty. It is the goal of impeachment to uncover for the finders of fact the witness's faulty perception, errant memory, or inability to communicate.

It follows that no witness is perfect, and a witness's imperfections, particularly of memory, constitute a fertile field for impeachment. If every witness had a perfect memory, there would never be a prior inconsistent statement. If every witness were able to communicate clearly to others the exact images remembered, the description conveyed each time would be the same. Again, we would not see every day the impeachment of a witness's testimony by showing that he or she has given a description materially different from that given on another occasion.

Some witnesses insist that their memories improve as time goes on, and that they are then in a better position to fill in more details based on their improved memory. This may be true in a rare case. Generally, however, the witness's imagination takes over and "fills in" details that were never perceived. When the mind prompts the memory to "remember" details that did not exist, another fruitful area for impeachment arises.[4]

§5.02 First Step: Identify the Adversary's Contradictions

To be successful at impeaching a witness, the attorney must be able to identify contradictions in the witness's testimony. The cross-examiner must be able to point up contradictions not only between the witness's current testimony and past statements or physical exhibits, but also between that testimony and contradictory positions taken by an opponent or other witnesses. Generally, this can be achieved only by the fully prepared cross-examiner.

Preparation begins long before a witness's direct testimony. Assume that proper discovery was conducted and that depositions of all opposing witnesses, along with relevant documents, exist. Further assume that all relevant materials from the client were obtained well before trial.

It is incumbent upon the good attorney to review all depositions and relevant documents in the final days and hours before trial. Even though it might be unlikely that the other side will call a particular witness, the deposition of that witness should be reviewed for possible contradictory material which may serve to help or hinder your opponent's position at trial. Having reviewed this material, it is beneficial for the advocate to figure out what the witness is expected to attest to and what the other side will attempt to prove. At this point, it is helpful to review the client's position and to review the theory of the case. The next step is to note down what each witness is expected to testify to and to plan the cross-examination of each witness. In formulating this plan, it is beneficial not to lose sight of the ultimate goal, namely, convincing the finder of the fact that the advocate's position argued at trial is the one that the fact-finder should follow.

After completing pretrial preparation, attempt to ascertain the order in which witnesses for the other side will testify. This enables the advocate to review relevant notes on each witness before the witness actually takes the

---

[4] For an extensive treatment of the problems of eyewitness testimony, see E. Arnolds, W. Carroll, M. Lewis, & M. Seng, Eyewitness Testimony: Strategies and Tactics (Shepard's/McGraw-Hill 1984).

stand. When the witness takes the stand, listen! Failure of litigators to listen to the witness's testimony occurs with amazing regularity. Beyond listening, make *written* notes of the testimony and be prepared to make proper objections. This is not "busy work," for it forges a strong position with the jury. When it comes time to examine the witness, such notes will prove invaluable as a reference to direct testimony, and thus enhance your credibility with the jury. Indicate on these notes which parts of the direct testimony may be contradicted either by the witness's prior testimony or by some other available information.

§5.03 Second Step: Determine the Witness's Achilles' Heel

Many jurors and potential jurors view lawyers as bullies and "nit-pickers," and an advocate who appears as such will lose sympathy and credibility with the jurors. When presented with extensive impeachment evidence raising an opportunity for lengthy cross-examination, the natural tendency is to address all possible contradictions and biases of the witness; however, that is the worst thing to do—the results may prove disastrous. The jury gets bored, pities the witness, and views the lawyer as a bully; unnecessary damage is thus done to the cross-examining attorney's client.

Experienced attorneys look for the witness's Achilles' heel, the softest spot in his or her testimonial armor. Of course, the points of attack must be relevant to the witness's direct testimony and not a broad attack on the witness's character.

Further, experienced cross-examiners set a finite amount of time during which the examination of the witness will be complete. This avoids the appearance of being a nit-picker or a bully.

Points intended to do the most damage to an opponent's case generally should be kept for the examination's finish. Several reasons support this tactic. First, the time to obtain helpful admissions from the witness is at the start of cross-examination, before impeachment is undertaken. Second, the cross-examiner wants to finish on a high by eliciting a supportive point. Last, the final piece of information presented to the jury, or to any listener, generally has the greatest impact.

§5.04 Control Yourself: Appear Confident

A successful cross-examiner never appears timorous, fearful, or lacking in self-confidence. Jurors will sense a lack of confidence in an advocate and may presume that the case is not worthy of any concentrated effort. On the other hand, swaggering self-confidence may be viewed by jurors as a thinly veiled cover for a nonmeritorious case.

How then should the litigator project self-confidence without false bravado? Preparation goes a long way in reducing trial butterflies. Moreover, never indicate, by facial expression or body language, that unexpected evidence was hurtful or damaging to your client's case. Be confident that damage is reparable!

Even if the damage at the moment appears insurmountable, something may yet save the case, making the damage appear negligible. Remember, jurors are never as well versed in the facts of the case as the litigants, and the jury may ignore or misinterpret damaging evidence.

This is not to suggest that the litigator should adopt an overly positive, unrealistic attitude. Honesty is important; a trial lawyer must recognize the weaknesses as well as the strengths of the case, especially when the situation turns awry. The client should be alerted to the difficulties in the case before trial commences. Even if, in the midst of trial, something goes wrong and nothing can repair the damage, the matter can still be settled.

Similarly, while the litigator should minimize the impact of damaging evidence by maintaining composure, he or she should likewise refrain from smugness or glee at revelations of the opponent's weaknesses. A smirk or a smile may be interpreted by the jury as conceit or superciliousness, and lead the jury to feel antagonistic toward the litigator. While a smile or a laugh at the jest of the judge or witness is fine, a smile in response to difficulties encountered by an adversary can spell disaster.

A winning attitude is just as important to a trial lawyer as it is to a champion athlete.[5] That winning attitude starts with self-confidence, built on a truthful recognition of one's own strengths and weaknesses. Most litigators have the education and requisite knowledge necessary for their calling. Knowledge of the instant case, however, is begotten only through hard work. Good trial attorneys have the will and motivation to devote the time and energy necessary to attain full knowledge of the case.

§5.05 Control Your Nonverbal Communication

During cross-examination, the litigator conducting the examination rarely looks at the jury. The litigator's eyes generally travel from his or her notes to the witness and back again. This "poker face" technique must be employed with the witness as well. Additionally, the examiner must appear thoroughly prepared and self-confident, a professional going about the business of the profession.

The lawyer should also recognize that communications are projected by body movement and facial expression as well as speech. A nervous movement and reproachful look indicates to both the witness and the jury that the lawyer has been surprised. Trial attorneys should strategically use nonverbal expressions during trial. Nonverbal communication should result from a conscious decision aimed at controlling the witness's answers and the courtroom situation. Such decisions must be designed to win over the hearts and minds of the jury.

Certain body movements must be avoided in practically every situation. The attorney should avoid touching his or her mouth area while asking questions. This action indicates nervousness and also makes it difficult for even those with acute hearing to comprehend what is being said. Similarly, "clucking" or mak-

---

[5] J. Kestler, Questioning Techniques and Tactics 86 (Shepard's/McGraw-Hill 1982).

ing a "tsk, tsk" sound in a disapproving way after the judge's adverse rulings gives the jury the impression that the judge, whom the jurors look to for guidance in the courtroom, believes that the advocate has a weak position.

§5.06 Repeating Parts of the Direct Examination

It is sometimes suggested that only the neophyte will have a witness repeat the direct examination on cross-examination, since by doing so the impact of the witness's direct examination is strengthened and emphasized. Generally, this results when the cross-examination lacks an aim or plan. However, repetition may be valuable in certain circumstances. Letting the witness repeat or review direct examination provides the witness the opportunity to expand on it, correct any mistakes, or explain it further. But at times it is advisable (and, indeed, necessary in some jurisdictions) for parts of the direct testimony to be repeated in order to lay the proper foundation for impeaching the witness. To lay a proper foundation, the cross-examiner should not only meet the requirements of the law, but also attempt to lock in the witness's position so that the witness is left without a plausible explanation for any inconsistency.

Taking good notes on the direct testimony is therefore important because a transcript is rarely available immediately after direct examination. If the witness denies having made a statement on direct, the cross-examiner can request that it be reread. At times this cannot be done, such as when more than one court reporter is assigned to the case or pertinent notes have been removed from the courtroom. Contradictions between what a witness said on direct and what the witness says on cross-examination go a long way to destroying the witness's credibility. The jury may evaluate such contradictions in several ways, including viewing the witness as having a poor memory for the facts at issue or as consciously shading the truth.

Repetition of a witness's direct testimony sets the stage for the more usual impeachment—that of being confronted with a prior inconsistent statement. This sort of impeachment is generally accomplished in the following manner.

Q: Mr. Pigeon, you testified on direct that the man you saw rob the bank was my client?

A: Yes, sir.

Q: At the time of the robbery, it was light and you had a good view of the bandit. Isn't that correct?

A: Yes, sir.

Q: Mr. Pigeon, how tall would you say my client is?

A: Your client is about five-foot-six-inches tall.

Q: And the defendant is very fair and has very light grey hair, isn't that true sir?

A: Yes, sir.

Q: Mr. Pigeon, after the robbery, you gave the police a description of the person that you allege you saw commit the robbery. Isn't that correct, sir?

A: Yes, sir.

Q: And the police officers wrote down what you said to them, isn't that correct, sir?

A: Yes, sir.

Q: Mr. Pigeon, isn't it true that you told the police officers that the perpetrator of the robbery was six-foot-four, young, and had black hair?

A: Yes, sir.

Note that this examination started with a rehash of part of the direct testimony. Such repetition focuses the jury on the contradiction to be revealed. Avoid having the witness repeat the entire story and confine the witness to areas where there are inconsistencies.

It is arguable that such confrontational impeachment is unnecessary because the failure to point up contradictions denies the witness an opportunity to correct, excuse, or explain the basis of the impeachment. This tactic may at times be helpful, but also can backfire if counsel waits until summation to raise the contradiction. In that situation some jurors may feel that counsel was "unfair" in not giving the witness an opportunity to explain contradictions. Besides, the impact of impeachment on the jury should be effected as soon after the direct testimony as is possible and before the jury can firmly set their impression of the witness's credibility.

§5.07 Asking Questions in "Installments"

When cross-examining a witness, various factors coalesce to challenge the lawyer's control of the examination. Be aware that the witness is generally hostile toward you. Witnesses do not ordinarily enjoy cross-examination, and may well feel that the cross-examination is unnecessary and demeaning. Even persons allied with the examiner's litigation position often feel that cross-examination is unnecessary. Often, the cross-examiner has not had recent contact with the witness. Answers on cross-examination are unprepared and unscripted. Thus, it is important for the cross-examiner to maintain control of the examination by breaking it up into questions that ask for one fact at a time. If questions are framed so as to include more than one new fact, the witness's denial of one part of the question may throw off the whole inquiry and confuse the jury.

Moreover, proper impeachment through use of "installment" questions prevents cross-examiners from "telegraphing their punches." For impeachment by inconsistent statements to be successful, it is necessary to force the witness into confirming the current version of a story, excluding avenues by which the witness may evade or excuse an inconsistency. If the witness becomes apprised of his or her inconsistency before the examiner wants to raise it, the witness may blunt the sting by blurting out an explanation. By proceeding with the cross-examination through installments, the advocate does not "telegraph the punches," assuring that the witness will not be able to avoid the impact of the inconsistency.

An example of asking questions in "installments" follows: Assume that you have to cross-examine a prosecution witness in a case where your client is accused of bank robbery. The witness, a young man, testified on direct examination that while driving down the street he saw your client running from the bank. The defendant has told you that he was running after a man who had knocked him down while he, the defendant, was merely passing the bank. Part of the cross-examination could proceed along the following lines:

> Q: Mr. Pigeon, you told us that you first saw my client while you were driving down Main Street, near where State Street crosses Main. Do I have that correct, sir?
>
> A: Yes.
>
> Q: At the time, you were driving your new Porsche?
>
> A: Yes, sir.
>
> Q: Doesn't that model have the marvelous hi-fidelity Grundig radio and tape deck?
>
> A: Yes, indeed, it does.
>
> Q: On the day in question, you were listening to your tapes, weren't you sir?
>
> A: Yeah, man.
>
> Q: Are you a fan of "heavy metal rock and roll"?
>
> A: Yes, absolutely.
>
> Q: And the tape that you were listening to when you were driving down Main Street on the day in question was a "heavy metal rock and roll" tape; isn't that true, sir?
>
> A: Yes, sir.
>
> Q: The day of the bank robbery, February second, was a very cold day, isn't that true, sir?
>
> A: Yes, and there was a cold rain.
>
> Q: Were you driving with the windows up?
>
> A: Of course I was.
>
> Q: As a good driver, you were paying attention to the other cars on the street and to the people who were attempting to cross the street?
>
> A: Yes, sir.

Note that, up to this point, the examiner has the witness testifying to details that might seem irrelevant to the identification, but which are properly before the jury to impeach the witness's ability to perceive the entire incident. The examination continues as follows:

Q: You were not paying attention to the folks on the sidewalk, is that correct, sir?

A: Yes, sir.

Q: In fact, there were parked cars on both side of the street, isn't that correct, sir?

A: Yes, sir.

Up to this point, the impeachment has generally been directed to the witness's ability to perceive. Each detail is filled in by a separate question. Each question is a leading question. The details are being filled in for the jury "in installments."

Q: Now, you testified on direct that you first noticed my client running from the bank. At that time, you were still about a block down Main Street from the corner where the bank is, on the corner of State and Main Streets. Did I understand your testimony correctly, sir?

A: Yes, sir.

Q: And you testified that you saw my client trip and fall on the sidewalk, and that you stopped to help him because he went down hard and you are with the local ambulance and rescue squad. Is that a fair summary of part of what you said?

A: Yes. That is part of my testimony.

Q: Did you see anyone else running on the sidewalk at that time?

A: Yes. There was another fellow in front of your client. It could have been an accomplice.

Q: Please, Mr. Pigeon. Just answer the questions. Since you suggest that this other runner could have been an accomplice, would you identify him and perhaps point him out in this courtroom?

A: (Pause). I cannot.

Q: You don't know who this other runner was, is that correct?

A: Yes.

Notice that the witness's volunteered speculation is turned back on him, and raises the possibility before the jury of hostility based on bias or prejudice.

Q: You gave a statement to the police immediately after the incident? Isn't that correct?

A: Yes.

Q: You went down to the precinct house with Sgt. Robinson and told him everything you remembered about the incident. Isn't that correct?

A: Yes.

Q: And Sgt. Robinson wrote down all you had to tell him. He then gave the statement to you; asked you to read it; add or strike out anything; and you did so and you signed it. Isn't that so?

A: Yes.

Here, the examiner breaks up the "installment" feature of the questioning. This is done only where the witness, by denying any part of the leading question, opens up an attack on the other side. Here, a denial of any part might suggest that the prosecution suppressed evidence.

Q: I am showing you the last page of Exhibit 3501. Isn't that your signature?

A: Yes.

Q: There is no mention of any other runner in the statement in Exhibit 3501, isn't that true, sir?

A: I guess not.

Q: At the time, no one asked you about anyone other than my client, isn't that so?

A: That's right.

A witness, upon being confronted with a prior inconsistency, often will look for an excuse or a scapegoat to explain the inconsistency. Suggesting such an explanation is not improper.

Q: And you told Police Sgt. Robinson that you first saw my client halfway down the block between the bank and where you were located in your car. Isn't that correct?

A: I guess so. If that is what is written there.

Q: I show you page 3 of Exhibit 3501, the part I have marked in yellow. I did read that part correctly, isn't that so?

A: Yes.

§5.08 Asking the Witness About Conversations Regarding Testimony

The trial lawyer should never call a witness to the stand unless the lawyer has had an opportunity to confer with and prepare the witness for the examination. The only exception is that rare circumstance when the advocate has no choice but to call a hostile witness. Witnesses often openly discuss with others the fact that they are about to testify at a trial, elaborating on the subject matter of their testimony. Merely eliciting on cross-examination the admission that the witness has discussed his or her testimony with your adversary is meaningless. Nonetheless, some witnesses are ignorant of the propriety of such conversations. Attorneys sometimes do not notify their witnesses that such preparation is appropriate or that the witness should be candid and freely admit on cross-examination that such conversation with counsel took place. Thus, it is incumbent on the trial lawyer to take careful measure of opposing counsel before trial. It is a waste of everybody's time to ask blindly whether such preparatory conversations took place!

In the appropriate case, however, it is wise to elicit from the witness whether such preparation occurred. If this tactic is successful, the witness will deny any pretrial discussions. The opponent then faces the unhappy prospect of impeaching his or her own witness, conceding that the preparation had in fact taken place. If the witness is well prepared and answers in the affirmative, move along swiftly to the next point. It is generally not advisable to ask this series of questions more than once in a trial.

If the cross-examiner knows that the witness has had a conversation with another person about the testimony, and knows of some inconsistency in the two tellings of the underlying facts, consideration should be given as to whether the inconsistency can be elicited at trial if the witness denies having had the conversation.

§5.09 Using Trick Questions

When confronted with the issue of "trick questions," ground rules must be set and a determination made as to the meaning of that term. If the term is intended to encompass unethical questions—ones that are misleading to both the witness and jury or intended to force the witness into testifying inaccurately and/or incompletely—then clearly the cross-examiner must avoid them at all costs. If, however, the term is restricted to the use of a verbal trick or unexpected question to obtain a truthful and complete response from an evasive, prejudiced, or perjurious witness, such trick questions are permissible but dangerous.[6] The Code of Professional Responsibility contains no specific section devoted solely to the conduct of cross-examination, but certain Ethical Considerations (EC) and Disciplinary Rules (DR) bear directly on cross-examination and on the use of trick questions. These include:[7]

> EC 7-10 The duty of a lawyer to represent his client with zeal does not militate against his concurrent obligation to treat with consideration all persons involved in the legal process and to avoid the infliction of needless harm.
>
> EC 7-25 Rules of evidence and procedure are designed to lead to just decisions and are part of the framework of the law. Thus . . . a lawyer . . . is not justified in consciously violating such rules and he should be diligent in his efforts to guard against his unintentional violation of them.

---

[6] For an extensive discussion as to the authors' view of the ethical problems involved in cross-examination, see R. Aron, K.T. Duffy, & J.L. Rosner, Cross-Examination of Witnesses: The Litigator's Puzzle §§5.01-5.04 (Shepard's/McGraw-Hill 1989).

[7] Model Code of Professional Responsibility EC 7-10, EC 7-25, EC 7-26, DR 7-102(A), DR 7-106(C) excerpted from the Model Code of Professional Responsibility, copyright by the American Bar Association. All rights reserved. Reprinted with permission.

> As examples . . . a lawyer should not ask a witness a question solely for the purpose of harassing or embarrassing him; and a lawyer should not by subterfuge put before a jury matters which it cannot properly consider.
>
> EC 7-26 The law and Disciplinary Rules prohibit the use of fraudulent, false or perjured testimony or evidence. A lawyer who knowingly participates in introduction of such testimony is subject to discipline. A lawyer should, however, present any admissible evidence his client desires to have presented unless he knows, or from facts within his knowledge should know, that such testimony or evidence is false, fraudulent, or perjured.
>
> DR 7-102(A) In his representation of a client, a lawyer shall not:
>
> > (1) . . . conduct a defense . . . or take other action on behalf of his client when he knows or when it is obvious that such action would serve merely to harass or maliciously injure another.
>
> DR 7-106(C) In appearing in his professional capacity before a tribunal, a lawyer shall not:
>
> > (1) State or allude to any matter that he has no reasonable basis to believe is relevant to the case or that will not be supported by admissible evidence.
> >
> > (2) Ask any question that he has no reasonable basis to believe is relevant to the case and that is intended to degrade a witness or other person.

The American College of Trial Lawyers' Code of Trial Conduct simply asserts that a

> . . . lawyer should never be unfair . . . abusive . . . inconsiderate to adverse witnesses or opposing litigants, or ask . . . questions intended only to insult . . . degrade the witness. He should never yield, in these matters, to suggestions or demands of his client or allow . . . malevolence or prejudice of . . . client to influence his actions.

While the language of the Code of Professional Responsibility (Code) appears clear, it does not supply a bright-line test for every situation that arises in the courtroom. It is up to the advocate's own conscience to determine whether, in the close situation, a particular question breaches the mandates of the Code. If it is clear that unethical behavior has occurred, the examiner will be subject to a swift and stinging rebuke from the court, to the examiner's own detriment as well as to the obvious detriment of case and client. It is almost impossible for a lawyer to rebound successfully from an accusation regarding the use of unethical tactics, either made by the opponent and sustained by the judge or raised by the court. Jurors are innately suspicious of lawyers; some indeed are only too willing to condemn a lawyer if there is any hint that the lawyer is guilty of unethical behavior.

More than losing the case is at stake for the lawyer who has been caught asking clearly unethical trick questions. Even in a hub like New York City, where there are a vast number of lawyers, the trial bar is made up of relatively few practitioners. An attorney who acquires a reputation for being unethical is treated, by both colleagues and the judiciary, with a great deal of suspicion. The resulting damage to an attorney's credibility and livelihood because of unethical tactics can be enormous. That consideration in and of itself should be reason enough for each member of the bar to eschew the use of trick questions.

A trick question which implies some "facts" that are untrue or not in evidence puts an examiner in the uncomfortable position of being called as a witness, before the judge and jury, to state the basis for the question. If there is no basis, the lawyer's credibility and integrity are destroyed in front of the jury and the client's case is lost. Of course, this implicates another concern, namely, the possibility of a malpractice action. If nothing else can convince the lawyer to refrain from behaving unethically, the specter of a malpractice suit should be a sufficient deterrent.

Finally we get to the trick question intended solely to bring out the complete truth from a recalcitrant witness. This situation is fraught with danger for both the novice and the experienced litigator. Trick questions can be the damnation of an advocate's case, making the advocate look foolish and switching the jury's attention away from the issues at hand. An example may suffice to illustrate this danger:

Q: Isn't it true that you met with your lawyer and went over the testimony you gave this morning?

A: Yes.

Q: And isn't it true that he had to instruct you to tell the truth?

A: No, he didn't have to tell me that, but he did tell me to watch you on cross-examination because you would try to trick me and give the jury a false impression both about me and about what the truth is.

Where the trickster has gotten this type of answer, even a motion to strike followed by a strong admonition to the jury will not prevent the jury from believing the examiner to be dishonest and cunning.

Trick questions should be used sparingly, if at all. They must have a basis in fact, be absolutely necessary, and be developed with extreme caution. Note that merely unexpected questions that may surprise a witness are not in the category of trick questions.

§5.10 Argumentative and "Why" Questions

"Why" questions should never be asked on cross-examination, and "why not" questions are even more dangerous. A question that begins with the word "why" asks a witness to reveal his or her own decision-making processes. Because the examiner cannot know at what stage these mental processes commenced, the use of a "why" question relinquishes the examiner's control over cross-examination. The witness then gains full control over his or her response.

Ceding control to the witness in this situation might amount to a disastrous summation on behalf of the opposition. Although the judge may cut off the witness's answer if it appears to be going on at length, the examiner should not count on being that lucky.

A "why not" question is even less effective than a "why" question. It does not ask for facts as to past mental processes, but for argument and current speculation as to why certain mental processes did not take place. "Why not" questions thus ask for opinion, not facts. Nonetheless, every day, questions are asked in courtrooms that start off with "why" and nothing disastrous happens to the lawyers or to the cases being tried. Such questions are the result of poor preparation of the witnesses and calamity is averted only through luck. The one exception to the rule against asking "why" questions is the somewhat rare situation where the cross-examiner has driven the witness into a corner without an escape, and any answer given by the witness to the question will reduce his or her stature and credibility in the eyes of the jury. An example of just this type of situation follows:

Q: And you told the F.B.I. and the prosecutors a story resulting in a trial of your uncle for serious felonies, isn't that true?

A: Yes.

Q: Your uncle was always good to you, isn't that true?

A: Yes.

Q: Your uncle brought you up after you became an orphan?

A: Yes.

Q: Your uncle was like a father to you?

A: Yes.

Q: When you were arrested and told this story about your uncle to the prosecutors, did you remember how much your uncle loved you and how much you owed him?

A: No.

Q: Why?

A: I don't know.

Thus, by this exchange, the cross-examiner abandons none of the control over his or her examination because the witness is placed in a position where there is no tenable response to the "why" question.

§5.11 Demanding Direct Answers

Breaking down the facts being elicited on cross-examination into "installments" suggests that there is no need for the witness to make a lengthy speech explaining his or her answers. Properly phrased questions on cross-examination generally can be answered by a simple "yes" or "no." The less you permit the witness to freewheel answers and the more control you exert over the witness, the better off your cross-examination. In order to exert this control, direct the witness to answer your questions only without any explanations. It can be helpful to start off each cross-examination with an admonition such as: "Mr. Witness, my name is Mr. Smith, and I am going to ask you some questions. Practically all of my questions can be answered by a simple yes or no. If you feel that you are unable to answer in that manner, please say so and I will rephrase the question for you." This approach informs the witness about what is expected and also alerts the jury to possible evasiveness on the part of the witness.

If the witness, after being admonished to respond directly to all questions, decides to launch into a diatribe, the examining attorney's recourse is to enlist the aid of the court to stop and control the witness. For example, "Your Honor, will you please instruct the witness to answer the questions put, without any explanation?" works nicely. Once the witness has gotten away with a long-winded answer, even after being told to respond by a simple yes or no, the more likely it is that the witness will try it again. However, in thwarting such an answer, it is unnecessary to be discourteous. It suffices to explain: "Mr. Witness, you will have the opportunity to give any explanation you desire for any of your answers, but that opportunity will come on re-direct when my learned opponent questions you again." Generally, this approach will not engender hostility in either the witness or the jury.

§5.12 Answering the Witness's Questions

Cross-examination should never degenerate into a debate. The lawyer's job is to ask questions; the witness's job is to answer the questions. If the lawyer is put in the position of having to respond to the witness's questions, the lawyer generally has lost control of the situation. This does not mean that the cross-examiner should ask the court to admonish the witness if the witness asks for a glass of water or a piece of paper and a pencil. Indeed, such simple requests can give the cross-examiner an opportunity to show the jury that he or she is a sympathetic and caring individual who is merely undertaking a proper and necessary duty of a professional lawyer.

But, it is an entirely different matter for the lawyer to be put in the position of being questioned by the witness. When a witness questions the lawyer's knowledge of the facts underlying the issues or the lawyer's tactics or motives, the lawyer may be unable to resist venting the anger engendered by such questions by replying with a sarcastic or smart answer. The lawyer, however, will then lose credibility with the jury, thus hurting the client's case. It is wiser and more appropriate to request the judge to instruct the witness that this is not a debate and that the matter will be resolved more quickly if everyone follows the rules. By remaining calm, and maturely handling what is often the frustrating experience of having a witness attempt to ask questions, the lawyer remains in control of the situation and often gains stature in the eyes of the jury.

Simply put, *do not* answer the questions of a witness!

§5.13 Using Witness Against Witness

Some lawyers believe that the only proper impeachment of a witness by inconsistency is through the use of an inconsistent statement made by that witness on the stand. There are other effective means, however. For example, if your opponent produces two witnesses who have inconsistent versions of the material facts, the opportunity arises to confront each with the statement of the other and point up the inconsistency. The cross-examiner has the chance to suggest to the jury that one or the other witness may not be telling the whole truth, and that perhaps neither should be believed. Such revelation of the inconsistencies between your opponent's witnesses can be particularly telling where your opponent bears the burden of proof.

It should be noted that such impeachment is best limited to revealing *material* inconsistencies. Do not waste time by pointing up minor inconsistencies or mere shadings of meaning that are of no importance. This tactic is often viewed by the jury as "nit-picking." That a witness uses a word different from, but synonymous with, that used by another witness is not a material inconsistency, and it is rarely advantageous for the examiner to point it out.

Often, however, there are significant differences between the testimony of the witnesses for one side. Although these inconsistencies are not material for impeachment *per se,* many advocates treat them in much the same way. Highlighting such inconsistencies can make the trial into a true test of credibility and offer the jury a clear choice between two versions of the facts.

§5.14 Referring to Witness Payments

That most "experts" are paid for time spent in the formulation of the opinion offered at trial, and for attendance at trial, is no longer shocking to jurors. At times, however, the amount of the payment is so great that it can make a difference in the weight that the jury or judge gives to the expert's testimony. For example, in a federal district court in New York City, a treating physician (not a specialist), who was called as a witness for the plaintiff, testified to being paid $10,000 for his preparation and time in court, which lasted about an hour. After returning a verdict for the defendant, the jury was later heard to comment that the physician was a thief, and that perhaps the plaintiff was also. The size of the payment to the doctor-witness was thus apparently an influential factor in the jury's consideration of the case and in the verdict that was rendered. Moreover, such information was properly put before the jury. The fact that a witness is being paid for time spent in court is relevant to determining whether the witness may have an interest or bias in the outcome of the case.

Expert witnesses are not the only witnesses who receive payment from a party to the litigation. A corporate officer or employee may properly be asked about the salary and other income, including the possibility of any bonus, received from the corporate litigant. Such witnesses often cannot be expected to bite the hand that feeds them, and such bias may properly be put before the jury. It is always proper to ask such a witness if he or she expects either a bonus or some type of advancement contingent upon the outcome of the trial. If such a question is answered in the affirmative, the potential bias or prejudice is obvious and it takes little effort to make clear to the jury that they should scrutinize that witness's testimony very carefully.

In criminal cases there have recently arisen a number of situations where "cooperating witnesses" not only receive "plea bargains" but also receive money, either in the form of a reward or of money on which to live. In addition, the United States Marshal's Service has spent substantial sums of money on witnesses in the federal Witness Protection Program to manufacture their new identities. All of these payments can properly be brought out on cross-examination. Dealing with a situation involving witness protection without making the defendant appear to be dangerous and potentially violent may be tricky. The generally accepted view is that the prosecutor in these circumstances must advise the defense counsel of all monies expended on the witness, provided that such information does not disclose where the witness has been relocated. After obtaining this information, one way of handling the matter is as follows:

Q: Mr. Pigeon, you were deeply involved with this illegal enterprise, isn't that true?

A: That is why I am here testifying.

Q: And isn't it also true that in return for your testimony the government has dropped all charges against you?

A: Yes.

Q: You don't expect to spend one day in jail on account of your criminal behavior in connection with this case?

A: That's correct.

Q: In addition to that bargain, isn't it true that you expect to get a percentage of the taxes which are to be assessed against my client?

A: That is what my lawyer told me I am entitled to.

Q: Isn't it also true that the government has been giving you $200 a week to live on?A: Yes, but that is not really a lot of money.

THE COURT:

Mr. Pigeon, please just answer the question without the editorial comment.

Q: And isn't it true, Mr. Pigeon, that the government has been putting you up in a hotel during this trial?

A: Yes.

Q: Mr. Pigeon, would it surprise you to find out that the government has spent $27,000 on you since you first made your deal with them?

A: I guess so.

Note that no mention was made of the Witness Protection Program, and yet this cross-examination leaves the record in such a posture that, on summation, the defense can argue that Mr. Pigeon's testimony was bought and paid for by the government. The government is hard put by this tactic because proof that the witness is in the Witness Protection Program may be excluded as irrelevant to the charges on trial or as proof of other crimes.

§5.15 Prefacing Each Question

Some lawyers on cross-examination have the habit of prefacing each and every question with the statement, "Answer yes or no," or something similar. Such a habit may not only bore or annoy the jury and the witness, but also show that the lawyer is lacking in confidence about himself or herself and the case. Properly phrased questions do not admit of answers other than "yes" or "no," unless the examiner is looking for an explanation. This is one of the many ways in which the lawyer's responsibilities while on trial differ from those of the lawyer during discovery.

On trial, it is sufficient at the beginning of the cross-examination of each witness to suggest that you would prefer that the witness answer yes or no, and that if the witness does not understand the question, he or she should say so in order that the question may be rephrased. This is ordinarily done by the cross-examiner as part of the introduction at the beginning of the cross-examination. This self-introduction is generally done even if the examiner has met the witness before, either in discovery or at a previous trial. The introduction may be accomplished in the following manner:

Q: Mr. Pigeon, my name is ____________. I represent the plaintiff. My job now is to ask you a few questions. Please answer these questions "yes" or "no," but if you do not understand the question or you believe that you cannot answer any question, please say so, and I will attempt to rephrase the question. Do you understand that, sir?

A: Yes.

Q: Now, you and I have met before. Isn't that correct?

A: Yes.

Q: During the discovery phase of this case, we were at a deposition, and I asked you some questions. Isn't that so?

A: Yes, sir.

By handling the introduction in this manner, and by weaving in your instructions to the witness concerning the answers expected, you treat the witness as an intelligent person who is capable of following instructions. If the witness then deliberately strays from your instructions as to the manner of answering, the witness's action may be viewed by the jury as either hostility, bias, or a penchant for prevarication.

Moreover, if, by your opening remarks to the witness, you make yourself clear and do not let the witness stray from your instructions, you will find that the judge is more willing to be helpful if you then request intervention by the court either to stop an uncalled for explanation or to strike an answer. Further, the judge's instructions will have a greater impact on both the witness and the jury.

However, there are some situations where prefacing a question with the instruction to answer "yes" or "no" is appropriate. One example is when the cross-examiner feels the danger lurking that the witness will blurt out information or an opinion harmful to the cross-examiner's client. But such a preface must be used selectively and not be permitted to become mere rote.

6 Impeaching Expert Witnesses

§6.01 Introduction

Most lawyers approach cross-examination of an expert witness with either trepidation, born of the belief that the witness is better prepared on the subject of his or her testimony than is the lawyer, or the smug cockiness resulting from the notion that the lawyer can control and conquer the expert witness. Neither emotion should infuse cross-examination of an expert witness. If adequately prepared, the litigating lawyer should approach cross-examination of an expert in the same manner as cross-examination of a fact witness.

However, differences in the decisions of whether and how to cross-examine an expert, in the preparation for and considerations regarding the cross-examination, and in the actual cross-examination of an expert witness are sufficiently significant and substantial to warrant separate treatment. Of course, to begin to understand those differences, it is essential to understand what an expert witness is and how the testimony of an expert witness differs from that of other witnesses. The two prerequisites to admissibility of expert testimony are an appropriate subject and a qualified witness—that is, the subject matter must be such that the law recognizes the need for expert evidence and the witness who is proffered must have the qualifications to testify as an expert.

Traditionally, the subject matter of expert testimony was limited to scientific or technical matters and the expert witness was a learned person possessed of knowledge in the scientific or technical area by education or training not available to, or experienced by, lay persons. As our society has become more complex and areas of human activity more specialized, the limitations on admissibility of expert testimony have been relaxed; many jurisdictions now permit expert testimony on subjects that lay persons have knowledge of, if the expert testimony will assist the trier of fact in understanding the evidence or deciding the factual issues.[1]

Unlike fact witnesses whose testimony was limited to statements of fact based on personal knowledge, expert witnesses traditionally testified to opinions predicated on facts they were asked to assume from evidence furnished the trier of fact by other witnesses. The trend has been to relax standards governing the testimony of expert witnesses. For example, in federal jurisdictions, it is not necessary that the factual predicate for the expert's opinion be admissible if it is information "reasonably relied upon by experts in the particular field in forming opinions or inferences upon the subject,"[2] and, unless the court directs otherwise, the expert's direct examination may include his or her opinion and supporting reasons for it, without disclosing its factual predicate.[3]

Thus, cross-examination and impeachment of expert witnesses is different from, and in some ways more challenging than, that of fact witnesses. However, the challenge exists only for the litigating lawyer who appreciates the need for thorough preparation and understands those many factors involved in determining whether, and how, to cross-examine an expert witness.

§6.02 Preparation for Impeachment of an Expert Witness

Preparation to cross-examine an expert witness should commence with the acceptance of representation of the client and recognition that the case very likely will involve one or more expert witnesses. The first step in preparing to cross-examine an expert witness should be the litigating lawyer's candid acknowledgment that, at that juncture, any adverse expert witness has greater knowledge of and familiarity with his or her area of expertise than does the litigating lawyer.

Selection of an Expert to Assist in Preparation

While the identity of the adverse expert witness will probably not be known during the early stages of a litigation, recognition that the case will very likely require or involve testimony from persons with expertise in identifiable areas suggests the next step in preparation: the selection of an expert with whom

---

[1] *See* Fed R Evid 702.

[2] Fed R Evid 703.

[3] Fed R Evid 705.

the litigating lawyer can work in pretrial, in preparing for trial, and in trying the case.

Selecting an expert requires time, effort, ingenuity, and substantially more than merely retaining the services of someone with education, training, or experience in the requisite area of activity. After identifying the expertise required, the litigating lawyer must focus on his or her precise needs for expertise, which may include one or more of the following:

1. Someone with whom the lawyer can establish a free and open dialogue to discuss the nature of the litigation and the relevance of expected expert testimony, who can give the lawyer a quick and early overview of the topic, who can direct the lawyer to material to read to become more familiar with the subject, and who, as the lawyer increases his or her knowledge and familiarity, can discuss the subject with the lawyer in greater depth to assist the lawyer in planning cross-examination of the adverse expert
2. Someone sufficiently familiar with other experts to be able to brief the litigating lawyer on the adverse expert witness once identified, and direct the litigating lawyer to writings authored by the adverse expert witness
3. Someone whose expertise, stature in the field, and communicative ability qualify him or her to be the responding expert witness

Though rarely attainable, one person may satisfy all of these criteria. Failing that, the person first selected should satisfy the needs other than that of being a witness, should be informed of the scope and importance of the relationship, and should be told that he or she may well be asked to recommend someone to testify as an expert.

If the litigating lawyer has no personal contacts that can offer the requisite expertise, the lawyer should network with friends, associates, and colleagues, whose judgment he or she trusts, to identify several persons who have expertise in the particular field or fields. In addition to obtaining each person's credentials, the litigating lawyer should ask each friend, associate, or colleague for a frank assessment of qualities of each expert under consideration in light of the three fundamental needs noted above.

Of singular importance, after identifying those few under serious consideration, the litigating lawyer should meet informally with each to confirm or reject the assessments from others and to determine whether the lawyer and the expert can establish that open and unimpaired relationship essential for the lawyer to maximize the relationship in the best interests of the client.

Developing Working Knowledge of the Area of Expertise

The litigating lawyer and the expert who is to assist in preparing for trial and, particularly, for cross-examination of the adverse expert should have an extended meeting at the earliest mutually convenient time. During that meeting, the expert should give the lawyer an overview of the area of expertise, which should be interrupted by a constant flow of questions from the lawyer so that, by the end of the session, a good working relationship of mutual trust and respect has developed.

By the conclusion of that first session, the lawyer should have a modest understanding of the area, some comprehension of its more important technical terms and concepts, and an idea of those matters which he or she must pursue in depth. Also, before parting at the end of the first session, the lawyer should obtain recommendations of texts, articles, and treatises to read to better understand the area of expertise and, perhaps, for beginning the development of a selection of acknowledged published matter to prepare for cross-examination of the adverse expert witness.

It should be made clear from the outset that the relationship between lawyer and expert is essentially one of partnership in which each is free to initiate communications with the other purposed solely to advance the client's cause within legal and ethical limits. Thus, each should be amenable to modifying focus, thoughts, and opinions based on the receipt of additional information. It is essential that the lawyer immediately share with the expert information concerning the adverse expert as it is received—his or her identity, qualifications, opinions, and the bases for those opinions. It should be understood that the ultimate purpose of the partnership is to enable the lawyer to persuade the trier of fact that the adverse expert witness or his or her opinions, or both, lack credibility.

Pretrial Discovery of the Adverse Expert Witness

Almost all jurisdictions have special rules which govern pretrial discovery of expert witnesses. Such special rules substantially limit what is discoverable, requiring judicial intervention for discovery of anything else.

For example, Rule 26(b)(1) of the Federal Rules of Evidence (Fed R Evid) permits discovery of evidence or "information . . . calculated to lead to the discovery of admissible evidence" on "any matter, not privileged . . . relevant to the subject matter involved in the pending action." However, as to "facts known and opinions held by experts . . . in anticipation of litigation or for trial," Rule 26(b)(4)(A) limits discovery to interrogatories seeking the identity of each expert whom the adverse party expects to call, the subject matter on which each expert will testify, the substance of facts and opinions as to which each expert will testify, and the grounds for each opinion of each expert witness. Any additional discovery of adverse experts requires judicial intervention. Many states have similar limitations on pretrial discovery of expert witnesses.[4]

To prepare properly to impeach an adverse expert, it is, of course, essential to exercise those limited discovery rights at the earliest moment. Identities, opinions, and the bases for the opinions of each adverse expert witness should be analyzed by the retained expert as early in pretrial preparation as possible.

However, while depositions of adverse expert witnesses are unavailable as a matter of right, the additional discovery available by application to the trial

---

[4] *E.g.*, NY Civ Prac L&R §3101(d)1, (i).

court, which includes depositions, should be pursued when expert testimony is central to the litigation. And, courts are exhibiting increasing interest in expanded reciprocal discovery of expert witnesses to enable each side to prepare adequately for trial.

Indeed, as earlier noted, Rules 703 and 705 of the Federal Rules of Evidence permit the expert witness to base his or her opinion on matters that are inadmissible and to testify on direct examination to his or her opinion, and the supporting reasons therefor, without disclosing the factual predicate. Thus, unless pretrial discovery has provided the cross-examiner with the factual predicate for the expert's opinion, the cross-examiner may unwittingly and unintentionally place inadmissible matter before the jury when, on cross-examination, he or she asks the expert for the factual predicate for the opinion to which the expert testified on direct examination. Thus, if the factual predicate for an adverse expert's opinion is not apparent and cannot be determined by other means, the litigating lawyer should use every effort to take the expert's deposition prior to trial.

Materials to Impeach Adverse Expert Witness

Beyond that direct discovery of adverse expert witnesses permitted by the relevant procedural rules, once the identities, opinions, and bases for opinions of adverse expert witnesses are known, the litigating lawyer can obtain materials to prepare for impeachment from a variety of sources, limited only by imagination and motivation.

The qualifications of adverse expert witnesses should be obtainable from professional directories or associations and governmental licensing authorities. Indeed, if an adverse expert witness is at all well known or has written extensively, computerized searches of periodicals and professional literature may well offer information on his or her qualifications.

A computerized search of professional literature may also offer leads to articles authored by the expert on the very subject matter of the expert's testimony; such articles should be analyzed by the retained expert for possible use during cross-examination. Further, a computerized search of periodicals may reveal articles reporting the activities or public pronouncements of the adverse expert witness or, possibly, even a list of trials where he or she testified as an expert.

If trials in which the adverse expert has testified can be identified by the litigating lawyer (whether by computerized search of periodicals or through other means), the transcripts of those prior testimonial appearances should be obtained and analyzed both for content as possible prior inconsistent statements and to ascertain the testimonial style of the adverse expert witness. Indeed, discussions with attorneys who have cross-examined the adverse expert witness can offer significant insights into the manner and style of the expert witness and uncover any weaknesses which might be exploited to impeach in cross-examination.

Of course, in-depth reading, analysis, and cataloguing of recognized authorities in the area of expertise on the specific subject of the expert witness's anticipated testimony and opinions are essential. The litigating lawyer should utilize the retained expert to identify the literature, respond to any questions the lawyer has when analyzing the literature, and brainstorm with the lawyer on utilization of the literature for cross-examination.

Finally, it may be beneficial to read transcripts of the cross-examination of other expert witnesses in the same field, conducted by experienced and respected litigating lawyers. While doing so will probably not provide specific impeaching material, it may offer tactical insights into approaches to be used to cross-examine an expert witness in that field with maximum effectiveness, and provide familiarity with particular phrases and questions normally employed in cross-examining an expert witness in that area.

§6.03 Deciding Whether and How to Impeach an Expert Witness

While there are more, and perhaps more sophisticated, factors to be considered in deciding whether and how to attack and impeach an expert witness on cross-examination than there are in deciding the same regarding a fact witness, assessing those factors and reaching a decision require no greater skill or sensitivity. Thus, the litigating lawyer who understands the factors to be considered, has adequately prepared for cross-examination, and has attentively audited direct examination need not approach with trepidation the task of deciding whether and how to impeach the expert witness; nor should the lawyer approach this task with smug cockiness.

As with a fact witness, the first consideration in deciding whether to assay impeachment of an expert witness on cross-examination is to determine the impact of the expert witness's testimony on direct examination. Did the testimony on direct examination inflict damage? If it did, what was the extent of the damage?

Of course, an objective assessment of the extent of damage caused by the adverse expert witness's direct examination necessarily requires that the litigating lawyer understand and appreciate the substance and significance of the adverse expert's opinion and the extent to which its substance and significance to the salient issues of the litigation are in conflict with the opinion of the litigating lawyer's expert witness.

If, from an objective evaluation, it is abundantly clear that the adverse expert witness's testimony on direct examination inflicted little, if any, damage, the better course would be to forgo cross-examination. If, as earlier suggested, the absence of damage from testimony on direct examination by a fact witness militates in favor of forgoing cross-examination, it does so all the more if the testimony on direct examination by an expert witness causes no serious damage. Generally, the expert witness will be an intelligent and educated person whose knowledge of the subject matter of the testimony is greater than that of the lawyer who may cross-examine. Unlike the fact witness, the expert witness may express opinions and furnish the bases for those opinions, which can present traps and snares for the unwary cross-examiner. Further, unlike most fact witnesses, the expert witness is likely to have had experience testifying and to be well prepared for cross-examination. Thus, if no articulable reason exists to seek to impeach an expert witness on cross-examination, the litigating lawyer is best advised to simply state, "No questions, Your Honor."

However, it is extremely rare that an expert witness's direct examination inflicts no serious damage on an opponent's case. Thus, in almost all circumstances where an adverse party has offered expert testimony, damage has been done. Indeed, if the testimony of an expert witness will not aid a client's cause and thus inflict damage on the opponent's, why would the adverse party call an expert to testify? Thus, an objective evaluation of the damage inflicted by the adverse expert witness's direct testimony will almost invariably result in a conclusion that damage was done, and is simply the first step in deciding whether and how to cross-examine to impeach an expert witness. It is then almost inevitable that the initial evaluation will require the litigating lawyer to take the next steps in deciding whether and how to assay impeaching the expert witness on cross-examination.

Hopefully, the lawyer has obtained, during pretrial preparation, substantial and valuable information concerning the adverse expert witness. With that information, the litigating lawyer must audit and observe the adverse expert witness during direct examination in order to evaluate the impression that the witness made on the trier of fact, whether judge or jury. That process of evaluation should also enable the litigating lawyer to form a plan for cross-examining the adverse expert witness for impeachment. The following questions can help the lawyer make the evaluation:

> How did the adverse expert witness's qualifications compare with those of the expert called, or to be called, by the cross-examining lawyer? More significantly, did the trier of fact seem to be impressed with those qualifications, or did the litany of qualifications appear to strike the trier of fact as so much window dressing for someone who is really simply a professional witness for hire?
>
> Did the adverse expert witness's testimony on direct examination, the manner in which it was delivered, and the expert witness's demeanor exude a quiet and reassuring confidence and suggest prior testimonial experience, or did the witness appear ill at ease, nervous, and uncomfortable, as though the witness had never testified as an expert before?
>
> Did the adverse expert testify on direct examination in a manner likely to persuade the trier of fact, explaining complex details in language that a lay trier of fact could readily understand with an evident interest in what the expert was doing? Or, did the direct examination appear to be rather routine, lacking a sense of interest and urgency, as though the witness were testifying from a script which had been used on prior occasions, employing technical jargon that the trier of fact very likely failed to comprehend, leaving the impression that the witness was simply giving a technical lecture?
>
> Did the adverse expert witness appear to be willing to acknowledge the possibility of an error in judgment or that another qualified expert could validly hold a contrary opinion, or did the witness seem inflexible, pedantic, and dogmatic, incapable of admitting the possibility that he or

she erred or that another expert could hold a contrary opinion in good faith?

In other words, the litigating lawyer must objectively evaluate whether cross-examination of the adverse expert witness is likely to accomplish a desired or necessary objective, and that analysis itself may give the litigating lawyer some idea of how to conduct the cross-examination for impeachment.

The litigating lawyer should bear in mind that the determination of whether and how to cross-examine the expert witness may depend on the nature and the posture of the case. Thus, while cross-examination to impeach an expert is generally purposed to tarnish the credibility of the witness or to undermine the substance or significance of the witness's opinion, the nature of the litigation and the party on whose behalf the expert appears may substantially impact the decision of whether to cross-examine and what the goal of impeachment should be.

For example, if the expert witness testifies on an issue or element as to which the party on whose behalf the expert is called has the burden, impeachment may be purposed simply to obtain a concession that other experts may reasonably hold a contrary opinion in good faith. If the expert witness is appearing for the prosecution in a criminal case, the purpose of impeachment may simply be to establish the possibility of error by the expert or that a contrary opinion may be valid, evidencing the reasonable doubt that precludes the trier of fact from returning a guilty verdict.

Thus, while planning and preparation for cross-examination are essential at all times, they are particularly important before commencing cross-examination to impeach an adverse expert witness. Indeed, if the litigating lawyer does not have definable purposes for cross-examination to impeach an adverse expert witness and articulable means to attain those purposes, it is better to forgo cross-examination.

§6.04 Impeachment of an Expert: Questioning Qualifications

As earlier noted, historical limitations on the permissible subjects for expert testimony have been relaxed. Many jurisdictions now permit expert testimony on matters of which lay persons have knowledge, if the expert testimony will assist the trier of fact to understand the evidence or decide the factual issues. There is also a trend to relax standards governing admissibility of testimony by expert witnesses. Thus, limited only by the imagination of litigating lawyers, utilization of expert witnesses has increased dramatically. Indeed, testimony of alleged expert witnesses is now offered on virtually every area of human endeavor which results in litigation and every damage theory that can sway a trier of fact.

No longer limited by subject matter or restricted to persons educated, trained, and experienced in the professions or other learned fields, demand for and financial rewards available to those who will testify for a fee as experts on an endless variety of subjects have substantially eroded the maxim that cross-examination to impeach qualifications is generally abjured. Indeed, today, in pretrial preparation, the point of departure to impeach an expert should be ascertainment and confirmation of the adverse expert's qualifications through the most reputable sources available. Although impeaching an expert witness by attacking the witness's qualifications is dangerous and to be assayed only after the most rigorous investigation and confirmation of the absence of substantial qualifications, the growing demand for persons who will appear as expert witnesses, and be financially rewarded for doing so, and the concomitant attraction of charlatans as experts, increase the possibilities of a successful attack on qualifications.

Assume that an expert witness testified on direct examination that his qualifications included a doctoral degree in sports nutrition, while pretrial preparation by the opposing lawyer suggested that the degree was of the mail order type.

Q: Dr. Hess, I believe you testified on direct examination that you have a doctoral degree in sports nutrition, didn't you?

A: Yes.

Q: What undergraduate degrees do you hold, Dr. Hess?

A: I have a baccalaureate degree.

Q: From what institution?

A: Florida Normal College.

Q: And when were you awarded the baccalaureate degree from Florida Normal College?

A: In 1968.

Q: When did you receive your doctoral degree, Doctor?

A: In 1983.

Q: From which institution of higher learning did you receive that degree?

A: Columbia College of the Pacific

Q: Were you a full-time student while you studied to obtain your doctoral degree?

A: Not really.

Q: Could you tell us some of the courses you took while studying for your doctoral degree in sports nutrition, Dr. Hess?

A: I really don't recall them all.

Q: Well, then, Dr. Hess, could you tell us the title of your doctoral thesis?

A: Yes, I believe it was "Appetite & Athletics."

Q: Isn't it a fact, Dr. Hess, that you never went to a single class at Columbia College of the Pacific?

A: It wasn't required.

Q: Dr. Hess, didn't you obtain your doctoral degree from Columbia College of the Pacific without doing anything but pursue your normal job and complete some forms reporting on your work?

A: I don't recall that, sir.

Q: I show you what has previously been marked as Defendant's Exhibit 9 and ask you if that refreshes your recollection, Dr. Hess.

A: I recognize that.

Q: What is it, sir?

A: What I sent Columbia College of the Pacific.

Q: And isn't it a fact, Dr. Hess, that within a month after sending Defendant's Exhibit 9 and a check for $500 to Columbia College of the Pacific, you received a diploma awarding you a doctoral degree in sports nutrition?

A: You may be right.

The tendency of lay persons to give great deference to the opinions of avowed experts counsels caution in venturing to impeach such persons. The interrogation should be either a very subtle probing to establish the basis to urge lack of credibility in summation or the infliction of a mortal blow. A failed impeachment leaves the witness in a stronger position than had impeachment not been attempted.

On the other hand, the qualifications of the adverse expert witness, while facially attractive, may be substantially less impressive than the qualifications of the expert witness called, or to be called, by the cross-examining lawyer. In that circumstance, probing the details of the adverse expert witness's qualifications in order to compare and contrast the qualifications of the parties' contending expert witnesses in summation may be profitable.

Q: Dr. Shippers, you told us earlier that you are a forensic pathologist and associate medical examiner for the County?

A: Yes.

Q: From what medical school did you obtain your degree?

A: The medical school of New Delhi.

Q: Are you board certified in forensic pathology?

A: No.

Q: Are you board certified in clinical or anatomic pathology?

A: No.

Q: Have you published any treatises, tracts, or monographs on forensic pathology?

A: No.

Q: How many associate medical examiners does the County employ?

A: Twelve.

Q: How long have you been an associate medical examiner for the County?

A: Five months.

Q: Is your employment as associate medical examiner for the County your first full-time employment as a forensic pathologist?

A: Yes.

However, if pretrial preparation indicates that the qualifications of the adverse expert witness are genuine and likely to impress the trier of fact if detailed during direct examination, the opposing lawyer should seriously consider standing, as the expert starts to set forth qualifications, and simply stating, "Your Honor, we are prepared to stipulate that Dr. Jones qualifies as an expert in forensic pathology." While opposing counsel is not required to accept the stipulation—indeed, an experienced lawyer who wants to impress the trier of fact with the expert's qualifications is likely to reject the stipulation—tendering the stipulation may take opposing counsel by surprise or evoke an observation by the court to the lawyer who called the expert: "All right, Counsel has stipulated to the expert's qualifications, so there's no need to spend any time on that."

On the other hand, while the opportunity does not occur with any frequency, occasionally, cross-examination of an expert witness's qualifications which seemingly enhances those qualifications is profitable. For example, assume that the adverse expert witness published a monograph or treatise, part of which supports the opinion of the expert to be called by the cross-examining lawyer, and the publication was not mentioned by the adverse expert witness in detailing his qualifications. Cross-examination which elicits an acknowledgment of the authorship of the publication might be appropriate and offer a foundation for subsequent impeachment of the adverse expert witness by prior inconsistent statement. It may also leave the trier of fact with the impression that the expert witness was trying to conceal the publication, enhancing its importance as a prior inconsistent statement.

Q: Dr. Hirsch, in addition to those qualifications you detailed during direct examination, you've also done some writing, haven't you?

A: Yes, sir.

Q: In fact, didn't you write Chapter 5 entitled "Sudden and Unexpected Deaths from Natural Causes in Adults" in a book edited by Drs. Spitz and Schnitzer entitled "Medical and Legal Investigations of Death"?

A: I did.

Q: When was that, sir?

A: The first edition was published in the early 1970s.

Q: Have you revised the chapter since?

A: The second edition is the latest edition.

Q: And when was that published, Dr. Hirsch?

A: I don't recall.

Q: Your Honor, might this book be deemed marked Defense Exhibit 12?

THE COURT:

Yes, it will be deemed marked.

Q: Dr. Hirsch, I show you what has been deemed marked Defense Exhibit 12. Is that the most recent edition of the book containing your Chapter 5 entitled "Sudden and Unexpected Deaths from Natural Causes in Adults"?

A: Yes, sir, it appears to be.

Thus, pretrial preparation should explore every facet of the adverse expert witness's qualifications to confirm his or her qualifications, discover the flaws, faults, or exaggerations in those qualifications, or ascertain the existence of material which, while apparently enhancing his or her qualifications, affords another vehicle for impeachment.

§6.05 Impeachment of an Expert: Interest, Bias, Motivation

As with all witnesses, the interest, bias, and motivation of an expert witness are proper subjects for cross-examination to impeach. Indeed, impeaching an expert witness by demonstrating interest, bias, or motivation for his or her testimony or views for or against the party for whom the expert is testifying is often more effective than impeaching a fact witness for interest, bias, or motivation. Since the jury usually assumes that an expert witness, unlike a fact witness, is a disinterested professional whose only interest is to help the jury understand complex matters, establishing the interest, bias, or motivation of an expert witness has an overwhelming impact on the expert witness's credibility.

Obviously, every expert witness is subject to impeachment for interest, bias, and motivation predicated on the compensation received for the expert testimony. However, effective cross-examination to impeach on the basis of such compensation should not be the commonplace, "How much are you receiving for testifying today?" It should be a bit creative.

Since it is common knowledge that expert witnesses are compensated for appearing in court, the fact of compensation alone may be a rather weak and unpersuasive basis for an assault on credibility for interest, bias, or motivation. As well, lack of planning and imprecise use of language can render impeachment for interest, bias, or motivation futile and leave the cross-examiner looking foolish.

Q: Dr. Jones, you appear here as an expert witness on behalf of the Plaintiff?

A: Yes.

Q: You are being paid for your testimony, aren't you?

A: No, I am not.

Q: You're not?

A: No, sir, I am not.

Q: Dr. Jones, are you saying that you appeared today for the Plaintiff without being compensated?

A: No.

Q: So you are being paid?

A: Yes, I am.

Q: But you just said earlier that you were not being paid, didn't you?

A: No, sir. I said I was not being paid *for my testimony.*

A little thought and precise use of language is a beginning for effective cross-examination.

Q: Dr. Jones, you're being compensated for appearing on behalf of the Plaintiff, aren't you?

A: Yes, I am.

Q: How much are you being paid for appearing on behalf of the Plaintiff?

A: Two thousand five hundred dollars.

Q: Is that your normal fee for testifying as an expert witness?

A: Yes, it is.

Since, as noted, it is common knowledge that expert witnesses receive compensation, the witness's acknowledgment that he is receiving that sum of money will most likely have little impeaching value. That is merely the foundation.

For example, although the jury may not consider the expert's receipt of compensation in the case on trial as significant evidence of interest, bias, or motivation, it may conclude otherwise if a substantial part of the expert witness's income is derived from testimonial appearances. Thus, continuing cross-examination beyond the pallid inquiry into compensation might be profitable.

Q: How many times have you testified as an expert witness?

A: I don't recall.

Q: How many times have you testified as an expert witness during the past 12 months?

A: Several.

Q: Were you compensated on each of those occasions as you have been for this appearance?

A: Yes, sir.

Q: Is a substantial percentage of your income derived from testifying as an expert witness?

If, as is likely, the witness says he does not know the percentage of his income which derives from testifying or seeks to elide the answer, the jury may draw the inference that, indeed, a substantial part of his income comes from testifying.

Countless other opportunities exist for cross-examination to impeach an expert witness for interest, bias, and motivation, assuming that there exists a reasonable basis for the particular avenue of interrogation. Of course, the absence of a reasonable basis for the inquiry constitutes an ethical violation and will most likely result in a failed impeachment effort, enhancing rather than impeaching the witness's credibility.

For example, if there is a reasonable basis for the inquiry, cross-examination to establish that the expert witness always testifies for the same party or proposition is persuasive impeaching material.

> Q: Dr. Hirsch, you testified today for the prosecution as an expert in forensic pathology?
>
> A: Yes, sir.
>
> Q: On how many occasions have you qualified and testified in criminal matters as an expert in forensic pathology?
>
> A: Over the course of the past 12 years, I would say several hundred times.
>
> Q: And on those several hundred occasions when you qualified and testified in criminal matters as an expert in forensic pathology, did you ever testify for the defendant?

Obviously, that line of questioning can be adapted to almost any expert witness in either civil or criminal cases, assuming that a reasonable basis exists for the inquiry.

> Q: Doctor, isn't it a fact that you do not testify for plaintiffs against other doctors who are sued for medical malpractice?

Cross-examination of an expert witness to demonstrate the existence of, or the basis for, a reasonable inference of the existence of personal or professional interest, bias, or motivation for or against a party or cause is appropriate cross-examination for impeachment, if the cross-examiner has a reasonable basis for the inquiry.

> Q: Dr. Smith, you testified as an expert in cardiovascular surgery on behalf of the defendant, Dr. Mishap, didn't you?
>
> A: Yes, I did.
>
> Q: And you testified that in your opinion, the conduct of Dr. Mishap, the defendant, with respect to the plaintiff, accorded with acceptable standards of medical practice?
>
> A: Yes.
>
> Q: Dr. Smith, you and the defendant are professional colleagues, aren't you?
>
> A: Well, yes, we are both doctors.
>
> Q: Dr. Smith, as well as both of you being doctors, aren't both of you on the staff of Central Hospital?

A: Well, yes, I suppose we are.

Q: And aren't you both affiliated with Memorial Hospital?

A: Yes, we are.

Q: And don't you and the defendant teach at State University Medical School?

A: Yes, we do.

Professional conflict and jealousy may be a most persuasive basis for impeaching the adverse expert witness for interest, bias, or motivation.

Q: Dr. Hoople, before you took the stand to testify, you were aware that Dr. Grant had testified for my client, weren't you?

A: Yes, I had been told that.

Q: Indeed, Dr. Hoople, didn't you see a copy of Dr. Grant's report and conclusions in this matter before you agreed to testify for the defense?

A: I believe I did.

Q: I think you told us during your direct examination that your opinion in this matter is based on a new theory in molecular biology which you have recently developed?

A: That is quite correct.

Q: Dr. Hoople, you have published articles and delivered papers at scientific meetings expounding that new theory, haven't you?

A: Yes, I have given quite a number of papers on that theory and expounded on it in a number of academic and scientific publications.

Q: And, Dr. Hoople, your new theory has not received unanimous acceptance, has it?

A: New theories never do.

Q: Indeed, haven't you been subjected to substantial scientific and academic criticism because of the new theory?

A: Yes, and it hasn't been pleasant.

Q: And, Dr. Hoople, hasn't Dr. Grant been one of the most vocal critics of your new theory?

A: Yes, he has been.

Q: And his leadership of critics of your new theory has substantially impeded its acceptance in the scientific and academic communities, hasn't it?

A: I believe it has.

Q: And, Dr. Hoople, you consider Dr. Grant personally responsible for that, don't you?

A: Well, he hasn't really been helpful to me.

Thus, as with the fact witness, almost anything that suggests the existence of interest, bias, or motivation of an adverse expert witness for testifying for or against one of the parties or for expressing certain conclusions and opinions is appropriate for inquiry to impeach. What is required is pretrial preparation to discover the basis for cross-examination to establish the interest, bias, or motivation of the adverse expert witness necessary to impeach.

§6.06 Impeachment of an Expert: Sources of Knowledge or Information

As earlier noted, while the testimony of the fact witness is restricted to recounting his or her sensory perceptions (subject to certain exceptions to the hearsay rule), the testimony of the expert witness is not so restricted. Indeed, were the expert witness limited to testifying to what the expert perceived, he or she could not fulfill the very purpose for calling an expert witness: to offer the trier of fact opinions based upon asserted expertise in order to assist in understanding or evaluating the factual evidence.

Thus, the opinions proffered the trier of fact in the testimony of the expert witness may be predicated on personal knowledge, information received from others, or facts assumed by the expert in formulating, or in questions posed to the expert in eliciting, his or her opinion. And even when the expert witness's testimony is predicated on the expert's own sensory perceptions, those sensory perceptions, unlike those of the fact witness, might not have been happenstance but, rather, might have been made precisely in order to formulate an opinion in order to testify as an expert.

Like the fact witness, the expert witness may be impeached by cross-examination which evidences or suggests defects or deficiencies in the witness's perception, memory, or ability to recall and recount. However, as just noted, unlike that of the fact witness, the testimony of the expert witness may be predicated on knowledge or information obtained for the very purpose of formulating an opinion, on information obtained from others, or on assumed facts. The expert witness, therefore, may also be impeached by cross-examination concerning the source of, and the manner of obtaining, the information, as well as its accuracy.

When assessing the credibility of an expert witness, both the source of the information and the manner of obtaining the information on which the expert's opinion is predicated may be critical. A trier of fact may well give greater credence to the testimony of an expert witness whose relevant information and knowledge were acquired as part of the expert's regular activities than to the testimony of one who sought and obtained his or her knowledge and information in order to formulate an opinion favorable to the party on whose behalf the expert is testifying.

For example, it is understandable that a jury would give greater weight to the testimony and opinion of a physician whose knowledge and information supporting his opinion came from treating a party over a prolonged period of time prior to the litigation than to the testimony and opinion of a physician employed and compensated for the purpose of examining the adverse party, formulating an opinion, and testifying to that opinion. Thus, cross-examination of an expert witness who was retained for the litigation might well seek to point up the differences between the source of and manner of obtaining the knowledge and information on which his opinion is predicated, and the source of and manner of obtaining the knowledge and information on which the opinion of the physician who treated a party over a prolonged period is predicated.

Q: Dr. Jones, your opinion is based on knowledge and information you obtained for the very purpose of forming your opinion, isn't that right?

A: No, sir, my knowledge and information is based on my examination of Mr. Maimed.

Q: But, Dr. Jones, you examined Mr. Maimed in order to form an opinion, didn't you?

A: Well, I couldn't form an opinion without examining him.

Q: But weren't you retained as the Defendant's expert witness before examining Mr. Maimed?

A: Yes, I was.

Q: So you never treated Mr. Maimed, did you?

A: No, I did not.

Q: How many times did you examine Mr. Maimed in order to form an opinion?

A: Three times.

Q: How long a period of time elapsed between your first examination of Mr. Maimed and your third and last examination of him?

A: Three weeks.

Q: And, Dr. Jones, prior to your three examinations, weren't you aware that Mr. Maimed was suing the Defendant?

A: Well, yes.

Q: And prior to your three examinations of Mr. Maimed, weren't you also aware that the lawsuit claimed that Mr. Maimed was suffering from traumatic arthritis?

A: I believe I was made aware of the lawsuit and the claim, yes.

Q: And after you were made aware of the fact that Mr. Maimed was suing the Defendant for causing him to suffer traumatic arthritis, you agreed to act as the Defendant's expert witness, didn't you?

A: Yes.

Q: And as part of that agreement you receive compensation, don't you?

A: Yes.

Q: And you examined Mr. Maimed three times and formed your opinion within three weeks only after agreeing to be Defendant's expert witness and agreeing on your compensation?

A: Well, I don't like that implication, counselor.

Q: But, Dr. Jones, isn't that accurate?

A: Well, I guess so, but my opinion is the result of my examinations of your client and it is an honest opinion, sir.

It would be gilding the lily and would evoke an objection from the proponent of the witness to ask the next question—"Dr. Jones, did I suggest that your opinion was not honest?"

When the knowledge or information on which the expert witness predicates his or her opinion derives from other persons, the expert cannot attest to its accuracy. Cross-examination which emphasizes the expert witness's lack of personal knowledge and his or her reliance on information obtained from other persons for the factual predicate for the opinion may seriously affect the weight that the trier of fact is willing to afford that opinion.

Q: Doctor, you neither performed nor observed the autopsy in this case, did you?

A: I did not, that's correct.

Q: In fact, Doctor, you base your opinion that the cause of death was strangulation on information you received from the Associate Medical Examiner who performed the autopsy report, don't you?

A: Yes, in part.

Q: And the Associate Medical Examiner informed you that her autopsy of the deceased disclosed a fractured hyoid bone and thyroid cartilage?

A: That is correct, but I also observed the fractured hyoid bone and thyroid cartilage preserved in the Medical Examiner's Office.

Q: Doctor, you did not observe the external skin of the deceased's neck, did you?

A: I did not, since the deceased was interred before I was asked to give an opinion as to the manner and cause of death.

Q: So again, you relied on information from the Associate Medical Examiner who performed the autopsy, didn't you?

A: As to the external marks on the deceased's neck, yes, I did.

Q: And at the time she did the autopsy, how long had the Associate Medical Examiner been in the Medical Examiner's Office?

A: Approximately five months.

Q: Doctor, in your years of experience as a forensic pathologist and as Chief Medical Examiner, you're familiar with cases where a hyoid bone and thyroid cartilage were broken by blows to the neck rather than sustained manual pressure, aren't you?

A: Yes, I am.

Q: And without marks on the external skin of the neck, you cannot state with a reasonable degree of medical certainty that the broken hyoid bone and thyroid cartilage resulted from sustained manual compression, can you?

A: That is correct.

Q: And since you did not personally observe the external skin of the deceased's neck, it is possible that your opinion that death was due to sustained manual compression might be incorrect, isn't it?

A: I don't think it is incorrect.

Q: But, Doctor, since you did not personally observe any marks on the external skin of the deceased's neck and those marks are essential to your opinion that the deceased was subjected to sustained manual compression of the neck, your opinion is based on information given you by the least experienced forensic pathologist in the Medical Examiner's Office, isn't it? Isn't that right?

A: Yes, that is correct.

As well, when the knowledge or information on which the expert witness predicates his opinion derives from other persons, the cross-examiner may consider employing hypothetical questions to impeach the opinion of the expert witness. Since it must be assumed that the adverse expert witness is both qualified and well prepared, cross-examination with hypothetical questions should be fully planned and prepared in advance with the assistance of the expert associated with the cross-examiner.

Cross-examination utilizing hypothetical questions (1) may isolate and question the expert concerning the individual factors on which he predicates his opinion, (2) may ask the expert to assume specific factors which were not included in the predicate for his opinion, but either have been, or will be, established by evidence offered, or to be offered, by the cross-examiner, or (3) may employ both of those tactics.

Q: Mr. Boeckmann, your appraisal concluded that the fair market value of the real estate is $1,500,000, didn't it?

A: Yes, sir.

Q: And as I understand your testimony on direct examination, that appraisal of fair market value is premised on the highest and best use of the property, is that right?

A: That is right.

Q: And in your opinion, the highest and best use would be institutional use of the existing buildings and subdividing the other acreage for construction of private residences on two-acre plots?

A: That was my opinion of the highest and best use to establish fair market value of the property.

Q: When you formulated that opinion, did you consider the existing zoning?

A: I believe that I did.

Q: And did the zoning allow institutional use of the existing buildings?

A: No, not without a special permit.

Q: Were you aware, at the time you formulated your opinion, that my client had entered into a contract to buy the property?

A: Yes, I was aware of that, yes.

Q: And were you aware that they entered into the contract for the purpose of using the existing buildings for a school?

A: I had heard that.

Q: Mr. Boeckmann, at the time of the contract, had the municipality issued a special permit authorizing institutional use of the building?

A: No.

Q: Since the contract was signed and you formulated your opinion that the highest and best use of the property is institutional use of the existing buildings and subdividing the remaining property for private residences, has the municipality issued a special permit authorizing institutional use of the existing buildings?

A: No, it has not.

Q: Thus, Mr. Boeckmann, the primary assumption on which your opinion of fair market value of the property is based never occurred, did it?

A: No, it did not.

Of course, cross-examination of an expert witness may combine two impeaching tactics—isolating one factor which is critical to the expert's opinion and impeaching the source of the information on which the opinion is predicated, thus undermining the credibility of the opinion itself.

Q: Doctor, you testified on direct examination that, in your opinion, sustained manual compression was exerted on the deceased's neck?

A: I did so testify.

Q: And you based that opinion on the existence of fractures of the hyoid bone and thyroid cartilage, didn't you?

A: And marks on the external skin of the neck.

Q: Which you did not personally observe, isn't that correct?

A: Yes.

Q: But you did observe the preserved fractured hyoid bone and thyroid cartilage, didn't you?

A: Yes, I did.

Q: You also personally observed extensive ossification and calcification of the deceased's hyoid bone and thyroid cartilage, didn't you?

A: Yes, I did.

Q: And, Doctor, when a hyoid bone and thyroid cartilage are extensively ossified and calcified, they are more brittle and can be fractured by less substantial force than if they were not as ossified and calcified, correct?

A: That is correct.

Q: Doctor, assume that there was a physical altercation between the deceased and the defendant in which each party struck blows. Are the fractured hyoid bone and thyroid cartilage you observed consistent with multiple blows to the deceased's neck by the defendant?

A: Yes, they would be consistent with multiple blows to the neck.

§6.07 Impeachment of an Expert: Treatises and Literature

While treatises and literature that support an expert witness's opinion or theory generally cannot be utilized during direct examination to corroborate the witness or bolster his or her opinion, treatises and literature that undermine, discredit, or distinguish the opinion of the adverse witness, or one of the opinion's premises, may generally be utilized to impeach the adverse expert witness on cross-examination. Indeed, cross-examination utilizing learned treatises or other literature is one of the most popular means of impeaching an adverse expert witness. Of course, as was suggested earlier, a substantial benefit to retaining an expert during the early stages of a litigation is obtaining assistance in identifying and securing access to relevant treatises and literature.[5]

Some jurisdictions require that the expert witness have relied upon a learned treatise or literature before that treatise or literature may be utilized during cross-examination to impeach the expert. However, more commonly, impeachment by cross-examination using learned treatises and literature is permitted if the expert witness recognizes or acknowledges that the particular treatise or publication is authoritative. Rule 803(18) of the Federal Rules of Evidence permits even broader opportunity to impeach an adverse expert witness using literature.

> To the extent called to the attention of an expert witness on cross-examination or relied upon . . . on direct examination, statements in . . . treatises, periodicals, or pamphlets on . . . history, medicine, or other science or art, established as reliable authority by the . . . witness or by other expert testimony or by judicial notice.

Thus, Rule 803(18) excepts those published writings from the hearsay rule and permits authentication not only by the adverse expert witness on cross-examination, but also by other expert witnesses and the court.

Authentication of a published work for impeachment purposes is not difficult. Obviously, the more substantial the acknowledgment during cross-examination of the adverse expert witness of the authority of the publication or its author, or both, the stronger the impeaching value of the work.

---

[5] *See* §6.02.

Q: Doctor, are you familiar with a treatise entitled "Forensic Pathology" by Dr. Schmidt?

A: Yes, I am.

Q: And, Doctor, do you recognize and accept "Forensic Pathology" by Dr. Schmidt as an authoritative work in the field?

A: Of course.

Q: Indeed, Doctor, you were a student of Dr. Schmidt's in medical school, weren't you?

A: Yes, I was.

Q: So you recognize Dr. Schmidt as an authority on forensic pathology and accept his book as a scholarly work in the field, don't you?

A: Yes.

Occasionally, an adverse expert witness may refuse to recognize a particular published work or its author as authoritative. In that circumstance, if the cross-examiner is satisfied from pretrial preparation that the work is accepted as authoritative almost universally, and is persuaded both that the adverse expert witness's refusal is frivolous and that the cross-examiner can authenticate the work through other means, cross-examination of the adverse expert witness may probe the expert's refusal to recognize the work, both to increase the focus of the trier of fact on the potential impeachment by learned treatise, or other literature, and to establish the frivolousness of the adverse expert's refusal to recognize the work.

Under Rule 803(18) of the Federal Rules of Evidence and likely decisions in other jurisdictions, there are two alternative ways to authenticate a publication. Assuming the work has universal acceptance and is known outside of the specific field, asking the court to take judicial notice is perhaps the easiest but least dramatic.

Q: Your Honor, I respectfully ask the Court to take judicial notice that Gray's Anatomy is and for many years has been accepted as the standard work on anatomy, used in virtually every medical school in the United States.

COURT:

Yes, I will take judicial notice that Gray's Anatomy is an authoritative work.

Although the cross-examiner can ask the court to take judicial notice of the authoritative nature of the work while the adverse expert witness is still testifying and thus limit the interruption of cross-examination, authenticating a work in that manner is rather bland. Calling another expert witness to authenticate a work makes more of the adverse expert witness's refusal to recognize the work as authoritative. To minimize the loss of continuity, courts will sometimes grant a request to interrupt cross-examination of the adverse expert witness to call another expert to authenticate a work being used to impeach. If the adverse expert witness refuses to authenticate a published work and the court will not permit interruption of cross-examination to permit another expert to authenticate it, the court may permit continued cross-examination using the work on the representation that another expert witness will authenticate it.

Q: Doctor Jones, what do you do?

A: I am a physician specializing and board certified in internal medicine and I teach at the University's Medical School.

Q: What do you teach?

A: I teach an honors course in anatomy.

Q: Have you ever heard of a treatise entitled Gray's Anatomy?

A: Of course.

Q: When did you first hear of Gray's Anatomy?

A: When I was in medical school.

Q: Was it then recognized as an authoritative work in the field?

A: I would say it was then recognized as *the* authoritative work in the field.

Q: And, forgive me, Doctor Jones, but you were in medical school several years ago. Is Gray's Anatomy still used in any way?

A: Of course. I use it as primary material in my honors course in anatomy and it is still recognized as *the* authoritative work in the field.

Q: Thank you, Doctor.

As suggested earlier, pretrial preparation should include a computerized or other search of published writings by the adverse expert witness on the subject matter of his or her testimony. *See* **§6.02.** It was also earlier observed that the relatively limited pretrial discovery of experts does not usually afford an opportunity to know precisely what the adverse expert will testify to during his or her direct examination.[6]

Published works by persons who appear as expert witnesses and the views and opinions expressed in those writings are generally rather conservative and guarded. Thus, if carefully analyzed and catalogued, those writings are likely to provide some materials inconsistent with the opinions and views expressed by the adverse expert witness during direct examination.

Moreover, if the adverse expert witness has had substantial experience and written extensively in the field, it is likely that, over a prolonged period of time, the expert's views have changed or been tempered; thus, some of those writings should offer material for impeachment. Of course, the adverse expert witness will try to explain that his or her earlier opinions or views, which are used to impeach the expert, have changed with the expert's experience and research; but, if the cross-examiner properly controls the adverse expert witness on

---

[6] *See* **§6.02.**

cross-examination, the explanation will come on re-direct examination and be substantially vitiated.

Where pretrial preparation discloses the opinions and views that the adverse expert witness will offer during his or her direct examination and such expert has published a writing which is inconsistent with those opinions and views, authentication of the published material and, if possible, its continued vitality, may be effected in the context of bolstering the adverse expert's qualifications. *See* **§6.04.**

Q: Dr. Hirsch, in addition to those qualifications you stated during direct examination, you've also done some writing, haven't you?

A: Yes, sir.

Q: Did you in fact co-author Chapter 5 entitled "Sudden and Unexpected Death from Natural Causes in Adults" in a book titled *Medical and Legal Investigation of Deaths* edited by Doctor Werner Spitz and Doctor Russell S. Schnitzer?

A: I did.

Q: How long ago was that, sir?

A: The first edition of that book was in the early 1970s, I believe. I don't recall the exact date.

Q: Have you amended, modified, or revised it from time to time?

A: There is currently a second edition and we made some modifications in the material for that edition.

Q: The second edition is the latest edition?

A: Yes.

Q: Thank you, Doctor.

As with impeachment by use of prior inconsistent statements, the adverse expert witness must, generally, be confronted with the writing to impeach with treatises or other published writings. Indeed, the best and most effective way to impeach an adverse expert witness by using a treatise or other published writing is substantially the same as the best and most effective way to impeach an adverse witness with a prior inconsistent statement.

Q: Doctor, are you saying that in your opinion the cause of death was a combination of trauma and disease?

A: That is my opinion, yes, sir.

Q: And these five pieces of paper marked as Exhibit 5 containing notes you made between January and May are the only writings you have relevant to your opinion that the cause of death was a combination of trauma and disease?

A: Yes, sir.

Q: Doctor, did you prepare a report in which you analyzed your findings and show the relative role of trauma and disease in causing the death of the deceased?

A: You have my notes, sir.

Q: I am aware of that, Doctor. Do those notes contain an analysis of your findings and show the relative role of trauma and disease?

A: I leave that to you, sir.

COURT:

No, Doctor, please answer the question "Yes" or "No."

A: No, sir, the notes do not.

Q: Do your recall telling us earlier that you wrote Chapter 5 entitled "Sudden and Unexpected Death from Natural Causes in Adults" in a book called *Medical and Legal Investigation of Deaths* edited by Doctor Werner Spitz and Doctor Russell S. Schnitzer?

A: Yes.

Q: In that Chapter 5 of the book at page 118, didn't you write, and I quote: "In any situation in which an individual is accused of causing the death of another and the investigation and autopsy findings indicate that there is a combination of injury and disease responsible for the death, the pathologist must analyze the situation carefully and show in his report and opinion the relative role of the two events in causing death"?

A: Yes, sir, I wrote that.

Q: Did you prepare such an opinion or report in this case, Doctor?

A: I'm here to express such an opinion.

COURT:

Excuse me, Doctor. Did you prepare such a report in the form referred to in the book?

A: No, sir, I did not.

Thus, the adverse expert witness should be committed to the testimony, opinion, or view to be impeached. Indeed, if possible, have the adverse expert witness become firmer and more fixed in the rightness of his or her testimony, opinion, or view. Such interrogation should focus the attention of the trier of fact on the testimony, opinion, or view to be impeached and close every avenue of escape and explanation.

The treatise or published writing should then be authenticated by the adverse expert witness. If the adverse expert witness refuses to authenticate the writing, the cross-examiner should authenticate it in the least intrusive manner possible or ask the court to permit cross-examination using the treatise or published writing with subsequent authentication.

As with a prior inconsistent statement, only after focusing the attention of the trier of fact on the testimony, opinion, or view to be impeached, closing means of escape or explanation, and authenticating the treatise or published writing should the cross-examiner confront the adverse expert witness with the impeaching material.

And, as with a prior inconsistent statement, impeaching an adverse expert witness with a learned treatise or other published writing should only be assayed if the subject for impeachment is significant, the impeaching material clear, and the cross-examiner thoroughly prepared and capable of controlling the adverse expert witness during cross-examination.

§6.08 Impeachment of an Expert: Control Is Essential

It was earlier suggested that the first step in preparing to cross-examine an adverse expert witness should be the candid acknowledgment that, at that juncture, every adverse expert witness has greater knowledge of and familiarity with his or her area of expertise than does the litigating lawyer. Indeed, the cross-examination of an adverse expert witness should be commenced, conducted, and completed with the assumption that the adverse expert witness has encyclopedic knowledge of and familiarity with his or her area of expertise and significant experience in testifying.

Thus, the cross-examiner must always bear in mind that maintaining control of the witness and the witness's responses to questions posed on cross-examination is critical to any meaningful cross-examination. No matter how thorough the pretrial discovery, preparation, and planning for cross-examination of an adverse expert witness, failure to control the adverse expert witness during cross-examination will most likely result in an ineffective or futile cross-examination.

Concededly, maintaining control of an experienced adverse expert witness is no easy task, and is made all the more difficult if the adverse expert witness seeks to or concludes that he or she can assume control of the flow and content of cross-examination.

Of course, without thorough knowledge of the area of expertise and preparation for cross-examination, any effort at control is doomed to failure. Assuming the existence of thorough preparation and planning, the first step in controlling the adverse expert witness is the framing or determining the phraseology of the questions: they must be posed in clear, concise, and nontechnical language, easily understood by the trier of fact, and capable of being answered with a simple "yes" or "no." If the question is such that the trier of fact readily comprehends it and expects a simple "yes" or "no" in response, an effort by the adverse expert witness to evade a simple affirmative or negative response, elide the question, or thrust and parry with the cross-examiner will most likely damage the credibility of that witness. Moreover, if the question is such that the trier of fact readily comprehends it and it can be answered with a simple "yes" or "no" in response, and the adverse expert witness tries to evade responding, elide the question, or engage in banter with the cross-examiner, the court may well intercede sua sponte and direct the witness to answer the question with a simple affirmative or negative response. Furthermore, in a jury trial, the court's intercession will very likely inflict damage on the adverse expert witness's credibility.

Beyond the framing and phraseology of questions, controlling the adverse expert witness requires the cross-examiner to exude a quiet confidence, neither arrogant nor supercilious. The cross-examiner's conduct, demeanor, and body language must evidence self-confidence in knowing what has to be done and how to do it. That message must be communicated to the adverse expert witness and the trier of fact so that the former is cautioned about seeking to seize control and the latter accepts any required interruption of the adverse expert's answer in order to assert control.

The cross-examiner must also understand that control of an adverse expert witness must be exercised from the very start of cross-examination. Once an adverse expert witness concludes that he or she can control the flow of the interrogation and the content and manner of responses to specific questions, the cross-examiner will have difficulty in asserting or reasserting control.

Thus, on the first occasion that the adverse expert witness seeks to evade a question by a nonresponsive answer or begins a narrative in response to a question which seeks, and may be answered by, a simple "yes" or "no," the cross-examiner must assert control. That control may be asserted in a number of ways.

Perhaps the worst method of trying to assert control over an errant or recalcitrant adverse expert witness is to taunt the witness or engage the witness in a debate. If the adverse expert witness gives a nonresponsive, evasive, or inadequate response to a question, the cross-examiner's inquiry, "Don't you understand the question?" will very likely evoke an unhelpful response: perhaps, "Yes, I understood the question, Counselor, did you?" or, "No, counselor, could you make it clearer?" or, "I think I understood it and answered it. Do you want to ask another question?" The cross-examiner will feel compelled to respond to the adverse expert witness's taunts; at that point, the adverse expert witness has seized control of the interrogation.

When controlling the adverse expert witness who has sought to evade, elide, or totally avoid responding to a clear and concise question, the simpler the approach, the better. Thus, if the first rule of control has been followed and the trier of fact understands the question and realizes that it can be answered with a simple "yes" or "no," the cross-examiner may simply say to the difficult expert witness, "Could you please answer the question," "Could you please answer the question I asked," or "Could you please answer the question simply 'yes' or 'no' "

If the cross-examiner adheres to the first rule of control and the adverse expert witness persists in trying to evade, elide, or avoid giving responsive answers, the cross-examiner may want to enlist the support of the court by simply saying, "Your Honor, would you please instruct the witness to respond to the question [I asked] [simply 'yes' or 'no']."

Some litigating lawyers exercise control over an adverse expert witness by initiating cross-examination with a simple series of questions. However, even in posing such introductory questions, the cross-examiner must maintain control over the adverse expert witness.

Q: Doctor, do you understand that I am going to ask you some questions about your testimony on direct examination?

A: Yes, I do.

Q: Do you also understand that you must answer each question I ask?

A: Yes.

Q: Doctor, I will ask each question so you can answer it simply "yes" or "no." Will you answer each question simply "yes" or "no?"

A: I will if I can.

Q: If you do not understand a question or find that you cannot answer a question simply "yes" or "no," will you tell me that, before you try to answer it another way?

A: As you wish.

Q: Does that mean you will?

A: Yes.

Having heard this introductory interrogation, the jury and the court will understand the cross-examiner's interruption of a response by the adverse expert witness other than "yes" or "no."

Q: Doctor, I believe you agreed that if you did not understand a question or could not respond simply "yes" or "no," you would tell me that, before you tried to answer the question another way?

A: Yes, I did.

Q: Well, then, would you please answer the last question simply "yes" or "no" or tell us why you cannot do so?

If the question is clearly susceptible of a simple "yes" or "no" response, the adverse expert will have to furnish that response or, likely, inflict damage to his or her credibility. The cross-examiner will thus have asserted continuing control over the flow of the interrogation and the content and manner of response.

7 Influence of Demeanor of Witnesses During Cross-Examination and Impeachment

§7.01 Introduction

"A witness' demeanor on the stand is an element of importance in the solution of the always difficult problem of determining the truthfulness of his testimony."[1]

Witnesses, testifying about what they have seen, heard, or observed, provide not only important information to the fact-finder, but also, in certain cases, the decisive information required for judging a case. The importance of witness testimony in general, and the significance of a witness's credibility in the impeachment process in particular, merit and require a thorough study of two aspects of human communication: the witness's message and its perception by the fact-finder.

As in any human communication, when a witness gives testimony at a trial, there are two languages which the jury, the judge, and the lawyers must understand: the verbal language (the significance of the words, including metacommunication—the meaning of the words over and above their literal sense) and the nonverbal language (facial expressions, eye contact, gestures, postures, etc.).

If the testimony of any witness is analyzed, the following main elements are found:

1. The witness's response to the questioning (the message)
2. How the witness's words are spoken
3. The body language accompanying the words

Based on these elements, some questions will arise:

1. Was what the witness said the real expression of what he or she intended to say?
2. Was the witness's message intended to hide the truth, or did the message express the truth about what the witness knows about a certain fact?
3. Did the witness's body language contradict the sense of the spoken words?
4. Was the witness's message spontaneous or the result of external influence (i.e., preparation by the lawyer presenting the witness)?

In the following sections we will analyze not only the witness's behavior during testimony and its influence on the perception of the finder of fact, but also the witness's silence during the testimony, and its interpretation and effect. From this analysis we will try to find answers to questions which arise regarding witness-lawyer communication and the way this dialogue influences the perception of juries and judges.

This study is based on our professional experience and also on the experience of other trial lawyers, psychologists, and judges in the interpretation of

---

[1] William J. Riddle, 102 F Supp 884, 887 (SDNY), *affd,* 200 F2d 608 (2d Cir 1952).

verbal and nonverbal communication, and the influence of these factors on the demeanor of witnesses during their testimony. Our examination of the conduct of witnesses will be based on the study and analyses of various research works included in the following books: *How to Prepare Witnesses for Trial,*[2] *Trial Communication Skills,*[3] and *Cross-Examination of Witnesses: The Litigator's Puzzle.*[4]

§7.02 The Ability and Capacity to Testify

Rule 601 of the Federal Rules of Evidence establishes that "[e]very person is competent to be a witness except as otherwise provided in these rules." Is it enough for a prospective witness to have seen, heard, or observed an event in order to be able to testify about that event? Certainly not. Also required are the capabilities to recall and communicate—to tell the trier of fact in understandable and credible terms what the witness knows about the event.

In this chapter, two aspects of testimony are discussed: the witness's ability to communicate in a credible manner, and the different ways in which the witness's message and behavior can be interpreted by the jury or the judge.

A person could have the ability to communicate, but his or her message might not be believable. For example, a witness could testify that he saw the face of the murderer when he attacked the victim, but the witness was more than 100 yards from the place of the attack, the event occurred at night, the place of the attack lacked illumination, and the attack happened on a dark night with no moon. In this example, the witness may have had the ability to communicate, but his communication lacked credibility. A witness's credibility can also be affected by contradictions or incongruencies in the testimony, avoiding a straight answer, confusion of words, lack of concordance between the spoken words and the witness's body gestures, etc.

The expectation of a lawyer presenting a witness at a trial is that the witness's testimony will persuade the trier of fact that events happened as the witness says. If the witness's communication does not lead to this result and the witness's testimony is impeached, the consequences could be serious—not only for the witness during cross-examination or impeachment, but also for the case itself and for the lawyer who, in preparing the witness, did not foresee the witness's weaknesses or inability to testify.

§7.03 The Structure of Witnesses' Testimony

Two principal parties participate during testimony at trial: a lawyer (and sometimes also the judge) asking questions, and a witness responding.

---

[2] R. Aron & J. Rosner, How to Prepare Witnesses for Trial (Shepard's/McGraw-Hill 1985).

[3] R. Aron, J. Fast, & R. Klein, Trial Communication Skills (Shepard's/McGraw-Hill 1986).

[4] R. Aron, K.T. Duffy, & J.L. Rosner, Cross-Examination of Witnesses: The Litigator's Puzzle (Shepard's/McGraw-Hill 1989).

Lawyers' attitudes toward witnesses in direct examination are different than in cross-examination; witnesses' attitudes toward lawyers during direct examination are also different than in cross-examination.

In direct examination, the lawyer-witness relationship is cordial. The lawyer acts like a friend, asking questions about subjects previously discussed with the witness during the preparation process. At this stage, there is no confrontation or antagonism between the two characters. Moreover, if the direct examination was well prepared, the lawyer does not need to resort to leading questions, which are forbidden; the lawyer knows what to ask in order to obtain the answer expected from the witness.

Seldom during direct examination does one hear answers such as: "I don't remember," "I don't know," or "I don't understand the question." The reason is obvious: during the preparation process, the lawyer presenting the witness learned what the witness knows about a given fact, and the witness knows what questions the lawyer will ask.

There are exceptions to the friendly questioning, when the witness can be qualified as a hostile witness. In such case, leading questions are permitted.[5]

During cross-examination, the lawyer-witness relationship is generally antagonistic. The lawyer's main purpose is to prove that the witness's testimony during direct examination, or at least part of it, was untrue or incredible.

During a trial, each party's lawyer has a theory of the case which he or she tries to prove to the court through witnesses or other evidence. Witnesses are among the chief pillars by which a lawyer supports his or her theory.

The goal of the cross-examiner's questioning of the witness is to prove that the opposing lawyer's theory of the case is incorrect. The cross-examiner knows that the result of destroying or weakening the credibility of the opposing witnesses will be to weaken or destroy the other lawyer's theory of the case.[6]

The main character, caught in the middle of the lawyers' battle, is the person called "the witness." (We are referring to an impartial and disinterested witness.)

An interesting description of what a witness is was presented in *How to Prepare Witnesses for Trial:*

> [W]e dedicate this book to THE WITNESS—that participant in the litigating process who has been at once the most essential and the least considered, of whom greater participation has been required and less training provided, whose reward for providing critical elements to the litigating process has often been doubt, criticism, and castigation, and who has survived centuries of cross-examination.[7]

---

[5] Fed R Evid 611. For a more complete study of preparation of witnesses for direct examination, see R. Aron & J. Rosner, How to Prepare Witnesses for Trial ch 12 (Shepard's/McGraw-Hill 1985).

[6] For a more compete study of preparation of witnesses for cross-examination, see R. Aron & J. Rosner, *supra* note 5, at ch 13.

[7] *See* R. Aron & J. Rosner, *supra* note 5, at dedication page.

Generally, the witness is the only "impartial" participant in a trial (parties and lawyers are interested in a favorable verdict). The witness's only sin is to have observed an event which is the basis for the trial, or to be needed for some other purpose in the trial.

Seldom are a person's words so important and decisive as in the witness process of testimony. The witness's words not only transmit information, but also make possible a determination of patterns of conduct of the parties involved in the case.

Each word pronounced by the witness during direct examination may be examined with a microscope during cross-examination; the meaning of each sentence may be analyzed meticulously during closing arguments. Moreover, each silence, each hesitation, and the intonation of each word may become the subjects of lengthy dissertations and interpretations by the lawyers for both parties.

Sometimes a witness wants to avoid the responsibility of giving an answer or does not know what to say and remains silent. He or she looks at the lawyer and does not say anything. This is actually a means of communication. The witness's face is telling the lawyer, "I don't know what you are asking," "I am not so stupid as to answer your question," or, simply, "I don't know."

When questions and the witness's testimony involve short and/or simple sentences, such as during the preliminary questioning, no problems of interpretation will arise, usually. For example:

Q: What is your name?

A: My name is Peter Smith

Q: Where do you live?

A: I live at 555 Eighth Avenue in New York City, Apartment 89.

But at times, the witness must answer more complicated questions:

Q: During direct examination, you stated the time at which you arrived at the scene of the crime, but I did not pay attention to your answer; could you be so kind as to repeat the time at which you arrived? (The lawyer's statement that the lawyer did not pay attention to the witness's answer is not to be taken literally.)

A: I said that it was a quarter past twelve at night. (This demonstrates the other lawyer's first mistake by not advising the witness, during the preparation process, to say "approximately.")

Q: How do you know that it was a quarter past twelve?

A: Uh . . . because I looked at my watch.

Q: Do you mean to tell us that you arrived at the place where a person had just been murdered, you saw the victim's corpse, and your first reaction was to look at your watch to find out what time it was?

A: Well, you know. . . .

Even though the time of the witness's arrival may not have been an important factor, the cross-examiner succeeded in confusing the witness.

It may be concluded that while *what* a witness says is important, even more important is *how* the words are spoken. If this has not complicated the analysis of a witness's testimony enough, we need to add the following factors: the demeanor of the witness during the testimony and the influence of the witness's behavior on the way that his or her message is perceived by the trier of fact. This theme is developed in the following sections.

§7.04 Witnesses' Verbal and Nonverbal Communication

In order to study the influence of a witness's demeanor, during testimony, on the determination of whether the testimony is truthful, and the influence of the witness's conduct on the perception of the trier of fact, it is necessary to analyze carefully the witness's verbal and nonverbal communication.

As mentioned in the introduction to this chapter, in any human communication there are two languages: the verbal expression (the words that are heard), and the nonverbal communication (the language that is seen).

To emphasize how important it is for judges, jurors, and lawyers to understand both languages, we present the following example: Suppose that a trial is conducted in two languages, English and Spanish. If the participants in the trial understand only one of the two languages, they will be severely handicapped in their comprehension of what is going on.

A similar situation exists if the characters participating in a trial understand verbal communication but are illiterate in or do not pay attention to nonverbal communication.

Furthermore, if, in a witness's testimony, there is a contradiction between verbal and nonverbal communication, the truth can usually be found in the witness's nonverbal communication. The reason for this is that *words* are easily manageable, while *body language or reactions* are more difficult to control. If a person wants to say, "I was there" or "I wasn't there," normally he or she will not have a problem pronouncing the desired words. But if a person does not want to sweat, it is not enough to give the body the order "don't sweat," since perspiring is the result of an organic and sometimes psychologic process. The following example of a witness's cross-examination applies these principles.

Q: Isn't it true that you were not present when the contract between the plaintiff and defendant was signed?

A: I don't understand to whom you are referring.

Q: I am referring to the parties in this trial, the plaintiff Mr. Robinson and the defendant Mrs. Wells. Were you present when they signed the contract?

A: To what contract are you referring?

Q: In your direct examination, you referred repeatedly to the sales contract in which Mrs. Wells sold her house to Mr. Robinson. I am referring to this contract, and I will repeat my question: Were you present when they signed the contract?

A: Now I understand; well . . . uh . . . (the witness is perspiring, maintains no eye contact with the cross-examiner, crosses his arms defensively, and, trying to win time, drinks water (with trembling hands)). Sure . . . you want to know if I was present when the contract was signed.

Q: Exactly, that is what I want to know.

A: Well (the witness clears his throat), I think that I was present when they signed the contract.

Q: You think or you are sure that you were present?

A: You know sir, your way of questioning makes me nervous; I am surprised that my lawyer is not objecting to your style of questioning me.

Q: Are you hesitating to tell the truth? Are you confused?

A: No, I am not hesitating and I am not confused.

In this example the witness said, "I think that I was present when they signed the contract." But, the witness's behavior on the stand, his hesitations, his tricks to avoid giving a straight answer, his body gestures, clearly indicated that he was not present when the contract was signed. Also, the witness's statement, "I am not hesitating and I am not confused," contradicted the witness's conduct during the interrogation.

Many authors and psychologists have studied the question of which is more important in human communication—verbal or nonverbal communication.[8] They have not arrived at a definitive conclusion. For example, Albert Mehrabian believes that 93% of human understanding is the result of nonverbal communication, and only 7% the result of verbal communication.[9] Other psychologists claim a 50-50 ratio, and others argue for different percentages.

§7.05 Analysis of Research Regarding Witnesses' Demeanor and Verbal and Nonverbal Communication

On these topics, there exist research works in which trial lawyers, judges, and psychologists were asked their opinions as to which is the predominant factor in human understanding—verbal or nonverbal communications—and

---

[8] R.L. Birdwhistell, Introduction to Kinesics (1952); C. Darwin, The Expression of the Emotion in Man and Animals (1872); J. Fast, Body Language (1979); E. Goffman, Behavior in Public Places (1969); E.T. Hall, The Hidden Dimension (1966); A. Mehrabian, Silent Messages 42-47 (1971); Ekman, Sorenson, & Frieson, *Pan Cultural Elements in Facial Display of Emotion,* 3 Sci 37, 58 (1970); Scheflen, *Human Communications,* 13 Behavioral Sci 13 (1968); Griffith, *Body Language Politics,* Time, Feb 6, 1984, at 59.

[9] A. Mehrabian, mentioned in R. Aron, J. Fast, & R. Klein, Trial Communication Skills 27 (Shepard's/McGraw-Hill 1986).

what, in a witness's testimony, indicates that the witness is truthful. The results of some of these studies are summarized in the following subsections.

§7.06 —Witnesses' Truthfulness: Research and Commentary

In *How to Prepare Witnesses for Trial,*[10] question 13 of a questionnaire sent to "Professors of Trial Advocacy and to Outstanding Trial Lawyers"[11] asked: "In your opinion, what are the indications that a witness is truthful" or "is a liar"?[12]

In response to the first part of question 13, regarding what characteristics the respondents looked for, when interviewing a witness, in order to assess whether the witness was telling the truth, the researchers received the following comments.[13]

The truthful witness' body language:

1. Eye contact (mentioned 4 times)
2. Body language (mentioned 4 times)
3. Their intonation
4. Nonverbal actions
5. Looking in the eyes at the appropriate time, body position, fidgeting
6. Relaxed, natural
7. Lack of hesitation

Appearance and behavior of the witness:

1. Appearance (mentioned 5 times)
2. Demeanor (mentioned 9 times)
3. Naturalness, directness
4. If the witness act[s] normally
5. Sincerity, desire to help
6. Spontaneous testimony, responsive answers
7. He or she is responsive
8. Appearance of candor, objectivity, accurate, thoughtful, and reflective
9. Even nature of dealing with both direct and cross-examination
10. Firmness in opinion

---

[10] Reprinted from R. Aron & J. Rosner, How to Prepare Witnesses for Trial 326-28 (Shepard's/McGraw-Hill 1985), copyright 1985 by Shepard's/McGraw-Hill, Inc. Reprinted by permission of Shepard's/McGraw-Hill, Inc. Further reproduction is strictly prohibited.

[11] *Id* 306.

[12] *Id* 307.

[13] *Id* 326.

Consistency, corroboration, and coherence of story:

1. Consistency; not interested in other than compensation for expenses
2. Consistency of testimony; consistency with documents
3. Observation, consistency of statements
4. Story is internally consistent over time, suggested by other evidence and common sense
5. His or her story is logical, internally consistent, and tracks the other facts of the case
6. His or her story is reasonable and is corroborated by independent witnesses
7. Corroboration
8. Comparison to other facts
9. Substance of testimony
10. Tells a constant story
11. Straightforward answers, few contradictions, understandable testimony, coherence of story
12. The witness is not evasive, not argumentative, and the testimony is logical
13. Usually contradictions
14. Contradictory statements.

How truthful witnesses tell their stories:

1. Ability to recall
2. Concise, full answers on direct and cross-examination (mock)
3. Direct and clear answers to questions
4. Nonevasive answers
5. No evidence of lies, evasive or similar testimony
6. Aside from good recall of events and independent corroboration, a witness who will not say something he or she does not remember clearly
7. Not an advocate of either party, is nonargumentative and usually tells the story as known to him or her
8. Recalls adverse as well as helpful parts
9. Admitting to things that hurt as well as things that help
10. The witness must be open and candid. The witness must answer quickly and directly, telling the good with the bad
11. Has an opportunity to embarrass or exaggerate and refrains

How the attorney and the witness interact:

1. Lack of animus on the witness' part
2. Ability to withstand cross-examination

3. Cross-examine the witnesses; if they are truthful, they demonstrate it
4. If unable to trap the witness, then the witness must be telling the truth[14]

In response to the second part of question 13, "What are the indications that a witness is a liar," the responses were as follows:

The big three telltale signs:

1. Evasive (mentioned 12 times)
2. Inconsistent (mentioned 9 times)
3. Refuses eye contact (mentioned 9 times)

Body language traits:

1. Halting speech
2. Hesitation
3. Nervousness (mentioned 8 times)
4. Putting hand on mouth
5. Averting eyes

Appearance and behavior of the lying witness:

1. Demeanor (mentioned 7 times)
2. Deceit
3. Conduct
4. Smug
5. Greedy
6. Not logical
7. Argumentative

How lying witnesses tell their stories:

1. Protestations of truthfulness (e.g., I wouldn't lie)
2. Inconsistent reiteration of the witness' testimony
3. Story is internally disjointed; the witness keeps changing it; forgets what prior statements have been
4. Inability to answer *office* cross-examination; changed accounts
5. Story too pat
6. Certain inflexibility; too definite
7. Set testimony
8. Witnesses are too exact

---

[14] *Id* 326-28.

9. Selective memory only
10. One-sided recollection or changing recollection
11. Constantly enlarging role
12. More than necessary correction
13. Comparison with other facts
14. Contradictions
15. Equivocating
16. Hedging
17. Witnesses trying to sell their position too hard
18. Under-answering and over-selling

How they interact with the attorney:

1. Animus to attorney or client
2. Show animosity to attorney
3. Argumentative advocates
4. Take an adversary approach
5. Unwillingness to concede any point
6. Reluctance to relay information to the lawyer
7. Change in attitude on cross-examination
8. Evident bias; interest[15]

Commentary: From the answers to both parts of this question, we can learn that there is no one determining factor that can help to establish with certainty when a witness is telling the truth and when a witness is lying. This is true because we are dealing with witnesses, who are human beings with unique and individual characteristics. The logical conclusion of the research is that to determine whether a witness is truthful or not, it is necessary to analyze the behavior of the witness during his or her testimony.

Other research relating to witness demeanor during testimony will be discussed in this chapter and, at the end of the chapter, the results of all of the research presented are coordinated in order to arrive at the most concrete conclusions possible.

§7.07 —Verbal and Nonverbal Communication: Research and Commentary

This subsection discusses part of a questionnaire in *Trial Communication Skills*

---

[15] *Id* 328-30.

which was answered by clinical psychologists.[16] Selected from this research are various questions and answers applicable, directly or indirectly, to witness behavior during testimony.

> *[Question] 4:* In your opinion, how much of any communication between people depends on nonverbal signals and how much on verbal?
>
> * * *
>
> *[Responses:]* The following table shows the exact breakdown of the respondents' answers:

Number of Respondents	Nonverbal	Verbal
1	.01	99.99
2	5	95
4	15	85
12	20	80
16	25	75
4	30	70
10	40	60
2	45	55
2	50	50
2	75	25
2	85	15[17]

Commentary: The researchers were surprised by the low rating given by most of the respondents to nonverbal communication, especially considering that most of the researchers in this field have estimated 60 per cent or more for nonverbal communication. They received an explanation from a clinical psychologist, who examined the results and said: "Clinical psychologists . . . deal with the spoken word. Unlike researchers, they are not overly concerned with body language. They spend their working time concentrating on nuances of speech and since most therapy sessions do not even involve eye contact, they tend to gloss over body language."[18]

> *[Question] 5:* Which, of all the elements of nonverbal communication, do you consider most important? Please rate the rest in descending order. Gestures . . . Handling Space. . . . Eye Contact. . . . Touch. . . . Appearance. . . . Other. . . .

---

[16] Reprinted from R. Aron, J. Fast, & R. Klein, Trial Communication Skills (Shepard's/McGraw-Hill 1986) copyright 1986 by Shepard's/McGraw-Hill, Inc. Reprinted by permission of Shepard's/McGraw-Hill, Inc. Further reproduction is strictly prohibited.

[17] *Id* 427-30.

[18] *Id* 431

* * *

[Responses:] A list of all the elements suggested plus those the respondents added, in order of importance, would read like this:

Elements	Order of Importance
Gestures	First
Eye Contact	Second
Appearance	Third
Facial Expression	Fourth
Touch and Metacommunication	Fifth
Pose and Assurance	Sixth
Handling Space	Seventh

* * *

Below is a breakdown of the various elements and the importance assigned to each by the respondents.

Elements	The Order in Which They Were Listed					
	1st	2nd	3rd	4th	5th	6th
	(number of respondents listing each element)					
Gestures	24	18	14	8	2	2
Eye Contact	20	20	18	6	4	-
Appearance	12	18	12	18	6	2
Facial Expression	6	2	-	-	-	2
Touch	4	4	8	18	24	6
Metacommunication	4	2	-	-	-	-
Poise and Assurance	3	1	-	-	-	-
Handling Space	0	4	12	14	28	2
Posture	0	0	3	-	-	-[19]

Commentary: We think that for trial lawyers, it is important to keep in mind, during the questioning of witnesses, the relevance of the different elements of non-verbal communication. It is interesting to note that most of the respondent psychologists attributed the most importance to three elements: gestures, eye contact, and appearance.

In our opinion also, gestures and eye contact are the most influential factors of body language in human communication. Gestures are like accents given to the words that a person is saying. Eye contact is the visual link between two persons during the communication process. A witness who, while testifying, looks constantly at the floor or at the ceiling and avoids eye contact with the interrogating lawyer gives the impression that the witness is not sure how to answer, or, worse, that the witness is hiding something or lying. If in addition to the absence of eye contact, the witness is covers or intends to cover his or her mouth when speaking, the conclusion of untruthfulness is inevitable.

---

19 *Id* 427, 432-33.

Suppose that during a trial, the judge is speaking to the lawyer, and the lawyer, instead of paying attention to the judge's words and looking at the judge, is looking the other way. The lawyer's nonverbal message to the judge is, "You can say what you want, but I am not interested in what you say." Or, imagine that the lawyer is speaking to the judge, and the judge, instead of paying attention to the lawyer's words, is looking at his or her papers or at the other side. The judge's body language is clear: "Don't annoy me with your arguments." In both cases, the unspoken messages can have serious consequences: the judge believes that the lawyer's attitude is one of disrespect; the lawyer believes that the judge's attitude is like a red light, saying to the attorney, "I don't like your performance so far," and the lawyer must ask himself or herself, "What am I doing wrong?"

The other relevant element noted by the psychologists is *appearance.* The importance of a witness's appearance is also related to credibility. Imagine the impression given to the jury and the judge if an expert witness, a medical professor, for example, appears on the stand in a jogging suit, or with his or her hair tinted in different colors. . . .

It is the lawyer's responsibility to advise a witness how to dress and how to appear at court when giving testimony.

> *QUESTION 6:* Do you believe it is possible to change a person's nonverbal communication?
>
> * * *
>
> *RESPONSES:* Seventy of the 76 respondents (92 percent) answered positively, asserting that a person's nonverbal communication could be changed. There were no negative answers, but five were undecided and one respondent did not answer this question.[20]

Commentary: When a trial lawyer is preparing witnesses for depositions or testimony at a trial, it is of extreme importance to pay attention to the witness's nonverbal communication. The fact that 92 per cent of the psychologists responding to question 6 agreed that it is possible to change a person's body language represents good news for trial lawyers.

There are unconscious gestures that a witness makes which may negatively influence his or her appearance during the testimony. The witness generally is not aware of these gestures. Some examples of such gestures are not making eye contact with the lawyer, covering the mouth when speaking, or constantly scratching the head or rubbing the nose, etc. All of these gestures can be corrected and eliminated easily. It is the lawyer's task during witness preparation to call the witness's attention to such unnecessary and negative gestures.

> *Question 7:* If it can be changed, is it advisable to do so.
>
> * * *

---

[20] *Id* 427, 433.

> *Responses:* [This question] was answered by 55 respondents, and of these, 48 (87 percent) answered yes. Only two said no, it was not desirable, and three were undecided. Twenty-six qualified their positive answer. These qualifications included the following. Four respondents said, "Yes, if the present nonverbal communication is poor" (a condition the authors took for granted). Six felt it "depended upon the situation." Three said, "sometimes," without expanding. Five answered "Yes and no" (the authors interpreted this as "depending upon the situation"). One believed it depended on the verbal communication. If this was poor, yes. If this was good, no. Three held that it was desirable, but questioned the purpose. Two wanted to know when, and under what circumstances.[21]

Commentary: Based on the affirmative answer given by psychologists to question 6, regarding the possibility of changing a person's body language, our commentary to the responses to question 7 is that it is not only advisable but also a lawyer's obligation to change a witness's body language, not only if the witness's verbal communication is poor, as some respondents said, but also if the witness has an exaggerated body language—for example, if the witness, when speaking, moves his or her arms like a windmill.

> *[Question] 8:* Would you give your reasons for your answer to question 7 [Is it advisable to change body language?].
>
> * * *
>
> *[Responses:* The following are some of the answers.]
>
> It aids communicationTo make people more expressive
>
> To improve the effect of communication
>
> To control what one wants to communicate
>
> To increase impact
>
> Change should be attempted when communication is dissonant, suggesting conflict
>
> If one's cause is just and the opponent's is corrupt
>
> To command proper attention and regard
>
> Any signs of uneasiness, doubt, and aggression are better contained or removed
>
> When there are contrary messages
>
> If the changes in nonverbal communication match or are followed by other changes that can increase a person's ability to function
>
> When relationships depend on adaptability in communication, both verbal and nonverbal
>
> Change would be difficult, but it can happen with training. Sincerity and spontaneity as well as "natural" expressions of warmth are to be emphasized. Some will be more natural than others

---

[21] *Id* 427, 433.

The question seems to imply that nonverbal is the same as involuntary. In general it isn't, though some nonverbal communication may be. It is advisable to communicate, nonverbally, to the extent that it is voluntary

In most cases, nonverbal communication is controlled by an unconscious motivation. At times it needs to be inspected and changed

This would depend on the reasons for attempting change. Nonverbal communication is pretty deeply inbedded in the personality structure, as are semantics and syntax

* * *

Eye contact, not staring, is of prime importance with the jury

For both verbal and nonverbal behavior, instead of advising, I would emphasize "telling it like it is"[22]

Commentary: If we only pay attention to the first four answers of the psychologists to this question ("It aids communication; To make people more expressive; To improve the effect of communication; and To control what one wants to communicate"), we arrive at the conclusion that it would be of great help for trial lawyers to read and remember the psychologists' opinions of when it is recommended to change body language, in order to apply this knowledge later in the preparation of their witnesses. We said in a previous section that not only *what* the witness says on the stand is important, but also *how* the witness communicates his or her knowledge about a certain fact. With a little effort by the lawyer during the preparation process, it is possible to change a mediocre performance by a witness to a good or even excellent one.

[Question] 9: In terms of nonverbal communication, how you detect resistance?

* * *

[Responses:] The most commonly cited element of nonverbal communication in this section was facial expression, listed 28 times. The next three in importance, listed 24 times each, were the avoidance of eye contact, stiffening and tension in body posture, and physically pulling away. Arms folded across the chest was listed 10 times. Gestures indicating a negative attitude was listed 8 times. Dissonance or incongruity between words and actions was listed 6 times, and the following were all listed once:

Rapid breathing

Aggressive behavior

Reducing or inhibiting body movement

Shrugging the shoulders

Carelessness in dress

---

[22] *Id* 427, 433.

Hand to face gestures[23]

Commentary: When trial lawyers begin their cross-examination or impeachment, there is a natural attitude of resistance by the witness to the lawyer. This attitude may result not only because the witness may be under the influence of movies with dramatic cross-examinations and impeachments where the lawyer destroys the witness psychologically, but also because the lawyer presenting the witness has probably put the witness on guard against the cross-examiner. During cross-examination and impeachment, an objective observer can see in the witness's body expressions of tension and nervousness, such as tics, rapid breathing, stiffness in posture, etc.

During cross-examination and impeachment, one of the most difficult tasks of a trial lawyer is to break this instinctive resistance of the witness. Different tactics may be used in order to succeed in this endeavor.

There are trial lawyers who, in order to win a witness's sympathy, begin the questioning by saying, "I will ask you only a few questions in order to clarify what you said during direct examination," or "If you tell the truth, we will finish in a couple of minutes." Trial lawyers using the tactic of, "I am a good guy, trust me" think that by gaining the cooperation and confidence of the witness, they may obtain more information from the witness and perhaps even the confirmation of important points for their theory of the case.

On the other hand, there are trial lawyers who think that during cross-examination or impeachment, it is better to maintain the witness in a constant state of panic and nervousness. They are sure that under these circumstances, the witness will become confused and tense, and will contradict himself or herself more easily. As a consequence, the witness's message to the trier of fact will be less credible.

Which method of interrogation produces better results? There is not a definite rule in favor of one strategy or the other. It depends on the personality and character of the witness and the lawyer, and perhaps also on the circumstances of the case.

[Question] 10: Can you change that resistance?

* * *

[Responses:] While the answers to this segment varied, a number seemed consistent with each other and should offer help in dealing with resistant witnesses, jurors, or jurists. Most, however, would apparently work best on a one-to-one basis. Realizing that often each respondent offered more than one solution, following is a summary of the answers: The advice given most often was a variation of the suggestion of making the resistant person aware of his or her own resistance by bringing it to a conscious level. This suggestion was expressed in various ways:

Make the client aware of resistance

---

[23] *Id* 427, 435.

Address it directly

Let the other realize the results of resistant behavior

Bring resistance to the surface

Make the person aware of discordance

Let the resistant person know what he or she is doing

Urge the resistant person to speak out about resistance

* * *

Other suggestions were varied and in general suggested that the recipient of resistance show understanding and warmth.

Appear friendly, nonthreatening, agree when possible

Sympathy, considerate approval, a supportive role

Reasoning appeal, a softer voice

Be warm in your experiencing

Show real interest

Some suggested nonverbal approaches:

Keep eye contact

Get close

Use a softer voice

Use gestures expressive of courtesy and regard[24]

Commentary: We must understand that the respondents, as psychologists, gave their answers based on what they have learned and experienced in practicing their profession. For this reason, not all of their advice can be applied to break the resistance of a witness, a judge, or the opposing lawyer.

At a trial, some of the psychologists' advice can be effective. For example, if the lawyer wants to break the resistance or the hostility of a witness, by softening the voice and asking questions in a nonthreatening form, the lawyer can tell the witness in unspoken words, "You are wasting time being aggressive; I am your friend, I am not trying to hurt you."

As in our commentary to the preceding question, it is necessary to mention that there are trial lawyers who, when faced with a witness's resistance, aggressiveness, or hostility, try to irritate or provoke the witness further in order to bring the witness to a state of exasperation, causing confusion in the witness's mind. This tactic can be effective with certain witnesses. It will never succeed in changing a judge's hostility towards the lawyer. In this case, the best advice is not to provoke the judge, but, rather, to swallow the judge's words and not be polemic with him or her. If, as a result of the judge's attitude, there is a decision that the lawyer considers unjust, the lawyer always has the right to appeal.

---

24 *Id* 427, 436.

[Question] 15: Are there any nonverbal cues that will allow you to detect a lie?

* * *

[Question] 16: If yes, what are they?

* * *

[Responses:] Seventy-three of the 76 respondents answered this question; 42 (58 percent) said "yes," there were nonverbal cues. Fourteen (19 percent) said "no." Seventeen (23 percent) were uncertain.

It surprised the authors that such a large percentage believed that there were no nonverbal cues or were uncertain about it. A similar percentage felt that there were no verbal cues to lying, and, coming from therapists trained to deal with patients who tend to hold back the truth, this, too, surprised the authors.

Psychologists, the authors believed, would be the group most likely to know about lying and the methods used to conceal a lie. The research in the literature contradicted this finding in the questionnaire. A little more light is shed by question 16 in which the respondents were asked about the nonverbal cues to lying.

Fifty-nine respondents (75 percent) listed some type of cue, while 17 (22 percent) left this question blank. One simply noted "all sorts of cues" and another, rather wryly, commented, "in my experience the guilty lie with far more poise and conviction than the innocent." . . . Following is a list of the various nonverbal elements and how often they were cited.

Element	Times Cited
Eye contact	25
Posture	11
Hesitation	11
Facial expression	10
Sweating	8
Conflict between verbal and nonverbal	7
Flushing	5
Gestures	4
A break in the flow of movement	4
Tension	2

The following elements were listed only once:

A slight smile
Narrowing of pupils
Paleness
Heavy breathing
Fidgeting
Cold hands

The following elements the authors consider metacommunication, and perhaps should be listed under verbal elements:

Tone of voice	5

Change in voice tone	4
A rapid pace in speaking	1[25]

Commentary: Evidently, it is important to know what characteristic elements could give clues to detecting lies. But in the trial lawyers' specialty, this knowledge is, in general, not as important as for psychologists or for other professionals.

A well-prepared trial lawyer has had the opportunity to prepare for direct examination by checking the prospective witness's truthfulness with the client and other witnesses, and by proper investigations.

During cross-examination and impeachment, trial lawyers normally follow the principle of not asking questions without knowing what the answers will be. In other words, if a witness lies in his or her response, the interrogator has the resources to detect the lie. Notwithstanding this, the trial lawyer will not always know whether a witness is lying. In such a case, it will be of great help for the attorney to know the nonverbal clues to discovering when a witness is not telling the truth.

[Question] 17: Are there any verbal cues that will tell you whether a person is lying?

* * *

[Question] 18: If yes, what are they?

* * *

[Responses:] There were 74 answers. Thirty-eight (50 percent) said "yes," and ten (16 percent) said "no." Nineteen (25 per cent) were uncertain and seven (9 percent) said it depended on other factors.

[On] question 18, . . . twenty-seven chose not to answer. . . . Forty-nine did answer it, and their replies can be summarized as follows.

Verbal Method for Detecting a Lie	Number of Times Cited
Changes of pitch, tone, and inflection	15
Glibness or overtalking	13
Slips of the tongue, inconsistencies	9
Incongruence between actions and words	8
Hesitations	5
Anger	4
Intuition on the part of psychologist	3
Use of phrases such as, "To be frank," "To be perfectly honest," "To tell you the truth"	3
Too slow or too fast a reply	3
Accusations	3
Circumlocutions	3

[25] *Id* 427, 438-39.

Stalling	2
Repeating	2
Counterquestions	2
Raising the voice	2

The following were cited once each:

Changes in detail
A flat and even response
Stammering
Confused elaboration
Increased tension (a nonverbal element)[26]

Commentary: Just as it is important to know what the nonverbal clues to lying are, it is also essential for a trial lawyer to determine the verbal clues.

It is interesting to note that the psychologists' answers mention factors that we have observed many times in the courtroom. The difference is that when, for example, we have seen witnesses on the stand changing their pitch, tone, or inflections, we have thought that the reason was nervousness or insecurity—not that such a change signified a lie. The same is true regarding most of the other characteristics mentioned by the psychologists in their responses.

One method of lying particularly grabs our attention: the use of phrases such as, "To be frank,", "To be perfectly honest," and, "To tell you the truth." Perhaps with certain naiveté, we have always interpreted these phrases positively, as signs of sincerity. Now, having read the psychologists' answers, we think that, indeed, when a person is telling the truth, it is not necessary to use statements such as, "To be perfectly honest," "To tell you the truth," or, "I cannot lie to you," such statements could mean that the person normally is not used to telling the truth.

> *[Question] 27:* Do you believe the clothes one wears, their style and color, can have a psychological impact on another person?
>
> * * *
>
> *[Question] 28:* If yes, how strong an impact? Very strong. . . . Moderate . . . Slight . . .
>
> * * *
>
> *[Responses:* The first question] was a yes/no question, and was answered by all the respondents. In every case, the answer was "yes," a most unusual 100 percent agreement.
>
> The second question in the series requested an evaluation of the impact of clothes. . . . Sixty-nine respondents answered, and forty-three of them (62 percent) felt that the style and color of the clothes one wears have a very strong effect on other people. Twenty-one (30 percent) felt they had a moderate impact, and five respondents felt the impact was slight.[27]

---

[26] *Id* 17 & 18.

[27] *Id* 428, 444.

Commentary: The impact of a witness's clothing is not always considered important by the lawyer presenting the witness. Sometimes, lawyers forget to advise the witness how to appear in court.

If a witness appears slovenly in his or her appearance, a man unshaven or a woman with her hair in disarray, the result is not only to make a bad impression on the jury and the judge, but also to distract the trier of fact from paying complete attention to the witness's words; judges or jurors cannot avoid wondering why the witness has appeared in court in such neglected shape.

The foregoing words do not mean that the witness must go to the other extreme and appear on the stand wearing a tuxedo or a gala dress.

Each witness should dress in accordance with his or her social and economic status. The quality or style of the witness's clothes is not important; what is important is naturalness, cleanliness, and orderliness.

§7.08 —Assessing Verbal and Nonverbal Communication of Trial Lawyers and Witnesses: Research and Commentary

This section will deal with a questionnaire in *Trial Communication Skills,*[28] which was sent to professors of trial advocacy and to practitioners. From this questionnaire, we will discuss questions numbered 11 and 12, which relate to the theme of this chapter.

> *Question 11:* What a lawyer says and how he or she says it are both important to effective courtroom presentation. In a *jury* trial, how much do you think depends on what the lawyer says and how much depends on how the lawyer says it (body language, inflection and nonverbal messages)?
>
> * * *
>
> *[Responses:]* Of the 55 respondents, 51 answered this question, while 4 did not. Since it follows that a practitioner who sees body language as 45 percent of the process sees words as 55 percent, the focus in presenting the breakdown of these 51 replies will be on groupings based on the respondents' estimates as to the importance of *nonverbal communication.* These were:

Under 25%	8
25% to 40%	16
Equal—50%	15
60% to 75%	10
Over 75%	2[29]

[28] Reprinted from R. Aron, J. Fast, & R. Klein, Trial Communication Skills (Shepard's/McGraw-Hill 1986) copyright 1986 by Shepard's/McGraw-Hill, Inc. Reprinted by permission of Shepard's/McGraw-Hill, Inc. Further reproduction is strictly prohibited.

[29] *Id* 482, 483.

Commentary: First of all, we must note that question number 11 refers to the influence of verbal and nonverbal communication in lawyers' presentations in jury trials, and does not refer to witness testimony. In spite of this fact, the results of the survey could also be of interest in assessing witness performances and the influence of verbal and nonverbal communication of witnesses during jury trials, and how each factor could affect a witness's message to the jurors.

In order to draw the clearest conclusions possible from the responses, we determined that from the 51 respondents there are three groups of answers (16, 15, and 10) which make up a total of 41 who stated that the influence of nonverbal communication varies between 25%-40% to 60%-75%, which means a rough average of 50%.

If we apply these results to witnesses' testimony in a jury trial, one can deduce that the average influence of nonverbal communication in a person's testimony could be considered to be about 50%. If this is so, it confirms the importance of nonverbal communication during jury trials, and that a witness's body language can influence the trier of facts.

> *Question 12:* In a *bench* trial, how much do you think depends on what the lawyer says and how much depends on how the lawyer says it (body language, inflection, and nonverbal messages)?
>
> * * *
>
> *[Responses:]* Of the 55 respondents, 52 answered this question, while 3 did not. Since it follows that a practitioner who sees nonverbal communication as 45 percent of the process sees words as 55 percent, the breakdown of these 52 replies falls into groupings based on the respondents' estimates as to the importance of nonverbal communication. These were:

Under 25%	21
25% to 40%	26
Equal—50%	2
60% to 75%	2
Over 75%	1[30]

The commentary of the authors of the research was:

> These results when compared with answers to the previous question on jury trials are markedly different. While only 8 practitioners saw nonverbal factors as less than 25 percent of communication in a jury trial, when considering bench trials, almost half—21 respondents—viewed nonverbal as under 25 percent. Only 1 in 10 considered nonverbal factors to be more than 40 percent of communication with a judge, compared with 1 out of 2 who viewed this as the case in jury trials.
>
> This change is understandable. A jury, composed of a panel of laypersons, requires a more explicit and vivid explanation, and that situation was certainly the influencing factor in the respondents' replies to question

30 *Id* 483, 484.

> 11. In bench trials, the judge has not only a complete knowledge of trial procedures but also experience in understanding the lawyers' arguments. This is the reason why lawyers' performances during a jury trial are more emotive and, when arguing in a bench trial, more legalistic. It is necessary to clarify one point to avoid misinterpretation: the emphasis in jury trials must be put on emotions, but they also require a big dose of logic and explanations of the legal situation. In the same manner, in bench trials, a legalistic approach does not mean only to make a dry and passionless presentation. As some lawyers said, "the judge is also a human being," and in a trial the lawyer must support his or her arguments with all the skills in the attorney's arsenal.[31]

Commentary: In this case, as noted in our commentary to question 11, the query was about the influence of lawyers' verbal and nonverbal language during a bench trial, and not the influence of witnesses' language during the same kind of trial.

Supposing again that, in a trial, there is a similarity in the influence of verbal and nonverbal communication of lawyers and of witnesses, we can arrive at the conclusion that the fact that in one case (the situation mentioned in question 11) the message is directed to a jury, and in the other case (the situation mentioned in question 12) is directed to a judge, explains the big difference in the responses in these cases.

It is logical that, when a witness is testifying at a jury trial, he or she will be less inhibited in speaking to the jurors, who, in general, are, like the witness, laypersons, than he or she would be when speaking only to a judge. Being less inhibited permits the witness to be more natural and to use his or her normal verbal and nonverbal language.

Instead, when giving testimony at a bench trial, the witness is more tense, and both verbal and nonverbal language will be more restrained.

From a different point of view, judges, with their experience hearing witnesses day after day, are less impressed with the emotional tone or the intense body language that a witness may put into his or her testimony.

§7.09 —Adjusting Witnesses' Examinations to the Reactions of the Finder of Fact: Research and Commentary

This section deals with question 18 of the same questionnaire discussed in **§7.08,** which was sent to professors of trial advocacy and to practitioners.

> *Question 18:* Do you adjust your examination of witnesses based upon the jury's or judge's reactions?

* * *

---

[31] *Id* 484.

[Responses:] There were 54 answers to this question:
46 "yes"
4 "no"
4 "sometimes"

* * *

The following reasons were given by some of the respondents in the teaching advocacy group for their attitude:

1. It is essential to adjust the presentation to the jury's (or court's) reaction. Persuasion is an exchange between speaker and audience
2. Absolutely. A lawyer must adjust his presentation to the court's reaction
3. No. I never know how the jury is reacting. I do not believe that other attorneys know this either
4. Sometimes, yes. Yet it is so instinctive that it is hard to quantify
5. No, because I usually anticipate correctly.[32]

The authors of the research made the following comments:

> It is clear that the majority adjust their presentation to the reactions of the jury or the judge. This was true also in the earlier questionnaire.
>
> The basis for the technique of adapting the argumentation to the audience's reaction is knowledge of how to interpret psychological behavior and nonverbal communication, and how to react to that impalpable something called "intinct" or "perception." These factors are improved by "experience" in courtroom litigation.
>
> As mentioned, one respondent answered that not only did he not adjust his presentation, but he did not believe that other attorneys could really know what the reaction of the jury was. While appreciating the sincerity in this reply, it is difficult to believe that, for example, a lawyer who sees that some of the jurors are sleeping during a presentation will not understand that his or her way of speaking or presenting the case is boring. What sense is there in continuing an argument when part of the audience is not hearing?[33]

Commentary: First of all, we want to explain why we mention this question 18 here.

We are studying in this chapter the witness's conduct during testimony and how the witness's demeanor affects and influences the jury and the judge.

In question 18, practitioners were asked if they adjust their examination of witnesses based upon the jury's or judge's reactions. The great majority of

---

[32] Reprinted from R. Aron, J. Fast, & R. Klein, Trial Communication Skills 501, 502 (Shepard's/McGraw-Hill 1986) copyright 1986 by Shepard's/McGraw-Hill, Inc. Reprinted by permission of Shepard's/McGraw-Hill, Inc. Further reproduction is strictly prohibited.

[33] *Id* 502.

respondents (46 out of 54) answered positively. That means that the questions directed by the litigators to the witnesses, the way of asking the questions, the aggressiveness or absence of aggressiveness when asking questions—all of this verbal and nonverbal communication is adjusted by trial lawyers to the reactions of the jury and/or the judge.

The witness, during direct examination and cross-examination, is in one respect a passive figure—he or she *reacts* to the litigators' questions.

Knowing the importance of a witness's demeanor during interrogation, especially when being cross-examined or impeached, would it not be important for the lawyer, during the witness's preparation process, to instruct the witness on how to adjust his or her testimony, taking into consideration the jury's or judge's reactions in the development of the witness's testimony?

§7.10 —Judges' Opinions Regarding Verbal and Nonverbal Communication: Introduction

The following two sections discuss questions 3, 8, and 9 of a questionnaire in *Trial Communication Skills,*[34] which was sent to 280 judges from 6 jurisdictions. Responses to the questionnaire were received from 90 judges from the different jurisdictions.

Questions 3, 8, and 9 involve communication skills. (The responses are from judges in large jurisdictions (large juris.), small jurisdictions (small juris.), and criminal and civil courts.

§7.11 —A Witness's Anti-Impeachment Profile

[Question] 3: From your experience observing trial lawyers, how would you rank the following communication skills and attributes in order of importance? (Please use a scale of 1-6, "1" being the most important and "6" being the least important.)

[1]—Knowledge of trial techniques
[2]—Knowledge of persuasion skills
[3]—Natural talent
[4]—Thorough knowledge of facts of case
[5]—Thorough knowledge of law of the case
[6]—Pleasing personality

[Responses:]

	Total	Large Juris.	Small Juris.	Criminal	Civil
[No. 4]	5.33	5.30	5.39	5.33	5.32

[34] R. Aron, J. Fast, & R. Klein, Trial Communication Skills (Shepard's/McGraw-Hill 1986).

[No. 5]	3.54	3.67	3.22	3.66	3.45
[No. 2]	3.42	3.18	4.00	3.44	3.41
[No. 1]	3.31	3.20	3.56	3.32	3.30
[No. 3]	2.76	2.80	2.67	3.08	2.54
[No. 6]	2.42	2.55	2.11	2.24	2.54

[The judges were also asked to list other skills and abilities they thought important to a lawyer's ability to communicate. The following were the responses, in descending order of frequency.]

A good voice	14
The ability to present ideas clearly	13
Sincerity	12
Being well groomed, dressing well	10
Being courteous	9
Working out a theory of the case and law	8
Using English correctly	8
Being concise but thorough	7
Knowing psychology and human nature	6
Thorough preparation of witness and case	6
Eye contact	4
Good fact analysis	4
Speak to jurors and witnesses	3
Integrity	3
Calmness	2
Judgment	2
Organization	2
Logical thinking	2[35]

Commentary: In various sections of this book we have referred to how and when to impeach witnesses, but we have not discussed how to prepare witnesses to *avoid* impeachment. After reading the opinions of an important group of judges regarding the ranking of lawyers' communication skills, we think that perhaps it would be advisable to try to establish an "anti-impeachment profile" to be used by practitioners during witness preparation.

Suppose that in a given case, a lawyer has 20 or more prospective witnesses. The lawyer wants to present 6 to 8 witnesses at trial. In this situation, the lawyer is confronted with two problems: (a) whom to select, and (b) in what order to present the witness selected.

Adapting to witnesses' testimony the judges' scale for trial communication skills, we can establish a scale of priorities in the selection of witnesses in order to produce a good testimony and avoid the risk of impeachment. The following could be the priorities in the selection of witnesses:

---

[35] Reprinted from R. Aron, J. Fast, & R. Klein, Trial Communication Skills 532-33, 545 (Shepard's/McGraw-Hill 1986) copyright 1986 by Shepard's/McGraw-Hill, Inc. Reprinted by permission of Shepard's/McGraw-Hill, Inc. Further reproduction is strictly prohibited.

—The ability to present the facts clearly

—Sincerity and veracity

—Being concise but thorough (good analysis of facts and persuasive presentation of them)

—Eye contact (speaking to the lawyer and/or to the judge)

—Integrity

—Absence of contradictory statements (written or spoken)

—Appropriate appearance

Once the selection of witnesses has been made, following the foregoing criteria, the lawyer must decide the order in which to present the witnesses. To this task the lawyer can apply the theories of *primacy* and *regency*,[36] considering the circumstances of the case.

§7.12 —What a Lawyer Says and How a Lawyer Says It: Research and Commentary

[Question] 8: Both what a lawyer says and how he or she says it is important to effective courtroom presentation. In a jury trial, how much do you think depends on what the lawyer says and how much depends on how the lawyer says it (body language, inflection, and nonverbal messages)?

* * *

[Responses:]

	Total	Large Juris.	Small Juris.	Criminal	Civil
What the lawyer says	61.6%	63.5%	56.1%	62.6%	60.8%
How the lawyer says it (body language, etc.)	38.4%	36.5%	43.9%	37.4%	39.2%

[Question] 9: In a nonjury trial, how much do you think depends on what the lawyer says and how much depends on how the lawyer says it (body language, inflection, and non-verbal messages)?

* * *

	Total	Large Juris.	Small Juris.	Criminal	Civil
What the lawyer says	80.7%	81.4%	78.7%	80.4%	80.7%
How the lawyer says it (body language, etc.)	19.3%	18.6%	21.3%	19.6%	19.3%[37]

[36] *Id* 196-98.

[37] Reprinted from R. Aron, J. Fast, & R. Klein, Trial Communicarion Skills 533, 546

The following is from the comments of the authors of the research.

> The judges most strongly agreed with the statement that it was important for lawyers to vary their technique when talking to a judge as opposed to talking to a jury. Again, this may reflect a bias rather than being a most important factor in communications. Lawyers naturally tend to be more dramatic before a lay audience of jurors. This takes longer. Nothing bothers a busy judge more than having a lawyer make a long, emotional pitch on a simple issue. This may be behind the total agreement of judges that lawyers should vary their style when arguing to the court.[38]

Commentary: We gave our opinion on this matter when commenting on questions 11 and 12 of the questionnaire sent to professors on trial advocacy and practitioners. (*See* **§7.08.**) In **§7.17** (Conclusions), we will elaborate on this theme.

§7.13 —Credibility of Witnesses: Introduction

The following three sections discuss parts of questionnaires, regarding cross-examination and impeachment, in *Cross-Examination of Witnesses: The Litigator's Puzzle,*[39] which were sent to trial lawyers as part of a research project. Because of their connection with the subject of this chapter, questions 8, 15, and 16 are discussed.

§7.14 —Facts Affecting Witnesses' Credibility: Research and Commentary

> *[Question] 8:* Do you think that the credibility of a witness is more greatly affected by (Please use a scale of 1-6, "1" being the most important and "6" the least important):
>
> a) Evidence of the witness's inability to perceive what the witness testified to
> b) Evidence of the witness's inability to understand what the witness testified to
> c) Evidence of the witness's inability to recall events the witness testified to

---

[38] *Id* 542.

[39] R. Aron, K.T. Duffy, & J.L. Rosner, Cross-Examination of Witnesses: The Litigator's Puzzle (Shepard's/McGraw-Hill 1989).

d) Evidence the witness made a prior statement inconsistent with what the witness testified to
e) Evidence the witness was convicted of a crime: Generally [or] Involving dishonesty
f) Evidence of the witness's bias or prejudice in favor of the party that called the witness or against the adverse party to testify

* * *

[Responses:] The results of the survey are as follows (remembering that number "1" is the most important factor affecting the witness's credibility and number "6" the least important factor):

To letter (a): 8 responses saying "1"
2 responses saying "2"
7 responses saying "3"
4 responses saying "4"
2 responses saying "5"
3 responses saying "6"

To letter (b): 4 responses saying "1"
8 responses saying "2"
8 responses saying "3"
3 responses saying "4"
2 responses saying "5"
5 responses saying "6"

To letter (c) 5 responses saying "1"
8 responses saying "2"
11 responses saying "3"
4 responses saying "4"
1 response saying "5"
2 responses saying "6"

To letter (d) 17 responses saying "1"
7 responses saying "2"
4 responses saying "3"
2 responses saying "4"
0 responses saying "5"
1 response saying "6"

To letter (e), generally: 0 responses saying "1"
8 responses saying "2"
4 responses saying "3"
4 responses saying "4"
4 responses saying "5"
7 responses saying "6"

To letter (e), involving dishonesty: 10 responses saying "1"
3 responses saying "2"
4 responses saying "3"
5 responses saying "4"

5 responses saying "5"
3 responses saying "6"

To letter (f): 6 responses saying "1"
9 responses saying "2"
9 responses saying "3"
2 responses saying "4"
3 responses saying "5"
3 responses saying "6"[40]

The authors of the research made the following analysis of the results.

> Question number 8 refers to a very controversial element, "credibility." It is a subjective term because what may be reliable or believable to one person may not be reliable or believable to another, depending on the circumstances. The disparity between what a witness says and the actual facts can be interpreted in different ways, depending, for example, on the importance that a particular fact has in the case on trial.
>
> The foregoing commentary explains why, in the respondents' answers, there are such different opinions about just what factors most affect "credibility" in a witness's testimony.[41]

Commentary: First of all, it is necessary to underline the great disparity of opinions among the respondents. For example, the researchers received 26 answers to question (a), divided into 6 categories. Each category received less than ⅓ of the opinions. There were 30 answers to question (b), divided into 6 categories, but each of them received less than 27% of the votes; etc. Only question (d) received anything close to a consensus: 31 answers produced 17 responses saying "1."

The three first questions (a), (b), and (c), involve the abilities of a witness to perceive, to understand, and to recall what the witness testified to. The question is, what is the most serious problem in a witness's performance? Not to perceive, not to understand, or not to recall?

In order to better understand the questions, it is helpful to add to each question the element of *bona fides.* The following are examples of bona fides: if a witness says that he saw the red light when the car accident happened, and he honestly believes that the light was red; if the witness honestly says that he understood the question; if the witness honestly says that he or she recalled a given event. This element of bona fides will place the witness in the category of *inability* if he or she believes the truth of his or her statement, but, actually, is wrong.

---

[40] Reprinted from R. Aron, K.T. Duffy, & J.L. Rosner, Cross-Examination of Witnesses: The Litigator's Puzzle 489, 490 (Shepard's/McGraw-Hill 1989) copyright 1989 by Shepard's/McGraw-Hill, Inc. Reprinted by permission of Shepard's/McGraw-Hill, Inc. Further reproduction is strictly prohibited.

[41] *Id* 490.

On the other hand, if the same witnesses were knowingly lying (for example, the witness said that the light was red, knowing that it was green; the witness had the ability to understand the question, but intentionally claimed not to understand it; or the witness remembered what happened, but claimed not to remember), the witnesses are in the category of *untruthful* witnesses.

But, as the researchers said, the element of "credibility" is subjective and controversial.

For the purpose of the present chapter, trying to determine the influence of a witness's conduct during testimony, question 8 of the inquiry is important because it underlines the point at which the credibility of a witness's testimony can be affected.

§7.15 —Different Strategies in Criminal and Civil Cases: Research and Commentary

> *[Question] 15(a):* When cross-examining a witness in a criminal case do you use different tactics and strategies than you use in a civil case?
>
> *15(b):* If the answer is YES, please describe the main differences.
>
> * * *
>
> *[Responses:]* . . . [W]e received 5 "yes" and 8 "no" answers from respondents who practice law in both civil and criminal matters; some gave the following answers:
>
> -I'm a little rougher in criminal cases on witnesses that are adverse to my client—more cynical or sarcastic.
>
> -The main difference is that in a criminal case you might ask more questions that would help emphasize the higher burden of proof—by asking, for example, questions that emphasize that [the] witness's description of the facts is open to other interpretations.
>
> -I try to show more doubt, contradiction.
>
> -To the extent I deal with a professional witness such as a police officer, the questions are strictly leading. I have a greater tendency to imply I know the correct answer.[42]

The researchers made the following analysis:

> In our opinion, the big difference in tactics and strategies between cross-examining witnesses in civil cases and in criminal cases is that in criminal cases it is necessary to prove *beyond a reasonable doubt* that the defendant is guilty; in civil cases it is necessary to show a fair preponder-

---

[42] Reprinted from R. Aron, K.T. Duffy, & R.L. Rosner, Cross-Examination of Witnesses: The Litigator's Puzzle 502, 503 (Shepard's/McGraw-Hill 1989) copyright 1989 by Shepard's/McGraw-Hill, Inc. Reprinted by permission of Shepard's/McGraw-Hill, Inc. Further reproduction is strictly prohibited.

ance of the evidence or a higher grade of proof, clear and convincing evidence.

This difference in the burden of proof evidently has an influence not only on the tactics and strategies followed during cross-examination, but also on the tone and style of the cross-examination. For example, the dramatics that a lawyer can use in the case of a rape of a young girl cannot be used in the case of a debtor in default of a debt for one thousand dollars.

Another important difference is that in civil cases it is possible to obtain information through the deposition process about the case and the witness; in criminal cases, there are no depositions.[43]

Commentary: For the purpose of the present chapter, it is important to alert witnesses, during the preparation process, to the different kinds of interrogation they can expect. Even more important is to advise the witness how to give his or her testimony. For example, the tone, voice inflection, and body language cannot be the same if the witness says, "I saw when the defendant stabbed his knife in the victim's back," as if the witness says, "I saw when they signed the contract."

§7.16 —Control of Witnesses During Cross-Examination: Research and Commentary

[Question] 16: What tactics do you use in order to control a witness during cross-examination?

[Responses:] The respondents' comments were as follows:

1. Only one—know every answer (or close to it); make sure questions can be answered yes and no only. Don't let him talk!
2. I don't raise the decibel level until the crucial questions.
3. Pace length of questions, speed of interrogation; volume and tone; use of exhibits; physical position; order of examination.
4. N/A.
5. If you master the circumstances of the testimony better than the witness you'll control him.
6. N/A.
7. Ask only leading questions, and only questions that must be answered my way.
8. Phrase question so no room to make speeches—no open-ended questions.

---

[43] *Id* 503.

9. Keep the question simple, short, and devoid of subjective qualifiers. Keep eye contact. Use the deposition and documents. Never ask a question if I am not prepared to prove my point if the witness disagrees.
10. Calmness and easy questions. All leading questions. 1. Start—it is my understanding that you say or said 2. —isn't it true that (different story) 3. End—evidence proof of the difference between one and two.
11. Self-confidence, poise, command and the ability to recognize where you cannot take command.
12. Leading questions that can be answered yes or no. Assistance from court if the witness insists on giving an unsolicited narrative. A very short leash.
13. Questions with yes or no answers—question only when I know the answer—tell them counsel will be able to elicit further explanation if necessary.
14. Self-control, persistence, ask for help from the judge if necessary.
15. 1. Ask leading questions. 2. Avoid asking questions which permit an explanation. 3. Avoid argument.
16. Yes and no questions.
17. Ask short and to the point questions and elicit judge's assistance in having witness address the question asked.
18. Say "Please" when he wanders—Interrupt with "Please—just answer the question."
19. Short questions. Short answers (yes or no). Stick to prior testimony in deposition.
20. I use short, simple questions in order to avoid claims of ambiguity.
21. Bully him or be nice to him. Be patient or overbearing. Use the judge! Quote the law! Ask for his cooperation. Point out his behavior.
22. Pose questions for yes or no responses. Direct questions at prior trial or pretrial testimony of witness.
23. I am particularly careful to insist that the witness give a responsive answer and to call him on it every time he does not. This not only assures responsive answers but also establishes the proper relationships with the witness.
24. Extensive use of leading questions—use of the trial judge to admonish a witness who gives speeches instead of answers—use of deposition transcript to frame questions.
25. First, I repeat the question. Second, I say "I'm sorry, I didn't ask the question very well." (Then I repeat it again.) Third, I say "sir my question is simple (then I repeat again).
26. Leading question. Get court to compel answer.
27. Get him to answer the question asked.
28. Ask only "yes" or "no" questions or questions which cannot hurt.

29. I ask the witness if he knows what it means to be responsive to the question asked in view of the numerous times he has testified.
30. Ask good questions—confine answers to yes/no, I don't know, or other brief answers. Nicely appeal to witness and then to judge.
31. Having prior inconsistent statements. Making the witness believe I have prior inconsistent statements. Convincing the witness I know what he's talking about.[44]

Commentary: Question 16 asks about the different ways that trial lawyers control witnesses during cross-examination.

But it refers only to one side of the coin. In this chapter, about the influence of the demeanor of witnesses during impeachment, we must mention the other side of the coin: What is the task of a lawyer, during the witness's preparation? What instructions must be given to the witness in order to diminish the impact of the control of the witness by the opposing lawyer who cross-examines or tries to impeach the witness? How must the witness's answer be given, in order not to make a bad impression?

During the witness's preparation process, the lawyer must use the opportunity to instruct the witness about how to react during cross-examination or impeachment, in order to send a message of truthfulness to the trier of fact.

We know that a lawyer, before deciding to include a person as a witness, must consider the person's:

1. Competency to testify
2. Integrity
3. Credibility
4. Capacity to perceive
5. Capacity to recall
6. Capacity to communicate
7. Capacity to understand and follow the lawyer's instructions
8. Attractiveness[45]

In other words, the lawyer must study the witness's personality and character. This will permit the lawyer to know what kind of person he or she will call to the witness stand and what kind of instructions the witness will be able to receive and understand.

After the preliminary examination, the first basic advice must be to "tell the truth," followed by other explanations and advice to prevent the witness from being caught off guard.

---

[44] Reprinted from R. Aron, K.T. Duffy, & J.L. Rosner, Cross-Examination of Witnesses: The Litigator's Puzzle 503-05 (Shepard's/McGraw-Hill 1989) copyright 1989 by Shepard's/McGraw-Hill, Inc. Reprinted by permission of Shepard's/McGraw-Hill, Inc. Further reproduction is strictly prohibited.

[45] R. Aron, J. Fast, & R. Klein, Trial Communication Skills 234 (Shepard's/McGraw-Hill 1986).

The following may be a good check list of advice to give the witness:

1. Explain to the witness what "leading questions" are
2. Advise the witness that if the witness does not know the answer to a question, he or she must say, "I don't know"
3. Explain to the witness that his or her only tool on the stand is "memory," and not "imagination"
4. Advise the witness not to try to make speeches
5. Advise the witness that when the witness speaks, he or she should look at the lawyer who is questioning the witness, and answer without hesitation
6. Advise the witness not to look at his or her presenting lawyer, asking for help; at this stage, the lawyer cannot help the witness, and this look will make a bad impression on the jury and the judge
7. Advise the witness to only answer the question that was asked
8. Advise the witness to pause and think about what the answer will be, before answering a question; this pause will also give the lawyer who presented the witness the time and opportunity to object to the question if the lawyer thinks that the question is not proper or relevant
9. Explain to the witness what "objections" are
10. Explain to the witness the judge's right to ask questions and to interrupt during the witness's testimony
11. Explain to the witness that if the lawyer wants to introduce evidence through the witness, the witness must know about it
12. Advise the witness to control his or her nerves and not to lose his or her temper

We know that it is impossible to foresee all of the things that can happen when a witness is cross-examined or impeached. But, it is the lawyer's obligation to try to cover all possible angles of questioning. In this way, the lawyer is protecting not only the witness, but also the case itself and the lawyer's professional responsibility.

§7.17 Conclusions

In writing this chapter about the influence of the demeanor of witnesses during cross-examination and impeachment, we analyzed the ability and capacity of a person to testify, the structure of testimony, and witnesses' verbal and nonverbal communication during the trial. With communication in mind, we analyzed various research works in the field of witnesses' conduct during their testimony.

We emphasized certain subjects related to witnesses' demeanor, such as indications of when a witness is lying, or the elements of nonverbal communication which could influence the witness's message either favorably or unfavorably.

For each question from the research that we examined, we tried, in our commentary, to adapt the subject of the question to the theme of this chapter.

In examining the influence of verbal and nonverbal communication during a trial, we found a difference of opinion among the respondents in the different research studies. In the opinion of scientists who have done research in the field of human communication, the influence of nonverbal communication is 60%; the influence of verbal communication, 40%. In the opinion of psychologists, who were considering the subject from a more general point of view, the proportion is 55% to 80% for verbal communication, and 20% to 45% for nonverbal communication. In the opinion of judges and lawyers, who specifically were considering the subject of trial communication, the proportion is 60% for what the communicator says, and 40% for nonverbal communication.

Even if we believe that the percentage of influence of nonverbal communication—20% to 45%, according to psychologists—is lower than that of verbal communication, we still can see the importance of body language and the imperative for trial lawyers to know how to control their own nonverbal communication and their witnesses' nonverbal communication during a trial.

What we want to emphasize in this chapter is that in the study of witnesses' demeanor during cross-examination and impeachment, nonverbal communication is a matter of great relevance.

We hope that the subject matter of this chapter will help trial lawyers in two ways: (1) determining how to prepare their court presentations and interrogatories, and (2) determining how to instruct their witnesses in their body language when testifying during cross-examination and impeachment, so that their body language will convince the trier of fact of their truthfulness.

Part Two
Contributions by Other Authors

Buskin v Raytheon: Cross-Examination of Thomas L. Phillips, Chairman & CEO, Raytheon, by F. Lee Bailey, Esq.

Nibbling (Cross-Examination and Impeachment of the Medical Expert), by Norman Leonard Cousins, Esq.

Impeachment of an Undercover Police Officer, by William E. Johnson, Esq.

Civil RICO—Plaintiffs' Cross-Examination of a Defendant and the Defendant's Lawyer, by Kenneth Michael Robinson, Esq.

Impeaching the Professional Informant, by Karl F. Salzer, Esq.

Impeachment with Prior Inconsistent Statement, by Patrick A. Tuite, Esq.

Cross-Examination/Impeachment, by Dianne Jay Weaver, Esq.

Bushkin v Raytheon: Cross-Examination of Thomas L. Phillips, Chairman & CEO, Raytheon*

The litigation in the *Bushkin* case has a long and tortured history. When it finally went to jury verdict in July, 1989, it was more than fourteen years old, and nearly ten years had passed since the date of first demand for payment by the plaintiff.[1] It began this way.

Merle J. Bushkin was an investment banker who had graduated from Harvard Business School in 1960, and who had worked for the Raytheon Company of Lexington, Massachusetts, while a student. He held a number of positions in the investment banking field, and, in 1973, went into business for himself in New York City. He struck up a relationship with Raytheon through its then Vice-President for Planning and Acquisitions, and over a period of five years, or so, submitted more than sixty proposals to Raytheon; on two of these, he dealt directly with Raytheon's Chief Executive Officer, Thomas L. Phillips.

In February, 1974, another client—Ethyl Corporation—expressed an interest in acquiring Beech Aircraft Company of Wichita, Kansas, the "Mercedes" of the general aviation manufacturers. A meeting was held in Wichita between the Gottwald Brothers (who controlled Ethyl) and Olive Ann Beech (Chairperson) and Frank Hedrick (President)[2] of Beechcraft; Bushkin was in attendance.

In the course of the meeting, it was disclosed that because of advancing age, the principals were interested in being acquired by a larger company that could, among other things, help Beech finance the development of a corporate jet airplane to compete with Cessna and Lear. Beech management was to stay in place, its name was to remain in the fore, and the asking price was twelve times earnings, or about $130,000,000. Negotiations stumbled along for a year, then terminated. Bushkin was free to look elsewhere.

He immediately[3] got in touch with Vice-President Robert Seaman at Raytheon, and put forward a strong pitch. Raytheon thought of itself as being much too heavily committed to military contracts, and wanted to diversify. Beech was a premier company, and Raytheon had a lot of experience which was at least tangential to aviation (radar, etc.). Raytheon fit Mrs. Beech's requirements almost "to a T," and Bushkin thought that Beech would grow rapidly in the latter part of the decade. Bushkin asked for a one per cent fee, to which he claimed Seaman agreed. Seaman promised to think about the matter and to bring it to Phillips's attention; a month or so later, he said Raytheon wasn't interested.

But in June, Seaman called Bushkin to say that Phillips's interest in Beech had been heightened in the wake of another "failed deal," and that Seaman

---

* By F. Lee Bailey. Mr. Bailey, who tried his first case in June, 1954, is a litigation specialist, a frequent lecturer on cross-examination, and the author of 17 books. He is believed to have tried cases in more jurisdictions, and before more different judges, than any lawyer in the history of the United States.

[1] In Massachusetts, interest runs from the date of demand for payment by the plaintiff.

[2] Together these two owned 19% of the stock of this public company.

[3] On January 25, 1975—dates are critical to this case, as will be seen.

would be making a formal presentation of the Beech acquisition within a week. At the same time, Bushkin's name was recorded on Raytheon's "acquisition log" as the broker for the Beech deal, and a few days thereafter, Seaman wrote a memo to Phillips describing Bushkin as "our contact man in this [Beech] matter."

At the end of July, Phillips decided that the General Aviation industry was too "cyclical" for his tastes, and declined to go further. Bushkin looked elsewhere for a Beech buyer, with no success.

In November, 1975, Bushkin met Phillips personally for the first time, in a hotel in New York, in connection with another potential acquisition, and, in the course of the meeting, mentioned that Beech deserved another look. Phillips replied, "It's a good company, but too cyclical."

In September, 1976, Raytheon signed a contract with Royal Little, then nearing eighty, as an acquisition consultant. Little, the former CEO of Textron, was revered by many in corporate America as the "father" of the modern conglomerate concept. In late November of that year, Little mentioned Beech Aircraft to Phillips as a worthwhile company to scrutinize.

On February 12, 1977, Phillips directed Little to pursue Beech. A week later, Phillips was riding in the Raytheon company jet with Bushkin, in connection with a possible petro-chemical acquisition, when Bushkin mentioned that Beech had grown even more than he had earlier predicted, and was worthy of a further evaluation. Phillips replied, "We have *no interest* in a general aviation company." Despite this disclaimer, Raytheon's pursuit of Beech continued apace.

Negotiations dragged along, but in October, 1979, it was announced in the *Wall Street Journal* that Raytheon had struck a deal to acquire Beech for $815,000,000 in Raytheon stock. In a press statement, Phillips disclosed that he had been working on the deal since "early 1977." When Bushkin saw that, his eyes popped out; he immediately dashed off a letter to Phillips congratulating him on his acquisition, and demanding payment of the one per cent commission he claimed to have been promised by Seaman in January, 1975. When no response was forthcoming, Bushkin filed suit in the United States District Court for the District of Massachusetts, claiming an express oral contract for a commission on the sale.

Raytheon filed a motion for summary judgment, contending that New York law applied, and that New York required all such agreements to be in writing if they were to be enforceable. Judge Joseph Tauro agreed, and granted the motion. Appeal was taken to the United States Court of Appeals for the First Circuit; that court determined that it was confronting a question of Massachusetts state law of first impression, and transferred the case to the Massachusetts Supreme Judicial Court.[4] That court ruled for Bushkin, and the case was thereafter remanded for trial before Judge Walter Jay Skinner.

---

[4] *After* oral argument, Raytheon's counsel sent a letter to the Massachusetts Supreme Judicial Court calling its attention to the fact that Governor Michael Dukakis had just signed into a law a new Massachusetts statute changing the law relating to brokers to match that of New York. Counsel for Bushkin quickly responded with a letter showing that the statute had been sponsored by a paid lobbyist for Raytheon. This exchange

At the close of the plaintiff's case, Judge Skinner ruled that Bushkin's entitlement lapsed two years after his original contact with Raytheon's Seaman (January 25, 1975), and that there was no evidence that Raytheon set out to acquire Beech until February, 1977; on that basis, he directed a verdict. Once more the case went to the First Circuit. It was reversed again and remanded for new trial, this time with a virtual road map for the trial judge to follow in dealing with the convoluted legal issues which had infected the litigation. Two years was indeed the limit, ruled the court, but Bushkin might show with *circumstantial* evidence that Raytheon's interest was in fact "rekindled" prior to January 24, 1977. In this respect, the court noted that a jury might well find that Phillips's "disingenuous" denial to Bushkin—in February, 1977—of any interest in "general aviation," when he had in fact already given the order to attempt Beech's acquisition, could easily be construed by a jury as an attempt to cover Raytheon's known liability. The court also ruled that in addition to the express oral contract claimed, the facts would support a contract implied in fact or a contract implied in law (*quantum meruit*). It was plain that if the facts did not change substantially, all three of these theories would be submitted to the jury.

On the eve of the second trial, the new trial judge—the Hon. Edward F. Harrington—discovered that plaintiff's counsel had interviewed some of the Skinner trial jurors, a practice expressly forbidden in the District of Massachusetts absent court permission. Judge Harrington struck counsel's appearance, and ordered Bushkin to find a new lawyer. This led to our first face-to-face contact in Tampa, Florida, in February, 1989, where I was studying to take the Florida bar. Merle Bushkin proved to be a very perceptive and intelligent man in his early fifties who knew exactly what he wanted. Armed with his appellate opinion guaranteeing that his case would go to a jury, he had interviewed many of the best advocates in practice in the northeast. He felt—correctly, I believe—that his best chance of recovery lay in the effective cross-examination of Raytheon Chairman Thomas L. Phillips. A highly respected New York trial lawyer—Michael F. Armstrong—had advised him, "If your life depends on cross-examination, get Lee Bailey."[5] Bushkin took the advice to heart, and shortly we had a contract.[6]

With many depositions and a prior trial to confront, trial preparation for *Bushkin v Raytheon* required the concentration of most of our Boston office staff. As far as I was concerned, there were three players whose stories would rest in the forefront of the jury's consciousness when it finally retired to deliberate the case: Bushkin, Phillips, and Bob Seaman. If Bushkin's account of the events held up, then playing Seaman's testimony off against that of CEO Phillips

---

was noticed as insignificant in a footnote in the opinion. My effort to use this incident to show "consciousness of liability" on Raytheon's part was rejected by Judge Harrington.

[5] Upon reading this admission, Mike will doubtless hit me up for season tickets to all Jets and Giants games for life.

[6] With appropriate provision for "removed" counsel, who had skillfully handled the second appeal and prepared much of the case for trial.

offered the best chance to find a "smoking pistol." For whatever reason, neither witness had been attacked very aggressively in the first trial,[7] whereas Bushkin had been the subject of a blistering and derisive onslaught by Ed Masterman, one of the most seasoned and skillful advocates in the region. But the Seaman v Phillips ploy was never to be. Seaman claimed a heart condition which would preclude his appearance at trial. We protested, but a court-appointed physician opined that although the patient was healthy and played tennis regularly, cross-examination might prove to be an intolerable strain.[8] We would have to live with Seaman's prior utterances.

Which left us exactly where Bushkin had thought us to be, in a Bushkin v Phillips swearing match. Of the documents which flooded the file boxes, some cut one way and some another. On balance, I thought Raytheon's "acquisition log" and the Seaman to Phillips memo about "Bushkin, our contact man . . ." gave us a slight edge in the paper department. Nonetheless, to win more than a token recovery, I felt that the jury would have to like Bushkin and resent Raytheon's attitude in trying to brush him aside. It became our objective either (1) to force Phillips to defend his position that Bushkin was entitled to nothing, or (2) to get Phillips to admit that he had neglected Bushkin's position in the deal through oversight.

Although experienced lawyers are not in total agreement on the point, it has been my practice over the years in civil litigation from the plaintiff's side to call the defendants early on in the game, sometimes as the opening plaintiff's witness. There are drawbacks, to be sure, in this approach, but the single advantage of having control of the opposition's mainstay while he or she attempts to get a story told outweighs any disadvantages, in my view. For those who rely more on their ability to "build" a positive case for the plaintiff, rather than ripping into the opposition early on, a different approach might well work better.

Bushkin led off and—on balance—made an excellent witness. He had kept copious notes as a business habit, and his reconstruction of detail was formidable. Most important, he accepted our repeated insistence that the shortest fair answer to a cross-examiner is the best answer, and gave Ed Masterman very little new matter to work with. This is not to say that Masterman didn't score from time to time. His mere presence—tall, slender, handsome, and articulate—coupled with a wealth of experience in poking holes through witnesses could probably have enabled him to impeach an archbishop to a degree. But when Merle left the stand, our case was very much alive.[9]When Raytheon Chair-

---

[7] Which, in fairness to the strategy of trial counsel, was aborted before that strategy could be played out.

[8] The learned doctor was perhaps more correct than he had reason to know. Seaman had in the past claimed a lack of recollection as to the details of what proved to be the largest acquisition in Raytheon's history. I love to find witnesses with recollection problems on my opponent's side.

[9] Before the trial, settlement negotiations died and were buried. Raytheon would not offer more than $100,000 ("nuisance value"), and Bushkin would not accept less than $1,000,000. We were a "fur piece" apart.

man Thomas Phillips finally took the stand under plaintiff's subpoena, there was more than a little electricity in the air. The courtroom was packed, partly by Assistant United States Attorneys. Phillips was reputed to be a very strong and self-confident executive who brooked little nonsense from subordinates or those who sought to disagree with him. In his earlier appearances, he had ridiculed Bushkin's contribution to the Beech acquisition as silly, virtually non-existent, and a chiseler's effort to climb on someone else's bandwagon. He was anything but bashful. Nonetheless, he was tall, fit, and an imposing man, known to be very devout, and hardly one to be trifled with. We began our encounter this way:

THOMAS L. PHILLIPS, duly sworn
DIRECT EXAMINATION

BY MR. BAILEY:

Q. Tell us your name for the record, please, sir.

A. Thomas L. Phillips.

Q. Where are you employed?

A. Am I employed?

Q. Where are you employed?

A. I'm employed at the Raytheon Company.

Q. In what capacity?

A. Chairman, chief executive officer.

Q. How long have you held the position of chairman?

A. Chairman, since 1975.

Q. How long have you held the position of chief executive officer?

A. Chief executive officer since 1968.

Q. Prior to being chief executive, what was your position? I realize there's an overlap.

A. I was president.

Q. When was that?

A. 1964.

Q. So from '64 to '68, you were the president and chief operating officer, is that correct?

A. Yes.

Q. And who was the chief executive officer?

A. Mr. Adams.

Q. In 1975 when you became the chairman, did Mr. Adams leave the company?

A. He retired.

Q. Now, can you tell us your educational background, Mr. Phillips?

A. I'm a graduate of Boston Latin School, and I have a bachelor of science degree and a master of science degree from the Virginia Polytechnic Institute.[10]

Q. And a bachelor of science degree, was there any specialty within that degree?

A. Electrical engineering.

Q. What was your first employment?

A. My first employment, I became an instructor at New York University in February of 1948.

Q. I wonder if you can get just a little closer to the microphone. I'm having some trouble.

A. Sure.

I was an instructor at New York University in February of 1948.

Q. Thank you very much.

Did you subsequent to that go to work for the Raytheon Company?

A. Yes, I did.

Q. When?

A. In June of '48.

Q. What capacity?

A. As a junior engineer.

Q. Could you tell us, not in great detail but just progressively, how you worked your way up the ladder to becoming the CE?

A. Yes. I was a junior engineer, then a senior engineer. In 1951 I became a department manager. In 1958 I became a laboratory manager. In 1960 I became a vice president. In 1961 I became executive vice president. In 1964 I became president. In 1968 I became chief executive.

Q. Your original training, that was your college training, was not in business, was it?

A. That's right.

Q. Have you subsequently gone to any formal courses of instruction that deal with business such as finance, corporate management, that sort of thing?

A. Not formally, no.

Q. All right. Has it been your practice to attend conferences, seminars, and other things where instruction in these areas is offered?

A. Yes.

---

[10] In stalking one's quarry, his or her basic discipline is important to know. Virtually all of Phillips's formal education was in science, and more specifically engineering. Engineers think differently than lawyers, artists or philosophers, a fact which should be ever borne in mind when formulating questions.

Q. And prior to becoming executive vice president, had you acquired some experience and expertise in the fields of operation of the company other than engineering?

A. I would say yes.

Q. Did there come a time in the 1960s when you decided that Raytheon was too heavily concentrated in defense work for its own corporate health?

A. That's correct.

Q. Why was that, sir?

A. Because I had witnessed Raytheon go through the ups and downs of defense contracting, and I wanted Raytheon to have a commercial base of business so during the down periods of the defense contracting, Raytheon's fortunes would not be so adversely affected.

Q. And the ups and downs that you had witnessed, had they been directly related to the existence of hostilities in which the United States was involved directly or indirectly?

A. Sometimes. But sometimes no. Sometimes it was political.

Q. All right. What size company was Raytheon when you became president in 1964 in terms of gross annual sales?

A. About $500 million.

Q. And what percentage of that was sold to the Government or to branches of Government?

A. About 85 percent.

Q. What things did Raytheon make in 1964 for the commercial or civilian market?

A. Radio receiving tubes, semiconducters, a line on marine electronics, and some commercial apparatus such as welders and power supplies and that sort of thing.

Q. Raytheon had since World War II been a pioneer in radar detection and ranging commonly known as radar?

A. That's right.

Q. When you made this decision—is this a decision that was made to— between you and the Board of Directors or between you and the chief executive officer? How did it come about?

A. Yes. I worked with the staff at the time, and then presented it to the chief executive and the Board. And they accepted it as the philosophy of Raytheon that we would diversify into commercial markets.

Q. Is a decision of this size one that necessarily requires Board action according to Raytheon's policies?

A. Board concurrence.

Q. All right. Well, was it your understanding when you were the president and Mr. Adams was the chief executive officer that he could make a decision and then later ask the Board to agree with it even after it had been implemented? Was that the way you operated?

A. That's not the preferred way. The preferred way would be to have a course of action, to take it to the Board, get their concurrence, and then implement it after that.

Q. Now, in 1968 when you became the CEO and Mr. Adams remained on as chairman, was there a new chief operating officer appointed?

A. No. I was both the chief executive and the chief operating officers.

Q. Tell the jury, at least at Raytheon, the difference between those two when there are two.

A. When there are two of them, the chief executive determines policy and is responsible to the Board. The chief operating officer normally has all the operating entities reporting to him. The divisions, subsidiaries, and staff report to him, and he implements the policies of the company.

Q. So that the chief executive will set the policy, and the chief operating officer's job is to carry it out?

A. Right.

Q. All right. Now, in 1968 when you became the chief executive officer and remained the president and Mr. Adams remained chairman, did he have any executive operational authority remaining after he retired as CEO?

A. No. I was the final authority starting in 1968.

Q. Are you familiar with the bylaws of the Raytheon Corporation, its corporate charter?

A. I've read them. I haven't seen them for years, so I'm not familiar—I couldn't recite them for you right now.

Q. In 1968 was there a cutting line where a decision would become sufficiently significant to all of Raytheon that you would require the Board to participate in it before implementing that decision?

A. Possibly. I don't—

Q. Well, you say "possibly." Try to remember. I'm trying to learn whether the Board was advisory or whether the Board made decisions based on recommendations which you then carried out.

A. I think the course of action was for me to make recommendations to the Board, for the Board to approve them, and then for me to go up and carry them out.

Q. Okay. What I'm trying to—obviously, if you were buying new pencil sharpeners, that didn't go to the Board. I'm trying to find out at what level of seriousness, if there was one, did you determine that you had to go to the Board before issuing operating orders on that decision.

A. Well, for example, if you made an acquisition, that would commit company resources, we want the Board to approve that—

Q. All right.

A. —typically. A major capital investment in a new plant is something we would take to the Board and have them approve it before we implement it.

Q. So that major financial decisions that could impact upon the company as a whole, I take it, were for the Board to consider before anything was done.

A. Right.

Q. You would make an investigation, come up with your own views on the matter and recommendations, and present them to the Board and they would vote?

A. Right.

Q. How did you go about mechanically your program to diversify Raytheon out of the defense field?

A. I organized a study team under the office of the Vice President of Planning.

Q. Who was that in 1964?

A. I think it was Donald Yeats.

Q. Go ahead.

A. And he had a staff of two or three people with him. And we also issued to our investment banker, who I believe at that time was Morgan Stanley, our interest in diversifying.

Q. What is an investment banker insofar as Raytheon was concerned back in '64?

A. An investment banker in '64 was someone who advised the company on its capital formation, on going public, taking on long-term debt, or on mergers and acquisitions.

Q. Okay. And did Morgan Stanley do that for you exclusively, or were there others in the picture?

A. Well, the whole field of investment banking has changed over the years. When I first came aboard in '64, it was common to have, quote, unquote, your investment banker, and he would know all about your business and advise you on all aspects of it.

With time, those close ties with companies and investment bankers have diminished, and now companies work with multiple investment bankers and, of course, investment bankers work with multiple companies. But in '64 we were a lot closer to a one-on-one relationship.

Q. All right. Now move up, if you will, to 1971. And I ask you whether or not the Vice Presidency of Planning was still an office at Raytheon.

A. I believe so.

Q. Was Mr. Frank Fox the holder of that title?[11]

A. It's possible. You know, I'm not really sure. In the '70s we had Frank Fox for a period of time as Vice President of Planning and Bob Seaman in Planning and Analysis, and they worked together. And whether 71 was the time that Fox held that title or not, I can't answer for sure. He had it at a period of time.

Q. Did you own a publishing subsidiary in 1971 or '2 named D. C. Heath Company?

A. Yes, we did.

Q. Did Mr. Fox leave the office of Vice President of Planning in 1972 to become the president of D. C. Heath Company?

A. Quite possibly, yes.

Q. Well, is Mr. Fox someone that in the early 70s before he switched jobs you would see on a regular basis?

A. Yes.

Q. What would you see him about?

A. Depending on what his responsibility was at the time, I would see him either on the operations of D. C. Heath or during his time on the planning scene on the—on his activities in mergers and acquisitions.

Q. Now, have you learned anywhere along the way, Mr. Phillips, the legal concept of apparent authority? Has that ever been brought to your attention?

A. No.[12]

Q. Did you have any notion in 1971 that a person who carried a business card properly saying "Vice President of Planning" might have authority to bind the corporation in certain situations?

A. He didn't in our corporation; did not.

---

[11] This was a test question. *I* knew that Frank Fox had held the title, because I had learned this information in preparation for the trial. Did Phillips really *not know* this information? Here was a man who had been embroiled in this controversy—about which he had strong personal feelings, we were told—for almost ten years. Either he had done little preparation for his testimony, or he had a bad memory, or he was erecting the "I don't remember" defense early in the game. This sort of event should cause the hackles on the back of the cross-examiner's neck to stand up.

[12] Score! In view of the fact that Phillips had earlier taken the position that his vice-president (Seaman) had no authority to contract with Bushkin, it was inconceivable to us that his very able counsel had not discussed with him the legal concept of "apparent authority." Phillips's subsequent suggestion that he had given little thought to the fact that the laws of Massachusetts recognized this concept even though Raytheon did not was important, because it conferred a license on the cross-examiner to paint him as a person of some arrogance without much risk of jury backlash.

Q. I'm asking you whether or not you learned by 1971 that regardless of what you thought, a vice president might have apparent authority to bind the corporation.

MR. MASTERMAN: He's answered the question.

THE COURT: Overruled. Just what his belief is. He says in his company someone didn't have authority, but I'll let the question—

A. It could be in other companies, someone with that title might have the authority. I don't know.

Q. Mr. Phillips, please listen to the question. I'm not asking about Raytheon. I'm asking about whether you knew of the legal concept that your corporation could be bound by someone who was a vice president in fact and held out as such by you. Did you know that?

A. I don't know that I thought about it very much. I'm sorry.

Q. You didn't. Okay.

Well, were you dealing at the time—was Raytheon dealing with a number of investment bankers and brokers in its acquisition program?

A. By '71, yes, I would say so.

Q. Were you continuing at that time to look for acquisitions?

A. Yes.

Q. Major? Minor?

A. '71. Uhm—

(Pause)

A. Our plate had become quite full by '71. We had made several acquisitions in the late 60s.

Q. Can you think of any of them?

A. Yes.

Q. Please name them.

A. Amana—

Q. Excuse me. What does Amana do?

A. Amana does refrigeration, appliances.

Q. How big a company were they?

A. How big were they then?

Q. When you bought them.

A. When we bought them, 28 million.

Q. All right. Others?

A. Caloric. Gas ranges.

Q. Yes.

A. Badger.

Q. How much did you pay for Caloric?

A. How much did we pay for Caloric? Oh, you're asking me a lot of detailed questions. $15 million, maybe.

Q. Maybe 15?

A. Yes, in that vicinity.

Q. Now, is this memory, by the way, that you were telling us about today something that comes from the late '60s to the present time?

A. What memory? I'm sorry?

Q. You're testifying to some acquisitions made in the late 60s, including their approximate prices, and I'm asking you if that's something you now remember.

A. Yes. I'm telling you what I remember off the top of my head.

Q. All right. Thank you.

The next company was Badger.

A. Badger.

Q. What did they do?

A. Chemical engineering plants.

Q. Chemical engineering.

Can you be any more specific?

A. Chemical and oil refineries.

Q. All right. Was this your first acquisition in the energy field?

A. No, it was the second. Actually, we acquired Seismograph first; Seismograph Service Corporation of Tulsa, Oklahoma, was before that.

Q. They're a service company?

A. Service company. Exploration of oil and gas.

Q. And what did you pay for Badger, if you can recall?

A. What did we pay for Badger. I suspect between $60- and $70 million.

Q. And for the service company?

A. I would say $30 to $40 million.

Q. Okay. By 1971 can you tell us what the gross sales of Raytheon, including its subsidiaries, were?

A. I don't have '71 in mind very clearly. My guess is a billion and a half by then or maybe two billion.

Q. All right. When a company like Raytheon buys other companies that are already in business and already have sales and those sales continue, they become part of the gross sales of the parent, in business language, do they not?

A. That's correct.

Q. All right. Now, if you were asked to put a value upon Raytheon in 1971, whether you remember what it was or not, how would you have gone about it? How would you tell anybody what Raytheon is worth?

A. Well, very simple. You look at the price of the stock and multiply it by the number of shares, and that's the market value of Raytheon.

Q. Regardless of its debt?

A. Yes.

Q. Do you have any idea using that formula what the market value was in 1971?

A. I don't. I do not know what it was.

Q. All right. Were you a shareholder by that time?

A. Yes, I'm sure I was.

Q. Now, Mr. Phillips, what policy did you have when Mr. Fox was in Planning with respect to dealing with outsiders, that is, investment brokers and bankers who wanted to do business with Raytheon in any fashion?

A. Mr. Fox was to find opportunities for us that were possible merger candidates. Mr. Seaman was to analyze these. I was to make all decisions.[13]

Q. Okay. Was there any written document that was given out to investment bankers and brokers in 1971 when Mr. Fox was still there advising them of your policies?

A. I don't recall that.

Q. Isn't it a fact, Mr. Phillips, that you know that the first published policy for investment bankers and brokers is dated in April 1976?

A. That's possibly true.

Q. Do you know of any publicly—or I should say published policy in writing prior to that date which was put out by Raytheon?

A. I don't know.

Q. Do you know of any means by which an innocent investment banker attempting to contract with your Vice President of Planning would be on notice that that vice president didn't have any authority?

MR. MASTERMAN: I object.

THE COURT: Sustained. You can have the question, but whether someone is innocent or not innocent is irrelevant.

MR. BAILEY: Okay.

BY MR. BAILEY:

Q. Do you know of any means by which a broker dealing with Raytheon's Vice President of Planning in 1971 would be on notice that the vice president had no power to contract with him?

---

[13] This assertion characterized the witness as one who was all things to all people, and delegated no authority to anyone. This was an important step in the process of painting Raytheon as a tyrannical monarchy, where the king often stomped about in ignorance of the doings of his subordinates.

A. I don't know how you would know except our vice president would tell him because I had told him.

Q. And your vice presidents always did everything you told them, is that right?

A. Not always.

Q. You mean that it's possible that some broker might make a contract with the vice president and think it was a good contract?

MR. MASTERMAN: I object.

THE COURT: Overruled.

A. My vice president has no authority to make a contract; therefore, that's not possible. Had no authority.

Q. I see. And if a broker thought a vice president might have that authority and hadn't been told to the contrary, he should have figured out that you didn't allow it?

MR. MASTERMAN: I object.

THE COURT: Overruled.

A. Our vice presidents would not defy me[14] on something as binding as making a contract with anyone on the outside.

Q. You say they would not; but you were not present at all the meetings your vice presidents had with brokers, were you?

A. I was not.

Q. And you know personally of a case where without your authority your vice president bound the company and you honored it, don't you?

A. I'm not sure of that.

Q. You're not.

A. No.

Q. Do you recall the name of a company called Allyn & Bacon?

A. Yes.

Q. Do you recall a gentleman named Merle Bushkin who sits at the plaintiffs' table?

A. Yes.

Q. Do you recall Mr. Bushkin coming to you and telling you he had an agreement with Raytheon during your very first meeting?

A. I authorized that agreement.

Q. Okay.

---

[14] The word "defy" is a strong clue to the relationship between Phillips and his minions. These subordinates *would* not do something they physically *could* do, he was sure, because such conduct would constitute the unthinkable: insubordination. One often hears attitudes of this sort from career military witnesses.

A. That's different. I can tell my vice president he is authorized and he can do it.

Q. Then why did you tell Mr. Bushkin in the course of the meeting that no one could authorize it but you?

A. Uhm—

(Pause)

A. I don't know if I told him that. Did I?

Q. Sure.

A. Well, on any significant—

Q. Assuming that you told him that, would you tell us why?

A. I don't know.

Q. Okay. Thank you, Mr. Phillips.

Now, when Mr. Bushkin came to you for the very first time, were you aware of how many different cases he had brought to Raytheon?

A. I was not.

Q. Had you ever prior to that time authorized a fee for Mr. Bushkin that you can remember?

A. I authorized a fee to be paid on Allyn & Bacon.

Q. When?

A. I don't recall.

Q. Well, was it when Mr. Bushkin first proposed Allyn & Bacon or was it sometime later, if you know?

A. I do not recall.

Q. Is that the only case prior to your first meeting with Mr. Bushkin that you ever authorized a fee be paid if there was a successful acquisition?

A. I don't recall.

THE COURT:

For my information, when was the so-called first meeting? What does the evidence indicate?

MR. BAILEY: November 6, 1975.

BY MR. BAILEY:

Q. Do you recall that, Mr. Phillips?

A. What am I to recall?

Q. Did you have a hotel suite in New York—at the Hilton to be precise—get introduced to Merle Bushkin for the first time in your life on November 6, 1975, by Frank Fox?

A. I don't recall how I met Mr. Bushkin.

Q. Did you meet him?

A. I met him.

Q. Did Frank Fox introduce you?

A. I don't recall.

Q. Was it about Allyn & Bacon?

A. Yes. My—my first contact with Mr. Bushkin was with regard to Allyn & Bacon.

Q. As you sit here today, do you have no memory at all of the meeting in New York with Fox present?

A. There was a meeting in New York. I don't recall whether Fox was present or not.

Q. Do you recall getting a letter from Mr. Bushkin written the following day enclosing information that you had requested?

A. On Allyn & Bacon I requested information from Mr. Bushkin and I received it, yes.

MR. BAILEY: Your Honor, I don't have a recollection as to whether this document is an exhibit.

(Defense counsel examining document)

THE COURT: Any objection?

MR. MASTERMAN: I object on the grounds of relevance, your Honor.

THE COURT: Let me see it.

SIDE BAR CONFERENCE. . . .

(Court examining document)

THE COURT:

At this time I'm going to sustain it. But why don't you ask him whether he received it?

MR. BAILEY:

I was going to do that. I wanted to mark it first.

THE COURT:

You want to mark it first for identification?

MR. BAILEY:

That he's received it and reviewed it.

THE COURT:

He can mark it at this time for identification.

MR. BAILEY:

Okay.

MR. MASTERMAN:

Rather than keep jumping up, because he is then going to offer it—

THE COURT:

I can't rule unless I know what his answer is. If he says, Yeah, I read it—

MR. MASTERMAN:

Then I'm going to come back and make another objection.

THE COURT:

All right.

MR. MASTERMAN:

All right.

. . . END SIDE BAR CONFERENCE

THE CLERK:

Plaintiffs' 40 for identification.

(Plaintiff's Item 40 was marked for identification)

BY MR. BAILEY:

Q. Mr. Phillips, please examine Plaintiffs' 40 for identification and tell us whether or not you recognize that as a copy of a letter you read some years ago.

A. I recognize the letter.

Q. What is the date of the letter?

A. November 7, 1975.

Q. Does that help you remember that you met with Mr. Bushkin the day before?

A. No, it does not.

Q. It doesn't.

A. It says in the letter I did, but *that doesn't help me remember.*[15]

Q. You don't know how long after you asked for information that Mr. Bushkin sent it to you?

A. No.

Q. No recollection at all?

A. No.

Q. Could it have been a year?

A. No. I don't think it could have been a year, no.

Q. Have you reviewed that letter since this litigation began?

---

[15] A witness's attempted handling of his own ostensible ability to "recollect" is almost always a crucial factor in the tactics of cross-examination, and should be identified early on. Many witnesses—even very bright ones, like Phillips—become convinced that an alleged failure of recollection is an impregnable bunker in which one should seek refuge whenever even the most trivial threat is perceived. To be confronted with a document specifically detailing a meeting which has already been recalled, and thereafter assert that it does not help to revive a recollection, leaves one in a delicate position. The implication is that one is either stupid, or being a bit coy. No one in the courtroom ever thought that Tom Phillips was even the least bit stupid. (An extreme example: I once had a doctor tell me, hard on the heels of failing a polygraph examination relating to the murder of his wife, "Well, *if* I killed her, *I don't remember it.*")

A. I've seen the letter since the litigation began, yes.

Q. All right. Have you reviewed the accompanying document?

A. I glanced at it.

Q. Do you now recall, having looked at the document, why you asked that it be sent to you by Mr. Bushkin?

A. Why, did I recall?

Q. Right.

A. Do you want me to give you the rationale of why we were looking at Allyn & Bacon?

Q. No, sir.

A. What are you looking for?

Q. I'm asking if you remember why you asked Mr. Bushkin to send you a certain document, which document you are now examining as an attachment to the letter of November 7 to you from Bushkin.

Do you remember why you wanted a document of that sort?

A. Yes, because it's unusual. It's an unusual kind of combination of notes and cash that Mr. Bushkin reported a stockholder of Allyn & Bacon would be receptive to, and that's what Mr. Bushkin presented.

Q. Now, from the meeting you had with Mr. Bushkin and from what you remember of it, is it apparent to you that Bushkin and Fox had been working on this Allyn & Bacon deal before the meeting?

A. I would think so, yes.

Q. And they had made some examination of who the principals were and what they wanted and so forth and so on?

A. I would guess that's right.

Q. All right. Do you remember what it was they were asking you for? Why were you there?

A. Why was I there?

Q. Why did you have Mr. Bushkin in your suite?

A. Because Raytheon was interested in Allyn & Bacon, and Mr. Bushkin reported that he had a way of reaching the principal shareholder.

Q. All right. Now, prior to—do you know if he had done so by that time?

A. Mr. Bushkin reported he knew Mr. Ettinger, who was the principal shareholder.

Q. What did Allyn & Bacon do?

A. I beg your pardon?

Q. What did they do?

A. They're a publisher.

Q. And you thought they would be a good subsidiary for D. C. Heath?

A. D. C. Heath, that's right.

Q. And in 1975, of course, Mr. Fox was the president of D. C. Heath, wasn't he?

A. I'm vague on that. Probably was, yes, but I'm not sure of that.

Q. Not sure?

A. Because he went in and out of the Planning job, and I don't know the dates.

Q. Okay. Now, you've told us that prior to your knowledge of any published policy, there was an unwritten policy that only you could approve fees, isn't that right?

A. That's right.

Q. So that no investment banker or broker who brought anything to one of your subordinates, Fox or Seaman, and continued to work on it had any assurance he would be paid anything even if you acquired the company? Is that the way it was?

A. That's not true.

Q. Okay. Tell us how it was.

What would a broker get if he didn't get your personal assurance of a fee?

A. I think very often we wrote down our fee agreements with people. We had started dealing with very major investment bankers, like Morgan Stanley, like Goldman Sacks, and so forth, where I knew the principals very well, they knew me very well, and it's only in the period around 74, '75, that a lot of lesser investment bankers started to come into our picture, like Mr. Bushkin, and also at the same time appeared many charlatans.

Q. That was '74 and '75?

A. Yes. Many charlatans who—

Q. Mr. Phillips, do you remember my question?

MR. MASTERMAN:

May he finish his answer?

THE WITNESS:

I'd like to finish my answer, please.

MR. BAILEY:

I'd like him to answer it, your Honor.

THE COURT:

Let him answer.

A. And these people would put their brand on any company that you might think of wanting and subsequently come back and ask for a fee. And I was very cautious about this kind of investment banker.

And my approach had been as soon as, you know, something came to us, that I would ascertain that, in fact, the finder had some legitimate contact with the company, and it wasn't just something he read in the paper and submitted to us.

You know, there was a period of—

THE COURT:

All right.

Q. No, please. Could you answer the question, Mr. Phillips?

THE COURT:

What's your next question?

Q. Could a broker be in a position to collect a fee for his legitimate work short of getting that permission from you or through you? Could he?

A. It would have to be with approval from me.

Q. So that if brokers were continuing to bring deals and work on deals and present deals in expectation of fees in each case where you hadn't approved it, they were out of luck, is that right?

A. After I ascertained they had something legitimate to offer, then a fee would be—would be—would be ascertained.

Q. When is the first time you ever heard Mr. Bushkin's name, Mr. Phillips, if you recall?

A. When is the first time?

Q. Right.

A. Probably about this time of this letter.

Q. About 1975?

A. 1975, yes.

Q. Now, are you including him with one of the charlatans that showed up in 1974 and 5?[16]

A. Uhm—Mr. Bushkin had a habit of dropping names.

Q. Please answer the question. Was he in 1974 and '5 a person you knew to be a charlatan broker?

A. No. In '75, no.

Q. If that had been the case, would you have invited him into your hotel suite and asked him to work on a deal?

A. In '75 I did not think that. I thought he had legitimate ties to Mr. Ettinger.

Q. Did you know how long Mr. Bushkin had been bringing matters to Raytheon?

---

[16] Since the witness has succeeded in getting before the jury (in a nonresponsive answer) the notion that "charlatan" brokers were beginning to besiege Raytheon in 1974-75, I thought it best to get him to turn his hole card face up and take a position: Was Bushkin—in his view—a "charlatan" in 1975, or wasn't he. Phillips backed down, as well he should, else he might have had to explain why, with his apparent personal approval, he allowed this *public* company to continue to do business with Bushkin through *1977.*

A. I did not know.

Q. Did you know with whose authority he had been bringing them to Raytheon?

A. Had to be either Seaman or Fox, one or the other.

Q. Did you know that when Fox turned over the post to Seaman, he said that Bushkin was one of the top ten people he dealt with? Did you know that?

A. I did not know that.

Q. All right. Did you know that prior to leaving his post, Mr. Fox had entertained 18 different proposals from Mr. Bushkin?

A. I did not know that.

MR. MASTERMAN:

I object to that, your Honor.

THE COURT:

Overruled.

MR. MASTERMAN:

"Entertain" means what? Telephone call for a minute?

THE COURT:

Next question.

BY MR. BAILEY:

Q. Did you know that the Allyn & Bacon deal wherein you met Mr. Bushkin was the 26th deal he had brought to Raytheon?

A. I did not know that.

Q. All right.

A. The other 25 did not come to my attention evidently.

Q. Okay. So that if your vice president asked for information, it never came to you or, if it did, you don't associate the name "Bushkin," is that correct?

A. I associate the name "Bushkin" for the first time with Allyn & Bacon.

Q. So if the vice president was saying about any of these, Tom Phillips says he doesn't want it, that would have been made up, wouldn't it?

A. What do you mean by "made up"?

Q. Well, if the vice president never brought you the information and went back and told the broker, Tom's looked at it and doesn't like it, that would be false, wouldn't it?

A. It would be if he said that.

Q. Okay.

A. If somebody lied it would be a lie, I agree with that.

Q. Yes. A lie is a lie, isn't it?

A. That's right.

Q. Did you ever hear of Mohasco?
A. Vaguely.
Q. Did you ever hear of Fuqua Industries?
A. Vaguely.
Q. Did you ever hear of Gable Industries?
A. No.
Q. Victor Comptometry?
A. Vaguely.
Q. U.S. Truck Lines of Delaware?
A. No.
Q. NCR Information Systems?
A. Yes.
Q. Avco, New Holland Division?
A. Never heard of it.
Q. Standard Kollsman Instrument Manufacturer?
A. Yes.
Q. Do you have any idea how it was that you heard of these companies?
A. I've heard of them because they're in the public domain.
Q. Were they ever presented to you, sir?
A. Not to my recollection.
Q. None of these companies that I've mentioned were ever presented—
A. Not that it left any impact with me.
Q. Did you ever look at Fuqua Industries?
A. Possibly.
Q. Where do you think it came from, or don't you know?
A. I have no idea.
Q. Did you ever inquire?
A. No.
Q. When Mr. Bushkin made a claim against you in 1979 before you had even acquired Beech, did you cause an inquiry to be made of your corporate records to find out who he was and where he came from?
A. When he made a claim on Beech, it's the first time I ever heard of Bushkin related to Beech.
Q. I didn't ask you that. I asked you whether or not you caused an inquiry to be made by one of your staff members as to who Mr. Bushkin was relating to Raytheon and where he came from.
A. I'm sure I went to my general counsel and I got his letter and turned it over to him to look at the records.

Q. And did someone bring to your attention that according to your own corporate records Mr. Bushkin had been bringing deals to Raytheon since 1971?

A. No. That did not come out.[17]

Q. Are you learning that for the first time today, if it is the truth?

A. '71? Yes. I don't recall Mr. Bushkin back in '71.

Q. Would you be learning for the first time today, if it turns out to be the truth, that Mr. Bushkin brought deals to your company in 1972?

A. As I told you, as I testified, I first learned of Mr. Bushkin with regard to Allyn & Bacon in 1975.

Q. I'm asking you now whether you have since learned since this has become a controversy about any deals that were done in 1971, '2, '3 or '4.

A. No. Didn't know about them.

Q. Okay. So if what I'm telling you turns out to be correct, you are learning it for the first time today, Mr. Phillips, is that right?

A. That's probably true, yeah.

Q. Okay. That's probably true?

A. It's true.

Q. It is true. Okay.

A. It's true.

Q. Thank you.

When was an investment banker prior to the published fee policy, which we'll get to in a while—when was an investment banker entitled to anything from Raytheon if he dealt with him and Raytheon made an acquisition?

A. An investment banker would be due a fee if he brought a company

---

[17] Louis Nizer always counseled that in testing a witness's credibility, always keep one eye on the "probabilities" that arise from the human experience. Coupled to that is the notion that a cross-examiner's dream is a sharply pointed question where any answer offered leaves the witness badly wounded. Such was the case here. If in 1979 when the Bushkin claim was received Raytheon's corporate records were not combed for all evidence of Bushkin which they might reveal, there were three possibilities:

(1) Raytheon viewed Bushkin as too puny—no matter the merits of his claim—to put up a serious fight for his money against the mighty corporate juggernaut that was Raytheon

(2) Raytheon's legal department was too incompetent to perceive the urgent need for such information; or

(3) (And most likely) Phillips had been given a complete background on Bushkin, and promptly forgot what he had been told as if it were trivia.

Any of the above were just dandy from the plaintiff's viewpoint.

to us and effected an introduction to the principals and later on a deal was consummated. Then an investment banker would be due a fee.[18]

Q. Okay. If an investment banker did all of those things or tried to—

A. Or tried to?

Q. Or tried to.

—and before being given an opportunity to perform, you switched bankers on him, would he be entitled to anything?

A. It all depends on whether he had something substantive to bring to the party or not when he mentioned the company.

Q. Okay.

A. Just calling up and mentioning a company does not entitle him to a fee.

Q. Well, supposing that he had met with the principals of the company to be acquired, the one he was proposing; supposing that he had learned of their specific conditions and desires and requirements as to who could acquire them, what kind of company it would have to be and what the terms would be; and supposing for a whole year he stayed abreast of that situation when dealing with another client and brought that information to Raytheon based upon which you bought the company.

Would he be entitled to a fee?

MR. MASTERMAN: Is this a hypothetical?

THE COURT: It appears to be.

MR. MASTERMAN: If it's a hypothetical—

THE COURT: It's a hypothetical.

MR. MASTERMAN: —it's certainly not based on the facts in this case.

THE COURT: It's up to the jury what the facts are.

MR. MASTERMAN: If it's a hypothetical, then you may answer.

Is that a hypothetical?

MR. BAILEY: Yes.

THE COURT: It's a hypothetical. Overruled.

You may answer.

---

[18] In view of Phillips's earlier derisive remarks about "little" investment bankers and brokers, I thought the time was ripe to pin him down as to just what criteria *he* recognized as being sufficient to earn a fee. He obliged in what he thought, no doubt, was a clever fashion, for he knew full well that Bushkin had *not* accomplished his (Phillips's) introduction to the principals of Beech. I finally felt that I had one hand on the witness's throat, since it was manifest from the undisputed evidence that Bushkin had done all that Phillips had required *except* the personal introduction. Of that he was obviously capable—he had done it for the Ethyl Corporation in 1974—but *Phillips never gave him the chance to perform,* a no-no in the world of contracts.

A. If we acquired the company based on the facts he brought, he would be due a fee.

Q. All right. At what point in his activity, Mr. Phillips, would that entitlement arise? If he brought the company, furnished information, was requested to get more, furnished more information, at what point did he have any claim on that acquisition as the basis for a fee?

A. Don't forget, I also said—

Q. Can you, please, answer the question?

A. Yes.

Q. At what point in the transaction does he have any basis for a claim for a fee?

A. If he accomplished the introduction, as well, and then we went on and acquired the company, he would be due a fee.

Q. Supposing he offered to accomplish the introduction and you wouldn't let him.

A. He would have to accomplish the introduction.

Q. Oh. So any time that a broker worked hard to bring you a company and offered to introduce you to the principals, which meeting you wanted, you could shut him off and get rid of him. Is that right, sir?

A. I could shut him off. But if I didn't know he existed, I couldn't very well shut him off because even though he was there—

Q. If he existed according to documents with your own company and you forgot it, is that his fault, Mr. Phillips?

A. I forgot it?

Q. Yes. Assume that you forgot it. Is that his fault?

A. If a company—if he brought a company to us—

Q. No, please. Could you answer the question?

If you forget the broker, is that his fault?

A. No, it's not his fault.[19]

Q. Oh. Now, based on all that you have learned about this transaction since your company got sued from your employees and documents, particularly those addressed to you and others, is it your claim as you

---

[19] This one answer probably governed—more than any other single factor—the outcome of the trial. In a way, it may have been both deliberate and brilliant on Phillips's (or counsel's) part to make this concession, or it may have been simply the snare grabbing the witness by the foot, rather than the throat. To have "overlooked" Bushkin's entitlement to compensation is certainly a much more acceptable human foible than a deliberate attempt to strong-arm or cheat him out of it. Nonetheless, there was a remaining and formidable hurdle, one which had not been accomplished directly in the first trial: the establishment of Raytheon's "rekindled" interest in Beech prior to January 24, 1977.

sit here today that in 1975 Merle Bushkin had nothing to do with Raytheon about the Beech Corporation?

A. Merle Bushkin brought the Beech Corporation suggestion to Mr. Seaman. Mr. Seaman took it to me. I told Mr. Seaman, We have absolutely no interest in it. Mr. Bushkin was promptly notified. Based on that, Mr. Bushkin did not earn a fee.

Q. Because you told Mr. Seaman that even though Mr. Bushkin had brought the material and even though you asked him to augment it—

A. I did not ask him to augment it, I'm sorry.

Q. When Mr. Seaman called Mr. Bushkin and said, Tom Phillips wants additional information, that was false?

A. I did not recall—I do not recall asking for additional information. I do not recall the presentation.

Q. You don't recall anything about it, do you, Mr. Phillips?

A. I don't recall that presentation because I had no interest in Beech at all at the time.

Q. You had an interest in Beech in 1969, didn't you?

A. I did.

Q. And they turned you away.

A. They didn't turn us away. In 1971 we went away from that, and I didn't rekindle any interest in general aviation until 1977.

Q. Mr. Phillips, you didn't dissipate your interest in Beech totally until October 8, 1973, at which point you wrote it off as an acquisition. Isn't that true?

A. In October 1973 I think there is documentation from me to Seaman that says, We have absolutely no interest in general aviation and Beech, but probably that lack of interest preceded that, as well.

Q. All right.

A. And also followed it.

Q. Fine.

Mr. Phillips, do you remember anything about Beech Aircraft Company in 1974 and '5?

A. Nothing.

Q. Nothing.

A. No. Let me qualify that. I do remember one thing, please.

Q. Okay.

A. Beech Aircraft was mentioned in a trivial way to us four or five times in the early '70s, '71, '2, '3, '4, '5, '6 possibly.

Q. Name the people who mentioned them.

A. Don't know them, any of them.

Q. Any way we can find it out?

A. It was trivial all the way.

Q. Any kind of records?

A. No records because the chief executive had no interest.

Q. Any memo from the chief executive saying, Seaman, this is the fifth time. Don't bring me Beech anymore?

A. The chief executive said, Go away. I don't want to hear about general aviation. I don't want to hear about Beech.

Q. And you permitted Bob Seaman to defy you, Mr. Phillips?

A. I don't know. I can't understand to this day why Bob Seaman studied Beech in 1975. I had no interest in it whatsoever.

Q. But you do know, sir, don't you, isn't that so? It was because you were making him feel good, isn't that true?

(The witness gave no response.)

Q. You were humoring him.

A. I listened to his presentations from time to time just to maintain my position as his supervisor and go over it. In 1975 I was totally consumed with the energy field and stayed that way for the next two years.

Q. Did you turn Beech away in June and July of 1975 because you were so consummately tied up with ITE Imperial's acquisition?

A. That's right. That was the energy company I was looking at then, energy distribution.

Q. Are you really sure of that, sir?

A. Well, sometime in that period.

Q. The fact is the presentation to you of Beech Aircraft occurred on June 27, 1975. Do you deny that?

A. It's on the record, I think.

Q. The fact is your company said under oath that the ITE Imperial deal died 14 days before. Do you deny that?

A. I don't know that. You have the records. I don't.

Q. I'll show you an interrogatory put to you and ask you to publish it, please. The one that's answered June 13, 1975.

(Witness examining document)

THE COURT: All right. We're going to take a twenty-minute—you didn't get your twenty minutes before, so we'll take a twenty-minute break at this time.

(Morning recess at 11:20 a.m.)

(Court reconvened at 11:43 a.m.)

(The jury entered the courtroom.)

THE CLERK:

Court is reopened. You may be seated.

BY MR. BAILEY:

Q. Mr. Phillips, when we adjourned I asked you to compare Interrogatory "I" with Answer "I", and tell the court whether or not Raytheon on its oath admits that the negotiations with ITE Imperial terminated on June 13, 1975.

A. It says here—I'll read "I."

This is the date when negotiations between ITE Imperial and Raytheon regarding an acquisition and merger—

(Off the record)

A. Starting with "I," I read:

The date when negotiations between ITE Imperial and Raytheon regarding an acquisition or a merger between ITE Imperial and Raytheon terminated and the amounts of any fees paid by Raytheon and ITE Imperial to investment bankers, brokers—

Q. Please, Mr. Phillips—

A. —or finders—

Q. —read "I" and the answer to "I," if you will, not "J."

A. I don't know what the answer to "I" is.

Q. It's on the next page. Would you look at it and read it? It's your answer.

A. Answer No. 4. Excuse me.

(Pause)

A. "June 13, 1975."

Q. All right. Now, when a deal is done, it's done, isn't it, Mr. Phillips?

A. Yes.

Q. When a deal is terminated, you don't hang around and waste your time or Raytheon's ruminating about it, do you?

A. That's right.

Q. So any claim on your part that a presentation in late June of 1975 when this terminated in mid-June was of no importance because you were agonizing with ITE wouldn't be correct, would it, Mr. Phillips?

A. The ITE deal terminated on June 13, 1975, but my interest in energy did not terminate.

Q. Oh?

A. It stayed on.

Q. Do you recall giving a deposition on January 22, 1981?

A. I gave a deposition sometime. I don't know the date.

Q. All right. Have you reviewed a deposition that you gave in 1981 recently?

A. Yes. I reviewed my deposition recently.

Q. How recently?

A. Last week.

Q. How carefully?

A. I read it.

Q. All right. Is your recollection good enough to remember what you read substantively?

A. Probably, yeah.

Q. Now, how recently have you reviewed your testimony from 1985? December 5, I think, was the date.

A. Last week, as well.

Q. And how much time did you spend reviewing it, Mr. Phillips?

A. Long enough to read it.

Q. In other words, you just read it; you didn't study it, check it?

A. I read it; that's all.

Q. Did you ever compare the two?

A. No, not really. I just read them.

Q. All right. Now, have you generally as an executive officer with a very large corporation enjoyed a good memory to help you through each day?

A. Let me qualify that, Mr. Bailey.[20]

Q. Yeah.

A. I have a good memory on substance, on important things that happened.

Q. All right.

A. I do not have a good memory on dates.

Q. Dates give you trouble?

A. Dates give me trouble; that's right, sir.

Q. But memories can be refreshed by things like corporate records?

A. That's right.

Q. And, in fact, your memory is so good that you never take notes of phone conversations, do you?

A. I didn't say my memory was that good that I don't take notes. I just don't take notes.

---

[20] Having been punched around a bit on matters of memory, Phillips decided to take a stance: Memory good for *substance*—"on important things"—not for *dates.* Subsequently, it was conceded that *names* did not stick in Phillips's memory, either. This tactic immediately rose up to bite the witness on the rump, since he quickly conceded that he had *no* memory of discussing the acquisition of Beech in 1975, even though that would have been even as of that date and at that (much lower) price, Raytheon's largest acquisition ever.

Q. Well, is that because you don't need to in order to remember things that are important?
A. Things that are important in the time scale that I might use them, that's right.
Q. And also when you go to meetings you don't take notes, do you?
A. I sometimes scribble notes to myself. I never publish a memo on my impressions of a meeting.
Q. Did you right at the outset of your deposition which you read last week say, I do not take notes of phone calls or at meetings? Did you say that?
A. I did say that.
Q. All right. Was it true?
A. Subsequently, someone was able to give me some scribbling that I did take.
Q. That was in Kewanee, wasn't it?
A. At Kewanee I did do some scribbling.
Q. We'll get to that. But that, you said, was extraordinary?
A. It was unusual. I normally do not take notes.
Q. You said, I believe, that it was because you had trouble remembering names and you wrote down all the names, right?
A. Probably.
Q. Those notes didn't have dates; they had names, didn't they?
A. They had names and what the business of Kewanee was, things to remind me.
Q. Okay. Now, do you have trouble with names as well as dates in your memory?
A. Probably yes, yeah.
Q. Okay. Do you recall saying in the deposition, I don't remember having conversation with anyone in 1975 with regard to Beech Aircraft Corporation?
A. Yes, I said that.
Q. All right. Is it true?
A. I believe that.
Q. As you sit there today, you have absolutely no recollection of discussing what was proposed as a $130 million acquisition?
A. What $130 million acquisition? Excuse me?
Q. That was the price of Beech in 1975, sir. Not 800; 130. Did you know that?
A. No, I didn't know that.
Q. No?

A. No, I do not recall discussing Beech in 1975.

Q. So if Mr. Seaman made a presentation to you, thought you had some interest and, pursuant to your direction, wrote you a memo telling you who brought the deal and the answers to the questions you had posed, all of that has so little substance, it could slip out of your memory, is that right?

A. Yeah. Mr. Bailey, you will recall in 1973 when the Beech deal fell apart with Grumman—

Q. What do you mean, I would recall?

A. Let me finish, please.

—Mr. Seaman also brought Beech to me then. And I distinctly have in writing and it's in the record: Bob, this may be a good deal for Grumman; it's not for Raytheon. We have no interest.

Q. That was October 8, 1973, wasn't it?

A. And that's stayed through '74, '5 and '6.

Q. When I brought that to your attention little while ago, you said your last interest had been in '71, hadn't it?

A. Mr. Bailey—

Q. Didn't you?

A. —our interest in Beech was in '69.

Q. Did you say that, sir?

A. In '69 was the time we visited Beech. How long after that we stayed interested, I really don't know.

Q. Did you testify that it ended in '71?

A. I testified it ended in '71. It could have ended in '74. I don't know.

Q. Did I then bring to your attention that you talked about it in '73 on October 8?

A. We talked about it only to reject it.

Q. Isn't that the date on which you said, It's a good deal for Grumman, Bob, but not for us?

A. I said that.

Q. All right.

A. It's in my handwriting.

Q. Was Raytheon in 1973 not interested in acquiring a general aviation company?

A. That's absolutely correct.

Q. Was Raytheon in 1969 interested in acquiring a general aviation company?

A. Possibly then, yes. We explored it then seriously.

Q. You authorized your people to go make it.

A. We did explore it. We were interested then, that's right.

Q. What changed?

A. Well, you'll have to give me an opportunity to explain this.

Q. I asked a question that invites an explanation. Have at it.

A. Yes. Please let me explain.

Q. Yes.

A. During the late '60s we acquired companies in appliances, in energy services, in publishing, and in construction. And this lasted into 1972 or '3. With each successive acquisition of fields, it became increasingly difficult for us to manage yet one additional field of endeavor. And, therefore, in '69 general aviation was still acceptable. By the time 1972 or '3 had come, it would be too great a burden for us to take on yet another field of endeavor.

Q. Okay. So—

A. One of the reasons I got interested in energy, in addition to the energy crunch, I thought because we were already in energy services, we could handle that. But general aviation seemed beyond our ability to really get to know the market and manage it well. And, therefore, during that period of time I rejected it because I thought it would overburden Raytheon and overburden me.

Q. In '73 you rejected it.

A. Yes.

Q. With your note to Bob Seaman.

A. That's right.

Q. All right. When is your next recollection of ever hearing the name "Beechcraft" uttered in connection with Raytheon?

A. I suspect the first time was when Royal Little brought it to me as something we ought to reconsider.

Q. That was November 1976, was it not?

A. I think so.

Q. And you told him, Yes, I'm interested, didn't you?

A. Not right away, no. No, that's not true. At that time Mr. Little was looking to interest me in something because we had paid him a $50,000 fee, and up until then he had brought nothing to us. He suggested we look at two companies: one was Beloit in Wisconsin, in the field of paper and forestry; and the other was Beech.

I told him I was willing to go see Beloit. And in February of 1977 I told him, Yes, go try to organize a meeting with Mrs. Beech. I'm willing to have meetings. That does not say we were hell-bent for acquiring either company at those times.

Q. Is that your answer?

A. That's right.

Q. Now, I'll put the question to you: Did you tell Royal Little on November 29, 1976, I am interested in Beech? Yes or no?

A. I am interested in having a meeting with Mrs. Beech.[21]

Q. Did you tell Angus MacDonald in December 1976, I am interested in Beech?

A. I'm interested in having a meeting with Mrs. Beech.

Q. Now, what is Raytheon's policy as to broker protection if they bring Raytheon a deal in terms of years, sir?

A. Well, our policy writes, It's good for two years.

Q. Was it in 1975 and 6 the same policy that was published in April of '76?

A. I would think so.

Q. The two years didn't change, did it, Mr. Phillips?

A. No.

Q. All right. Did Mr. Seaman have the authority to entertain from an investment banker a proposal?

A. Mr. Seaman carried on studies in hundreds of companies and hundreds of fields.

Q. Please answer the question.

Did he have the authority to entertain—

A. "Entertaining" means only taking it under consideration and performing studies.

Q. Would you answer the question: Did he have the authority to entertain it? Don't define it for me.

A. Yes. To entertain it, yes.

Q. That was his job, wasn't it?

A. Yes.

Q. Had Mr. Fox before him had that authority?

A. Mr. Fox worked in conjunction with Mr. Seaman doing that, yes.

---

[21] Bingo! Although the witness may not have appreciated the legal significance of his answer, everyone else in the case did. His admission that in *1976*—well before the two-year cutoff date—he had expressed a wish to meet with Mrs. Beech was more than sufficient to get us "rekindled" within the essential window of time. From this point forward, Judge Harrington observed that the case was in "quite a different posture" than it had been before Judge Skinner at the first trial.One might have terminated the examination at this juncture, since the two points theretofore made were sufficient to support a sound argument that Phillips had *conceded,* in essence, that Bushkin had a right to *some* compensation. Certainly a decision to quit and sit down could not have been faulted. However, I thought that a little additional "witness bashing" might bear favorably on *how much* Raytheon might be ordered to pay. In view of the fact that Bushkin could show little more than a few hours of actual work on the Raytheon-Beech deal, a jury tolerant of Phillips's conduct might return a modest verdict indeed.

Q. Do you think that's why prior to the time you ever met Mr. Bushkin he had made 25 presentations to Raytheon that you didn't know about because he—

A. He may have made 25 mentions, but—in that time scale. I don't know how many of them came to me at all.

Q. Have you any doubt that on January 28, 1975, Bushkin called Seaman and said, You guys should look at Beech? Any doubt?

A. The record says so.

Q. Okay. Is it also true that in March 1975 ITE was hot and occupying your time?

A. That's correct.

Q. So that if Mr. Seaman said to Mr. Bushkin in March, "Put this on hold, ITE Imperial is everything for the moment," that would be substantively correct, wouldn't it?

A. Probably, yes.

Q. Okay. Now, if Mr. Seaman called Mr. Bushkin on June 18, 1975, and said, ITE died last week and Beechcraft is number one, I would like to present it to Mr. Phillips, I want you to know that, would that have been in correct time sequence?

A. You'll have to ask Mr. Seaman that.

Q. We will. I'm asking you if it would have been in the correct time sequence.

A. It could have been, yes.

Q. All right. What is an acquisition log at Raytheon Company, Mr. Phillips?

A. An acquisition log is all the hundreds and thousands of companies that we consider over the number of years. It's a matter of the—the team, the Planning team, keeping track of what they're doing.

Q. What is the purpose of the acquisition log? Just for them to keep track of the—

A. Keep track of what they're doing, that's right; what's active and what isn't.

Q. Isn't it also the purpose of the acquisition log to keep a record of which broker brings which idea first?

A. That was included in the log, yes.

Q. All right. Now, was this acquisition log created with your authority, sir?

A. I knew of it.

Q. All right. Did you know of it because you were told, We have logged so-and-so in on such-and-such a deal, to keep it straight?

A. Yeah. I very seldom looked at the acquisition log.

Q. I understand that. Did you ever look at it?

A. Very rarely. Once in a while.

Q. But you were aware it existed?

A. I was aware it existed.

Q. And you were aware that it was being used to keep track of what brokers came on what dates with what deals?

A. Not necessarily what brokers, what companies, what—what—what situations, what fields, was the primary thing. The broker was additional information that was included in the log.

Q. Well, the log form called for the name of the broker. Was that an accident?

A. That was one of the entries.

Q. Okay.

A. One of the entries in the log.

Q. Did you learn in 1975 in June that on the 17th day of that month someone at Raytheon had entered Mr. Bushkin's name as the person who suggested or offered Beech to Raytheon?

A. I did not know that.

Q. All right. But it would have been done in the ordinary course of business if it was done, right?

A. If it was done, it would have been in there, that's right.

Q. And if you had wanted to know when Beech was presented to you—whether you remember it or not, if you had wanted to know who was in the deal, the acquisition log could have told you, right?

A. That's correct.

Q. Particularly since the entry was ten days before the presentation, right?

A. Right.

Q. Okay. Now, do you have any idea what Beech was worth in 1975?

A. I had no interest in Beech in 1975.

Q. I didn't ask you that.

A. I did not know what it was worth.

Q. Had no idea?

A. None whatsoever.

Q. Did you have an idea what its earnings were?

A. None.

Q. What was your earnings multiple in '75? About twelve to one?

A. I don't know in '75.

Q. Okay. Do you remember when you first authorized the use of an acquisition log?

A. I don't think the acquisition log originated with me.

I think that the Planning people started it by themselves to keep track of things, and it was in the picture.

Q. Did they do it without telling you, or did you know about it?

A. I saw it. You know, people have a right to keep records of what they're doing, to keep track of things.

Q. Sure.

A. They did it for their own benefit.

Q. Do you have any idea when you first saw it?

A. I don't know.

Q. Do you remember what it looked like?

Excuse me a minute, sir.

(Pause)

(Plaintiffs' counsel examining plaintiffs' exhibits)

Q. Mr. Phillips, I show you Plaintiffs' 8, which purports to be from the records of Raytheon Company and is described on its face as an acquisition log, and I ask you whether or not that's a form with which you are familiar.

A. Yes. I've seen this form before.

Q. Okay. Can you tell us when?

A. When I saw this particular one?

Q. Mm-hm.

A. I don't recall this particular one. I've seen forms of our acquisition log in different times. This particular copy of 1975 I don't recall.

Q. I'm not asking you about the copy. I'm asking you about the page.

Now, you're aware that this case has been under litigation since 1980.

A. Yes. I have seen this in—Mr. Masterman has showed it to me as part of the evidence. I've seen it recently. I haven't seen it in 1975 or '76 or '77. I saw it just now, just—

Q. But you saw it before Mr. Masterman showed it to you, didn't you?

A. Yes. I saw it when Mr. Masterman showed it to me, absolutely.

Q. When Royal Little said to you on November 29, 1981, (sic) You ought to go take a look at Beech, I looked at them for Textron, they look good, You ought to look at Beech—

A. I don't think 1981 is the correct date.

THE COURT: What date?

MR. BAILEY: I'm sorry, November 29, '76.

THE COURT: Rephrase the whole question.

MR. BAILEY: Certainly.

BY MR. BAILEY:

Q. When Mr. Royal Little suggested Beech late November of '76—

A. Right.

Q. —did you check the acquisition log to see if anybody was there ahead of him?

A. No.

Q. No. Is that because, sir, you had no idea that one existed and, therefore, couldn't resort to it?

A. That an acquisition log existed?

Q. Right.

A. No, that's not true. I knew it existed. I just—I just knew since we had no interest in Beech that Beech would not have been studied. That's what I assumed.

Q. But, Mr. Phillips, it turned out it was studied, whether you forgot it or not.

A. I know. Seaman did it on his own. I don't know why to this day he studied it in '75.

Q. He made the presentation on his own to you. And what did you do?

A. Frankly, I don't know—you know, as I said in my prior testimony, as a good supervisor, I listened to Seaman. Why in the world he was studying Beech in 1975, I have no idea. Please ask him. He wasn't authorized to do it.

Q. Mr. Phillips, did you on January 22, 1981, say on your oath that you had never heard of an acquisition log prior to that date?

A. I probably did. That was in error.

Q. Error?

A. Error.

Q. You were pressed on whether or not you heard of an acquisition log and denied it categorically, didn't you?

A. I just didn't think of the acquisition log as I saw it so seldom.

Q. You denied ever knowing of an acquisition log, did you not?

A. I probably did.[22]

Q. And you knew that part of Bushkin's case was based on entries in your records—

A. I did not know in 1981, I'm sorry.

---

[22] In his deposition early in the litigation, Phillips denied any knowledge that his own company kept a log showing which broker/investment bankers brought which deals to Raytheon for consideration. He went on to explain that the log was such an "unimportant" document that it "slipped his mind" when the question was asked. If he was in fact the sole source of authority as to which brokers were hired, and if he never consulted the acquisition log to determine who had been first to the door in a given case, there must have been a number of broker lawsuits against Raytheon comparable to this one.

Q. What would have caused you to say in 1981, I never heard of an acquisition log, which you tell us today you knew all about?

A. Because I saw it so seldom. It meant so little to me.

Q. Oh. In other words, when the question was put to you, Do you know about an acquisition log? you had seen it so seldom, you thought you were justified in saying no, is that right?

A. That's not true.

Q. Oh.

A. It just slipped my mind. It's an irrelevant piece of paper that I looked at very seldom.

Q. Okay.

A. So when the question was asked then, I didn't think I saw it before so I said no. Subsequently, it's right. On a few occasions I have seen an acquisition log, but very rarely.

Q. After you said no, did you say, I'm not even familiar with that term, "acquisition log"? Did you say that?

A. I don't recall that.

Q. All right. We have your deposition. Would you like a copy?

(Transcript handed to the witness)

A. You'll have to take me to where it is. I don't know where to find it.

Q. I will take you there, sir. Try page 53.

MR. MASTERMAN: What volume?

MR. BAILEY: Deposition. There's only one.

Q. I ask you whether or not—

THE COURT: What page?

MR. MASTERMAN: May we have a page or a line.

MR. BAILEY: Page 53, January 22, 1981.

Question: Have you ever heard of an acquisition log being maintained by anyone from Raytheon?

Answer: No. I'm not familiar with that term.

A. Yeah. I said, "I can't recall it. But it would—you know, it would appear to be the make-up of not a slide presentation but, you know—"

Q. Answer the question.

A. "He would have gone over this document with me."

That's what I read here. I didn't recall, Mr. Bailey.

Q. Did you say no—

A. I am a chief executive who has thousands of things come up on my desk week after week. To recall something that happened in 1975 and 1981 is asking a lot.

Q. All right.

Question: Do you recall having any conversation with Seaman in June 1975 relative to Beech?

Answer: No, not at all.

Question: Are you familiar with the term "acquisition log," sir?

Answer: Not really, no.

Question: Have you ever heard of an acquisition log being maintained by anyone from Raytheon?

Answer: No.

Are those the answers you gave on that day?

A. Yes.

Q. Are those incorrect answers attributed to the fact that you're a busy chief executive?

A. At the time I didn't recall the acquisition log.

Q. When you were being questioned on your oath, did you know why you were there?

A. Yeah.

Q. Did you know it was to sort out the claim made by Mr. Bushkin that he is the one that brought Beech to you and offered to set up a meeting with Mrs. Beech as he had done before? Did you know that when you gave this deposition, sir?

A. When I gave the deposition in '81?

Q. That's right.

A. Did I know that Mr. Bushkin offered to set up a meeting then?

Q. Did you know he claimed that he had brought Beech to your attention, offered to set up a meeting, and that he was entitled to a fee? Did you know that when you gave this deposition?

A. I knew that because he had written me a letter claiming a fee and shocked me with the letter.

MR. BAILEY: May that go out, your Honor, the shock? Nonresponsive.

MR. MASTERMAN: Why?

THE COURT: Overruled. It can stay in.

MR. BAILEY: All right.

BY MR. BAILEY:

Q. Did you understand in 1981, over a year after the shock wore off, that Mr. Bushkin was serious and had brought a lawsuit?

A. Yes.

Q. And that he claimed that he had been promised 1 percent by your subordinate? Did you learn that that was his claim?

A. I learned that from Mr. Bushkin.

Q. All right. Now, did you know that a part of the evidence he was relying on were your own corporate records in this litigation?

A. I didn't know it. I assumed it.

Q. Had you ever heard the term "acquisition log" before you were asked about it in this deposition?

A. I probably did.

Q. All right. So you heard about it, forgot about it, and denied it; is that the sequence?

A. That's right.

Q. Okay.

A. That's right.

Q. Has this happened to you often, sir?

A. Only on things that are very vague in my past recollection that I haven't had much contact with. If I have had substantive contact with it, I don't forget.

Q. What did you pay ultimately for Beechcraft, sir?

A. What did we pay? Somewhere in the vicinity of $800 million.

Q. All right. Would a claim for 1 percent of that money, should it be valid, be of any interest to the chief executive officer of Raytheon?

A. Very much so.

Q. Okay. And is it a matter that you would have researched rather carefully before coming in to give statements under oath about?

A. I should have.

Q. All right. Did you realize that in your very own acquisition file on Beechcraft was located the original of a June 30, 1975, memo to you from Seaman naming Bushkin and giving information about Beech?

A. At the time I didn't know it.

Q. All right. But when you did know it, did you brush it aside as something that you weren't going to be troubled with?

A. Since I had no memory of Bushkin with Beech, my testimony was very simple: I don't recall Bushkin with regard to Beech in any way whatsoever.

Q. All right.

A. That's my testimony today.

Q. Did you testify in 1981 when questioned about this June 30 memo: I saw one document, a memo from Mr. Seaman to me in '75. I spent all of two minutes looking on it—looking at it.

Did you say that?

A. I don't know if I did or not.

Q. Well, look in your deposition at page 43 and see if you said it.

(Witness examining transcript)

A. Yes. It says that here, that I said that in my deposition.

Q. All right. So you mean that you had no recollection of it. Even though it was in your file, when it was brought to your attention, you spent two minutes looking at it?

A. I should have said I must have spent two minutes looking at it because I don't remember it.

Q. You said, I spent all of two minutes looking at it.

A. Yes, I did say that.

Q. And you meant to say by that, That's the most I spent.

A. I meant to say it left no impression on me.

Q. You meant to say that that's all it was worth was two minutes, didn't you?

A. I meant to say I had no interest in Beech.

Q. Take a look at that letter, if you will, sir, and see whether or not that is, in fact, addressed to you. Give us the exhibit number, if you will.

A. What do you want me to read on this?

Q. I want you to give us the exhibit number, which is in pink, and tell us whether or not that's addressed to you.

A. Plaintiffs' Exhibit 11. It's a memo from R.L. Seaman to T.L. Phillips, June 30, 1975.

THE COURT: Is that in evidence?

MR. BAILEY: Pardon me?

THE COURT: Is that in evidence?

MR. BAILEY: Oh, yes, your Honor.

BY MR. BAILEY:

Q. Do memos sent by Mr. Seaman to you normally get any attention from you?

A. Normally, yes. But if I have no interest in the subject, they could be filed from one incoming file to the other without even being read.

Q. Now, you said that you had no memory of being—even hearing the word "Beech" in 1975, isn't that right?

A. That's right.

Q. Okay. So then you could not have said to Mr. Seaman, Don't bother me with Beech. I'm tied up with ITE.

You couldn't have said that, could you?

A. I could have said, I'm tied up with energy. I don't know what I said. All I know is I wasn't interested in Beech.

Q. Sir, please, try to answer the question.

Could you have said to Mr. Seaman in 1975, Don't bother me with Beech. I'm tied up with ETE?

A. "ITE."

Q. "ITE."

A. That's right.

Q. Did you say to Seaman, Don't bother me with Beech. I'm tied up with ITE?

A. I don't know what I said to Seaman.

Q. Did you say on your oath in January of 1981 that that is precisely what you said to Seaman, on page 58 of your deposition, top of the page?

(Witness examining transcript)

A. That's what it—I said I said that to Seaman, that's right.

Q. Now, were you trying to tell the truth there?

A. I testified earlier—

Q. No. Were you—

A. —that I don't remember dates. It was about that time—

Q. Sir—

A. —that I was working very hard on ITE.

Q. You were working hard.

A. Very hard on it. And, therefore, for Seaman to bring me something else was irrelevant and tying me up when I was a very busy guy running all over the country looking at ITE plants.

And, therefore, it's quite possible in 1981 I thought the two coincided. If one ended a few days before, that's irrelevant. I was exhausted from looking at ITE.

Q. You were exhausted.

Do you have severe dysfunction when you're tired?

A. I did not want to take on something else I wasn't interested in shortly after the time when we went through an exhaustive investigation of a major acquisition.

Q. Were you exhausted when you gave this deposition?

A. I don't recall.

Q. All right. Did you say that you told Seaman you were tied up with ITE, don't talk Beech? Did you say that in 1981?

A. I said that.

Q. Was it true in '81 that you said that?

A. Well, it probably missed by a few days. It was effectively true.

Q. If you said, Don't bother me with Beech, then you had to have talked with Seaman prior to June 13th, right, to be tied up with ITE?

A. I don't recall talking to Seaman about Beech in 1975 at all.

Q. But here you said you did recall. Do you want to change that?

MR. MASTERMAN: He didn't say that. Where does he say he talked about it?

Q. Did you tell Mr.—

(Simultaneous speakers)

THE COURT: Is there any objection?

MR. MASTERMAN: I object.

THE COURT: Well, it's effectively cross-examination. Overruled.

MR. MASTERMAN: He is suggesting he said something, and I don't see it in the deposition.

THE COURT: Well—

MR. MASTERMAN: He said, Don't bother me about Beech.

MR. BAILEY: Okay.

THE COURT: The objection is overruled.

BY MR. BAILEY:

Q. That's the question I read. In 1981 you said, I told Seaman that, don't bother me about Beech.

Do you wish to change that now?

A. I essentially must have told Seaman, Don't bother me about any acquisition while I'm tied up.

Q. That wasn't the question.

The question was: Did you say, Bob, don't bother me with Beech?

You said yes.

Do you want to change that? Was Beech in the statement?

A. Since I don't recall anything about Beech in 1975, obviously, I couldn't have specifically recalled to say Don't bother me about Beech.

Q. Well, then, that testimony wasn't true, was it?

A. That's right.

Q. Okay. Does that bother you at all—

A. Uh—

Q. —that you took an oath and didn't give truthful testimony?

A. It bothers me that it isn't precisely correct. But the essence of it was, I am not interested in Beech. Don't bother me with other acquisitions while I'm busy, Seaman. Go away. That's the testimony.

Q. Look at that memo from Seaman to you on June 30 and tell me whether or not that is a memo you would tolerate from an executive who had been told to get out with Beechcraft.

Look at it. Two minutes, if you will, if you need it.

(Witness examining document)

A. If I had read that memo, Mr. Bailey, I would have considered it trivial information.

Q. I didn't ask you that.

When you got the memo with two pages of information about Beech from an officer that had been thrown out of your office for talking about Beech, would you have tolerated this insubordination?

A. Would I have tolerated this insubordination?

MR. MASTERMAN: I object.

A. I'm a very tolerant man, Mr. Bailey.[23]

Q. You are?

A. I'm a very tolerant man.

MR. MASTERMAN: What officer was thrown out of his office? I object.

MR. BAILEY: I'm sorry—

THE COURT: Overruled.

BY MR. BAILEY:

Q. I thought "Don't bother me with Beech" meant go away.
Isn't that what it meant?

A. Go away and let me be because I'm busy.

Q. Okay. And when asked to explain what you meant by that, you said you were "obligated as a staff officer to listen to him when he came in just to keep his morale up, but there was no interest on my part."
Did you make that statement?

A. Yes, I did.

Q. Is that true? Would you listen to your vice president—

A. Yes, I would from time to time.

Q. All right.

A. I listen to my treasurer when he brings all kinds of loan situations and I'm not very interested, but I'm obligated to listen to him so he can go out and do his job well.

Q. When you say, Don't bother me with Beech and then he comes in with Beech, do you keep his morale up by forgetting your orders? Is that what happens?

A. I don't—I told him in '73, Don't bother me with Beech, and several other times that it came up from several other brokers.

Q. Okay.

A. As I testified, I don't know why Seaman studied Beech. I really don't.

Q. Okay.

---

[23] When St. Peter greets Tom Phillips at the gate—as I have no doubt he will some day do—he will probably commend him for many enviable earthly accomplishments. In my view—based on a study of his three different testimonial experiences in this case—tolerance will not be high on the list. I glanced at the jury when this answer was uttered, and picked up two winks.

A. It's possible as a former aviator he is interested in flying. I don't know. But it was an irrelevancy in 1975.

Q. I see. Did you tell Mr. Seaman, Bob, go away. I'll listen to your presentations, but I have no interest.

Did you make that statement to your own vice president?

A. Probably something like that, sure. I'm tolerant but frank.

Q. When you tell Bob Seaman to go away, does he do it or does he just keep coming on back?

(The witness gave no response.)

Q. What's been your experience with him? Defiance?

A. My experience is on major issues of committing the company, he is very good. On conducting studies on his own, he will go off on a tangent once in a while. That's my experience with him.

Q. Now, looking at that memo, is there anything in there that would give a reasonably prudent chief executive officer some hint that there was an investment banker in the picture on Beech as of 1975?

A. Yes. It mentioned Bushkin.

Q. Okay. Is that the kind of thing that would slip your memory immediately you read it?

A. I don't know that I even read it.

Q. You don't know if you read it, so you can't know that you didn't, can you?

A. I can't—since I don't recall Beech or Bushkin or anything else in 1975, I don't know whether I read the memo.

Q. But if Mr. Seaman says he had talked with you about it and you asked him questions and asked Bushkin for more information through him, are we to believe he made that up?

A. I can't believe I asked for more questions because I wasn't interested. And, therefore, if—if Seaman asked Bushkin additional questions, he asked them on his own.[24] I could not have asked for more information. I had no interest in Beech.

Q. So on June 27, which is the established date of the presentation to you of Beech, you said, Go away. Right? Is that right?

A. Something equivalent to that.

---

[24] Finally! Even if we had no Seaman in the courtroom to set off against his former boss, we had both his memorandum and his deposition which clearly showed that in June, 1975, Phillips's interest in Beech was such that he had *directed* Seaman to get additional information from Bushkin, which was done. The assertion that Seaman was in fact taking such steps "on his own" was the kind of flat contradiction that makes for a dream final argument: "Ladies and gentlemen, *at least one* of these two rascals isn't being truthful with you. *You* can decide which one that might be."

Q. Do you now remember the presentation on June 27?

A. No. No, I do not.

Q. If you don't remember it, sir, how can you tell this jury under oath what you did in response to it?

A. Because it all went away. It went away. The whole—

Q. What went away?

A. The whole Beech issue went away in '75.

Q. But the acquisition log didn't go away, did it?

A. No. But Raytheon did nothing on Beech in '75, wanted to do nothing.

Q. Wait a minute now. You said Raytheon did nothing.

Are you Raytheon?

A. Yes.

Q. All right.

A. I'm the chief executive; I'm Raytheon.[25]

Q. You're the boss.

A. That's right.

Q. Okay. And anybody who does anything in the name of Raytheon other than you is not acting for Raytheon despite his title, isn't that so?

(The witness gave no response.)

Q. Isn't that so?

A. People can make studies and evaluate things. But to take actions, affirm contracts, then they have to come to me for authority.

Q. Isn't it apparent to you as you look at that memo now, sir, that Mr. Seaman was leading Mr. Bushkin down the primrose path in asking him for more information for you?

A. I don't see "more information" in this memo, Mr. Bailey.

THE COURT: What's the date of that memo?

MR. BAILEY: July 30, 1975—June 30.

THE WITNESS: June 30, 1975.

Q. Would you read it, please? Would you read the memo and then we'll talk about.

A. You want me to read the whole memo?

---

[25] "I'm Raytheon." That was really what the litigation was all about. Had the Securities and Exchange Commission been a party to this lawsuit, a much more keen interest might have been shown in the assertion that one individual was in fact the *persona* of a company in which millions of shareholders had invested millions of dollars. As it was, this bold proposition was an automatic weapon for the plaintiff's closing, triggered again and again to argue why the irascible and patently unfair position of the defendant had made litigation necessary.

Q. Yes.

A. All right.

Further to my recent conversation on Beech Aircraft Corporation, the following information has been obtained.

1. In conversation with Harry Evans—

Q. I'm sorry, sir—

A. —I learned that his original contact—

You asked me to read the memo. I'm going to read it.

Q. Please, sir. You're reading so fast that the court reporter is having trouble again. I can't understand you. I have doubts that the jury can.

Is the first word you read "further to"?

A. All right.

Further to my recent conversation on Beech Aircraft Corporation, the following information has been obtained:

1. In conversation with Harry Evans, I learned that his original contact at Beech was with the Marketing Manager (Roy McGregor) on a proposed joint program. During this and in a subsequent meeting, Harry discussed the advantages of joining with a larger company and, in particular, promoted Raytheon as a likely candidate.

   He had discussed this issue because there apparently was an opportunity to buy a 22 percent block of Beech at $18 a share through Merrill Lynch. Joe Hoyt was involved, and Harry thought, as well, a Morgan Stanley man whose name he could not recall. In any event, he was not sure that Mr. McGregor ever advanced these views to Beech senior management.

2. In a further conversation this morning with Mr. Merle Bushkin, our contact on this matter, it was confirmed that Mrs. Beech is interested in getting some protection for her investment against cyclical pressures and thought that a merger might be the best way inasmuch as capital gains taxes could be avoided through this route as distinct from selling part of her shares and reinvesting.

   Also, Mr. Bushkin said that Frank Hedrick, Olive Beech's nephew and Beech president, told him that Beech must develop a jet of its own rather than continue to sell only the Hawker BH 125-600 plane and that this kind of project could be carried out better if Beech had the backing of a larger and stronger company. Additionally, Mr. Hedrick suggested that more financing could be done by Beech if they were associated with a company of greater financial strength.

   Mr. Bushkin mentioned again the importance of the dividend payout to Mrs. Beech and other members of her family. It will take some creative work to handle this problem and still be able to pool.

3. We have reviewed all of the public commentary on the Grumman-Beech merger discussions, but none have anything to say about a possible exchange rate or the value of a possible arrangement. I have the feeling that the announcements were quite premature. Incidentally, the Grumman-Navy argument had been settled before the Beech matter was announced.

I will be back from my New York trip before the weekend, so perhaps we could discuss what might be a rational next step in this investigation.

Q. All right. Now, Mr. Phillips, is it apparent to you from the face of that letter and your familiarity with Mr. Seaman that he would not say "further to our recent conversation" if there never had been one? Is that apparent to you?

MR. MASTERMAN: It doesn't say that at all.

MR. BAILEY: Read the words again, the first words.

A. "Further to my recent conversation"—

Q. Thank you.

A. —"on Beech Aircraft"—

MR. MASTERMAN: You said "our." You said "our," sir. You were misstating the record.

MR. BAILEY: I'm sorry.

BY MR. BAILEY:

Q. When Mr. Seaman says to you "further to my recent conversation," does that mean with you or somebody else?

A. I don't know.

Q. You don't know.

A. No.

Q. All right. When Mr. Seaman suggests to you that he has gotten information from Mr. Bushkin that comes directly from the principals of the company being looked at and suggests to you that he has a trip and when he gets back he ought to discuss it further, is that consistent with Mr. Seaman having been told, I don't want to talk about Beech?

(The witness gave no response.)

Q. Is that consistent with your having told him, Forget Beech in 1975, sir?

A. I can't reconcile that.

Q. If he had been told, I don't want anything to do with Beech, and he is sending you memos and asking for further meetings, he's got a little something in the head, hasn't he, to do that?

A. Must have.

Q. Was Mr. Seaman under any psychiatric care in 1975?

A. I don't know.

Q. Did you suggest that maybe he needed some time off for doing that which you ordered him not to do?

A. I don't think so.

Q. Did you remonstrate with him about that memo or send him a terse one back saying, How many times do I have to tell you, keep Beech out of my office? Do you remember doing that?

A. Jeez, I don't remember. I can't tell you that.

Q. Did you look in your records for any response to the memo?

A. There was no response.

Q. That's right?

A. Right.

Q. Is it fair to say that on July 29, 1975, you informed Seaman that you decided against going forward with Beech because it was too cyclical?

A. The records state it. I don't remember it.

Q. If Seaman says that happened and he told that to Bushkin, are you saying that he made that up?

A. If Seaman told Bushkin, We have no interest in Beech, he would be consistent for the first time.

Q. If Seaman told Bushkin, Tom Phillips said today the business is too cyclical, we have no further interest, is that something you would have made up, that you said that?

A. Probably not.

Q. Okay. So it appears that on June 27, 1975, you received a presentation; that on June 30, you received a follow-up memo, Further to our—to my recent conversation; and that a month later and a couple of days you informed your executive of a decision not to buy. That's what appears.

Now, do you say—

A. Not to do anything.

Q. —that you have no memory of any of that?

A. I do not.

Q. Okay. Now, assume that Mr. Bushkin labored under some terrible delusion that someone in the company other than you might have some authority to make a deal with him. Assume that, if you will. And assume that in good faith from January until July—

A. Assume what, please?

Q. Assume that in good faith—

A. Yes.

Q. —from January until July believing that Seaman invited him to go forward—

A. Right.

Q. —he brought you information and offered to arrange a meeting with the principals, which he had done before. Assume that.

A. Assume that. Okay.

Q. Does he now fall within the protection of Raytheon's two-year policy against other brokers?

A. I would have to ascertain that he is capable of arranging such a meeting.

Q. Wouldn't the fact that he had done it before in considerable detail and a full day spent there be some evidence—

A. Not necessarily.

Q. —that would cause you to check it out?

A. Not necessarily.

Q. Oh, it wouldn't.

Did you have any information that Bushkin's relations with Beech were in any way hostile?

A. I had no information. I didn't know he had any relations with Beech.

Q. You didn't even know who he was, you tell us now, right?

A. I knew who he was for the first time when he brought Allyn & Bacon to me.

Q. When you read Bushkin is our contact man in this matter, what did you think he was?

A. I didn't read it.

Q. Oh, you never read that memo?

A. I never read "our contact in this matter" until long afterwards, until after he sued us.

Q. I'm sorry. Are you now taking the position that despite the fact that it has your date stamp on it as received by Tom Phillips, that you never saw that memo until after you bought Beech? Is that what you're telling us?

A. I don't remember it.

Q. Okay. Well—

A. And it's possible I never read it.

Q. It's possible you never read it.

A. It's possible. Quite possible.

Q. It's quite possible you did read it, isn't it?

A. It's possible I read it and paid no attention to it. It's possible I never read it.

Q. If you read it, Mr. Phillips, are your reading habits such that the words "our contact in this matter" would have slipped by you?

A. "Our contact in this matter" would have no importance whatsoever if we had no interest in doing anything with the company. First of all, you have to do something with the company and perform a transaction before "our contact in this matter" has any meaning at all.

Q. Oh?

A. If the deal fell through and nothing happened, our contact is irrelevant.

Q. And there's no need for an acquisition log, is there?

A. During the time you're working on it, you probably should have an acquisition log.

Q. I think I understand.

If you make a decision not to buy something that's presented to you, you are then free to go buy it from someone else. Is that your position, Mr. Phillips?

A. No.

Q. Okay. So since you have no memory one way or the other and since your corporate records show Mr. Bushkin's presence in the case offering to do anything you might ask—

A. I beg your pardon?

Q. —offering to do anything you might ask—

A. Yes.

Q. —do you say you have the right to cut him out?

A. I would have to think that if I—if I were serious about—about an acquisition after this happens, I would have to feel that the broker bringing it to us has a good opportunity to bring off what he purports to say.

Q. Okay.

A. If he doesn't, then I would think I would—I would use some other channel to go to.

Q. Now, Mr. Phillips, did you ever test Mr. Bushkin's ability to arrange the meeting with Olive Beech that you ultimately sought through Little and MacDonald and Robinson? Did you ever test it?

A. Of course not. I didn't even know Bushkin was in the case.

Q. Did he have any right to try to finish what he had started with Raytheon within that two-year period?

A. Didn't know he was involved.

Q. I didn't ask you that.

Did he have any right, sir, to try to finish what he had started if he were capable of doing so?

A. If he were capable.

Q. All right.

A. That's—that has to be tested.

Q. Oh. Doesn't he have a right to show that he can create a meeting, particularly when he's done precisely that same thing before? Doesn't he have that right with you, sir?

A. Possibly.

Q. Are you the kind of man that puts someone down without giving them a chance?

A. In the acquisition business you have to have very credible contacts in order to make out—

Q. Mr. Phillips—

A. —and—

MR. MASTERMAN: May he finish?

MR. BAILEY: He is not answering the question.

Q. Are you the kind of man that puts someone down without giving them a chance?

A. I don't know that Mr. Bushkin was up to the level of arranging the right meetings with Mrs. Beech.

Q. You don't know that he wasn't, do you?

A. No, I don't know that.

Q. All right.

A. The whole thing is hypothetical, anyway, since I've testified and continue to testify I didn't know Bushkin was involved.

Q. Do you think that your testimony, sir, is conclusive on the point by any means? Do you?

A. I don't know.

Q. All right.

A. It's up to the jury to decide that.

Q. And supposing it is found that due to memory flaws on your part of a significant type, you simply forgot that Bushkin's entitlement went past the end of 1976 and brought another broker in, does that justify your act because you forgot?

A. There was no substantive contact between Bushkin and me. There was no contact that I know of with regard to Beech in 1975.

Q. Can you answer the question I put to you; not the one you would like to have heard, but the one I put to you, sir?

A. Repeat it, please.

Q. Certainly. If you simply forgot that there had been brought to your attention both directly and indirectly the name of Bushkin with Beech and he had a two-year entitlement that went past the end of 1976, should the fact that you forgot about it deny him his just compensation, Mr. Phillips?

A. Probably not.

Q. All right. That would be your mistake, not his, wouldn't it?

A. Right.

Q. All right. Now, if someone was thought to be of sufficiently high quality to bring 65 proposals in toto over a period of years to Raytheon and to command the respect and presence of his chief executive officer in a substantial acquisition where he was the only investment broker, wouldn't that show that he was a person of some ability?

MR. MASTERMAN: Which case is he talking about?

MR. BAILEY: Kewanee.

MR. MASTERMAN: Which 65 proposals? Which case are you talking about?

THE COURT: Overruled. Overruled. That's been testified before.

BY MR. BAILEY:

Q. Did you hear the question?

A. Repeat the question.

Q. Assume that Mr. Bushkin in 1971 through 1978 ultimately with your knowledge and approval brought deals to Raytheon, some of which you were personally involved with, and that you urged him to go forward.

Isn't that an indication that he is very good at what he does, in your view?

A. I worked with Mr. Bushkin with Allyn & Bacon. I traveled with him to see Kewanee. I had no other contacts with him on any other acquisition.

My experience with him after Kewanee is that he was a name-dropper; he dropped names of all possible companies far and wide to put his stamp of prior claim on the companies; and, therefore, you could accumulate 300 companies that way, not 78.

Q. Mr. Phillips, name the companies where he dropped the name. Name them.

A. He informed me of Babcock & Wilcox being available—

Q. Mm-hm.

A. —sometime after that. I recall telling him, You're the fifth guy to bring Babcock & Wilcox to me. I'm not interested.

Q. Did he know about the other four?

A. No, I don't—I don't know.

Q. Was he wrong to bring you something without knowing someone else had?

A. He brought me Eastern Gas and Fuel. Eastern Gas and Fuel had their chief executive on our Board for eight years. He was going to introduce me to Eastern Gas and Fuel for a fee. That's ridiculous. You know, that's staking a claim on something that doesn't belong to you.

Q. Mr. Phillips, he told you he knew that the man was on your Board, and you both knew he was dead, didn't you?

(The witness gave no response.)

Q. Didn't you?

A. He was dead, but I knew him for eight years prior to that. And for him to bring me a company that I knew so well is the height of ridiculousness.

Q. Okay.

A. So some of the—many of the 78 you're mentioning I am sure are of that category.

Q. Have you got any other examples to justify this attack, sir, other than the one's you've mentioned?

A. I don't know the names. Harnischfeger. All kinds of name that are sort of wild memories of the past now but, you know, Bushkin had no claim to those companies.

Q. Wait a minute. Harnischfeger in 1973, you said you've got another broker.

A. That's right.

Q. Okay. Within three years, didn't you? We're going to protect him for three years, isn't that what you said in '73?

A. I don't recall.

Q. You don't recall that, but the document would speak for itself if that were true.

A. Right.

Q. Now, you said that Mr. Bushkin had not shown you that he was a person capable of performing what you wanted—that is, a meeting with Olive Ann Beech—right?

A. I don't know that. I doubt that he was capable of doing that but—

Q. And the fact that he had done it for Mr. Gottwald from Ethyl, which was another sizeable company, that doesn't mean a thing, does it?

A. It's irrelevant because I didn't know Bushkin was involved in Beech at all.

Q. Is something in this world irrelevant simply because Tom Phillips doesn't know about it?

A. I wasn't involved; therefore, Raytheon wasn't involved.

Q. You were called upon, I thought you told us a few moments ago, to make a decision as to whether or not Mr. Bushkin was capable of doing something, and you decided maybe he wasn't, you didn't know. Right?

A. Right. It's a hypothetical question whether he would be capable or not, and I don't know. Sitting here to this day, I don't know.

Q. Let's focus late in 1976 when you agree that you went to another broker and talked about Beech. There's no question about that.

A. Another broker brought Beech to us.

Q. All right. If you had known that Bushkin was the first broker to do so and that he had done so less than two years before, you wouldn't have talked to the other broker, would you?

A. That's correct.

Q. All right.

A. I would have said, Let's go back to the original broker.

Q. So you made a mistake, right?

A. I made a mistake. I didn't know Bushkin was involved in Beech.

Q. Well, then he's entitled to be paid, isn't he, Mr. Phillips?

A. Paid for what? He didn't do anything.

Q. For being the broker in the deal that you cut him out of because you got a bad memory.

(Pause)

Q. You don't follow that?

A. He brought something to us at a time we were not interested. We became interested later and, therefore, we paid the broker who brought it to us—

Q. Mr. Phillips—

A. —and arranged the meeting for us.

Q. Please try to focus on late '76.

You had a broker in the picture that you have forgotten about, you say—

A. I never knew of him.

Q. If your records knew about him, Mr. Phillips, Raytheon knew about him, even though you say you're Raytheon. Do you understand that?

A. Mm. I guess so.

Q. All right. Now, if that's the case and if you mistakenly, for failing to keep track of what your people were doing, didn't know that Bushkin was in the case and hired another person in violation of his rights, isn't he entitled to be paid?

(The witness gave no response.)

Q. In fairness, Mr. Phillips?

A. I would guess so.

Q. All right. Thank you.

Now, then, did you authorize Royal Little in November of '76 to go get Beech for you?

A. I don't think so.

THE COURT: I missed that question.

MR. BAILEY: I'm sorry, your Honor. I asked whether or not he authorized Royal Little in November of 1976 to, quote, go and get Beech for you.

A. Not true.

Q. Not true?

A. No.

Q. Did you have an agreement with Royal Little prior to that time about acquisitions?

A. Yes, we did.

Q. Was that agreement, in addition to a cash retainer which had been paid in 1976, I think September 1, also an agreement for certain percentage fees with Mr. Little and Lonsdale? Do you remember that?

A. Yes, I probably did. Right.

Q. All right. Did that call for a half of 1 percent for acquisitions which went together brought to them by you if they were over a hundred million?

A. Right.

Q. Okay. Was that agreement in force and effect in November of 1976, 14 months later?

A. Fourteen months later than what? When was that agreement signed? I don't know.

Q. I'm sorry. September 1 of '76 it was signed.

Was it renewed a year later without an additional retainer?

A. In September of '77?

Q. Yes.

A. Yes. I recall having a one-year agreement where we paid a fee—a retainer of $50,000 and then a subsequent renewal without retainer.

Q. All right. So you had agreed that if Mr. Little could bring you a company that you acquired, that you pay him half of 1 percent of the value of the transaction, right?

A. Yes, I think that's right.

Q. And you agree that Mr. Little, because you had forgotten Mr. Bushkin is the first person—

MR. MASTERMAN: I object.

MR. BAILEY: I'm sorry. I thought he said that.

MR. MASTERMAN: You said that.

Q. Is the—

MR. BAILEY: He said he forgot Mr. Bushkin.

MR. MASTERMAN: You said that.

I object.

(Simultaneous speakers)

THE COURT: Objection sustained.

MR. BAILEY: All right.

THE COURT: I think the evidence is that he has no memory of it.

MR. BAILEY: All right.

THE COURT: It's argumentative. Rephrase the question.

BY MR. BAILEY:

Q. Without awareness of any commitment to Mr. Bushkin, there's no question but in 1976 in November you talked about Beech with Little.

MR. MASTERMAN: I object to that, as well, your Honor. It begs the question. Without awareness of anything. There is no record or evidence that there was any commitment to be aware of or unaware of.

THE COURT: This is, in effect, cross-examination. Objection overruled.

BY MR. BAILEY:

Q. Can you answer the question?

A. Royal Little asked me if his one-year—if his one-year program where we paid him a $50,000 fee could be extended for another year without fee, and I agreed. So essentially Royal Little was under contract to us to bring us acquisitions for an additional year but no fee and with a finder's fee for anything that was consummated.

Q. In 1976 he was in the first year of this contract, wasn't he?

A. I don't recall dates that well. I don't know when—when the contract started and when it ended. I'm sorry. It was two years total.

Q. You assume that it was begun in September of '76?

A. Is that when it started? I don't know. So that must have—that must have been the year we paid him $50,000 retainer then.

Q. Yes.

A. The first year we paid him; the second year we didn't. I remember that.

Q. And by November you had only heard two names brought to you, Beech and Beloit, right?

A. Right.

Q. And November 29 there is no doubt in your mind, is there, that it was Royal Little who suggested that you purchase Beech?

A. That we look at Beech, we look again at Beech. We had looked at it. We had looked at it before. He said, Look at it again.

Q. Okay. "Pursue Beech Aircraft."

A. "Look at it."

Q. All right.

A. He also said to me, Let's look at Beloit.

We looked at both. We wanted to look at both.

Q. When did you look at Beloit?

A. I don't know. Somewhere in that period of time.

Q. Did you have conversation when you looked at Beloit about Beech with anyone in December of 1976?

A. Since I went out there with Royal Little and he was interested in those two companies, that could well have been.

Q. Who else was at that meeting with Beloit?

A. Probably Robison, his partner, but I don't recall exactly. I think Robison.

Q. If they say you went to talk about Beech when you went to look at Beloit, is that—

A. Probably true, yeah.

Q. I ask you whether or not in 1985 on December 5th, page 81—

MR. BAILEY: Has he got a copy of his testimony?

THE COURT: Keep your voice up. I missed that last question.

MR. BAILEY: I just asked if he had a copy of his testimony, your Honor. I'm going to afford him one to refer to.

BY MR. BAILEY:

Q. Would you look at page 81, Mr. Phillips. I ask you if you heard this question and gave an answer under oath as follows.

Question: There's no doubt in your mind, is there, that it was Royal Little who in November 1976 suggested to you that Raytheon pursue Beech Aircraft Corporation?

Answer: Yes. But they had expected to do a lot more, except the deal got away from them. There was nothing further they could do once it got out of their hands. And they understood that.

Do you recall that answer?

A. Yes.

Q. And were you giving that answer because you had brought in another firm in addition to Royal Little to complete the transaction?

A. That's right.

Q. All right. Now, when you originally made the deal with Royal Little for half of 1 percent, had you expected him to do the entire thing?

A. Yes, I did.

Q. Okay. He was to set up meetings with the principals?

A. Right.

Q. Assist you in the negotiations?

A. Yes. Put in a good word for us, help Mrs. Beech out, do all those things.

Q. How many of those things did he do?

A. He set up the meeting.

Q. Okay. Did he put in a good word for you?

A. Probably.

Q. Did Angus MacDonald, who knew her very well, we're told by Raytheon, did he put in a good word for you?

A. Yes. He wrote constantly to her, visited her, called her and so forth, and said, Raytheon is a great company. And Mrs. Beech responded.

Q. Mr. Phillips, is there any question in your mind that if at the moment you had these conversations in late '76 and were considering looking at Beech again, you had been handed notice that Merle Bushkin brought this thing to you in mid-1975, that you would have had to defer that engagement?

A. I would have had to defer that engagement, that's right.

Q. Okay. Is there anything Mr. Bushkin did to cause you to be unaware in December of '76 that he was a Beech man as to Raytheon, anything he did?

A. Never heard of Bushkin with Beech.

Q. Okay. Well, recall, if you will, something we talked about earlier. You have an exhibit before you which is a letter dated November 7, 1975, am I correct?

A. What's that again?

Q. You have an exhibit before you, it's been sitting there for awhile over by your left hand, a letter to you from Bushkin, November 7, '75.

A. Right.

Q. Okay.

THE COURT: What's the exhibit number on that?

THE WITNESS: 40.

Q. And you've identified that as a letter you received with attachment—

A. Right.

Q. —after a meeting with Bushkin, and you can't recall where and when the meeting took place.

A. I suspect it was New York. I suspect the meeting first took place in New York.

Q. All right. Now, if he recalls it being in your hotel suite with Frank Fox present, would you dispute that, Mr. Phillips?

A. No. Frank Fox probably invited him into the suite to meet me.

Q. Frank Fox was very involved with Allyn & Bacon, wasn't he?

A. Yes.

Q. At that point you didn't know anything about the fee arrangement with Mr. Bushkin, did you, sir, in November of '75?

MR. MASTERMAN: What fee arrangement, sir?

THE COURT: Sustained. Which one?

MR. BAILEY: Allyn & Bacon. That's why they were there at the meeting.

BY MR. BAILEY:

Q. Did you know anything about a fee in November of '75 when you met Bushkin?

A. Not when I first met him, no.

Q. Did you talk about an Allyn & Bacon fee at the meeting?

A. No.

Q. Did you talk about him doing work to acquire Allyn & Bacon?

A. We talked about that.

Q. Did you inquire of him as to whether he thought he had any fee arrangement without having talked to you?

A. I did not.

Q. Did you think he was working because Raytheon is a charitable institution?

A. I am sure that if Allyn & Bacon had been consummated, we would have owed Mr. Bushkin a fee.

Q. Okay.

A. I'm sure of that.

Q. All right. Why is that, sir?

A. Because he had a substantive contact. He would have—he would have arranged the introduction. And he did some analysis. He did real work on Allyn & Bacon which I remember.

Q. Okay. So that the real difference in this case is that if he did real work, you don't remember it. Isn't that the only difference, sir?

A. I remember it because it was real, substantive work.

Q. No, no. What I'm asking you is assuming that the evidence shows he did about the same real and substantive work in this case—

A. Which case?

Q. Beechcraft. The reason we're here, sir—

A. Yeah, but I have no knowledge—

Q. Please, let me finish the question.

If the evidence shows that even though you didn't know it, Mr. Phillips, he did real substantive work on Beech within the time period similar to Allyn & Bacon, you would agree he is entitled to a fee on the same basis, would you not?

A. We also require a broker—

Q. No. What's your answer to that?

A. —to perform the introduction.

Q. Could you answer that?

A. If he had done substantive work, he would be required a fee.

Q. If he was able to introduce and willing to introduce and you forgot about him and he never got the chance, that wouldn't diminish his right to the fee, would it?

A. I don't know. Probably not.

Q. In June of '76 you learned about Mr. Bushkin's fee, didn't you?

A. In June of '76?

Q. In the Allyn & Bacon case you learned about his fee, didn't you?

A. I don't recall the exact dates.

Q. All right.

A. I knew it was perfectly right for him to have a fee for Allyn & Bacon.

Q. Strike that out. Go back to November of '75.

THE COURT: Where are we now, what date?

MR. BAILEY: November 6, '75, your Honor, the meeting in New York.

BY MR. BAILEY:

Q. Do you recall talking about the means of acquiring Allyn & Bacon which generated the proposal in your letter there?

A. Yes.

Q. Okay. Do you recall Mr. Bushkin saying, I can send you a proposal similar to the one I sent Mr. Seaman on Beechcraft? You should have bought them.

Do you remember him saying that?

A. Absolutely not.

Q. Are you saying that a meeting you can't even remember the whereabouts of, you specifically recall he didn't say that?

A. I don't remember any reference to Beech.

Q. In other words, he might have said it and once again you've forgotten it?

A. Very dubious, but I don't remember.

Q. You managed to forget a memo with his name in it, didn't you?

A. Yeah. I may not have seen that memo.

Q. May not.

A. Yeah. We haven't established that I read that memo at the time.

Q. All we've established is that Seaman sent it to you and it's got your date-stamp on it.

A. We've established that my secretary saw it and stamped it, that's for sure.

Q. Does your secretary screen out your memos from your senior vice presidents?

A. No. She probably puts them in my in basket; and if they're on a subject I'm not interested in, at a busy time, it's quite possible they go from the "In" basket right to the "Out" basket.

Q. You can't tell us on your oath that that ever happened, can you?

A. No. But it has happened on other matters—

Q. All right.

A. —that I'm not interested in.

Q. Go forward to June of '76, and I ask you whether or not Mr. Bushkin came to you and said, I have a complaint about Seaman. He's impinging on my right to earn a fee in this case.

MR. MASTERMAN: I object. May I approach the bench?

SIDE BAR CONFERENCE . . .

THE COURT: Wait a minute. What was the question?

(The record was read as requested.)

THE COURT: I still don't—

MR. BAILEY: That it's news to him that a 1 percent fee was agreed on and he now tells Bushkin for the first time, despite the conversation of six months earlier, that he has to approve the fee.

THE COURT: Rephrase the question again just for me.

MR. BAILEY: Okay.

Did Mr. Seaman or did Bushkin come to Phillips—

THE COURT: Did Bushkin come to Phillips.

MR. BAILEY: —six months after they personally talked about Allyn & Bacon.

THE COURT: This is in 1976.

MR. BAILEY: June of '76.

THE COURT: Yes.

MR. BAILEY: —and say, Seaman has brought another broker into the Allyn & Bacon case that we're working on, and did Phillips say, Well, that's not right. You're entitled there. And did Bushkin say, My fee is 1 percent? And did he say, Well, this time as a favor to me, would you split it with the other broker?

THE COURT: What's the relevance?

MR. BAILEY: He has testified in prior cases he sent it to Seaman and said, Resolve it.

Number one, it shows he is on notice of a 1 percent fee that Seaman engaged in without his knowledge and he never protested it and he never denied it; he just tried to settle it. So I think it's impeaching in that respect.

Number two, it shows his method of dealing with the broker.

THE COURT: What's your objection?

MR. MASTERMAN: My objection is that it isn't at all relevant to the case at issue here, which is what is Mr. Bushkin entitled to on an alleged contract January 28, 1975. How does it bear upon the express contract claim, the quantum meruit claim, the implied contract claim? It has no relevance to that at all.

THE COURT: The only thing is, this Allyn & Bacon has been part and parcel of the case both in direct and in cross-examination.

MR. MASTERMAN: Well, it's been referred to but carefully limited to its relevance. And at the moment it's getting into an area that it has no relevance at all.

THE COURT: Since this is in effect cross, I'll let him have it. Overruled.

. . . END SIDE BAR CONFERENCE

BY MR. BAILEY:

Q. Did Mr. Seaman come to you in June of '76—I'm sorry—Mr. Bushkin with a complaint about Mr. Seaman that you can recall?

A. June of '76.

Q. Yes. About seven months after your meeting in New York re Allyn & Bacon.

A. Yes. There was a time Mr. Bushkin thought that Mr. Seaman probably was not totally receptive and fair to him.

Q. Well, didn't he say, in effect, He's brought in another broker on a case I'm working with you, Mr. Kramer? Didn't he tell you that?

A. No, that's not the way it happened. I remember the case very well. The case is—if I may describe the case, please.

Q. Sure. Where did the conversation take place, if you can tell us?

A. Let me explain the case, please—first, please, so I can tell you the sequence of events.

Mr. Bushkin had represented Allyn & Bacon to us. He was the first finder of it, and he represented that he knew Mr. Ettinger, who was the 30 percent shareholder; and, therefore, if he could go to him with this investment plan, that he could sell Mr. Ettinger and Mr. Ettinger, in turn, could sell the management, and we could acquire Allyn & Bacon.

It turned out I authorized Mr. Bushkin to do that. He went to Mr. Ettinger and Mr. Ettinger struck out. Mr. Ettinger could not—could not reach the management of Allyn & Bacon, so the deal died.

Some eight or nine months later another broker whose name I don't recall represented to Mr. Seaman that he had a way to get to Allyn & Bacon and Mr. Ettinger that was a sure-fire way, and Mr. Seaman brought it to me. I responded immediately, There's another broker in this case. You cannot go ahead with this. You've got to resolve the differences between the two finders. Go back and talk to Mr. Bushkin properly and resolve the matter of fees.

Mr. Seaman went back to Mr. Bushkin and asked him if he would waive his claim since another person could now reach it. Mr. Bushkin refused. The two brokers put—both put in their full fees. The deal got to be too expensive and I canceled it. So, therefore, we did not go ahead with Allyn & Bacon because the two brokers could not settle between them.

But I want to put on the record that when I knew a prior broker was involved, I instructed Mr. Seaman to go back and settle with that broker. And that's how it came about, and that's when Bushkin called me up and said, Seaman isn't being fair to me.

Q. Didn't you, in fact, try to get Seaman to resolve it after you failed to resolve it yourself between the brokers?

A. Say that again?

Q. Did you not yourself ultimately resolve the dispute by asking Mr. Bushkin to take half his fee and share with Kramer? Didn't you do that?

A. I don't recall how it did it, but we eventually ended up with two fees and the deal got too rich and we weren't interested. I doubt that we could have made it, anyway, so the deal died.

Q. You just told us that the two fees were added together.

A. Yes.

Q. Right on top of the other.

I'm asking you whether or not it was you personally, sir, who arranged them each to take half so Raytheon wouldn't have to pay any more. Isn't that so?

A. I couldn't have because I never—I never met the other broker, so there's no way I could have reached him. I didn't know who he was.

Q. All you had to do was get Bushkin to agree, didn't you, and get Seaman to get the other fellow to agree?

A. Well, I don't know how he did it.

Q. Okay. You don't know, do you?

A. I don't know how he did it. But, eventually, they decided on a fee splitting, and it got to be too rich.

Q. Okay.

A. And, therefore, we lost interest in the deal.

Q. Mr. Phillips, a moment ago you told us it got too rich because they both insisted on a full fee.

A. Yes. I don't know—

Q. Now you remember that they were fee splitting.

A. I don't know if they split one fee or split two fees. Frankly, I don't remember that.

Q. Sir, when you don't remember something, would you be good enough to say "I don't remember"?

A. Yeah.

Q. All right.

A. I remember the deal got too rich.

Q. Did you testify under oath about this matter last time that Mr. Bushkin met you in your office?

A. Say that again?

Q. Did you testify that you remember meeting Mr. Bushkin in your office to have this conversation?

A. I don't recall, sir.

Q. He's never been in your office, has he?

A. I think he has once, maybe twice. I don't know.

Q. Now, did you and Mr. Bushkin agree at that time that because of his inability to work with Mr. Seaman based on an incident, that he would work with you personally?

A. What's the date of that, please?

A. June of '76.

Q. Yes. From June '76 until I took the trip with him to Kewanee, I had given him that permission because I thought perhaps Seaman wasn't treating him fairly. I couldn't tell.

Q. Okay.

A. From Seaman's standpoint, he told me he couldn't trust him.

THE COURT: That may go out.

MR. BAILEY: Move to strike.

A. Say that again?

Q. I move to strike. The judge has stricken what you said.

THE COURT: Motion to strike granted.

Unresponsive.

BY MR. BAILEY:

Q. All right. How many deals did you work on with Bushkin personally after he refused to work with Seaman anymore?

A. The one I recall is I took a trip to see Kewanee with him.

Q. My question was, How many deals?

A. I have no idea.

Q. You have no recollection of dealing with him on other potential acquisitions?

A. He probably mentioned names to me that didn't take hold at all. Nothing happened from any of them.

Q. Okay. Let's talk about some of them.

Do you remember in 1976 Harnischfeger?

A. I have no idea. He may have mentioned Harnischfeger to me. He mentioned lots of names. He was a name-mentioner, a frequent—

Q. Try and answer the question.

Did he mention it or didn't he—

A. He may have mentioned it. I don't know.

Q. You have trouble remembering the names, don't you?

A. When just a name is mentioned, it's hard to remember 13 years later.

Q. So there would have been no occasion to send him a letter in '76 about a prior broker, would there, Mr. Phillips?

A. Harnischfeger is a case that one of our directors, Gordon Jones, brought to us originally and, therefore, we felt we had an obligation to go back through him.

Q. Did you send Mr. Bushkin a letter to that effect?

A. I may have.

Q. All right. Assume that Raytheon did that. That was the proper thing to do, wasn't it?

A. Right.

Q. Okay. And Mr. Bushkin had no way of knowing whether you had a prior broker in a case without asking you, didn't he?

A. Right.

Q. Okay. So sending you a proposal with no knowledge of a prior broker in the picture wasn't improper, was it Mr. Phillips?

A. No.

Q. Okay.

A. No.

Q. Now, do you know whether, for instance, he had ever talked personally with anyone at Harnischfeger?

A. I don't know.

Q. Well, then putting him down for name-dropping on Harnischfeger is just a little unfair, isn't it, Mr. Phillips?

A. Probably on that one it is, but several others it isn't.

Q. Okay. Let's talk about some others.

Cameron Iron Works, is he a name-dropper?

A. I don't recall Cameron Iron Works. He probably—undoubtedly, it was mentioned during that time.

Q. Did you send him a letter saying, We have a prior broker within three—three—years? Did you send that letter?

A. I don't recall.

Q. If he mentioned Cameron Iron Works, do you have any knowledge as to whether he knew any of the principals?

A. I have no knowledge.

Q. But if he could bring something substantive to the party like direct contact with the principals, that would be the kind of thing you would be looking for if you didn't have a prior broker, right?

A. If we were interested in Cameron Iron Works. I'm not sure we ever were.

Q. Well, there wasn't any way he could find out you were interested in something without asking, was there?

A. No.

Q. What about Wadsworth Publishing, Mr. Phillips? That was submitted to you on January 10, 1977. Remember that one?

(The witness gave no response.)

Q. Wadsworth Publishing?

A. Vaguely.

Q. Skipping Kewanee for a minute, do you remember in April Babcock & Wilcox?

A. Yes. That's the one that four other guys had brought to me.

Q. And you sent him a letter saying, We have four other brokers in the picture, didn't you?

A. Yes.

Q. That's the perfectly decent thing to do in this business, isn't it?

A. Yes. Mr. Bailey—

Q. Thank you.

A. —dealing with Mr. Bushkin was not my primary responsibility. That should have been done with Mr. Seaman.

MR. BAILEY: May that go out?

THE COURT: That answer may go out. You have to answer whatever the question is.

BY MR. BAILEY:

Q. What about Fruehauf, Mr. Phillips? Did you ever hear of Fruehauf?

A. I heard of it. It just went bankrupt.

Q. But in 1977 they were one of the biggest manufacturers of trucks around, weren't they, truck bodies?

A. Probably were.

Q. Did they ever come to your attention in 1977 through Mr. Bushkin?

A. I heard of Fruehauf through somebody sometime.

Q. Did Mr. Bushkin on April 14, 1977, propose that you take a look at Fruehauf, Mr. Phillips?

A. I have no idea.

Q. And do you know, if he did make that proposal, whether or not he had direct contact with anyone at Fruehauf?

A. I have no idea.

Q. Okay. Now, let's talk about Kewanee.

THE COURT: Before we get into that, let's take about a ten-minute break, fifteen minutes, and then we'll be able to go on until two o'clock.

(Recess at 12:58 p.m.)

(Court reconvened at 1:10 p.m.)

THE CLERK: Court is reopened. You may be seated.

MR. BAILEY: May it please the court, the staff brought to my attention that I may occasionally step out and block the view of the juror in the close quarters. Would you simply invite the jurors to bring that to somebody's attention? Because I'm—

THE COURT: If you can't see the witness, just let me know.

Next question.

MR. BAILEY: Thank you.

BY MR. BAILEY:

Q. Do you recall Mr. Bushkin in connection with Kewanee Industries, Mr. Phillips?

A. Yes, I do. Yes, I do.

Q. What was Kewanee Industries in 1977?

A. Kewanee Industries was a combination company that had oil and gas properties and two specialty chemical companies.

Q. Was Raytheon in pretty good economic health in 1977?

A. Yes.

Q. Did Raytheon have in the bank about $700 million cash?

A. Probably so.

Q. In your experience in the corporate world, Mr. Phillips, is that sometimes an invitation to a raider to come and try to take over your company, that much cash?

A. Yes.

Q. All right. Would it have been prudent corporate policy, then, to make an investment, a good investment, that would turn some of that cash into something else?

A. Probably, yes.
Q. In early February of 1977 was your relationship with Mr. Bushkin a good one?
A. Yes.
Q. Had you at any time told him you thought he was a charlatan, name-dropper, or any of those bad things you were talking about earlier?
A. No.
Q. The fact is until you wrote him a letter in 1978 about Eastern Gas saying you were impatient because he had mentioned it, you never had any cross words with Mr. Bushkin, did you?
A. I became aware of Mr. Bushkin's name-dropping on the trip back from Kewanee in February of 1977. I became wary of him after that.
Q. Okay. Well, let's go through Kewanee.
In early February of 1977 he sent you a package on Kewanee, right?
A. Right.
Q. And asked if you were interested in meeting with the principals.
A. Right.
Q. Now, this was the first of your involvements with Mr. Bushkin where him arranging a meeting with the principals was requested, isn't that true?
A. True.
Q. He was never asked to do that in the Beech case, was he, to your knowledge?
A. Didn't know he was involved in Beech.
Q. Then, I take it, you never asked him to set up a meeting with Olive Ann Beech, did you?
A. Correct.
Q. Okay. Do you know who was the principal stockholder of Kewanee?
A. A woman named Smith.
Q. And was that about a $450 million company?
A. Approximately.
Q. And you were, in fact, interested enough in acquiring it to attempt to get a meeting with the principals of Kewanee, correct?
A. Right.
Q. That company was located in the suburbs of Philadelphia, wasn't it?
A. Correct.
Q. And when you initially asked for a meeting, it was suggested that maybe everybody would be there but Mrs. Smith, correct?
A. The chairman of the Board at the company would be there originally, that's right.

Q. But not Mrs. Smith, who was a shareholder, right?

A. Right.

Q. And you said, Mr. Bushkin, if you can't get Mrs. Smith at the meeting, I won't go, didn't you?

A. Right.

Q. And Mr. Bushkin did get Mrs. Smith at the meeting, didn't he?

A. He did.

Q. The only time you ever tested his ability to deliver a meeting with the principals, he came through, didn't he, Mr. Phillips?

A. He was terrific.

Q. Okay. Now, let's talk about just how terrific he was.

You thought enough of Mr. Bushkin to pick him up at the Westchester County Airport in the suburbs of New York City on the way to Philadelphia so he wouldn't have to take a commercial flight and wait around for it, right?

A. Because he asked me to.

Q. Well, he says you offered to.

A. Not so. I thought it was an imposition.

Q. You thought it was an imposition.

A. That's right, but I did it anyway.

Q. When is the first time you have had a memory that you were imposed upon that day? Is it today, sir?

A. When he first asked me.

Q. All right. Have you ever—

A. I said, A broker shouldn't be doing that. He should be showing up to serve.

But he didn't do that. So I picked him up because I was a nice guy.

Q. Did Mr. Phillips—Mr. Phillips, did Mr. Bushkin intimidate you, sir?

A. Not at all.

Q. When you said, A broker shouldn't be doing that—

A. I thought he had a lot of gall.

Q. He had a lot of gall.

A. That's what I thought.

Q. Has it been your experience that when people treat you with a lot of gall, you accede to their wishes. You?

A. It would facilitate the trip in us arriving there in the shortest possible time, so I did it.

Q. Mr. Phillips, he can drive from New York to Philadelphia in a couple of hours, couldn't he?

A. Yeah. That's what he should have done.

Q. All right. Your corporate jet is used for your transportation, isn't it?

A. Right.

Q. About a $10 million airplane, isn't it?

A. I don't think so. I wish they were. We sell them at Beechcraft, and we would like to make more money for it, but we don't get that kind of money for it.

Q. I thought it was a Canada Air Challenger.

A. We've never owned a Canada Air Challenger.

Q. What did you have in 1977?

A. Probably a Hawker, but I'm not sure of that. A Hawker Siddeley.

Q. Was the trip from Philadelphia nonstop to Boston about 40 minutes, 45?

A. Probably an hour.

Q. It's 225 nautical miles. Did you know that?

A. I didn't know that. Thank you very much.

Q. And your jet cruises at 440 knots. Did you know that?

A. It takes time to get up airborne and land.

THE COURT: Let's go. Let's get on with the trip.

Q. How much longer does it take if you have to stop in Westchester to pick up a rude broker?

A. Probably another half hour to come down again and go up again and fight air traffic and so forth.

Q. All right. Did you have a meeting in Philadelphia about Kewanee?

A. Did I do what?

Q. Did you have the meeting you went down there to have?

A. Oh, yes. Yes, we met.

Q. Was it a pleasant meeting?

A. Very pleasant.

Q. Was it productive?

A. No.

Q. It was not?

A. No.

Q. When you left the meeting, was there any possibility of doing anything with Kewanee?

A. Not really.

Q. Well, what shut it down, can you tell the court?

A. Yeah, it's very simple. My interests were in energy, as I've said—testified before, and the oil and gas properties were very interesting to me. But the company wasn't only energy; it had two chemical companies besides.

I asked the chairman of the Board, who did all the talking at the meeting, whether our expert people could look at the chemical companies. He said no, and I said good-bye.

We're not interested in a company we can't look at because the chemicals companies that—they were foreign to us and, therefore, it would have been a big risk for us to go ahead with companies we knew nothing about.

The oil and gas, we were interested. But they weren't selling just the oil and gas; they were selling the whole package. That's the reason.

Q. How long did it take you to find out that Kewanee would not permit you to inspect their chemical divisions?

A. When the chairman told me so.

Q. How long into the meeting?

A. Oh, I don't know. I don't recall.

Q. How much time did you waste before you found you had a deal breaker?

A. Darned if I know.

Q. All right.

A. That was '77. This is '89.

Q. All right. Did you once again succumb to Mr. Bushkin's insistence and drop him off in New York on the way back?

MR. MASTERMAN: If your Honor please, I object to the question.

THE COURT: Overruled.

A. We dropped him on the way back—I dropped him on the way back.

Q. All right. Was this another case where he shouldn't have asked you, you felt he was imposing on you, but you did it because you were a nice guy?

A. No. Because I had picked him up, naturally the right thing to do is to drop him off again.

Q. If you take him to the dance, you have to take him home.

A. Absolutely. You have to take your date back home.

Q. Did you talk with him on the way back?

A. Undoubtedly did. We were together in the cabin, just the two of us. Had to talk.

Q. Did you talk about Kewanee?

A. Probably.

Q. Do you usually spend time talking with a broker after a deal is dead?

A. I probably told him why I thought it couldn't go ahead.

Q. Now, this was February 28, 1977, wasn't it?

A. Yes.

Q. Okay. On February 16, 1977, or at some earlier time in 1977—

A. Yes.

Q. —you had issued a directive to set the Beech acquisition in motion, had you not?

MR. MASTERMAN: I object, your Honor.

THE COURT: He can answer it. Overruled.

A. I didn't issue a directive. I told Royal Little to please go ahead and arrange for me to meet with Mrs. Beech. That's what I did on February 16, 1977.

Q. All right.

A. That is not a directive to go ahead with the company. I said, Let's organize a meeting.

Q. It's a directive to pursue the acquisition—

A. It's a directive to take a look.

Q. And your interest from that day forward continued until you did acquire it, right?

A. My interest to have a meeting was very much alive. For reasons beyond our control, the meeting did not take place for a full year afterwards. In the meantime, my interest went away. I went back to energy and came back in 1978.

Q. So if you testified at an earlier time on your oath that your interest never waned from early '77 until the date of acquisition, you now say that testimony was false, is that correct?

A. I don't know. I don't think so. I don't think I testified to that.

Q. They couldn't both be true, could they, Mr. Phillips?

A. No, they couldn't.

Q. Then we'll have to check it, won't we?

A. We'll have to check it.

Q. Yes.

A. Okay.

Q. In any event, Mr. Phillips, isn't it true that Mr. Bushkin said to you on February 28, 1977, in your aircraft at about 23,000 feet en route from Philadelphia to Westchester County, Tom, look at what's happened to Beechcraft. You really ought to take another look at that. Isn't that so?

A. The answer is, I don't recall.

Q. All right. Thank you.

A. But I must qualify that.

Q. Do you partially recall it?

A. No. I qualify it this way: I do not believe that conversation took place.

MR. BAILEY: Your Honor, the answer "I don't recall" should stand.

THE WITNESS: I don't recall, and the conversation could not have taken place.

BY MR. BAILEY:

Q. Wouldn't you say that's trying to have your cake and eat it, too, Mr. Phillips?

A. Had Mr. Bushkin made that comment and I had told Royal Little just seven days before to—to force me to—to arrange a meeting with Beech, I would have told Mr. Bushkin, We have a prior claim on that.

Q. You would have.

A. I would have, just the way I did it on Allyn & Bacon.

Q. On Allyn & Bacon—

A. That would be consistent with what I did with Allyn & Bacon when a second broker came in.

Had Mr. Bushkin mentioned Beech at that point, it would have rung bells. That would not be something I can forget.

Q. You're saying that the fact that Mr. Phillips' bell didn't get rung is some evidence that he didn't say it because you don't recall it. Is that what you mean?

A. I don't recall it, but it's something highly recallable.

Q. Highly recallable?

A. Highly recallable. And, therefore, I believe it did not happen.

Q. Is it any more highly recallable than your being told in writing by your own vice president in 1975 that Bushkin brings Beech? Is it more recallable?

A. Oh, much more recallable, much more, because now my interest is rekindled in Beech and, therefore, it would ring bells. In 1975 it was a trivial event that several brokers had mentioned, and I said to all of them, No interest.

But in 1977, a different ballgame. Now I'm telling Royal Little, Go arrange a meeting. So if Bushkin mentioned it then, it would have rung bells immediately and that's not something I would forget.

Q. Okay. See if this is something you have forgotten.

Did you in 1985 on December 5—page 120, if you will, of your trial transcript—get this question put to you and give this answer:

Is it your testimony, sir, however—

THE COURT: Wait until he gets an opportunity to refer to it.

MR. BAILEY: Oh, I'm sorry.

Line 12, Mr. Phillips.

THE COURT: What page?

MR. BAILEY: 120.

THE COURT: Have you got it?

THE WITNESS: Yes.

THE COURT: Go ahead. What's the question?

BY MR. BAILEY:

Q. Is it your testimony, sir, however, that once you decided to pursue Beech Aircraft Corporation, that interest continued on your part?

Answer: Once we decided in '77, the interest continued because our studies in general aviation indicated a pretty good growth in that business at that point in time.

Did I read that correctly?

A. You read it correctly.

Q. Did the court reporter take it down correctly in 1985?

A. Probably did.

Q. Does that mean you probably said it in 1985?

A. Probably did.

Q. Was there anything in that answer about your interest going away for a year?

A. Well, I looked at the records since then.

Q. No. In that answer do you find any reference to your interest going away for a year?

A. No. Just a second. Let me tell you—

THE COURT: No. You've answered the question.

What's the question?

MR. BAILEY: The question is, In that answer does he see a reference to his interest going away for a year?

THE WITNESS: No.

MR. BAILEY: Thank you.

BY MR. BAILEY:

Q. Now, isn't it true, Mr. Phillips, that the approximate purchase price at 12 times earnings of Beech Aircraft, had it been made in 1975, would have been in the range of $130 million?

A. I don't know. I don't know the numbers in 1975.

Q. Okay. Do you know whether or not Mr. Seaman was told by Mr. Bushkin for the purpose of passing on to you that it looked like the growth in general aviation products would be expansive in 1975? Do you know if that was said?

A. No, since I don't recall Bushkin in 1975 and Beech.

Q. If that was a prediction Mr. Bushkin offered as a basis for recommending purchase, wouldn't you say that it was brilliantly perceived—

MR. MASTERMAN: I object.

Q. —looking back?

MR. MASTERMAN: I object.

THE COURT: It's a hypothetical, but I'll let him have it.

A. "Brilliantly perceived." I never thought of Mr. Bushkin as brilliant.

MR. BAILEY: May that go out, your Honor?

THE COURT: That may go out.

The question is, Was his prognostication brilliant?

A. In fact, the general aviation industry was growing during the '70s, that's correct.

Q. By the time you got around to purchasing it, you paid five times more than you originally had to, didn't you?

A. It's because Hedrick and Mrs. Beech weren't babies. They weren't going to sell their company cheap. They were—they were just giving everyone a come-on until they were ready. That's the issue. It isn't that we were dumb.

You know, Hedrick dragged out the deal for two years until he built up Beech adequately to gain the maximum amount of money. It isn't because Bushkin said so in '75, he would have sold in '75. That's stupid.

Q. And you say that without ever having met him, without having remembered anything, you're able to tell this court that Hedrick would not have sold in '75?

A. Absolutely. I got to know Hedrick very well. He worked for me for a few years.

Q. Would you say he seems to have conned you a little bit?

A. He got the better part of the deal. I'll admit that, Mr. Bailey.

Q. Yes. Beech hasn't really been a very good acquisition, has it?

A. Not to date. It's going to be, but not to date it hasn't been.

Q. Well, after nine years of running it, you haven't brought it around the corner yet; is that what you're telling us?

A. No. I'm saying that the general aviation industry is going to demise in the '80s just like it was growing in the '70s. That's the facts of life.

Q. Okay. Was Mr. Hedrick working for you in 1985 when he gave testimony in this court about this case?

A. '85?

Q. Yes.

A. I think in '85 Mr. Hedrick was virtually retired.

Q. Did he have any—

A. I don't think he was an active officer of Beech Aircraft at that time.

Q. Did he have any kind of pension or remaining ties?

A. Yes. He was on the Raytheon Board. He was a director of the Raytheon Board and probably on the Beech Board, but that was his active role. Other people were running the company then.

Q. He didn't elect himself to that Board; he didn't have enough stock. Is that right?

A. To the Raytheon Board? No. When we made the merger, we invited Mrs. Beech and Hedrick to join our Board.

Q. Okay. But he was a member of a Board, you say, which you were the chairman in 1985 when he gave his testimony in this case.

A. That's right. I think that's right.

Q. How old a man was he at that time, Mr. Phillips?

A. Oh, I lose track. Let me see. '85 is four years ago. I would say '74 then.

Q. Did you ever talk to him about the meeting with Bushkin in January of '74?

A. I don't know that I talked to him directly. I think I heard his comments maybe indirectly through other people.

Q. Was Mr. Hedrick in any way interested in a jet aircraft?

THE COURT: When? When?

MR. BAILEY: From the first time he met him.

A. He was interested in a jet aircraft if he could get it, you know, very cheaply, for free and not spend the money to develop it.

Q. Did he ever suggest to you that one of the good things about a merger with Raytheon would be the deeper pockets of the Raytheon Company when it came to the risks of research and development?

A. No, he didn't.

Q. That was never discussed?

A. No. That wasn't—Mr. Hedrick was not a great builder for the future. He was a profitmaker. So building—he was typical of a man of his age, you know, past retirement age. He was looking not to the future but to the past; and, therefore, his interest on the future jet or other things was very limited.

Q. And as of what date is this that you became familiar with—

A. Since I got to know him, really. We forced a jet on Beech really over his objections.

Q. You forced a jet on Beech?

A. Yeah. Yeah.

Q. Over his objections?

A. Yeah. He was not enthusiastic for a jet, that's right.

Q. Okay. So if he told a bunch of people in '74 he wanted a lot of money to build a jet, he had changed his mind by the time he met you?

A. I don't know that he said that. I'm sorry. I don't know who he said that to. That's not my testimony. I'm telling you my contact with him is I didn't find great enthusiasm for spending a lot of money on a jet.

Q. Well, you have spent more money than a jet costs on a turboprop investment, haven't you, the Starship?

A. Yes.

Q. Okay.

A. But we also got a jet for one-tenth the price since then.

Q. You bought a jet that Mitsubishi Company makes in Japan and imports it?

A. No. We're now making it in Wichita, Mr. Bailey.

Q. The whole thing?

A. The whole thing.

Q. This is one designed and certified by Mitsubishi, right?

A. It was designed, certified, and transferred to Wichita and it's going to be an American-made plane. You'll be happy to know that.

Q. And you bought it for a song because it was a disaster, is that true?

A. Not true.

Q. You bought it very cheaply?

A. We bought it very cheaply because the Japanese couldn't sell it in America because they had no home market, and, therefore, they couldn't make a go of it.

Q. You mean they can't sell in America generally or just airplanes?

MR. MASTERMAN: Objection.

THE COURT: Sustained. Let's move on.

MR. BAILEY: All right.

BY MR. BAILEY:

Q. Now, do you recall agreeing the last time that you testified that a statement appears in a memorandum February 16, 1977—and I'll pull it out if we have to—that:

> Tom Phillips called Royal Little and wants to meet Olive Beech. Very much interested in taking over Beechcraft. Arranged that through Angus MacDonald.

I believe you agreed at that time that that happened the way it's described, is that correct?

A. I recall asking Royal Little to arrange a meeting. The words of enthusiasm and taking over Beech are his words, not mine.

Q. Okay. So—

A. But I authorized, Let's get a meeting going.

Q. Okay. So when he says "very much interested in taking over Beech Aircraft," that's his opinion of the way you felt?

A. That's his words.

Q. That's the way you felt; that was his interpretation of your direction?

A. I said, Let's meet with Mrs. Beech. Let's explore.

Q. Okay. And can you tell us today, bearing in mind your conversations in late '76 with Mr. Little—

A. With whom, please?

Q. Mr. Little.

A. Mr. Little.

Q. —when your interest in Beech was rekindled?

A. I suspect the first sign of my interest in Beech being rekindled is when I authorized him to go organize a meeting.

Q. Well, haven't you earlier told us in 1985 that your interest was rekindled in 1977, but you can't say when?

A. Yeah, I didn't look—I didn't look at the records that carefully then.

Q. Well, look back at page 120 where we were a moment ago and see whether or not you testified that you arrived at the decision to go forward sometime in 1977, but you can't be more specific.

A. That's right.

Q. That's where you said, "Once we decided to go forward, our interest continued until acquisition."

A. Yes. But that—the date now that I associate with that is the date I asked Royal Little to organize a meeting because now I have some records in front of me to look at dates.

Q. You had the same records in front of you at the last trial, didn't you, Mr. Phillips?

A. I didn't look at them, I'm sorry.

Q. You didn't look at them?

A. I didn't look at them in the detail that I did this time. Sorry.

Q. Do you wish to change the testimony you gave under oath in this court four years ago almost?

MR. MASTERMAN: I—

A. I'm not changing anything.

Q. Excuse me. Listen to the question and then make answer, if you will.

Do you wish to change the testimony you gave then that you knew you had rekindled interest in 1977 but could not be more specific than that and now say it was February 16?

MR. MASTERMAN: I object to the question.

THE COURT: Overruled.

MR. MASTERMAN: It's—

THE COURT: Overruled. "Cross-examination."

A. Yes.

MR. MASTERMAN: Where's the change?

THE COURT: Let him answer.

MR. BAILEY: He says he wants to change it. Change it.

MR. MASTERMAN: You say he wants to change it.

THE WITNESS: I'm not changing anything.

THE COURT: Objection overruled.

A. I am not changing a thing. I said sometime in 1977 because that's as well as I had it pinpointed when I testified in 1985.

Since then I have looked at the Royal Little letter to Angus MacDonald and have thought about it, and it had to be then, the February 16th date of 1977.

Both within '77. More precise this time. I studied the records more precisely this time. No—no inconsistency in that.

Q. And your statement four years ago was inaccurate?

A. No.

Q. When you said—

A. It didn't bracket it closely enough because I didn't know adequately enough. I said sometime in '77. That was correct.

Q. Is it the purpose of your statement, Mr. Phillips, that that would put it beyond the two-year date and deny Mr. Bushkin the fee you've already admitted you might owe him? Is that your purpose?

MR. MASTERMAN: If your Honor please—

THE COURT: Overruled. "Cross-examination."

A. Not at all.

Q. Is it a coincidence?

A. Not at all.

Q. If, Mr. Phillips, it is found that Bushkin was legitimately in contact with Seaman in June of '75 after ITE fell through and made presentations to Seaman which, despite your lack of recollection, came to you and generated further requests, if that is found to be the case, would you say under Raytheon's policy that the two years should run from the date that his name was recognized in your books? Wouldn't that be fair?

A. I don't think so, no. I think the date would have to run from the time it was first brought to us.

Q. But you said it wasn't brought to you on January 28 because nobody told you about it, is that right?

A. I also don't recollect it in June of '75, either.

Q. But in June we have written evidence about it that it came to Tom Phillips, at least in writing.

A. Except Seaman knows it came in January of '75.

Q. I see. Okay.

Do you normally buy manufacturing companies in the $800 million range with a snap of the fingers, or do you do a little homework first to see if you can swallow that big a company?

A. We do a little homework.

Q. All right. Now, Mr. Phillips, prior to 1977 what did you know about manufacturing aircraft?

A. Manufacturing aircraft?

Q. That's right.

A. That's an irrelevant question. I don't have to know manufacturing. I have to know the business of aircraft rather than manufacturing. I don't have to make it with my own hands.

Q. What is Beechcraft? Are they a manufacturer?

A. They're a manufacturer and a seller and a developer of aircraft.

Q. Okay.

A. They're in the aircraft market. We have to know what the market and where it's going.

Q. Were you interested in knowing how good a company they were before you laid out $800 million for it?

A. Absolutely.

Q. Okay. In order to know that, wouldn't you have to know the quality of their personnel?

A. Yes.

Q. Wouldn't you have to know whether any of the aircraft they were bringing to market at that time were obsolete and needed replacement?

A. Yes.

Q. Wouldn't you have to know whether or not they had any certification problems?

A. Yes.

Q. Wouldn't you need to know what their prospective liability was for products claims following crashes?

A. All of those things.

Q. All of them.

A. Right.

Q. Wouldn't you know whether or not they had any new projects on the drawing board that were going to cost a lot of money to bring to market?

A. Yes.

Q. And when you bring a new product to market, whether it be a jet or a tailfin, you have to invest money to develop it and get the FAA to certify it, don't you?

A. Right.

Q. And you have to sell enough of those items to write off the whole original investment and then start making a profit.

A. Correct.

Q. Okay. Now, even though you are Raytheon, isn't it fair to say you wouldn't spend $800 million of your shareholders' public money without going very carefully over some analyses of these kinds of health of that company?

A. That's correct. And we did.

Q. All right. Tell me who began to bring you this data that enabled you to decide to pursue it in '77 on February 16. Who had brought you data?

A. In '77 we agreed to look. The first meeting at Beech did not take place until '78. I began meeting with Mr. Hedrick in 1978 and met with him over a year and a half. During that time we conducted in-house analyses of all these relevant factors, including what's happening in the market.

Sometime in '79 Mr. Hedrick confronted me with a book some two or three inches thick that Mr. Kinloch had prepared on the value of Beech. This book analyzed their—all of their 23 airplanes, their marketing structure, their holdings, their R & D, and so forth.

We not only studied that book ourselves, but we hired Lazard Freres to give us a fairness evaluation of whether all of that was worth what Beech was asking for. We looked at their financial records. We finally made the acquisition advisedly. Now, subsequently to that the market went to pot.

Q. The market—

A. And, therefore, general aviation did not turn out to be the good acquisition we thought it was going to be in the '80s. The school's still out for the '90s, you know. I'm not sure Beech isn't good for Raytheon for the long pull, but the '80s have not been good for the Raytheon/Beech merger.

But we did do our homework for an $800 million thing. We took it to the Board several times.

Q. When did you bring in Lazard Freres?

A. Oh, undoubtedly, '79.

Q. The delay of the year from the time you wanted to meet with Mrs. Beech until you could reach Mrs. Beech was beyond your control, wasn't it?

A. That's right.

Q. When you brought them in, in '79, had you used Mr. Little and Lonsdale up to that point?

A. Little and Lonsdale did some—some preliminary studies in '77. We did some preliminary studies ourselves that I'm familiar with before—in preparation for my meeting with Mrs. Beech.

It turned out we could not use that because the meeting with Mrs. Beech never took place in '77 because of circumstances beyond our control again.

Q. All right. Did Little and Lonsdale—by the way—strike that out.

You had known Royal Little for quite awhile before you ever made this contract with them, hadn't you?

A. Mostly by reputation rather than personally. I had met him personally, but I didn't know him well.

Q. He had a very fine reputation as a businessman, didn't he?

A. He had a reputation as the originator of the modern conglomerate. He was the archetype acquisitor in building Textron.

Q. All right.

A. And, therefore, he had many contacts in the field. And even though he was old, I respected him.

Q. How old was he?

A. At the time? When we concluded the deal, he was 80.

Q. All right.

A. I don't know what he was then.

Q. And you had given him $50,000 and a promise of a half a point of—one-half of 1 percent if a deal of more than a hundred million went together after he brought it to you, right?

A. Right.

Q. Okay. Did you ever ask Mr. Little to do something for you, as Raytheon, in the Beech deal that he refused or was unable to do?

A. No. We had expected him to do a lot, but he couldn't because the situation got away from both of us.

Q. What couldn't he do? What got away from you and Mr. Little?

A. What got away from us, in the process of trying to arrange a meeting with Mrs. Beech, Mr. Hedrick played golf with Dave Lewis of General Dynamics. They came off the golf course and announced a merger of Beech and General Dynamics. That, obviously, threw our meeting with Mrs. Beech out the window, and we could do nothing while that merger was ongoing.

Q. He—

A. And therefore, even Lonsdale failed to arrange the meeting at the prescribed time because—

Q. And Angus MacDonald?

A. And Angus MacDonald.

They all failed because Hedrick, instead, played golf with Lewis, and they are the guys that took the play away from us. And, therefore, Lonsdale was left out in the cold because of that.

Q. When you have a contract with the broker which is interrupted by some event over which he has no control, such as Beech talking about a marriage with General Dynamics, does that mean the broker's contract is modified, sir?

A. No, except Mr. Little and I had an agreement, an understanding, that he would do several things for us in this merger, not just arrange a meeting. And he was unable to perform because, in fact, you know, events interrupted it.

Q. That deal fell through, didn't it?

A. What deal fell through?

Q. General Dynamics.

A. The General Dynamics deal finally fell through.

Q. And then a meeting was arranged where you met with Beech and Hedrick, right?

A. Eventually. Not right away.

Q. Who arranged that meeting?

A. Probably Angus MacDonald.

Q. Wasn't he one of the three—

A. One of the three, that's right.

Q. They were working together?

A. Right, with a team.

Q. So he did what you asked him to do.

Now, when was the first time that a member of this team was unable to do what you asked him to do, Mr. Phillips?

A. They were really unable to fulfill their obligations when Hedrick first confronted me with the Loeb Rhoades very thick report that this gentleman Kinloch had put together.

Q. Okay.

A. Then we required a very detailed analysis and a fairness evaluation that I thought was beyond their means to handle.

Q. You hired Lazard Freres, in your own words, in self-defense against Beech's team, didn't you?

A. Right.

Q. Okay. Now, are you telling us that the reason you went out and got those people in 1979 is because Royal Little and his crowd couldn't stand up against Mr. Kinloch? Is that what you're saying?

A. Probably.

Q. A question of size?

A. Yeah, probably, and ability to analyze, and resources from an investment banking firm. I needed a major leaguer at that point in time because we were going to play against a major leagueer.

Q. What was Lazard Freres able to do?

A. Well, they had an analysis team that could look at a whole bunch of things. They had Felix Rohitan. They had style, size, pizazz.

Q. Style, size, and pizazz?

A. That's right. And they had analysis. And, therefore, a fairness evaluation by them would be worth a lot more than a fairness evaluation of a couple of partners.

Q. Okay. But when you agreed to pay a couple of partners a fee and decide you want someone else to do something, do you normally take it out of those partners? Is that your practice?

A. I don't normally do anything.

Q. Okay.

A. I called Royal Little and we discussed it, and we decided, you know, in fairness for the fee we had to pay Lazard, his fee ought to be reduced.

Q. Are you representing that he agreed with you on that?

A. Absolutely.

Q. The fact is he didn't know he had the protection of a written contract and, therefore, agreed to a reduction, right?

A. I called him on the phone and I said, A million dollars seems fair for you guys just organizing an introduction. And he agreed with me.

And I said, How would you like it paid?

He said, Pay my partner in cash, but pay me over five years.

And I agreed with that. And that was totally amicable.

Q. You paid him a million-one?

A. Paid—yeah, paid Royal Little 600,000 and Angus MacDonald 500,000, that's right.

Q. You represent that your understanding as you sit here today was that Mr. Little was quite happy with being reduced from almost $4 million down to one by you, is that your testimony?

A. I discussed it with him. He was perfectly happy with it.

MR. MASTERMAN: Your Honor, please, I object to the question. It contained a lot in it that is not in evidence.

THE COURT: Well, he answered it. He answered it. Objection overruled.

BY MR. BAILEY:

Q. Wouldn't the fee have been over 3-½ million to Royal Little if you hadn't reduced it?

A. I don't know what it would be.

Q. Did you say on page 78 in your testimony in December of 1985, sir:

I reduced Lonsdale's $3.5 million fee to $1 million because all they did was introduce us.Did you say that?

A. Probably did.

Q. Take a look.

A. What page again, please?

Q. It appears on page 78. Just before you talk about paying Lazard Freres 2 ½.

A. Which line, please?

THE COURT: What's the line?

(Pause)

BY MR. BAILEY:

Q. Right at the top:

Did you pay 3.5 million to Lonsdale Enterprises?

Answer: We did not.

Question: You didn't want to pay that much money to Lonsdale Enterprises, did you?

Answer: No, we did not.

Question: And you made a decision as to how much money you wanted to pay the finders in the case, didn't you?

Answer: We negotiated.

Question: You negotiated?

Answer: And we arrived at a mutually satisfactory amount.

Question: And you spoke with Royal Little in that connection?

Answer: I did.

Question: And did you tell Royal Little that you would pay not more than $1 million to all the finders in the case together?Answer: That's right.

Question: Notwithstanding the fact that you had obligated Raytheon to pay one-half of 1 percent of the transactions' value?

Answer: Notwithstanding—yes, the original assumption was that they would do more than just introduce us. As it ended up, that's all they ever did.

Was that your testimony?

A. That's right.

Q. Okay. Now, when you agreed that you told Royal Little that you would pay not more than $1 million, and that's in fact what you paid him, do you call that negotiation, sir?

A. Uh, we negotiated. We negotiated on the phone very amicably.

Q. Mr.—

A. I—I don't know exactly how I approached it. I said, You know, Roy, I think what you did is worth about a million dollars. What do you think?

I don't know how we ended up, but it was a very happy event.

Q. Your testimony—

A. Happy on both sides.

Q. Your testimony was you told him—

A. But we negotiated.

Q. And you know, don't you, sir, that Mr. Little subsequently said on his oath he was very unhappy with it?

A. I don't know that for a fact.

Q. Are you hearing that for the first time today, Mr. Phillips?

A. I heard it from Mr. Masterman last week, but I don't—I don't really—I never heard back from Royal Little that he was unhappy.

Q. Do you know he gave a deposition saying so on his oath prior to 1985?

A. I knew it as of last Friday.

Q. And up until then, you never heard that?

A. Every representation he made to me, he was happy with our negotiation.

Q. All right. Now, assuming, Mr. Phillips, that because you had forgotten or were unaware—that Raytheon, the corporation, was; you were not—that you engaged Mr. Little and his group within the two-year time frame that would have been the entitlement of Mr. Bushkin, wouldn't you agree, Mr. Phillips, that in no event should he get less than he would have gotten if he had continued in their shoes? Wouldn't you agree with that?

A. Should he have gotten less than who? I'm sorry. I'm mixed with up the—

Q. If the fault of him being disengaged was yours and not his.

A. No. It was events, not ours at all. It was Frank Hedrick and Dave Lewis playing golf. That's the fault.

THE COURT: Rephrase the question.

MR. BAILEY: Yes.

Q. If Mr. Bushkin because you had somehow remembered his talks with you in '75 or the documents you saw in '75 had been in the picture in November of '76, would you have reduced his fee to a million dollars, as well, if he made the introduction?

A. That's hypothetical.

MR. MASTERMAN: I object to the question. It contains facts not in evidence.

THE COURT: Objection overruled. A hypothetical was given to this witness on direct on the basis of facts that may or may not be determined by the jury. He has a right to phrase a hypothetical—

MR. BAILEY: Yes, your Honor.

THE COURT: —depending on the jury's ultimate finding of the facts.

Objection overruled.

A. I would think if I knew Mr. Bushkin was in the picture and I didn't think he was the best man to complete the deal, I would have done with him what I did with Royal Little. I would have got on the phone and said, Merle, you know, you can't—I don't think you can take it any further. I don't think we can succeed. What about this amount?

I suspect I would have done that. But since I didn't know he was in the picture, I didn't.

Q. Would you have given him the opportunity to arrange a meeting before telling him he was incapable of doing so?

A. I would have made that judgment as to who was the best person to arrange a meeting. It's our company, I'm making the decisions, and I have a right to decide who is the best person to make the right contact for the company.

Q. And do you have a right to cancel contracts that Raytheon's engaged in—

A. Not at all. Not at all.

Q. —because you're the chief?

A. Not at all. If a valid contract is engaged in, we honor it.

I'd like to see the writing that's a valid contract.

Q. You don't honor valid written contracts, do you? You cut Royal Little way down, didn't you?

A. I did after negotiation.

Q. Mr. Phillips—

A. With his agreement.

Q. —should it be the determination of this court that Mr. Bushkin was entitled to notice in '76 that he should continue to try and get the meeting you then wanted, wouldn't you agree that he should be compensated in all fairness, sir?

A. If he—if he didn't arrange the meeting or couldn't take it any further but was involved within a two-year period and I knew about it, I would have called him or had some contact with him to try to get an accommodation.

Q. Did you understand my question?

A. I'm not sure I did.

Q. I'll put it to you again.

If it should be found that Mr. Bushkin was entitled to the opportunity to arrange the meeting that you asked Little and others to arrange and that, due to your oversight, he never got that opportunity, would you not agree that he should be compensated?

MR. MASTERMAN: Isn't that for the jury, your Honor?

THE COURT: Overruled.

A. He should be compensated for not having the opportunity to arrange the meeting? Is that what you're asking?

Q. No. Because you cut him out of that opportunity through ignorance.

A. Uh—

(Pause)

A. Anybody that made a fair contribution should have some compensation. If he—if he made a contribution but I cut him out through ignorance, some fee would have been due him had I known about it.

Q. But when you don't know about it and never have the chance to negotiate with him or reduce his fee, is he entitled to the benefit of a valid contract with Raytheon if he made one, sir?

A. If he has a valid contract.

MR. BAILEY: That's all.

THE COURT: What we'll do is suspend at this time and continue tomorrow at nine o'clock. Is five hours difficult?

All right. Try it one more day. We're going to have Wednesday off. So don't talk about the case, and I'll see you tomorrow at nine o'clock.

The jury deliberated for nearly four days before returning a verdict on count three—a contract implied in law, or *quantum meruit*—for $600,000. To that was added interest and costs bringing the total to over $1,300,000.

Nibbling (Cross-Examination and Impeachment of the Medical Expert)*

In *My Life in Court,* Louis Nizer wrote:

> Preparation is everything. It makes the stupid man bright, the bright man brilliant and the brilliant man steady.

But what of the million dollar case that's poorly prepared? The depositions are worthless, the B/P (Bill of Particulars) inadequate, the Panel[1] made no finding or ruled against you. The hospital record has been so sterilized it's hard to tell the patient is your client. You have no idea who the defendant's experts are going to be. All you know is that the case is on for trial in two weeks.

If the accident occurred in the hospital (be it malpractice or negligence), a thorough knowledge of hospital protocol and a pad of subpoenas are your best friends. The mere fact that something is not reflected in the hospital record doesn't mean it didn't happen. *Topel v Long Island Jewish Medical Center,* 55 NY2d 682, 446 NYS2d 932, 431 NE2d 293 (1981).

Interview the patient and patient's family at length and in great detail. Lay testimony may force the defendant to bring in medical personnel to refute their testimony, which will give you the opportunity to cross-examine. If necessary, build a straw man issue (or issues). If the defendant feels compelled to respond to even one, he will bring in witnesses who may address that issue, but be wholly unprepared on a vast array of other matters which can be utilized to the plaintiff's advantage. The traditional caveat, "Never ask a question you don't know the answer to," must be replaced with, "Never be afraid to ask a question which may *help* you but can't *hurt* you." The trier of a poorly prepared case is going to have to prove his case through the mouths of defendant's witnesses. While it is always good advice, "Never to underestimate your adversary," it is more important that we not *over*estimate him—or his preparation. As in football, you must recognize and capitalize on every mistake your adversary makes and force your adversary to make them as often as possible. The trier of a poorly prepared case is behind the eight ball, and it's an uphill battle to put in a prima facie case.

If you truly have nothing to work with, then you have no choice but to subpoena the defendant-physician and call him to the stand first. Because he is "your witness," you may not have the same latitude in examining him as you would on cross. (*Ciaccio v Houseman,* 97 Misc 2d 367, 411 NYS2d 524 (Sup Ct 1978).) Nevertheless, the defendant-physician is the enemy, and most judges will give you a fair shot at examining him. (*Jordan v Partinello,* 144 AD2d 540,

---

* By Norman Leonard Cousins. Mr. Cousins is a member of the Bar of the State of New York. He is a specialist in the trial of medical malpractice cases and is the head of the Manhattan law firm which bears his name. He is listed in Who's Who in American Law (6th ed. 1990-1991).

[1] The Medical Malpractice Panel. In New York, the findings of the Medical Malpractice Panel, if unanimous, are revealed to the jury.

534 NYS2d 686 (1988); *McDermott v Manhattan Eye, Ear & Throat Hospital,* 15 NY2d 20, 255 NYS2d 65 (1964).

Before examining any witness (be it the main defendant or any of his experts), it is imperative that you accurately size him up and determine right off the bat whether the witness is basically a liar, a legitimate physician who had a bad result and really believes he did nothing wrong or an expert witness who was given a bill of goods (or an incomplete and misleading set of records) by the defendant in order to elicit his testimony.

If you decide that the defendant is basically a liar, you must then make a judgment as to the defendant's attorney. Is the attorney a party to the perjury, or a victim? (Because no lawyer is ever more vulnerable than when his client has lied to him.)

In a recent Manhattan Supreme Court case, the defendant physician told his lawyer that his "clinic" was licensed by the New York State Department of Health. His lawyer permitted him to testify accordingly. When documentary evidence was thereafter received into evidence from the New York State Department of Health that it never licensed the defendant's entity, the defendant's credibility was shattered. Had the defendant told his lawyer the truth, I'm sure the defendant's testimony would have been, "We are not required to be licensed." To see a competent trial lawyer sandbagged by his own client (as happened here) is painful.

Daily copy is a must. Keep the defendant on the stand and elicit as much testimony as possible. Make your questions as specific as possible. Have him explain every act and reason for it. Have him identify who was present for all events and conversations. Have him admit that doing A, B, and C was a departure from good and accepted medical practice (i.e., malpractice). (Half the battle is now won. Now all you have to do is prove that the defendant did it!)

Forget about sleeping. Evenings are for getting copies of the day's testimony of the defendant to your expert witnesses. Nights are for preparation for tomorrow.

If you are right in your judgment that the defendant is basically a liar and you keep him on the stand long enough, you will eventually give him enough rope to hang himself. Compare the defendant's testimony to the hospital record. If the defendant performed a procedure, where is the consent for it? If a test was performed, where is the order for it? If there is no consent, was it because there was an unexpected emergency which left no time to obtain consent before action was required? If there is no order, is it because orders are missing? If *some* orders are missing, what about *other* orders? Subpoena and put into evidence the standards of the Joint Commission on Accreditation of Hospitals (JCAH). Subpoena and put into evidence the hospital's by-laws of its medical staff and its nursing procedure manual. Were all of the doctor's orders carried out? Where's the documentation to prove it? Do the nurses' notes match the medication records? Subpoena the blood bank records (if transfusions are involved). Do the type and cross-matching entries in the hospital record match the blood bank records (or have they *both* been destroyed)?

While it is important to know as much about your subject matter as possible, it is more important that the defendant physician (or expert witness) *thinks* you do. If a doctor thinks he can snow you, he will. If a doctor thinks you are a physician or went to medical school or, for some reason, have as much medical knowledge as he does, he is much more inclined to give you answers that at least have some relationship to the truth.

Have the doctor define all of his terms. Often a physician (especially a negligent one) may not know the meaning of half the medical terms he is using. Even if the erroneous definition is not critical, it looks bad for the physician in front of a jury and provides another avenue of attack upon his or her "expertise." In a recent Manhattan Supreme Court malpractice case, the defendant physician, a board certified orthopedist, testified that Betadine was an antibiotic and had no idea what "parenterally"[2] meant.

It's very hard to win cases on technical testimony. It's much easier for a jury to conclude that the defendant is lying and therefore must be covering up his negligence. Give the jury as many opportunities as possible to conclude that the defendant is lying. In *Naveja v Hillcrest General Hospital,* 148 AD2d 429, 538 NYS2d 584 (1989), which resulted in a $1.9 million verdict for the plaintiff, the defendant physician was kept on the stand by plaintiff's counsel for three days. By the time redirect examination was concluded, he had, during the last two days of his examination, recanted virtually everything he had said during the first two days, admitted that if he had done certain things (which it appeared he had done), he was guilty of malpractice, and furnished a wealth of material with which to cross-examine his experts.

Again, *don't ever overestimate the opposition.* Size up your adversary's experts. If they have good credentials, are practicing physicians, and do not spend their lives in court testifying, there is a good chance they were conned into coming to court by the defendant by being given a distorted version of the facts and an incomplete set of hospital records to support them.

Take it slow. Feel out the adverse expert. *Nibble.* Was the expert aware of this? Was the expert aware of that? Was the expert shown this by the defendant's attorneys? Was the expert shown that by the defendant's attorneys? (Incidentally, if your adversary is obnoxious or dishonest, lump him with the defendant and let the jury hate them both.)

In the *Naveja* case, Dr. Alan Van Posnack, Professor of Anesthesiology and Pharmacology at New York Hospital-Cornell Medical Center, testified on behalf of the defendant. In listening to his direct examination, I was extremely impressed with his demeanor and sincerity. He *believed* that based upon the information he was given, the defendant had done nothing wrong. By the time he was finished with his direct examination, I was convinced he had been deliberately misled and brought to court under false pretenses. Fortified with the conviction of that belief, I initiated the following cross-examination:

Q. Given the medication that was given, would you agree that it would be a departure from good and accepted medical practice not to have this patient's vital signs being monitored throughout the procedure by a person competent to do so?

---

[2] The administration of something other than by mouth.

A. I would agree.

Q. Was an anesthesiologist present and monitoring vital signs throughout this procedure?

A. No.

Q. Was there an anesthetist present and monitoring the vital signs throughout this procedure?

A. No.

Q. Were you told by Dr. Kazemi's attorney that there *was* somebody present throughout the procedure monitoring the vital signs?

A. Yes.

Q. If that was not done at all by anyone, would you agree that that would be a departure?

A. Yes, that would be.

With five simple questions, the defendant's own witness destroyed the defense attorney's credibility with the jury and established the defendant's negligence.

An intellectually honest physician resents being sold a bill of goods by a lawyer, and I give the witness every opportunity—which the witness usually takes—to explain that he was misled by the attorney who retained him.

Juxtaposition is an incredibly effective tool. Plaintiff was able to make out a prima facie case of medical malpractice just by juxtaposing the defendant's answers against his expert's.

In the *Naveja* case, the defendant (plaintiff's first witness) testified that during the course of an operative procedure upon the plaintiff, he ligated the paracervical artery. Three days later he not only denied ligating the paracervical artery, he swore that he never testified to any such thing. When I cross-examined the defendant's expert witness, I read him the defendant's testimony wherein he stated that he ligated the paracervical artery. I asked the defendant's expert if it was good practice for the defendant to do so under the circumstances. The witness answered, "Yes." I asked him if it would have been a departure from good and accepted medical practice for the defendant *not* to have done so under the circumstances. He answered in the affirmative. *Guaranteed* he had not read the daily copy of the defendant's testimony. I did not read to him that portion of the defendant's testimony where he categorically denied ligating the paracervical artery or vehemently protested that he never testified to any such thing.

One of the most difficult problems that had to be overcome in the *Naveja* case was the destruction of the hospital records. Whole sections of the chart had been removed—but proving it was something else. (Proving what the missing portions of the chart *said* was even more difficult!)

By going back to basics (the JCAH Manual, the by-laws of the medical staff, and the hospital's nursing procedure manual), we were able to demonstrate to the jury the wholesale destruction of the hospital record and what the entries contained in the missing pages must have said.

Following the stroke which befell the young female plaintiff (*in the hospital*), she was transferred to the intensive care unit (ICU). *There* had *to be an order for that. It was missing.*

In the hours preceding her stroke, the female plaintiff received at least four units of blood. The problem was that the doctor's orders for the blood transfusion were missing, the notes of the nurses who gave the blood transfusion were missing, and even the laboratory (blood slips) were missing. But because I believed that one of the defendant's expert witnesses (a hematologist) was basically an intellectually honest man, I was able to utilize a single post-stroke blood count to work backwards and, through having the defendant's expert explain the principles of hemodynamics to the jury, show that the plaintiff-patient did, indeed, receive at least four units of whole blood during the critical pre-stroke period or that—as the defendant claims—it would have been criminal for her not to be given blood.

Don't be so quick to conceded a mistake. The jury may not know an honest mistake from a lie, so if the defendant makes an honest mistake in the course of lying his face off, don't be Mr. Nice Guy. The more corrections the defendant has to make in his testimony, the less credibility the defendant has in the eyes of the jury.

Be quick to take advantage of your adversary's mistakes. Recovering a fumble is nice. Picking it up and running for a touchdown is much better.

One of the defendant's experts was nasty. Aside from being uncalled for (because unfounded), his character assassination upon the plaintiff was irrelevant. (The defendant was either negligent or he wasn't. He either caused the plaintiff's stroke or he didn't.) The defendant's expert, who purported to be an authority on venereal disease, testified that the plaintiff had venereal disease as a result of her promiscuous life style and that the condition caused or contributed to her stroke (which just coincidentally happened to occur in the hospital which she entered for a routine D&C). There were five women and one father on the jury. The father had a daughter. The defendant's VD expert was so offensive and so insulting (and his testimony so entirely irrelevant) that I felt there was a good chance he had offended everybody on the jury as much as he had offended me. As I slowly rose to address the hostile witness, I conceded his impressive qualifications and extensive experience with venereal disease (both gonorrhea and syphilis). "Tell me doctor," I asked him, "was that knowledge acquired firsthand?" The judge admonished me, properly so, but the jury almost fell off their chairs laughing. There were so offended by the doctor's testimony, that they reveled in the opportunity to laugh at him. They had sat and listened to him sully the reputation of an innocent 22-year-old girl (who was brain damaged, paralyzed, and incontinent), and regaled in the opportunity to laugh in his face. Humor can be a dangerous tactic and should not be employed lightly, but it can be devastatingly effective when it is used appropriately.

What do you do with a harmless witness? The trial has been going on more than five weeks. The witness (a nurse) knows nothing about the facts of the case, was asked to testify by the defense about a few meaningless entries in the chart, and excused. She still works for the defendant hospital, so is presumably hostile. At the same time, she knows nothing and hasn't hurt you. In your mind, the jury has already reached a verdict in plaintiff's favor and wants to go home. The best response under those circumstances was three short questions:

Cross-Examination

Q. You have no recollection whatever of Miss Naveja, is that correct?

A. That's correct.

Q. You have no knowledge whatsoever of the facts of this case, correct?

A. Correct.

Q. So I take it you wouldn't be offended if I asked you no further questions?

A. Correct.

If you won the case, you did everything right. If you lost, no matter what you did it wasn't enough. So the difficult task is to know when you've won the case and it's time to shut up and sit down. (Oh, the stories we can tell of the one question too many!)

How far you should go with your adversary's expert depends on a number of factors: (1) what do you have on the expert; (2) how intellectually honest is the expert; (3) was the expert lied to by the attorney that retained him (and is the expert now angry about it); and (4) how much do I really need of what I might get out of the expert. If the expert has written an article or a chapter in a book supportive of your case, then see what you can get out of him or her. (Nibble.) If you sense that the expert resents being put in the position the defendant has put him or her in by deliberately misleading the expert, then give the expert an opportunity to bury the defendant. Always go slowly. Keep the answers short and sweet. Nibble. If you don't like the way it's going, shift to some conclusory question or repeat a favorable point you've already made and terminate the examination.

Don't ever overlook the possibility that your adversary is more unprepared than you are. In the field of personal injury and medical malpractice, that's frequently true. The plaintiff's lawyer who is not prepared to take advantage of that does himself and his client a disservice.

There is no substitute for preparation. The comments made herein are as applicable to the properly prepared case as they are to the poorly prepared one. Only here they are more urgent.

Impeachment of an Undercover Police Officer*

Scope of Article

This article deals with the impeachment, by cross-examination, of an undercover police officer. The specific examples of cross-examination show how to attack the officer's direct testimony and impeach his credibility as to (1) the manner of his investigation, (2) his failure to investigate fully, (3) his unjustified reliance on persons unworthy of trust, and (4) his willingness to use information that he knew was totally unreliable in attempting to make a case against a distinguished State Police officer.

The Facts

Houston McNeal, the undercover agent, had testified in an earlier trial which led to the conviction of Allen on the charge of conspiracy to commit murder. Frederick and Allen were indicted co-conspirators with Captain Campbell, commander of the Special Intelligence Unit of Eastern Kentucky, and a former Commissioner of the Kentucky State Police. Frederick, who plea bargained and pled guilty to one count, and Allen, after the earlier conviction, agreed to testify against Captain Campbell.

Agent McNeal had been glorified as a hero by the local media for performing dangerous services as an undercover agent in bringing about the arrest of Frederick, Allen, who was County Judge-Executive of Morgan County, Kentucky, and Captain Campbell.

Counsel for Captain Campbell knew that McNeal's credibility had to be weakened by cross-examination. Captain Campbell and his counsel knew, from pretrial discovery, that Agent McNeal had never attempted to give any money directly to Captain Campbell and appeared to have avoided having any contacts with Captain Campbell. This led to the defense belief that Agent McNeal and other police officers working with McNeal did not want to give Captain Campbell the opportunity to show his innocence. Instead, McNeal and his cohorts sought to rely upon people they knew to be unreliable.

Campbell was charged with conspiracy to extort money and with conspiracy to possess and distribute marijuana and cocaine.

Agent McNeal, during direct examination, testified that Campbell had received payoffs through McNeal. However, McNeal had never given any money to Campbell. He always gave money to either Frederick or Allen, who represented to McNeal that they gave the money to Campbell.

McNeal had been in the presence of Campbell on two occasions: once when Campbell traveled with Frederick and Allen to Florida, and once when Campbell met Allen and McNeal on a lane near Morehead, Kentucky. On nei-

---

* By William E. Johnson, member of the Kentucky and American Bar Associations and of the Association of Trial Lawyers of America, the Kentucky Academy of Trial Attorneys, and the Kentucky Criminal Rules Committee. Author, Maximizing Product Verdicts Through Trial Techniques, Trial Magazine, November, 1982. Contributing author, Kentucky Appellate Handbook, Banks-Baldwin, 1985.

ther occasion did McNeal offer any money to Campbell. However, during the meeting in Kentucky, McNeal had asked Campbell if it was all right to give information to Allen. McNeal testified that Allen had earlier told him that Campbell did not want the word *money* mentioned and that the word *information* would be the code word for *money.*

Campbell's defense was that he did not receive any money, did not know Frederick and Allen were trying to buy marijuana or cocaine from McNeal, and hoped that Frederick and Allen might be able to assist him as a police officer in apprehending drug dealers in eastern Kentucky.

Frederick and Allen testified that they were involved in a drug buying scheme and that Campbell was going to give them protection, including notifying them of any police activities. They testified they paid Campbell a portion of the money given to them by McNeal.

The government relied almost entirely on what Frederick and Allen told McNeal to prove the case against Campbell. It was therefore important to show that the testimony of Frederick and Allen was unreliable and that McNeal should have known, even during the ongoing investigation, that their statements were unreliable. It was also important to impeach the testimony of McNeal by showing that he, as an investigating officer, did not do what a good police officer should have done to establish a case against Campbell.

The Impeachment

The following cross-examination was for the purpose of impeaching McNeal's testimony that money had been paid to Campbell, and to show that he had not made any effort to see if the money was paid to Campbell.

MR. JOHNSON: Thank you, Your Honor.
CROSS-EXAMINATION.

BY MR. JOHNSON:

Q. Several times today I heard on the tape and I think I heard you testify to the term that you wanted to pay someone hand-to-hand. Does that mean that you have the money in your hand and that you hand it to the person that you want to pay?

A. Yes, sir, that's correct.

Q. That's what a payment hand-to-hand means.

A. Yes, sir.

Q. When Titus Frederick was telling you that he could take ten kilos at one time, and based on the numbers that have been mentioned, $33,000 a kilo, $330,000, was there ever an occasion when you said, Mr. Frederick, I'd like to see the money, let me see how it looks?

A. No, sir, I don't recall asking to see any money.

Q. Did you ever ask Gene Allen to see any money?

A. No, I didn't.

Q. Well, did you really plan on selling these people any drugs?

A. Absolutely not.

Q. Really, your purpose was to involve them in a situation where you could bring a charge against them by giving them money; isn't that true?

A. That's correct.

Q. And that's what you did after you had first told them that you were a heavy equipment stealer and a narcotics dealer and that you were available to sell drugs, then you go to them and say, well, I really want you to take money from me. That's what you did, isn't it?

A. I let it be known that I was a heavy equipment—that I could move heavy, stolen, heavy equipment and that I was in the narcotics business. Yes, I let that be known.

Q. And then you also let it be known, after you had gotten their interest and they had expressed an interest in buying drugs from you, then you changed your position and you said, I want to pay you money in order to feel protected. That's what you told them, isn't it?

A. Yes, sir.

Q. Now, let me ask you about the money that was paid to be sure. Gene Allen, you paid him the sum of $2,500 on October 30, 1985; isn't that correct?A. Yes, sir.

Q. And that amount of money was paid in West Liberty, Kentucky.

A. Yes, sir.

Q. Did you see what Gene Allen did with the money?

A. No, sir.

Q. Did you take any steps to see what he did with the money?

A. I don't know any way I could trace the flow of that money. No, sir, I didn't.

Q. Have you ever heard of the word surveillance?

A. I have heard of it, yes, sir.

Q. Isn't that a common police term? You put one under surveillance?

A. I was constantly under surveillance. I am very familiar with it, yes, sir.

Q. All right. So you know the meaning of the term. Do you know how to surveil someone, to watch them, to see what they do?

A. Yes, sir, I have had some experience with it.

Q. I will bet you have done it in your lifetime, haven't you?

A. Yes.

Q. You didn't do it in this case, though, did you?

A. No, sir, that was not my role.

Q. Well, there were other people, though, working on the case. There was Agent Keller of the FBI, who was in charge. There was an agent by the name of Owens who was an FBI agent, wasn't there, working on the case?

A. Yes, sir, Stewart K. Owens.

Q. Stewart K. Owens.

A. Yes.

Q. So there were people available in the United States Department of Justice or other governmental agencies that could have put Gene Allen under surveillance to see what he did after he received money from you. There were people there, weren't there?

A. Yes, sir, and I don't know what the surveillance team done. I don't know exactly what they were doing at all times.

Q. Well, are you telling me you had a surveillance team?

A. I am not saying that at all, sir. I did not, I did not do any surveillance on Judge Allen.

Q. I am not asking you whether you did, I am asking you if you know—

A. I don't know.

Q. -whether there was a surveillance team?

A. I don't know, sir.

Q. Mr. McNeal, I will apologize to you if I interrupt your answer. But for the sake of the reporter, you and I cannot both talk at the same time. So if you would wait until I get through with my question, I would appreciate your answer.

Now on October—Well, let me keep with Gene Allen. On December the 4th, 1985, you paid Gene Allen $2,500. Isn't that correct?

A. Yes.

Q. And that was paid in West Liberty, Kentucky.

A. At the home of Titus Frederick, yes.

Q. All right. Is Titus Frederick's home in West Liberty or is it outside of West Liberty?

A. It's outside the town of West Liberty.

Q. Is it in Morgan County, if you know?

A. It is my understanding it is in Morgan County.

Q. All right, sir. Now, on January 9, 1986, you paid Gene Allen $5,000; is that correct?

A. Yes.

Q. Now, all of these are what we call hand-to-hand transactions, aren't they? You took the money and you put it in Gene Allen's hand.

A. That's correct.

Q. All right. And that amount of money was paid in Florida.

A. Yes, sir.

Q. And then on January the 10th, 1986, you paid Gene Allen hand-to-hand $5,000.

A. That's correct, sir.

Q. And that was also paid in the State of Florida?

A. Right, sir.

Q. And then on January 23, 1986, immediately after you had been down in the boondocks, or on the road in Morgan County or between Morehead and West Liberty, wherever you were, you paid Gene Allen hand-to-hand $5,000 more dollars, didn't you?

A. Yes, sir.

Q. And that was paid where, in the shopping center there at Morehead where you had met him?

A. Yes, sir.

Q. Now Titus Frederick, on October 31, 1985, you paid him $2,500; is that correct?

A. Yes, sir, I believe that's correct.

Q. That was at Mr. Titus Frederick's house; is that correct?

A. Yes.

Q. And then on December, is it the—excuse me. On November the 7th, 1985, you paid him $2,500 more?

A. Paid Mr. Frederick $2,500, yes.

Q. Yes, sir. That was at Titus Frederick's house, wasn't it?

A. Yes.

Q. And on December 4, 1985, at Titus Frederick's house, you paid him $5,000.

A. Yes, sir, I gave him a total of $5,000.

Q. All right. And then on January 16, 1986, you paid Titus Frederick $5,000, and that was in Florida.

A. That's correct.

Q. All of those sums that you gave to Titus Frederick were hand-to-hand transactions. You handed it to him.

A. That is correct, sir.

Q. And on every occasion when you gave Titus Frederick money, Butch Campbell was not present, was he?

A. Absolutely not.

Q. And on every occasion when you hand-to-handed money to Gene Allen, Butch was not present, was he?

A. Absolutely not.

Q. Now, you expressed concern one time, did you not, about whether Butch was really getting the money. Didn't you say that on one occasion?

A. Yes, sir, I indicated on several occasions that I wanted to pay Mr. Campbell hand-to-hand, and satisfy myself that he was getting the money.

Q. And you never did pay Butch Campbell hand-to-hand, did you?

A. No, sir, I never did.

Q. Now, did you ever say, though, to Gene Allen, you know, Gene, it would just make me feel so much better if I could watch you give all or a part of that money to Butch, and would you tell me where you are going to give Butch his cut so that I can be hiding in the bushes and watch that, or words to that effect? Did you ever tell Gene you would like to do that?

A. No, sir.

Q. Did you ever say to Titus Frederick, Titus, I would feel more comfortable if I could be sure that Butch was getting some of the money, I would like to watch you hand it to him? Did you ever say that to Titus?

A. No, sir.

Q. Now—

Judge, how late do you plan on going? I am just trying to plot my course accordingly.

THE COURT: Well, how late do you plan on talking?

MR. JOHNSON: Judge, you run the show, I am just here whenever you say.

THE COURT: We will go another five or ten minutes.

MR. JOHNSON: That will be fine. Whenever you call time, I will be ready.

BY MR. JOHNSON:

Q. Now, when you would have these conversations with Titus Frederick, Titus frequently brought up how close he was to Butch, didn't he?

A. Yes, he did.

Q. Told you he was just a real good friend, didn't he?

A. Sure did.

Q. And didn't he tell you on one occasion that Captain Campbell frequently came around him and brought another trooper friend with him?

A. Yes, he's told me that.

Q. Now, on that occasion, though, he didn't give you the name of the other trooper friend, did he?

A. No, sir.

Q. Well, as a good investigator, though, wanting to have all the facts, you found his name, I am sure?

A. I don't know his name, no, sir.

Q. You never did try to find the name of the trooper friend?

A. No, sir.

Q. One time when you went to Titus's house, you took him two cases of beer, didn't you?

A. Yes, sir.

Q. Did that loosen his tongue?

A. I, I don't recall that it did. I don't know that he drank any of it.

Q. You know he is a pretty good drinker of beer, don't you?

A. I know he likes it, yes, sir.

Q. Was that the purpose, that you wanted him to be liberal of speech in your presence?

A. No, sir, it really wasn't. I took it by there because I know Titus likes beer and you can't buy it over there, so I took it just to—as a friendly gesture.

Q. Gosh, that's dry territory, isn't it?

A. Sir?

Q. That's dry territory where you hauled that beer?

A. I believe it is, yes, sir.

Q. You say you believe it?

A. Yes, sir, it is dry.

Q. You know it is, don't you?

A. Yes, sir.

Q. How many cases did you really take him?

A. I took two cases over that I remember.

Q. I see. Did you help him drink them?

A. I don't recall whether I had one or not.

Q. But you will, won't you?

A. Pardon?

Q. On occasion you will lift a beer, won't you?

A. Absolutely, yes, sir.

Q. Or maybe something a little stronger?

A. I have been known to do that, yes, sir.

Q. Yes, sir. Now, you only saw Butch Campbell on two occasions in your life, other than at the trial here, didn't you?

A. That's correct.

Q. Yes. And in fact, when he was down to Florida, you never spoke a word to him nor he to you?

A. No, we didn't talk.

Q. So, of course, you didn't offer him any money, did you?

A. No, sir.

Q. You remember the conversation of about, it's in October of 1985, it's before you flew the substance in there that you then showed in the presence of Gene Allen and Titus Frederick and you had an FBI agent with the money, and you got to look at it and then you all switched the stuff. In October, you remember that Titus Frederick said that he could have three Kentucky State Troopers block the road to the airport.

A. Yes, sir, I remember a conversation like that.

Q. And he named one of them. He said one of them was named Davis. Do you remember that?

A. I don't recall any name.

Q. Well, if you put that in your report to the FBI, October 9, 1985, if you said it, it more than likely was information that you had gotten then, wasn't it?

A. I'd say that if it's in the notes of the FBI, it's true, yes, sir.

Q. Yes.

A. But I don't recall.

Q. You don't recall that. But you recall him saying that he could get three Kentucky State Troopers to block the road to the airport?

A. Yes, sir, I remember that.

Q. All right. Now, that would be a pretty good way of testing whether Captain Campbell was on the take, wouldn't it? That is by seeing if at a time when you are bringing drugs in there, if Captain Campbell would block the road after you had notified him it was coming in, after, say, it had gone through Titus, that would be a good way of testing, wouldn't it?

A. Sir, I can't answer that. I don't know.

Q. You don't, you don't know about how you test a person, either by, one, offering them money or by, two, if somebody says that this person will block the road by really checking to see if they do block the road at a certain time?

A. Sir, I wasn't making these judgments. I that I—

Q. Well, weren't you trying to establish some facts so that then you could come into this courtroom and base your testimony on a factual basis? Sir?

A. I was seeking information, yes, sir.

Q. Well, let me ask you, let me put it this way. On the day that you are going to fly that cocaine into that airport, or whatever the stuff was you brought in there, on that date, did you take steps to see that somehow the word got to Captain Campbell that you were coming in so that you could check to see if he blocked the roads with Kentucky

State Police officers in order to find out whether he was involved? Did you do anything?

A. I didn't take any steps like that, no, sir.

Q. Well, do you know anybody that did, that was working with your group?

A. I am not familiar with it, if they did.

Q. If they did, they didn't tell you about it, huh?

A. I am not aware of it, no, sir.

Q. Well, were the roads blocked?

A. The ones I traveled weren't, no, sir.

Q. They were wide open, huh?

A. Yes, sir.

Q. In fact, when you went back that day after being down there on the 20th, you saw a State Police cruiser sitting up there pretty close to the airport, didn't you?

A. I didn't see it, but I heard somebody say there was a State Police car in the area.

Q. Well—

A. Parked.

Q. Didn't that interest you? Here you are, trying to find out about this scurrilous Police Captain Campbell, didn't that interest you that you saw a State Police cruiser parked there?

A. I didn't see it.

Q. Well, when somebody told you it was there, didn't you—

A. I was told after I was gone. I didn't see it.

Q. But you remember then when the subject came up that Gene Allen said, that belongs to Lieutenant Hensley, who is a Kentucky State Policeman that lives up here by the airport. Remember that?

A. It's possible he said it. I don't remember.

Q. Didn't you hear it on the tape today that was played? Didn't you hear that?

A. If I did, I don't remember it. We can play it again.

THE COURT: I think we'll stop—

Q. Do you have a hearing problem?

I am sorry. I will pick up in the morning.

THE COURT: We will stop.

Ladies and gentlemen of the jury, we are going to recess for the evening. . . .

It was also important to impeach the testimony of Frederick and Allen by showing that they had lied to Agent McNeal and that McNeal knew, at the time of their statements, that they were lying. This set up for final summation the argument that Agent McNeal should not have relied on Frederick and Allen but should have looked for other sources of information.

The impeaching cross-examination was as follows.

Q. Do you recall on October 30, 1985, when you were present at Titus Frederick's residence, Titus Frederick telling you that he and Gene Allen had made millions of dollars in dealing in Florida cocaine?

A. I recall the conversation on that date, whereby Titus had said that, indicated that other people had made millions of dollars, but he hadn't gotten anything out of it. That's my recollection.

Q. Didn't he say that he and Gene Allen had made millions of dollars?

A. That's not my interpretation of that conversation. It's possible.

Q. You remember making a report to the Federal Bureau of Investigation on or about November 3, 1985, concerning your report of the meeting with Titus Frederick on October 30, 1985?

A. I know that a debriefing was held concerning that meeting.

Q. All right, sir. Do you have a copy of the report that's been furnished to us by the prosecution showing it, showing that report?

A. I have a report here. It may not be the same as what you have.

Q. Look and see if you have one, it shows at the bottom, date dictated, 10-31-85, and up in the top right-hand corner, date of transcription, 11-3-85.

Your Honor, for the sake of time, may I approach the witness with the copy that has been furnished to him—furnished to me?

THE COURT: Yes, sir.

BY MR. JOHNSON:

Q. It's just been pointed out to me that there is a page number at the bottom, 110. Would that help you?

A. Thank you.

Q. All right.

A. All right. I have page 110.

Q. All right, sir. Would you make reference—First at the top, does it say H. E. McNeal, Special Agent, parenthesis, SA parenthesis close, for the Virginia State Police, parenthesis, VSP, parentheses close, utilizing an undercover name of Harry McBride, Special Deputy United States Marshal, furnished the following information at a debriefing at the Holiday Inn, in Winchester, Kentucky, room 112.

A. Yes.

Q. All right. Then dropping down to the very last paragraph, does it read, Titus Frederick and Judge Gene Allen have set up a connection in Florida for cocaine. Make millions of dollars. And eventually led to Titus Frederick getting shorted or not getting his cut.

A. Yes, it does.

Q. All right. Now, did you conduct any investigation to determine whether Titus Frederick and/or Gene Allen had made millions of dollars from the cocaine connection?

A. No, sir, that was not my role in this investigation. That was a judgment to be made entirely by the FBI, and more especially, Dade County.

Q. Did you see any evidence of Gene Allen or Titus Frederick being millionaires?

A. I really couldn't say, you know, whether they are millionaires or not, actually. Both of them seemed to own property, and I just couldn't answer that.

Q. Were you aware or did you become aware that throughout this period of time when your investigation was going on, that Gene Allen's bank account with the Commercial Bank in West Liberty always was on the negative side, that he never had a bank balance in the account?

A. Again, Mr. Johnson, I wasn't privy to that part of the investigation. And, again, Dave Keller can answer those questions for you, sir.

Q. So your answer was, no, that was not brought to your attention?

A. No, sir, not during the investigation.

Q. And you didn't attempt to find that out?

A. No, sir, I had all I could do operating as undercover agent. . . .

Q. Now, you heard Titus testify at an earlier trial here where Gene Allen and a fellow named Griggs were on trial. Maybe you didn't hear him testify.

A. Sir, I didn't hear him testify, no, sir.

Q. All right. Are you aware that Titus testified in that trial that he never gave any money to Butch Campbell?

A. I understood from sources that that was his statement.

Q. That that was his testimony?

A. That he kept the money, the first $2,500, the one we are talking about.

Q. I see. Well, from the same sources, weren't you advised that his testimony under oath at that trial was that he, Titus Frederick, never gave Butch Campbell any money?

A. No, sir, I am not aware of it in that way.

Q. All right. Well, he'll be the best one to ask—

A. I didn't get the information in that particular way.

Q. I see. Well, he would be the—his testimony would be the best, wouldn't it?

A. I would certainly think so, yes, sir.

Q. Yes. Now, but I believe you indicated yesterday that you didn't believe Titus Frederick a lot.

A. There is a whole lot that I didn't believe about him, but there was a whole lot that he said that he did do and produce. And certainly there are things that I don't believe. But on the other hand, he did prove some points, and also bore out the fact that he was involved in criminal activity and could produce and did do certain things.

Q. Well, are you saying that it's your belief that sometimes he told the truth and sometimes he didn't?

A. That's exactly right.

Q. That's the fellow that then, he certainly engages in deception on selected occasions, didn't he?

A. I am sorry, Mr. Johnson, I couldn't hear you.

Q. I am sorry. He gave you the impression he was a man who could engage in deception?

A. Well, my impression of Titus Frederick, that he likes to brag or blow a lot and build himself up as a—or kind of a martyr or a person of high political clout, this type.

Q. Well, is that the same as saying that when he brags and blows a lot, he's handling the truth recklessly?

A. Well, I am sure he does on a lot of occasions, and I am very much aware of that. . . .

Allen had represented to McNeal that he would bring Campbell to Florida during January, 1986. Allen represented to McNeal that Campbell had been to Florida and missed seeing McNeal. Allen then called a person named Griggs who posed as Campbell while speaking to McNeal. McNeal and other agents discovered Allen's deception within an hour of the call but wrote their reports as if Campbell had spoken to McNeal on the telephone. One of the overt acts alleged in the indictment gave the impression that Campbell had spoken to McNeal by telephone. It was important to show the deception practiced by Allen, the absence of any involvement by Campbell, and the unfairness of the investigation. The cross-examination was as follows:

Q. Well, he told you that he would have no trouble getting Butch Campbell to come to Florida in January of 1986. He told you that, didn't he?

A. Yes, sir.

Q. And Butch Campbell didn't come to Florida in 1986, did he?

A. I didn't see him down there.

Q. Well, didn't Gene Allen on January 9 or 10, 1986, represent to you that Butch had been to Florida and had left?

A. He certainly did.

Q. But you, you knew that wasn't true, didn't you?

A. I knew it was a lie, yes, I did.

Q. You knew that was a lie, you knew Butch hadn't been there. But didn't you also realize that Gene Allen felt it was important to convince you that Butch had come to Florida?

A. Well, it was obvious that he was trying to convince me that Butch had been there and left, yes.

Q. And Gene Allen had told you that he was going to bring Butch down to Florida so that you could make a hand-to-hand payment to Butch, didn't he?

A. Yes, this was told to me.

Q. And then when Butch wasn't there, you couldn't offer to make the hand-to-hand payment to him, could you?

A. No, obviously, if he wasn't there I couldn't do that.

Q. But then it was in, on or about January 9 when Butch wasn't in Florida, didn't Gene Allen say that he'd get him on the telephone and you would talk to him?

A. Yes, that's correct.

Q. Yes, and did you watch him make the call?

A. No, I didn't. He walked in the bedroom and made the call.

Q. And he talked to somebody and then he called you in and you talked to the person, didn't you?

A. That is true.

Q. And you know today that wasn't Butch Campbell, don't you?

A. I know it. I knew it at the time it wasn't Butch, or believed at the time it wasn't.

Q. But Gene Allen represented to you that he was going to make the call to Butch Campbell so that Butch would give you assurances that you could give Butch's money to Gene Allen; isn't that correct?

A. That, that was what happened.

Q. And a fellow came on the phone and you said to the man on the telephone, you asked him if he liked his Christmas present, didn't you?

A. I believe that's correct, yes, sir.

Q. And the fellow in the conversation indicated to you that it would be all right for you to give the money that Gene Allen said was for Butch Campbell, that that could be given to Gene Allen?

A. Yes, sir.

Q. And you knew that the person that you were talking to on the phone wasn't Butch Campbell.

A. I knew, almost positively knew at the time that it wasn't.

Q. In fact, you found out later on when you checked the telephone records that the call went from Okeechobee, Florida, where Gene Allen placed the call, to Burlington, North Carolina, didn't you?

A. I understand that that's correct.

Q. And you then found out that the telephone number where the call went to was to the residence of the wife of Gerald Griggs; is that correct?

A. I—Yes, sir . . .

Q. Let's go back to the telephone call on January 9. You, you make the call, you know that it wasn't to Captain Campbell, or you said you felt pretty sure it wasn't, right?

A. Yes, sir, that's right.

Q. Okay. Well, turn, if you would—Let me find the page here just a minute.

Turn, if you would, to page 158. When you find it, let me know.

A. I have 157 here.

Q. All right, sir. Is that a report that shows you acting as Special Agent and sets out your report that you made and shows the date dictated, January 15, 1986, and the date that this was typed, January 21, 1986? Is that your report?

A. Yes, sir.

Q. And that relates, does it not, portions of it, to the telephone call?

A. Right.

Q. All right.

A. Yes, sir.

Q. Let me see. Picking up the fifth paragraph down, does it say, McNeal—that's you, isn't it?

A. Yes, sir.

Q. McNeal advised that earlier on this date, while at the residence of Titus Frederick that was being occupied at the time by Gene Allen, Allen was noted to have been making several telephone calls from the bar in the kitchen. The calls were being made from telephone number 813-763-8837, a number which McNeal had copied off of the telephone. Apparently, Allen telephonically contacted Butch Campbell on the telephone and was believed to be at Campbell's residence, due to the information being supplied to McNeal by Allen. Apparently Allen was talking to Captain Campbell on the phone for approximately one minute in the back bedroom.

Is that the call we are talking about?

A. Yes, sir.

Q. It goes on then to say: McNeal advised that in the living room of the residence was Lester H. Burns, along with Robert William Coomer. Allen eventually calls out for McNeal to come into the bedroom, at which time he hands McNeal the telephone. McNeal covers the mouthpiece of the telephone with his hand and asked Allen who it was, and Allen stated that it was Butch, and indicated that Butch knew what was going on.

Then going to the next paragraph. McNeal advised that he then had a conversation with an individual he was told was Butch Campbell. He indicated that he was sorry that he missed McNeal and indicated that he was here for two or three days, referring to Okeechobee. Excuse me. He said that it would be fine to get with McNeal in order to discuss his problem. He said, quote, oh, yeah, the judge has told me all about it, end of quote.

McNeal indicated that he was sorry that McNeal missed Campbell and asked Campbell if he would wing it back down to Okeechobee, Florida. Campbell indicated that he was pretty much tied up right now, that if he had any stuff coming—Let's see. That if he had any stuff coming, just give it to the judge, and made reference that he had already discussed it with Allen. McNeal then stated okay. And it was obvious to McNeal that the individual on the other end of the line was very afraid that McNeal would say something over the telephone that should not be said. Allen then gets on the phone with him. Allen wants McNeal to meet Captain Campbell at Allen's residence in order to pay him for January protection. McNeal advised that there—McNeal advised that then there is discussion as to why McNeal wants to pay Campbell at least one time in person.

The reason I am asking you this, and feel free to read the rest of that report, but nowhere in that report that you made to the FBI do you state that you believe that the individual that you were talking to was not Butch Campbell.

A. That's true.

Q. And yet this was dictated on the 15th day of January, which would be six days after the telephone call, and you have told us this morning that on the date of the call you didn't believe that that was Butch.

A. First of all, Mr. Johnson, this—the fact that it was dictated sometime later has nothing to do with it. We immediately had a debriefing and it was just a matter of an hour that we knew that that was not Butch Campbell. After the debriefing, then we knew that it wasn't Butch. But this, the debriefing was held immediately after this telephone conversation.

Q. You made a report on an official form, and in that report you never said to Mr. Keller or any other agent that would ever see this report that Gene Allen had misled you and you knew that he had misled you, and that the person on the other end of the phone was not Butch Campbell. You didn't say it in this report, did you?

A. Not in this report, sir, but, again, I must lay some things off on Dave Keller. He can probably give some testimony as to this situation.

Q. Well, but I am asking you now, Mr. McNeal. Did you want people at that time to believe that the person you had talked to on the phone was Butch Campbell?

A. What people are you referring to, Mr. Johnson?

Q. Anyone that would ask you about it?

A. I was only in contact with the FBI, and more especially Dave Keller. That would be the only person that would be concerned. . . .

Agent McNeal had testified on direct examination about a controlled sale of cocaine that had taken place in Allen's house in Kentucky. One group of undercover agents "sold" the cocaine to another group of undercover agents in the presence of Allen and Frederick. Campbell was not present and there was no evidence offered indicating that he knew of this transaction. Prior to trial the defense discovered that Agent McNeal had tried to give two ounces of the cocaine to Allen's son. The following cross-examination occurred for the purpose of showing (1) that it was not a completely controlled transaction in that cocaine could have "gotten on the street," (2) that the cocaine was impure and potentially dangerous, and (3) that McNeal was the person who violated the controlled transaction plan.

Q. You flew in there with the cocaine and you had previously arranged for other agents to come down to West Liberty for the purpose of bringing money, and you met Titus Frederick and Gene Allen and went to Gene Allen's house. And it was there at the residence that you, carrying whatever the substance was, represented as cocaine, that it was shown to Allen, it was shown to Frederick, but they got none of it; is that correct?

A. No, sir, they didn't get any of it.

Q. Although you tried to give two grams of it to Gene Allen's son, a boy by the name of Steve Allen, didn't you?

A. This was done under the direction of the FBI and their guidelines as far as to how many grams of substance, which was just rotten stuff, that they let walk on the street.

Q. Well, the fact, whether it's good or bad doesn't mean—In fact, isn't it the worse stuff is, the quicker it kills you?

A. I am sorry, I didn't hear your question, Mr. Johnson.

Q. Yeah. The question is, the worse the stuff is, the quicker you die from sticking it in you?

A. Sir, I don't know. I really don't.

Q. You say it was rotten stuff, and you offered two grams of it to Gene Allen's son?

A. Yes, sir.

Conclusion

The impeachment of Agent McNeal, Frederick, and Allen contributed to a verdict of not guilty for Captain Campbell. Pretrial discovery and detailed preparation of the questions to be asked of Agent McNeal on cross-examination brought about successful impeachment of Agent McNeal. Counsel did not use written out questions in cross-examining, but, rather, focused on those areas where he believed that he could impeach McNeal. McNeal, an experienced police officer, had testified previously in court and had to be cross-examined with great caution. Defense counsel generally stayed in those areas where he knew, from pretrial discovery materials, that McNeal could not hurt the defense theory.

The defense theory was that McNeal had not conducted a thorough investigation and had relied too heavily on Frederick and Allen, who were unreliable persons.

Civil RICO—Plaintiffs' Cross-Examination of a Defendant and the Defendant's Lawyer*

The case was known as *Williams v Ashland,* tried in the Eastern District of Kentucky, Docket No. CV 84-149. The counts of the complaint basically charged civil racketeering (RICO), breach of contract, emotional distress, and wrongful discharge. Tony Fitch, Eleanor Bradley, and I represented plaintiff Williams, and John McCall, David Tachau, Ken Tuggle, and Bob Dibert represented plaintiff McKay. Ashland Oil, Inc. and the individual defendants were represented by a bevy of top, nationally known law firms, including Fulbright & Jaworski, Arnold & Porter, and Cravath, Swaine & Moore, and at trial by Stoll, Keenon & Park.

The key issues to prove for plaintiff Williams were whether Tim Landon and Yehia Omar had been government officials for the country of Oman when Ashland Oil paid several million dollars for a "worthless" chrome mine in Rhodesia in order that Ashland receive certain crude oil contracts worth many millions of dollars from Oman, and whether the payments or investments in the chrome deal were really no more than disguised bribes to two government officials, Landon and Omar, in order for Ashland to receive influence on the crude oil contracts. If said proof was beyond a preponderance of the evidence, then the jury of six would consider whether Ashland had violated the Foreign Corrupt Practices Act (F.C.P.A.) in paying bribes to get oil, and whether such acts, along with other evidence not to be covered in this article, formed a pattern of racketeering which led to the firing of Williams for later informing, "blowing the whistle," on Ashland to the United States Justice Department and the Securities and Exchange Commission.

The excerpts and discussion of cross-examinations for this article deal with two witnesses:

First, Sam Butler, the presiding partner of Cravath, Swaine & Moore, who sat on the Ashland Board of Directors and generally decided whether his law firm or another would represent Ashland on legal matters. He chaired a meeting of the CEO, Chief Operating Officer, and General Counsel along with other corporate officers and lawyers at his New York office on January 7, 1981, to discuss what to do about "illegal" payments that had been made over the "chrome deal."

The cross-examination excerpts presented here show how I brought out Mr. Butler's arrogance, his knowledge that Landon and Omar were government officials, how the chrome and crude oil deals were *linked,* thus exposing a bribe and that they were not unrelated deals, and how he participated in a cover-up of said knowledge by helping to retain a well-known law firm to do a report which would find that Omar and Landon were not government officials, that no laws had been violated, and, thus, that there was no duty to report their illegal actions to the Ashland Board of Directors or to the Securities and

---

* By Kenneth Michael Robinson of the newly created Washington, D.C. law firm of Robinson, Wood & Grimm, 301 I Street, N.W., Washington, D.C. 20001.

Exchange Commission as required by a 1975 Consent Decree, already in place, which disallowed Ashland's making improper payments and concealing them in the records with known fictitious entries.

Second, Dick Spears, who was a named defendant. He was the chief in-house lawyer for Ashland, a Senior Vice-President, and the head of all personnel for the company (which had more than 40,000 employees). He was the chief lawyer from whom defendant John Hall (CEO) sought legal advice. Hall, per our evidence, used Spears and McKay and Williams (the two plaintiffs) to discover improprieties committed by his predecessor, Orin E. Atkins, Chief Executive Officer and Chairman of the Board of Ashland Oil from 1970 to 1981, to report them to Spears who then took them to Hall. Thus, Atkins would be fired, Hall would replace him as CEO, a report would be prepared by outside counsel that Ashland had been involved in no wrongdoing, and business would proceed as usual. The problem was that the plaintiffs, Williams and McKay, did find and report evidence of Mr. Atkins's improper acts, but this information was used to have him fired and replaced by Hall. Thereafter, despite constant prodding by McKay and Williams, Ashland refused to voluntarily turn its evidence of misconduct over to authorities. After 18 months of receiving no response to their attempts to get Ashland to "do the right thing," Williams anonymously informed on Ashland to the Justice Department and the Securities and Exchange Commission. Within two months, Williams and McKay were fired in retaliation.

My cross-examination of Mr. Spears was very important because through four years of pleadings, interrogatories, and depositions, Ashland defended that Williams's job was abolished by a budgetary "reduction in forces" and that he was not fired. Thus, if Ashland were believed, Williams could not seek damages in court. The excerpts of the Spears cross-examination illustrate Spears's betrayal of Williams, a friend, which led to Spears admitting, much like a Perry Mason case, in front of the jury, for the first time, that Williams was in fact fired.

In order to keep your attention, I note that after seven weeks of trial and much evidence, the jury found against the defendants and a judgment was entered totaling $69,500,000. Two months later we settled for $25,000,000 and the matter was concluded.

I. Sam Butler, Cross-Examination

BY MR. ROBINSON:

Q. Mr. Butler, you really don't know Harry Williams, do you?

A. I don't what?

Q. Do you really know Harry Williams at all?

A. I do not. . . .

Q. Now, was the transition from Orin Atkins to John Hall in September of '81, would you call that a peaceful transition?

A. Yes, sir.

Q. Is this a peaceful passing of the baton, a friendly sort of thing?

A. Well, I—I mean it—it's—while it was Mr. Atkins' ultimate decision, he obviously received a good deal of—of persuasion to do so. But I—I mean it wasn't as if he retired as sixty-five and Mr. Hall was his then annointed successor. I mean it wasn't a—

Q. Now, I've kind of gotten the impression—you correct me if I'm wrong—that Orin Atkins had lost a little speed, was getting a little tired, was kind of time to go on home and rest. Is that what you're trying to tell us he was—

A. No, I don't really think that's what I'm trying to say. I think I was saying just the opposite, that Mr. Atkins was getting up too much speed and was flying off doing lots of different things as opposed to really focusing on what at least I thought—. . .

This was to set up how they set out to remove Atkins.

Q. Well, would you view that as an illegal proposal, if you'd said it, to suggest a 2.2 to a $5 million consulting agreement to pay Mr. Landon in order that you cannot have a problem about him being a government official? Would that be legal?

A. If you were to take it in context—if I had said it, which I hadn't. You're making an assumption. If it had been said by anyone it would have been said with assumptions that we would have gotten the necessary documentation, the necessary attestations, so that there wouldn't have been any problem about it under the FCPA.

This refers to a memo which credited Butler with proposing the above consulting agreement, which he denied but which we proved he made. We showed this suggestion to be an illegal proposal acting as a bribe to cover up previous illegal pay-offs.

Q. It could cost a man his law license if somebody prosecuted for having made that statement like that and it was actually brought about. Is that right?

A. No, sir. I don't agree with that because I don't agree with the premises on which you're making the statement.

Q. Well, you don't agree. But I believe Mr. Stephenson impresses you as a man who's able to read and write, does he not?

A. I'm sure Mr. Stephenson knows how to read and write.

Q. Well, you—now, there he is, he's saying that you said in paragraph 11—now I believe you made reference to this yesterday, but we didn't really read it to the jury yesterday. You recall reading this to the jury yesterday?

A. No, sir, I certainly didn't read that to the jury.

Q. "Mr. Butler suggested retaining Landon as an advisor on various projects around the world at a rate of 2.2 million to 5 million per year. Someone else (unidentified) suggested considering a service charge by Ashland re Landon's sale."

You deny saying that?

A. Yes, sir.

Q. Can you explain how it is that Jimmy Stephenson could be that wrong that he wrote that down in your own little paragraph there?

A. There is a first page of this. And I don't remember specifically. I haven't seen it recently. But I think it talks about this being a compilation of notes. And I don't think it's indicated that it is Mr. Stephenson's own notes.

Q. Well, he was in the meeting, wasn't he?

A. "The following is a summary of that discussion based upon a review of notes taken by Messrs. Mayne, Feazell and Stephenson. The combined notes were in no way inconsistent."

I haven't seen those notes. I don't know what it is that Mr. Stephenson based that statement on. I just know it is inaccurate; I didn't make that statement.

Q. Well, see that, Stephenson is saying Feazell, Mayne and he made notes. Is that right?

All three were Ashland in-house lawyers.

A. That's what he's saying.

Q. Did you make notes?

A. No, sir.

Q. When you were up there at Harvard did you take notes in class?

This was a dig at Butler's education for the jury's benefit.

A. In class I did, sir.

Q. And was the purpose so you could accurately write down what the professor said was important so you could study it and make an A and get a Supreme Court clerkship?

A. Yes, sir.

Q. And it worked?

A. It worked beautifully.

Butler's credentials are remarkable and here I sought to use them against him, poke fun at him, and make him show his arrogance. It worked.

Q. He made a mistake. Let's see if Arloe Mayne wrote something pretty similar down in his notes. You see that? I put it in green as in money. Sam Butler suggested retaining—SB—SB is your initials, Mr. Butler?

A. Yes, sir.

Q. Retaining T. L.—that's Mr. Landon—as an advisor on various proposals around the world, 2.2 to 5 per year. Seems pretty much identical to what Stephenson has in his notes, doesn't it?

A. I noticed that—I've never seen that. But I notice someone has written YO with a question mark above that. What does that mean?

Q. Who do you think that would be?

A. I assume that refers to Mr. Omar.

Q. Well, Mayne wrote this note. 2.2 to 5 million. That's pretty consistent with what Stephenson has as far as the his figures. It's right on the button, right?

A. The YO is—I don't think I made the suggestion about Mr. Omar. As I testified before, I never heard of anybody ever proposing a consulting a agreement for Mr. Landon. That wasn't the business he was in. It was Mr. Omar. And it is possible—I don't recall it—that I said something about a consulting agreement for Mr. Omar.

Q. Mr. Butler, on the line where he's writting down what you supposedly suggested, he has T. L. He has YO above it with a question mark, right? But on the line where he's paraphrasing apparently what he thinks you said he has T. L., right?

A. It's clear to me that Mr. Mayne obviously thought he made a mistake there. Because he probably didn't think—I don't know what was in Mr. Mayne's mind. But he thinks that I probably would not have said that.

Q. Okay. Well, did—did Mr. Stephenson put a YO above his Landon?

A. You'd have to ask Mr. Stephenson. As I said, I think Mr. Stephenson made a mistake.

Q. Assume Mr. Stephenson's testified that he made accurate notes and he can read and write. That's what he said happened.

A. You have the benefit of his testimony. I don't.

Q. My point is, sir, we've got two lawyers from Ashland. One's general counsel, one Jimmy Stephenson who's done right well since, writing notes that you said something as specific as 2.2 to $5 million a year. And you deny that you said it, right?A. Yes, sir. Everybody can make a mistake. I think Mr. Stephenson made a mistake.

Q. Those two made the mistake?

A. Yes, sir.

Q. You didn't make a mistake in saying it that you're now denying it. Is that the mistake that was made?

A. No, sir.

Q. Would that give motive to want to see Orin Atkins disappear when he's having Jimmy Stephenson write memos consistent with his Arloe Mayne that you may have made a suggestion that violates the law?

A. No, sir.

Q. All right.

A. I do not believe that if I had made that suggestion it would have violated law. I object to you saying that.

Q. If Tim Landon—if Tim Landon was the chairman of the planning review committee, a government official, and if the chrome deal was linked to crude you had an obligation on the '75 consent decree to take it in, didn't you?

A. None of that was evidence at the time. I didn't know any of that at the time. What I was told at the time was that Mr. Landon had retired; he was no longer an official. In any event, I didn't make the statements. So there's no point to—

Q. Well you knew before Queenan was hired that Landon was a government official, didn't you?

A. I did not.

Q. You didn't? Had you concluded that he was?

A. I had not. I certainly had indicated—certainly had concluded that he presented a serious problem because he might well be a government official.

Q. Let's get 388 out Mr. Butler, the chronology. And let's go to page 13.

This exhibit was a 27-page document Butler prepared in 1981. It showed his knowledge and was used to convince the jury that he knew Omar and Landon were government officials before he hired Queenan to do a "white wash" report, i.e., a violation of the law.

. . . Landon's a government official you shouldn't do it?

A. I don't recall that. I would have thought offhand meant reason to know that there was linkage between the two transactions but—

Q. Look at the next statements here in Stephenson's notes. If you're acting as an agent for Landon as is suggested in paragraph ten, quote, "Are we providing something of value to a government official."

Now, look at this tic tac toe. Landon government official, way to handle it according to Atkins, question, are you providing something of value to government official, and then the note, Butler suggests that two and a half to $5 million pay off to hide it. Did this happen in that chronology?

A. No, sir. It did not.

Q. If it happened in that chronology you admit do you not, Mr. Butler, with all your intelligence and knowledge that would violate the consent decree. Wouldn't it?

A. No, I do not.

Q. Why wouldn't it?

A. Because there are still more aspects of the Foreign Corrupt Practices Act. You go to the very next point, Mr. Queenan says it would be possible to solve the problem by getting a statement, an affidavit from the—not an affidavit but a letter from the Sultan that he had no problems with this.

Q. Mr. Butler, the Foreign Corrupt Practices Act and the '75 consent decree are two different matters, aren't they, two different matters, two different duties, aren't they?

A. They're certainly two different legal requirements.

Q. Seventy-five [1975] consent decree required directors with knowledge to disclose any known violation of fictitious entries in the books and records of Ashland?

A. Yes. And I don't know that there are any fictitious entries in here.

Q. Would it be a fictitious entry to conceal that some officials are getting some payments on a Mont d'Or payment by saying he's a consultant by giving him two million dollars to disguise getting the money? Would that be concealing or making a fict—

A. You keep making assumptions that have nothing to do with the facts. That wasn't proposed, that wasn't suggested, that wouldn't have happened.

Q. This little run that I just made, did any of this happen? Any of these notes happen, Mr. Butler, any of them?

A. There was certainly discussions about notes of those things, yes.

Q. You don't deny the things that Stephenson wrote other people say, you only deny what he says you said, right?

A. Only in that one point, that's correct sir.

Q. All right sir. Now, you were in fact a director in '75 weren't you, Mr. Butler?

A. Yes, I was.

Q. You were in fact a lawyer who negotiated the consent decree, Exhibit 23, weren't you?

A. Yes, sir.

Q. And this is the cover sheet of it sir. And you agree do you not—and this is really hard to read, defendant Ashland Oil, its officers, servants—you were one of their servants at that point in a sense. Don't mean to insult you, but you were a servant, weren't you?

A. I prefer to refer to myself as agent.

Here Butler shows his arrogance again; he could never be anyone's servant. The jury smiled here.

Q. All right. You're an agent, then.

A. I saw the word agents there.

Q. All right. Let me straighten that out. You're an agent. You helped write this proposal, didn't you?

A. The SEC wrote it. I certainly reviewed it.

Q. You agreed, didn't you?

A. I agreed to it. I signed it on behalf of Ashland.

Q. So you were an agent and you were a director?

A. Yes, sir.

Q. And it said certain duties did it not that dealt with violations of the securities law; is that right?

A. Yes, sir.

Q. You cannot aid and abet in the violation of those laws, right?

A. You can't—

Q. Aiding and abetting only means help out, doesn't it?

A. That's what it means.

Q. Page 2. Duty of directors and agents, both of which you were, right? Right?

A. Yes, sir.

Q. Duty, is it not, let's look at paragraphs A, B, C and D. Isn't it clear that the directors and agents, both of which you were, had a duty to disclose any fictitious entries in the books and records? This is a duty that's covered in paragraph D? You cannot omit to state the nature and extent of false or fictitious entries and if you do it's a violation of the consent decree, isn't it, Mr. Butler?

A. There's nothing about disclosure in here, which you keep talking about disclosure. There's nothing about disclosure. That says they're enjoined from violating the Securities Exchange Act if there were a nature or disclosure, agents and extent of false or fictitious entries.

If I knew of any such things certainly it would be my duty not to do so, or to prevent them from being made.

Q. There's no duty to disclose to the SEC violation of this?

A. The injunction is to prevent those violations from taking place.

Q. But that is a court order from a federal court, right?

A. Yes, sir.

Q. And there's language in there, I'm asking you as counsel—and by the way, you're the managing partner of Cravath Swain, or one of them?

Again, I deliberately did this so he would correct me and show his arrogance.

A. I'm the presiding partner.

Q. That means the number 1 man?

A. Yes, sir.

We were using his brains and powerful position to show that he could not be as dumb as he appeared on the stand; hence, he must be lying.

Q. All right. All right. You know do you not that there was an agreement with the federal court through this consent decree that Ashland would not do any of these things I've just got underlined up here, right?
A. Would not do any of those things, I'll agree with that sir.

Very important admission here.

Q. And if you do any of that it's a violation of the consent decree, right?
A. It's a violation of the consent decree.

A big admission as I was about to use his own memo to show his own knowledge.

Q. It's your promise?
A. Yes, sir.
Q. And if you breach that promise you have a duty to tell the SEC, do you not?
A. I don't agree with that.

This would be an issue for the jury and they concluded that Ashland Oil did have such a duty.

Q. What is your duty?
A. Duty to prevent it.
Q. What is your duty if you haven't prevented it. If it happens, what's your duty as a director with knowledge of a violation of the consent decree, what is your duty according to this consent decree, since you helped draft it?
A. I don't think the consent decree covers it in any way. I'd have to think about that. Certainly that would be something that I would have to, anyone would have to, you might consider just resigning from the board. I'm not quite sure what you would have to do, but the consent decree itself does not require you to go to the SEC.
Q. Well, what's the purpose of this?
A. To prevent people from violating the laws. That's what the purpose of it is. It's not designed to prevent disclosure.
Q. Okay. Well, once you learned of violations of the law, what did you do about it?
A. When you learn that somebody might be attempting to violate the law, which is what we were doing here at this time, that there might have been either advertent or inadvertent violation of the law to find out whether or not that had happened.

And then we would decide whether to go to the SEC or to the Department of Justice or anybody else. But it is not required in this consent decree that that be done.

Q. Okay.

A. Consent decree requires you not to violate the law, which we were not going to do.

Q. All right. And so you deny that there is a duty on the board members if they have knowledge of this to, one, bring it to the board's attention; and two, to bring it to the Securities and Exchange or the court's attention so that there could be a correction of the problem that the consent decree covers. You deny that?

A. I of course didn't say what you just said. It would clearly be something that should be brought to the board's attention. No question about that. Where it goes from there is consent—and that is not because the consent decree applies, it is just because you have a duty to prevent violations of the law.

Q. All right. Before Queenan was hired, we've got page 14, these are your notes—by the way, your chronology is accurate and truthful, isn't it?

A. Yes, sir, to the best of my knowledge.

Q. Everything in there, you intended to write it accurate and truthful, right?

A. I tried to do my best.

Q. And you don't know of anything in there that shouldn't be in there like in Stephenson's, right?

This was to prevent him from disputing some entries he made which I was about to use very effectively against him.

The next exchange was one I had never tried before, but I felt so confident with Mr. Butler that I proceeded. Remember, the issue was whether Landon or Omar were government officials. I used Butler's written entry in the next question and he bit the bait and focused on the word *appear.* Of course, *appear* means *more likely than not,* the precise burden of proof that we, as plaintiffs, had.

Q. All right. Deliberately put there by you.

A. I wrote it.

Q. Okay. Well, look at what you said. And you might want to go to page 13 since I can't find my 13 and read how come about this—this there is late April '81. You write, "It now appears clear to all concerned that Landon was without question, a foreign government official."

How, I just asked you, Mr. Butler, if you concluded this man was a government official and you said you didn't, didn't you?

A. I notice that I would focus on the word appear. It certainly appeared that there was serious problems, as I say, extremely dangerous. It now appeared clear that I was very concerned.

Q. Mr. Butler, what's the word appear mean? What's the word appear mean?

A. It means on the surface, likely that that's what it means.

Q. Likely of prima facie showing?

A. That's right. An investigation could have shown something else.

Q. Preponderance of the evidence?

Here, Butler admitted proof of one of our key elements.

A. That, I would agree with that, yes, sir.

Q. All right. So you concluded with a preponderance of the evidence prima facie showing at page 14 in April of '81 that without question Landon is a government official, right?

A. In September when I wrote that it's my recollection that at the time I thought it was very likely, appeared clear that he was a government official.

Q. And when you wrote it you back dated it because what you had to do on a chronology to April, so when you wrote in September you wrote your thoughts as they existed in April, right?

A. That's what I did my best to do. Yes.

Q. That's what you what?

A. I did my best to try to do that. To put it as I recall it at the time.

Q. So before Queenan is hired you made this prima facie finding. Preponderance. Now, look here. Mr. Atkins just says, indicated that the deals were related, that they're linked. Right? Right?

A. Yes, sir.

This was asked to show why thousands of dollars were spent for a legal report when they already had the answer, unless it is to cover up the truth they already knew.

Q. Now, you know do you not that linkage, if Landon is a government official and if the chairman of the board who did the deal in part says that chrome is linked to crude, that could be viewed by the SEC as a violation of the Foreign Corrupt Practices Act, couldn't it?

Again, the admission of a second key element to the case, i.e., payment to an official linked to the favor received; oil.

A. Certainly could.

Q. And it could be viewed as a violation of '75 consent decree, couldn't it? Because it's a fictitious entry, it's making it appear that Ashland is buying chrome when they're . . .

Q. Well, you concluded prima facie preponderance of the evidence, did you not, that Atkins showed there was linkage, and you supported it by looking at Mayne's notes, didn't you?

A. He said there was linkage. No question about that.

Q. And that really disturbed you, did it not?

A. I didn't hear what you said.

Q. That disturbed you.

A. It certainly did. . . .

Q. Look what he had concluded as early as March 12 as to who Landon was. "As I recall, the purpose of such an agreement would be separate payments to Omar from Oman crude contracts, since Tim Landon, who was clearly a government official, might also expect payments. Your partner was more involved in the trenches on a day-to-day basis than you, wasn't he?

A. Oh, not really, no. We intended to have it be that way but it didn't work out that way.

Q. He concluded Landon a month before you, if you want to quibble, a month and two weeks before you, that Landon was clearly a government official, didn't he?

A. That's what he says in September, that's correct.

Q. Do you have any reason to question your partner's veracity when he made that memo?

A. No.

Q. This is accurate, is it not?

A. It is the way he put it. I saw it before it was sent to Mr. Queenan, I did not disagree with it.

Q. He addressed it to you and you reviewed it and sent it on to Queenan, right?

A. Yes.

Q. So we've got two from Cravath, Swain & Moore. One the number one man, yourself, and your partner, saying without question Landon is a government official, right?

A. Yes, sir.

Q. Where you come from in Indiana that's a slam dunk, isn't it?

A. That's a slam dunk if he did something improper as a government official. There was no evidence at all to that.

Q. Well, that's a two-point slam dunk which you have to add up all the points. But that's one, government official Landon slammed in there, right, in our conclusion.

A. I think it was extremely likely that you would conclude that he was a government official. That does not answer the question.

Q. Now, Mr. Hall, did he tell you that he wanted letters from Landon that there was separability on the chrome and crude deals?

A. He might have, I don't remember that. I don't remember him telling me that.

Q. Let me ask you this, Mr. Butler: If in late April Atkins told you they were linked, and he's the chairman of the board, why would you want to get letters saying they weren't linked unless you're looking to cover it up? I mean, I don't understand that.

A. As I said, I don't remember Mr. Hall telling me that. I don't remember any conversations about getting the letters on linkage. The question was, what we were trying to do was to get a letter from the petroleum minister or the Sultan, which would say that Mr. Landon or Mr. Omar had not influenced any of those contracts. . . .

Q. Do you think it's appropriate for Hall to talk to Landon on April 17, 1981 and be told that in his opinion Yehia is a government official, and then turn right around and come back and write the boss and say my impression is that we can negotiate down the figure of 8.3 million for 25 percent of the chrome deal? Does that look like a possible pay off to Landon to get him to say something false in the letter?

MR. JOHNSON: Your Honor, I want to object because that's a mischaracterization of what Mr. Hall reported that Mr. Landon said to him.

THE COURT: Jury can figure it out.

Q. What did Mr. Landon say, Mr. Hall say to you about this?

Here, it is important to note that John Hall, then the number two man at Ashland, visited Tim Landon, an Omani government official per Butler's cross, on April 17, 1981. There Landon told Hall that "any reasonable person in Oman would consider Yehia Omar to be a government official . . . but the American lawyers might decide otherwise." We used Hall's memo of this discussion on Hall and Butler to show that one Omani official told Ashland that the other, Omar, was a government official and, rather than Ashland correcting the problem by telling the Board of Directors and the SEC, thus mitigating the damage, Ashland did as Landon suggested and hired American lawyers to render an opinion that Omar was not what "reasonable people *knew* he was" and thus cover up the crime. The cross-examination shows Butler admitting the significance of another element of proof, yet, still seeking to downplay the total significance of it all.

A. There certainly isn't any reference in my chronology because I didn't then and don't now remember this. I know as far as he is concerned that he, Omar, is a government official but that American lawyers might decide otherwise.

Q. Of which you're one, right?

A. I am an American lawyer, yes, sir.

Q. And he didn't tell you this, did he?

A. He didn't. No, I don't believe so.

Q. And is this the type thing that you would have liked to have been told back then in your search for the truth? I mean being honest about it, you'd like to have had this information, wouldn't you?

A. No, sir. I don't think so, because by this time, by the time he would have told me this, since I was away earlier as I said before, with my father's death, that we were fairly confident the money was coming back from the Mont d'Or, the 1.35 million.

Q. It's not significant to you that any reasonable person in the government of Oman would consider Yehia to be a government official? I mean, that doesn't look like a slam dunk to you?

A. That looks like Mr. Landon's opinion.

Q. Did it look like a slam dunk too?

A. No, sir. But it certainly is very good evidence.

Q. That looks close to Michael Jordan, doesn't it?

A. Well, it's getting close. As I said before, that isn't the only answer. There is another question. You keep saying that government official is the only thing. That's only a third of the problem. Only a third of the problem.

Q. You can only do one slam dunk at a time, can't you?

A. Yes, sir. Only one at a time.

Q. Two balls are hard to get in there?

A. Yes, sir. Don't make the second one till you get one.

Q. Do you consider the meeting of January 7 to be a facade, 1981?

A. No, sir.

Q. So you disagree with Mr. Hall's calling it a facade intended to divert attention from Yehia's problem? That's Exhibit 365. You disagree with Mr. Hall's conclusion as to the way that meeting was conducted, don't you?

A. I don't know what this document is. It says Hall says.

Q. That the meeting of January 7 in New York was a, quote, "facade."

A. Who says Hall says?

The next exchange brought the house down and, I believe, finished Mr. Butler off as a witness. Through a series of questions we showed him his chronology memo,[1] a memo from an earlier Board of Directors meeting prepared

---

[1] We did this by using transparencies of the pages and showing them on a 5′ by 7′ screen with an overhead projector. Key parts were underlined in red and green and

by Arlo Mayne, then General Counsel to Ashland Oil, and referred Mr. Butler to admitted conversations he had with Orin Atkins, CEO. It was during this exchange that defense counsel really objected and tried to protect Mr. Butler for what I perceived as the first time.

Q. I'm going to break it down please if I'm allowed. I'm asking you on a separate issue of linkage, you concluded beyond any question, did you not, in your memo at page 14, and please look at it again, that chrome and crude are linked.

That was your conclusion as a lawyer reading this document and talking to Mayne who wrote it and Orin Atkins who did the deal, that was your conclusion wasn't it, Mr. Butler?

A. Mr. Robinson, I am very pleased that you continually refer me back to my chronology, because my chronology exactly states what I have just said before.

It said Queenan and I both thought—let me go on to page 14, but if the chrome transaction was also tied to the Omar crude transaction the situation would again be extremely dangerous. And then we go on, since it now appeared clear to all concerned that Landon was without question a foreign government official.

Q. I want you to—

A. That's if, it's the if, Mr. Robinson, that I keep coming back to with you, is the if. If that is correct, if that accurately states the facts, that's Mr. Mayne's collection of a series of notes. If that is correct, we had an extremely dangerous situation.

Q. Sir, this is again counsel's notes of a board meeting in which Atkins presented the chrome and crude to the board, is it not?

A. That is not his notes.

Q. What is it?

A. He, as I say here, Mr.—after questioning Mayne admitted what he had shown me was not a simple transcript of his notes but rather a combination of notes and his recollections.

Q. May I borrow yours because surprisingly I can't find mine. Thank you. Okay. Now, I'm going to underline something for you. I don't want to nit pick, I'm asking you if you put in your chronology that after Orin Atkins told you they were linked and Arloe Mayne showed you this document, did you write in your notes that Mayne's notes proved this to be the case, period? Did you write that?

A. Would you let me read that now that you've read it?

Q. Yeah. I'm going to underline it so you can't miss it.

---

the judge and jury had each page in constant view while listening to the questions and answers.

MR. JOHNSON: Well, I'm going to object to that Your Honor. That's just lawyer's approach to—

THE COURT: He just said he was going to underline it.

MR. JOHNSON: Well, why should he seek in such an intimidating fashion to underline? He can read it.

THE COURT: Mr. Butler doesn't look intimidated to me.

Q. I don't believe Mr. Butler's scared one bit of me. Are you scared of me, Mr. Butler?

A. Well, I'm getting that way.

Q. Give me a job and I'll leave you alone.

A. You come in and see me tomorrow.

Q. Let me bring Harry down there.

A. Is he a lawyer?

Here I made a joke for my client, Harry Williams, a lawyer who per our complaint was unable to find a job since being fired by Ashland Oil.

Q. Look what I underlined there please. Now, just read what I underlined for us and then explain whatever you want to explain.

A. Could I read the whole sentence? Would that be all right?

Q. Yeah, but I want you when you get ready to read it stop and tell the jury what I underlined, reading the whole page if you like.

A. No. No, just read the whole sentence. "Atkins indicated that they were related, that"—this is where he starts in underlining "—that Mayne's notes prove this to be the case, and that McKay was attempting to conceal his own very active involvement in the chrome transaction."

Q. Now, did you conclude that Mayne's notes showed that clearly they're linked?

A. No. I did not so conclude. That was Mr. Atkins' statement.

Q. Okay.

A. I didn't say that. That's Atkins indicated that. I said if, and if I would be is what I meant.

Q. Did you think it was appropriate for Yehia to return 1.35 million dollars and at the same time get 3 million under a finders fee agreement and then get a letter from the oil minister saying everything's hunky dory? Would that be a proper way to solve this riddle?

A. Yes, sir. If all that happened in the way that I expected it to happen, not just the way you described it, I think that would have been perfectly appropriate.

Q. Well April 28, 1981, Exhibit 231 for Williams. If you look, I will get a copy for you sir. If I've got one. It's a letter to you Mr. Butler from Mr. Atkins, April 28, 231. Now this, if you notice the date, I'm going to get you one, this April 28 is the day after Atkins tells you on

April 27 that they're linked and shows you Arloe Mayne's notes which we just covered. You with me?

A. Yes, sir.

Q. And the next day Atkins writes you and suggests does he not that Yehia get 3 million upon the return of the million three, and that we can get a letter from the oil minister. Now, I'm asking you did you get this letter, sir?

A. Yes sir, I did get a letter.

Q. And did you call Mr. Atkins and say Orin, you can't do that. It looks like you're trying to cover up the problem. Did you tell him that?

A. No, sir. I did not.

Q. You should have, shouldn't you?

A. No, I shouldn't have.

Q. Well, I mean, here you got Yehia got a million 35, Landon has refused to give you letters, you know that by now don't you? You know that on April 17 Landon wouldn't give you letters, right?

A. Landon would make no attempt to get letters for our behalf.

Q. You know that Alan Stephenson and Jimmy Stephenson had been unable to get letters from Yehia on April 14, right?

A. That's correct.

Q. So now you've got Atkins telling you on April 27, according to your chronology, that the deals are linked showing you the document we covered, and then the next day Atkins writes you and suggests to you, Mr. Butler, 3 million for a million three with a letter from the oil minister. You don't think that appears that Orin Atkins was trying to buy the letters?

A. No, sir.

Q. Well, what does it look like to you? Explain what that means to you.

A. That we would rescind the Mont d'Or transaction. I didn't write this letter. This is what he is saying. The way I would interpret it, I'm not agreeing or disagreeing with the letter. I got it, I ignored it because I thought we had a big problem with respect to the chrome transaction.

Q. You ignored it?

A. Which this really doesn't address exactly, because we were going forward at that time looking toward the idea of having an independent counsel who could solve these problems. And indeed Mr. Atkins engaging in writing the letters about these really didn't add anything to the situation. I knew we were going to have to get to bottom of the problem. . . .

Q. Let me ask you this: Why do you have to write a letter for the people over there to write? Why can't you send somebody and say, put down the truth in a letter? Why do you have to write the letter?

A. Because we have, we'd like to give them a draft. The idea of the kind of thing we need.

Q. You'd like to give a draft to the person who is going to tell the truth about the status of these people? So you write the draft?

A. Do it all the time.

Q. Well, why don't you, if you're looking for the truth, ask a lawyer for the country of Oman to go to the Sultan or his people and let them draft the letter on the truth rather than you write it, a board member and lawyer for Ashland?

A. I don't think we knew who the lawyers for Oman were. How to approach somebody in the Oman government.

Q. You didn't?

A. No. We did not.

Q. Do you know who Baker & McKenzie was?

A. It's a law firm.

Q. You don't know whether they have access to people over there?

A. No sir, I do not.

Q. You know, do you not, I just took that off, that this is a copy of the first page of the draft for Mr. Omar prepared out of your law office by Alan Stephenson submitted on the day that Atkins sent the letter to you. The day, right?

A. Yes, sir. Mm-hmm.

Q. Okay. And this follows, does it not, the Atkins letter that talks about three for 1.35 and letters. That's the context in which this happens, isn't it?

A. This is all consistent with what he said in that letter that he had been working on these April 28 letters. . . .

Q. But I don't understand, if Mr. Landon tells Hall when he doesn't sign the letters that any reasonable person would say Yehia is a government official, why doesn't that stop it right there instead of then going and drafting a letter eleven days later at a time that you're proposing buying out 25 percent of a chrome mine for eight million dollars and send it to the very man who just told you the truth supposedly? Why do this?

A. Mr. Robinson, isn't it possible that Mr. Landon might change his mind, that we might be able to persuade him to give us that letter? Is that—

Q. Change his mind or change the facts?

A. We asked once, we asked once, he said no. There is no harm in asking again. . . .

Q. He says so we don't lose sight of the trees or the forest, whatever that thing says. Chrome transaction was approved the board was informed—he said up there, this statement squarely and directly tied the chrome transaction to a possible oil contract. That's your words, isn't it? That's your words.

A. No question about it, the linkage was there. I've testified to that. There is no question about that.

Q. Linkage is there. And four days later Atkins writes you and Queenan, who is going to do an independent study, to try to get Landon to get something from the Sultan that they're not and you don't think that that's wrong?

A. I don't think that's wrong because I told him we weren't going to do it and we didn't do it.

Q. The point is intent.

A. It was an idea of Atkins'. Atkins took the advice. . . .

I was wrapping up and then planted the seed that Mr. Queenan was hired to a "whitewash" job for Ashland where he and Ashland already knew the truth. The next exchange showed how Queenan and Butler first knew one another.

Q. Do you think it's proper for Mr. Queenan to conclude six weeks before he's hired that Yehia's not a government official? Would that be proper?

A. I don't know what you're addressing. I don't know whether they made any such conclusion. Are you asking me a hypothetical?

Q. Yes, sir. . . .

Q. If Arloe is right and three days later that Queenan said he'll try hard to give an opinion of counsel there is no violation of Foreign Corrupt Practices Act, that would be wrong too, wouldn't it?

A. If Queenan said that it would clearly be wrong. I can't believe Queenan said anything like that on May 4.

Q. I believe his daddy bought your daddy's business and you all went to Harvard together, right?

A. His daddy had nothing to do with the company.

Q. Your daddy had a company and sold it, his daddy became the owner of the company?

A. My daddy became head of the company long before his dad had anything to do with it.

Q. When you met him up there at Harvard his daddy was the head of the company that at one point bought your daddy's company?

A. Yes.

Q. You all went to Harvard together?

A. We were there a year or two together.

Q. Friends?

A. Not close, no.

Q. You referred him to Ashland in the first place, didn't you?
A. No, I did not.
Q. Referred him to them?
A. He was selected by Ashland. I didn't know anything about that.
Q. Well, Mr. Atkins knew that Landon was a government official, didn't he, in '81?
A. He certainly said that he had been a government official on January 7, that he had retired. That was his position. That he had been but had retired as a government official.
Q. And he sent this letter, 235-B, did he not and which I showed you the second page of a while ago, the eleven million dollar page, that Landon is probably the most influential man in the Omani government. That's an important fact to be thinking about at a time that you're studying the Foreign Corrupt Practices Act is it not?
A. No question about it. We were studying that all the time. We were concerned about that.
Q. So you know there had been payments to Landon for chrome and payments to Yehia for Mont d'Or, right?
A. Yes, sir.
Q. And you knew that Yehia was considered by some to be a government official, right?
A. Some people thought that he might be a government official.
Q. And Landon's a man of this kind of influence, right?
A. Yes, sir.
Q. You've got value and influence there, right?
A. Mm-hmm.

Butler admits two elements of the Foreign Corrupt Practices Act in one answer.

Q. And you've got a memo by Mayne about Orin Atkins intent on the chrome/crude deal is to get crude for chrome. That was a memo we read a while ago. You got intent, influence and value right there in one swoop, don't you? Right? Right or wrong?
A. We have, I'm not going to accept your words. We have there, as I repeatedly testify, indicia that were extremely dangerous that there might be a violation of law and that's what we wanted to investigate.

It was an influential, as I keep saying, the fact that he was influential, possibly government official does not indicate there was a violation of law. There still had to be proof that he, that we made the payment with the knowledge that he corruptly influenced the minister of Oman. We have no knowledge, information about that at all to this.
Q. That's the facts and a decision for the jury, you know that.

A. Yeah. Exactly. Mm-hmm. That's why we hired Mr. Queenan to make that factual decision.

Q. Might be why Harry hired me.

A. I don't know why Harry hired you.

Q. Anyway, 2/3/78, were you the secretary, Atkins secretary at this meeting on September 17?

This was the Board of Directors meeting where Atkins was terminated.

A. Yes, sir.

Q. Well, now, did you try to take more accurate notes than Jimmy Stephenson did?

A. I tried to take accurate notes.

Q. Well, now, this is what comes from the minutes. Now, my question is, I want to be fair, I don't know whether this is what you wrote or whether this is what somebody else wrote about what you were supposed to write. Did you write this? "Mr. Hall was advised that the understanding with Atkins was that while he would continue to have the title of chairman of the board and CEO until September 30, he would act in that capacity during the period only with respect to the investigation being made by the Kirkpatrick firm." Did you write that down?

A. That's the, following the minutes I believe because I was shown that the other day. I'm sure that I wrote that down. I was the acting secretary of that information.

Q. So you wrote that and that's what you wrote, right?

A. I did, sir.

Q. And what you wrote is what you wrote. It doesn't say that Orin doesn't have any power, it says he has that specific assignment, doesn't it? That's what we just read?

A. Yes, sir.

Q. And that's what Hall was told, right? . . .

A. Yes, sir. Mm-hmm.

Q. That's what you wrote?

A. That's what I wrote.

Q. That's what Hall was told, right?

In conclusion, Butler, the Harvard honors law review graduate, former clerk to Chief Justice Warren when the *Brown v. Board of Education* landmark segregation decision was handed down, presiding partner at Cravath, Swaine & Moore, and Board of Director member to Ashland Oil gave an incredible series of answers to a statement he made which clearly demonstrated an improper motive on his part to the Ashland jury.

A. Yes, sir. Not Hall, that's what the—I'm sorry, Hall. Hall was advised.

Q. And it appears—

A. By the board.

Q. And it appears that someone reading that almost seven years later that Orin Atkins was to act in the capacity of CEO with respect to the investigation of Kirkpatrick. That's what—

A. That's what the words say, yes, sir.

Q. Well okay. Would that be proper for Orin Atkins if in fact his remaining duty was to oversee the conclusion of the report since he was one of the targets of the report? Would that be proper?

A. For the life of me I can't understand why I wrote those opinions that way. Because I don't know what it means. I'm sorry.

Q. You don't know why you wrote it like that?

A. That's right.

Q. Don't know why Jimmy Stephenson wrote what he wrote, right?

That is, from the January 7, 1981 meeting where he wrote that Butler proposed a pay-off to an official to correct a problem. The deal, as recorded, had Butler suggesting that a $2.2 to $5.0 million consulting contract could be given to the person in exchange for something to cancel what we perceived as an earlier illegal act. Obviously, if that was the intent, the jury perceived then that the suggestion was criminal in nature.

A. That was different. I don't know what Mr. Stephenson says. That was a mistake.

Q. You don't know why Arloe wrote what he wrote.

A. That's true.

Q. But as a pattern, somebody is writing something and nobody . . .

I then stated that Butler was aware from Board meetings that my client, Williams, was considered to be the informant. At first, Butler denied knowledge, but I used his previous deposition to refresh his recollection.[2]

Q. Well, the board was also told were they not at some time that Harry Williams was the informant. Is that right or wrong?

A. I don't remember that ever having been said.

Q. You testify in the SEC?

A. Did I testify in the SEC?

Q. Well, you know, at a hearing.

---

[2] This was actually impeachment, but I chose to refresh his memory rather than impeach as I had already impeached him enough and preferred to refresh.

A. Yes, sir. I was interviewed. Not at hearing, but I was deposed by the SEC, yes, sir. Mm-hmm.

Q. Okay. I ask you if you recall being questioned at page 944. Question line six: "In that period, dealing with '82 and '83, whenever they started in '81 or before through the present day, have you heard any particular names suggested by anyone as to who the possible leaks are?" There is an an objection by Mr. Johnson. As a board member? Mr. Fitch, yes. Johnson, all right.

"Answer: At the board meetings I believe that it had been suggested by one or more board members that Mr. Hall or someone else would report about newspaper stories or SEC investigations, that kind of thing, that occasionally Mr. Hall might say it and occasionally other board members might say it and the information relating to that matter. I don't think anyone knew but they were speculating it had come from McKay. In later conversations, later board reports, I think there were speculations that they may have come from Mr. Harry Williams.

"Question: Can you provide us with any further information or details, approximate time, approximate subject matters, who the speakers were with respect to McKay and then with respect to Williams?"

"Answer: Nothing specific. I really don't have anything more specific."

Passed down to a question, line 12: "And do you have a recollection of Mr. Hall being one of the people who referred to Mr. Williams in that respect, meaning informant?"

"Answer: I think so. I'm a little vaguer about Mr. Williams. I think he did, others too." Do you recall that testimony?

A. Now that you've refreshed my recollection I do.

Q. Mr. Hall did in fact, as you best recall, suggest that Harry Williams might be one of the leaks or the informant to the board; is that right?

A. I wouldn't add any more to the answer I have in there. I have a very vague recollection.

Q. And you had nothing to do with the abolishing of Harry's job, did you?

A. No, sir. Nothing at all.

Q. And you weren't privy to the discussions that Spears Hall and McCowan and anybody else might have had to discuss whether he'd been fired or not, were you?

A. Say again.

Q. You were not privy to any discussions in June or July among them when Harry Williams job was discussed, were you?

A. No, sir.

Q. And you don't know in your own first-hand knowledge, since you were not a participant in that decision, why he was discharged, fired or abolished, do you? You only have the hearsay of what's come out in the litigation; is that right?

A. I have no direct knowledge at all.

Q. I ask you sir, to look at Exhibit 783 for McKay. Were you at this board meeting? I've got it marked right here?

A. Mm-hmm.

Q. And you see Jane there. Jane Pfeiffer testified that you were present and said some of those things. You were present at that board meeting, whatever date is on there?

A. January 26, '83. Yes, sir, I was.

Q. Were you present when somebody suggested that Mr. McKay was mentally ill?

A. Is that in here some place?

Q. Well, first let's see if you have a memory of it . . .

As a wrap-up, I then sarcastically suggested that Mr. Butler had nothing to do with Williams being fired and then showed him Mr. Feazell's notes (Arlo Mayne's replacement as General Counsel once Hall became CEO) from the January 7, 1981 meeting which we sought to prove was the "smoking gun" meeting where the cover-up was born.

Q. Tom Feazell is now the general counsel of Ashland since Mr. Mayne left; is that right?

A. Since Mr. Mayne retired, right.

Q. You have no reason to doubt his ability to take notes, do you?

A. Generally speaking, I consider Mr. Feazell's perfectly capable of taking notes.

Q. Seems like some of these lawyers ought to be able to read and write, doesn't it?

A. Well, notes are notes. Notes are what you jot down. You take them out of context they leave out a lot of things. Notes are what people want to remember.

Q. I will get up there and read this. SB, that looks like it's you at this January 7 meeting. "Fears leaving too many tracks, lead the government to you. If you start a monitoring procedure what do you do if you find something afoul."

Now, you say that you didn't say that, right?

A. No, sir. I didn't say any such thing.

Q. You gave an explanation yesterday about your recollection of it, right?

A. Right.

Q. Well, did you say what did you do if you find something afoul?
A. What I said and what she has truncated from those notes, is what notes are for, is that the problem procedure as detailed, and I was expressing there, the procedure as detailed that Mr. Queenan had proposed was that it, if you couldn't comply with it, it would lead the government or someone else who was investigating to say why didn't you follow your own guidelines. Guidelines were too strict that you couldn't always abide by them.
Q. What's truncated mean?
A. Truncated means shorten.
Q. Means shortened. Did you say you fear leaving too many tracks? Just yes or no Mr. Butler. Did you say that?
A. I don't believe I said that in those words. No, sir.
Q. What do you think he said that he could truncate into that?
A. I think what he said was that you didn't want to have too precise procedures which were impossible to meet so that you would give the government a guideline as to why you didn't do something you said you were going to do and then have them complain and assert that you had violated the law.
Q. Sir, you agree do you not that in these type cases involving documents, that the government from your experience trys to follow what's called a paper trail to solve the intent of the parties; is that true?
A. Yes, sir.
Q. And that if you can follow the paper trail the documents sometimes are more accurate as to what really happened in the puzzle than the testimony of the people who have an interest in the litigation; is that right?
A. No question about that.
Q. And there is a note being written that you fear too many tracks. And you've explained that, but I've shown you a lot of documents that happened in '81 that do leave somewhat of a paper trail about what everybody was thinking and saying back there even then; is that right?
A. There have been a lot of notes. There was no question that Ashland was leaving all kinds of paper around.

MR. ROBINSON: All right, that's all. Thank you.

THE COURT: Mr. McCall, any questions?

MR. McCALL: Yes I do, Your Honor. . . .

The cross-examination of Butler took from page 6549 to page 6618 of the transcript, just 69 pages, and in it we got Mr. Butler to admit the term *appeared* which meant proof by a *preponderance of evidence,* that Landon and Omar were foreign government officials, that the payment to them through the chrome deal was linked to getting the crude oil allowance from the Omani government (equivalent, to the jury, of a bribe), and that he could not explain his own notes he made as secretary to a very significant Board of Directors' meeting which allowed the outgoing CEO one last assignment, i.e., to oversee the conclusion of the Queenan report, a report we said was intended to *cover up* that CEO's illegal acts and thus permit Ashland Oil not to disclose its breaches of the SEC Consent Decree. Butler admitted that a "paper trail" leads to the truth more so than does biased testimony and, thus, his testimony was rejected.

As a footnote, I note that the *American Lawyer* did an article following the verdict and one juror told their reporter that she actually considered whether the jury could find punitive damages against Sam Butler, despite the fact that Butler was not named as a defendant.

II. The Defendant, Dick Spears, Cross-Examination

Dick Spears was a named defendant; he was a Senior Vice-President of Ashland Oil, Inc., Director of all of Ashland's 40,000 personnel, its chief in-house lawyer and advisor to the CEO, John R. Hall, and, purportedly, the former best friend to plaintiff Harry D. Williams. We sought to prove that Williams had nothing to do with the foreign operations where bribes were paid to the Omanis to get the crude oil. Our theory was that Spears solicited Williams's participation in bringing information about the illegal activities to Spears who would then give it to Hall, that Hall would use it to get rid of the then CEO, Orin E. Atkins, replace him, disclose it per the law, and clean up the company. Williams did as requested, and once Atkins was fired and Williams tried to follow through and have the new administration report it to the federal authorities, Spears and Hall isolated Williams and punished him to keep him quiet. Thereafter, in April, 1983 (19 months after Atkins was fired), Williams "blew the whistle" on Ashland Oil and the SEC began an investigation. Three months later, Spears and Hall fired Williams as retaliation. Ashland defended that Williams was not fired but, rather, was terminated as a part of a "force reduction" which was in no way related to retaliation for "blowing the whistle."

Ashland, Hall, Spears, and Atkins were sued. Punitive damages were sought from Ashland, Hall, and Spears.

The cross-examination of Spears began at page 5296 of the transcript and ended at page 5420. It followed a direct examination where Spears denied the bulk of Williams's testimony. Spears denied that he was a close friend to Williams, denied that Williams was put in motion by Spears to spy on Atkins and report back to Hall, denied that he, Williams, McKay, and Hall were "a team" working to collect data to get rid of Atkins for the good of the company, stated in 1982 and 1983 that Williams was doing a poor job in State Government Relations as a lobbyist, and denied that Williams was fired.

Q. You recall testifying in your deposition, number three—volume III, at page 474, that "I believe Mr. Bell and Mr. McCowan each have acknowledged to me that Mr. Williams in the 1980 time frame did a good job reorganizing the state government group and in getting fresh talent brought into that group. I think both those gentlemen have said words to that effect to me." That's a true statement, isn't it?

A. Yes, sir.

Q. So when you published there through Mr. Johnson's question this exhibit 24 for the defense talk about Harry Williams and then read "not enough strength in state government relations" you know Harry Williams had strong strength in state government relations, and you so testified. Is that right?

A. I thought that he did a good job building the group when he came to Ashland. The period that we were critical of did not relate to that activity.

Q. Well, you were being questioned at the time about a 1979 memo. And I just read to you what he did when he got to Ashland in 1980, right?

A. Yes.

Q. Did a right good job, right?

A. Yes, sir.

Q. Now, there was then a publication and attachment B, Mr. Spears—is Mr. Williams on this senior management and corporate officer list? Do you see that?

A. I've got an attachment B. What is it?

Q. You remember Mr. Johnson asked you if Harry Williams was listed on those corporate officers long range or primary list as an officer of the corporation and you said no?

A. Right.

Q. Now, this is March of '79, right?

A. Right.

Q. At about that time Mr. Hall was making you—recommending you to be the head of personnel, right?

A. I was the assistant at that point in time.

Q. You know, do you not, that Harry Williams was made a vice president by July of '79, right?

A. I didn't recall when it was.

Q. Well, you know it's '79 he made vice president, right, right?

A. I don't—I don't know necessarily. I don't have that in my head as a memory.

Q. Well, when you publish a document in March of '79 indicating Mr. Williams was not a long range corporate officer projection you know he made it by the end of '79, don't you?

A. If you tell me that, I will—I don't know the time frame. He became a vice president.

Q. All right. You accept, do you not, that if the impression was conveyed that Harry Williams as of March '79 didn't have much of a future at Ashland that within three months he was a vice president, right?
A. Okay.
Q. So you didn't mean to create that impression to this jury, did you?
A. I didn't make the connection at all.
Q. All right. Now, you say he's not a level II employee at any time he was at Ashland, right?
A. Right.
Q. And we have your word on that?
A. That's what I remember.
Q. You have any document that supports what you remember?
A. Not with me.
Q. Do you recall—the purpose of documents, as I understand it, is to have on paper something that is accurate, right? That's the purpose?
A. Right.
Q. All right. Now, what does the word incumbent mean to you as the head of the law department over at Ashland?
A. Incumbent means the person occupying a position.
Q. Well, you're familiar with Plaintiff's Exhibit 478, which looks like it's a 1983—this is my triple chart. You see this now. There was a reference by Mr. Johnson that potential, if you look at the top of the list, it says, does it not, "Level II Potential for Division President or Head of Major Corporate Function." That's the potential this list deals with, is it not?
A. Um-hum.
Q. The potential to go higher, right?
A. Right.
Q. To senior management. It doesn't deal with the potential to be a level II, does it?
A. Well, does it have level II on there?
Q. It has incumbent level II, if you'll look at it, Mr. Spears, which suggests that he already was?
A. Someone showed me this exhibit before. And I think it's simply an error.
Q. It's an error, right?
A. I think it is.
Q. It's an Ashland document that has incumbent level IIs, which Harry Williams is listed, right?
A. I think that's what it says.

Q. Then in all these papers over there on the defense side do you have a piece of paper that shows this is an error?

A. I think we could find one.

Q. You could?

A. Yeah.

Q. Okay. But you haven't thus far, have you?

A. No.

Q. Might find one over the weekend though, right?

A. No. . . .

Q. Okay. Now, Mr. Johnson asked you a question at some point before the break, did you ever tell Williams to stay away from McKay, get on board and go along with the cover-up and keep quiet? I don't recall having heard you say the answer to stay away from McKay. You did on repeated occasions tell Williams to stay away from McKay, didn't you?

A. Yes, I did.

Q. Who introduced him to McKay?

A. I have no idea. . . .

Q. And you're being sued for many millions dollars, right?

A. That's right.

Q. You're not biased at all, right?

A. I don't like being sued for millions of dollars. . . .

BY MR. ROBINSON:

Q. You said Mr. Williams was easy to deal with; it was easy to get rid of him. Is that your testimony?

A. I'm just not hearing you, sir.

Q. You said it was easy, as I recall, to sever Mr. Williams. You used the word easy?

A. That's correct.

Q. Didn't cause you any grief at all, did it?

A. That's right.

This answer really upset the jury, visibly.

Q. Um-hum. And he wasn't your friend, was he?

A. He was at one point. . . .

Q. Who was given the responsibility of telling Mr. Williams that he was finished at Ashland Oil? Who told him?

A. I believe his supervisor, Mr. Bell.

Q. And Mr. Bell had not at any time in the past told you, had he, that Mr. Williams was not doing his job, had he?

A. I had not had any conversations with Mr. Bell about Mr. Williams' job in some time.

Q. Did Mr. Bell didn't indicate any displeasure to you, suggest any displeasure as to Harry Williams' work product?

A. I don't remember it.

Q. Well, isn't that something you would remember, since you've testified earlier he wasn't doing his job?

A. I knew from my own personal belief that he was not carrying out the job properly during the period of '82 and '83.

Q. '83 he wasn't doing anything significant that you would consider doing his job properly. Is that your testimony, Mr. Spears?

A. Well, the—in the '83 period was a period when I was admonishing him to go to work, trying to get him to go to work and stay away from Bill McKay.

Q. Did you write him a memo commending him on the job he did in March of '83?

A. I probably did.

Q. How can you say he wasn't doing his job if you wrote him a memo telling him what a good job he was doing?

A. I was simply encouraging him. Totally consistent. "Good work. Here's what happens when you're working."

Q. Did you in fact write on a memo that he sent to his superiors: "This is a coup, Harry. Good work." Did you do that?

A. Yeah.

Q. I'm going to find it sooner or later. But did you do that? Did you do it?

A. Yes, sir.

Q. Now, I'm going to show you 475 that you were shown. Apparently Ashland wants 227,000 and some change back because Williams wasn't doing his job. Is that right?

This was Ashland's counterclaim against Williams.

A. Yes, sir.

Q. All right. You recall being questioned in transcript 1 at page 62:

"Question: And did Mr. Bell during 1982 indicate, at any time indicate to you any different appraisal than what is shown in the effective performance category in the very middle of this page?

"Answer: No, sir."

Did he ever—is that accurate?

A. Yes, sir.

Q. Mr. Bell in '82 never said Harry did anything else than how he evaluated; is that correct?

A. Yes, sir.

Q. And you know he evaluated him as 92, didn't you? Do you know?

A. I don't remember what it was.

Q. Well, I'll show you the bottom of my triple chart, exhibit 530 for Williams. You see this 92, graded by Robert Bell? Do you see that?

A. Yes, sir.

Q. What's wrong with a 92?

A. It's okay.

Q. What do you mean it's okay?

A. It's about an average score.

Q. Average score. So it's okay?

A. That's right.

Q. No criticism by Bell who was his immediate superior, correct?

A. Correct.

Q. What did McCowan give him?

A. I don't remember. I don't know.

Q. Well look above. 95?

A. Okay.

Q. You sent that to Mr. Hall, from Spears to Hall. It was exhibit 453, Harry Williams, 95, 1982, right? What's wrong with a 95?

A. Nothing wrong with a 95.

Q. Then why do you say he wasn't doing his job in 1982 when he is given a 92 and 95 and neither of them told him he wasn't doing his job? Why do you say that in here now?

A. Because of spending all his time with McKay. We were trying to warn him that McKay was in a disruptive mode and he ought to go to work. And the fact that he got a score at the end of the year like that does not preclude anyone from saying something like that to him if they observe it's going on.

Q. Well, let's see what you said about him in March of '83. And tell us whether or not this meant millions of dollars to Ashland Oil that you told him it was a coup. These are your words I believe, sir. Do you remember this memo? March 28, 1983, to Robert Bell from Harry Williams, copies to the core group. Talking about the "New York Gross Receipts Tax on Oil Companies in '83." Mr. Williams talks about what he had done. Whose handwriting is that on the bottom telling him it's a coup?

A. I fully remember it.

Q. Well, whose handwriting is it?

A. That's mine.

Q. Read it for us. Can you read it from up there?

A. "Harry, congratulations. This is a coup." . . .

Q. And that's what you're saying. You talk about force reduction, but he was dismissed because you all didn't like what he was doing. Isn't that the bottom line.

A. The force reduction—

Q. That's what you said.

A. The force reduction was—that's what I meant earlier when I said it was easy. It was easy to go along with the force reduction.

Q. Mr. Spears, you don't suggest to the folks on this jury, do you, that if Harry Williams went into the SEC and the Department of Justice and blew the whistle you have a right to fire him for doing that? Now are you telling these folks on the jury that that's what you have a right to do? Yes or no, and then explain it.

A. Yes.

This was an incredible admission which upset the jury and the Judge.

Q. Okay. Please explain that if Harry Williams had information—

A. If—

Q. Time out—

THE COURT: All right. Now, this. Just a minute. Just a minute.

THE WITNESS: If he is reporting a violation of the law—

THE COURT: Just a minute. Now, you asked the question. You're calling—I'll let him answer it. It's a matter of law. I'm interested in what he has to say. . . .

Q. Well, I know—

A. What I'm—what I am saying is we cannot fire someone for a violation—for violating the law—if we are violating the law. But if there is no violation of the law, as I understand Kentucky law, there's nothing to prevent us from firing him.

Q. Right. Now, of course you know, do you not, that under any law Ashland Oil doesn't decide whether you violate the law; that's reserved for a judge and jury? You know that as a lawyer, don't you?

A. Um-hum.

Q. Did I hear an "um-hum" in there somewhere?

A. Yes, sir.

Q. All right. Now, you were very complimentary of Mr. Williams' work in 1982, weren't you? Didn't you tell him that?

A. I—I've tried to encourage Harry all during this period. I probably did. . . .

Q. And then McKay got his suspension. And then thirty-six hours later Harry's job is abolished. Now as I heard you testify when Mr. Johnson questioned you, you didn't think that they were related in anyway. Is that your testimony?

A. That's right.

Q. That's just a coincidence, I guess?

A. No, it's not a coincidence. I think Bob Bell his supervisor just struck while the iron was hot, said, "Management's in a mood and he's spending a lot of time with McKay. And he needs to be force released. Let's do it." And that's what happened.

Q. Well, if Harry's doing his job according to these ratings and you're saying nice work, and nobody's complaining to you, which we've just covered in your deposition about the quality or the amount of work Harry's doing, what's wrong with him exercising the First Amendment right to talk to his friend McKay? Can you tell us that?

A. There's nothing wrong with his First Amendment right except when it enter, interfaces with the proper flow of the work and after we had a situation where McKay was disruptive and hostile to management. All I did was tell Harry, "Look, a word to the wise, son, stay out of this situation. Go on and do your other work."

Q. A word to the wise, son? That sounds almost like a threat, doesn't it?

A. No, I wouldn't call it a threat.

Q. What do you consider a man who's four years older than his friend saying, "A word to the wise, son. Stay away from McKay or else." What does that mean?

A. That may have been my—my vernacular I used here. I'm not sure I said that. What I'm trying to do is communicate with you that we were telling this gentleman you don't need to be over this confrontational situation.

Q. Well, you said it yesterday. I wrote it down. And you said it again today. So whether it's your vernacular or not, it must ring out in your mind that you said it, right?

A. Could have.

Q. "A word to the wise, son." You don't view that as a threat, some kind of an intimidation, "Harry, get in line, and do what we tell you, or it's Katy barred the door."

A. I don't think there was any doubt, Mr. Robinson, in that conversation that we were trying to say to him. It may not have been a threat, but we were trying to warn him, you're going down a path that may not lead you to any good result.

Q. Let me show you exhibit 321, January 11, '83, McCowan to Perrine, a copy to Hall. You know good and well, do you not, that a document about force reduction hasn't got one thing in the world to do about abolishing Harry Williams's executive job. Now you know that, don't you? And it does—please find the line in there that makes reference to it, that any reasonable person could read and conclude that you're telling the truth.

A. I'll tell the truth.

Q. Well, I know you took an oath so I suspect you will. So read it and show us where it's in there.

A. I don't see anything in here about state government relations.

Q. Well, but you were given that document by Mr. Johnson, as I recall, to suggest the impression that that's the document that started the force reduction that led to Harry losing his job. That was the impression I got when you read that document.

A. Well, I think the only implication of the document is that in this time frame of January 1983 the force reduction activities were going on and they continued. They started in '81. They went through January of '83. And this was simply an illustration of it. I don't think Mr. Johnson introduced it to relate to state government relations.

Q. Well, Mr. Johnson asked you if Harry told you of anything about Yehia and this problem in '79. You know good and well Harry was in Washington and had no idea there was a problem in '79, don't you?

A. I don't remember.

Q. Don't you?

A. I remember Harry coming to Ashland in '80.

Q. Well, Mr. Johnson asked you in front of this jury yesterday, did Mr. Williams complain to you about the Yehia matter in 1979? That doesn't make much sense, does it?

A. I answered no.

Q. Well, but it could create an impression that Harry wasn't complaining. That's the impression that could be created if somebody doesn't straighten it out. Is that right?

A. Okay.

Q. And the same question was asked in 1980. And Harry wasn't involved in 1980 either, was he, to your knowledge?

A. I don't think he was.

Q. Well, then a wrong impression could be conveyed with those questions and answers if somebody doesn't straighten it out. Isn't that right? Isn't that right?

A. Well, I'm not sure where you're going, Mr. Robinson.

Q. Well, I'm going at impressions, misimpressions to jurors who judge. What evidence is there that you have that Harry Williams should have complained about something in 1980 that he knew nothing about?

A. I didn't know he should have complained about something in 1980. . . .

BY MR. ROBINSON:

Q. Isn't it true the first time you have any idea of Harry Williams ever getting involved in participating in any discussions about the Yehia Omar deal was, whether you intended it or not, after he was at the luncheon with you and McKay the day they started had having been in Kentucky?

A. That's the first time I remember it.

Q. And that's just a coincidence, I suppose, that the first time he got involved was when he was at the dinner—lunch table with you drinking a beer in March of '81? That's just a coincidence?

A. That's as far as I know it was.

Q. And that's true when you say it's true?

A. That's true. . . .

Q. And while I'm—before I go to something else, you've told us that Mr. Bell never criticized Harry Williams' work during '82. The same holds true of Mr. McCowan, doesn't it? He never complained about Harry's work either, did he?

A. That's correct.

Q. And you'd agree that McCowan and Bell would know a whole lot more about the specifics of the job Harry was doing than you who was responsible for 40,000 employees?

A. That's correct.

Q. And neither of them complained about the job he was doing, did they?

A. That's correct. . . .

Q. Mr. Spears, did you ever when you were a younger have somebody you thought was your best friend?

A. Yes, sir.

Q. And sometimes be hurt that that best friend didn't think you were his best friend, right?

A. I don't know whether it ever got that complicated.

Q. Okay. Did you ever do anything in '80 and '81 to discourage Harry Williams from thinking that you were very close if not his best friend?

A. I went through that yesterday.

Q. Well, I'd like to go through it with my questions.

A. Okay.

Q. Did you ever discourage him, disown him like you did on the stand yesterday?

A. I told him beginning very early after Orin left when he started talking about jobs, what the rules were for getting jobs. And from then on

Harry—every time I saw him that's what he wanted to talk about was jobs.

Q. Well—

A. And the friendship—I couldn't spend that much time doing that. The friendship did—did fade away.

Q. Well, so it's clear, he was your friend. You're not saying you all weren't friends back in '80 and '81?

A. No, I didn't say—

Q. He used to come to the house and you'd see each other.

A. When he'd come to Ashland from Washington frequently he would stop by the house.

Q. Have a drink, watch the ball game on Sunday together?

A. Yes, sir.

Q. Your wife would send him birthday cards, didn't she?

A. She did.

Q. You're not trying to tell this jury you all weren't really chums? You were real close friends?

A. I was chums with a lot of people. Close—he's not my closest friend and never has been. I doubt if I am his closest friend.

Q. No, you're not. . . .

Q. And do you recall McCowan coming to see you and saying that you're the only friend Harry Williams has in the company. That you Dick Spears have a bright future, may be president some day. But would be better off for you if you dropped Harry Williams. McCowan continued by saying to Dick Spears, we probably shouldn't fire Harry Williams, waiting for you to say why not. But you didn't respond. Did you remember that conversation?

A. I'll give you my version.

Q. Well, you did discuss this matter with Harry Williams because there's no other way he'd have had this information. Isn't that right?

A. That's right.

Q. So you told Harry about that conversation?

A. Right after that conversation I called him up and told him to stop doing what he was doing.

Q. Well, that was because, was it not, McCowan told you you better drop it. "You have a good future, Dick. If you know what's good for you, drop Harry." Did he tell you that?

A. He also said Harry was criticizing him as a candidate for president.

Q. Mr. Spears, if Harry had not asked for a job for himself yet and was getting along fine with Bell and McCowan and getting these ratings coming up, and he goes and he recommends you over his boss, you can see how that would irritate Mr. McCowan if Mr. Hall told McCowan that Harry was sponsoring you and not McCowan, can't you?

A. I don't think either—I don't think McCowan wanted to be president. And I don't think the presidency was going to be an issue at all anyway. We didn't name a president for the next two or three years. So what you're talking about is gossip, idle gossip. And Harry went around the building talking about it. McCowan heard about it, came to me and said, "This is not attractive. It's not good for the company. And it's not good for you." And so I asked Harry to stop talking about it.

Q. It was after that that you dropped Harry, didn't you?

A. I didn't drop Harry. . . .

Q. Did Harry supposedly talk to Arnold before that or after that?

A. I have no idea. It was in spring of '83.

Q. Okay. Well, now Jimmy Stephenson told you on occasions after April 26th, '83, that Harry Williams was probably the informant, didn't he?

A. Well, I think several people speculated about Harry and . . .

Q. Okay. And was there a concern that somebody was an informant with them?

A. Yes.

Q. That would be a congressional committee probing this matter, right?

A. Yes.

Q. Why would that disturb you since you had such a powerful report of the Queenan report? Why would it disturb you if some committee wants to rummage around in there, see what went on?

A. Well, it didn't disturb us. We went and took it over there. . . .

Q. What do you think this means, John Hall—McKay says why is it so important to find out who the informant is? John Hall: "In order to stop him."

What does that mean to you as a lawyer, chairman of the board saying to Bill McKay, who had been disruptive according to you all, six days after they know that somebody blew the whistle? What did that mean to you?

A. You're talking about loose language which may have been sometime later. I've said repeatedly the emphasis was on stopping all the documents going to the papers. I know we didn't care about the informant. And if an informant was over there that's fine. We had to go respond to it. And we were going to. And we had stayed in touch with the SEC from 1981 right through. And if they wanted to send us a subpoena or if they wanted to insist we get the documents all together all they had to do was ask.

Q. Why would you send your secretary—

A. We weren't going to stop an informant.

Q. If you weren't concerned about it, why would John Hall have you send your secretary to bring Bill McKay up, ask him who is the informant and then say we want to stop him?

A. All I'm suggesting is that what John really had his mind on—and I can't speak for him.

Q. Then don't.

A. Was—

Q. Do you know what he had his mind on?

A. —the documents.

Q. The documents, so we can stop him. The informant at this point has called the Department of Justice and SEC. You knew that, didn't you? You knew this wasn't the newspaper. This was sure enough law enforcement had been called?

A. Yes.

Q. And John Hall had been called, right? Right?

A. Right.

Q. And you know, do you not, that to try to interfere with an informant providing information to a government—investigative branch of the government could be construed as an obstruction of justice? Didn't you know that? Didn't you?

A. Yes.

Q. And John Hall according to Harry's notes, "So we can stop him," right?

A. Yes.

Q. And you and Hall have no notes nor with Jackie Zornes of your recollections of that day and that discussion of Bill McKay?

A. We didn't keep 500-page diaries.

Williams kept a 500-page diary.

Q. And the only document is Harry Williams' notes made that day that Hall says so we can stop him, right?

A. I've explained it three times, what I believe the situation is.

Q. Something that could be construed as an obstruction of justice?

A. Could be construed.

Q. All right. Now, there is not a document in Ashland's files as of that day is there, sir—and if there is please tell me where we can find it—that has one piece of information that Harry's job is going to be abolished as of the day John Hall said "so we can stop him." Where is the document that Harry's job's going to be abolished as of May the 2nd, 1983?

A. I have no idea where the documents are on the force reduction.

Q. You know it doesn't exist as of May 2nd, don't you, sir?

A. No, I don't know it doesn't exist.

Q. Then where is it in all this discovery, stacks of documents, where is it?

A. It may exist; it may not exist. I'm simply telling you I don't know anything about it.

Q. If it is exists, Mr. Johnson didn't show it to you during your four hours of questioning, did he?

A. No, I suppose he didn't.

Q. And nobody showed it to you during your six or seven days of depositions, did they?

A. No, sir.

Q. But it may be out there somewhere, right?

A. It may be.

Q. In Mr. Queenan's safe or something, right?

MR. ROBINSON: I'll strike that, your Honor. I'm sorry. Nothing like organization, your Honor.

BY MR. ROBINSON:

Q. While you can't refer us to that document that deals with Harry's job being abolished, do you recall a document coming in to Mr. Hall's attention shortly thereafter from an outside director suggesting what he thought should happen to the informant?

A. Are you talking about the Erickson letter?

Q. Yeah, that's the one.

A. Yes.

Q. Now, what did Mr. Erickson suggest should happen to the informant?

A. Should be fired.

Q. All right. Now, he was on the board when Orin Atkins went down. Is that right?

A. Yes, sir.

Q. All right. So exhibit 496, May 24, twenty-two days after Hall says "so we can stop the informant," Mr. Erickson says, "I strongly feel that if we have internal, insider leaks from employees that we should make every effort to locate them, and they should be either be discharged or severely reprimanded," right?

A. Correct.

Q. McKay gets reprimanded with the suspension and on Saturday, July 23rd Williams' job vanishes, right?

A. Right.

Q. And by that time the suspicions had focused that Harry Williams was without any doubt the prime suspect as the informant, right?

A. No.

Q. Who was?

A. I don't think anybody knew who the prime suspect was.

Q. And you heard Mr. Hall testify? . . .

Others had testified that it was Williams.

At this point I knew that Spears had to be impeached in a major way before the jury. The momentum of the questions on how it was that Williams was discharged unless it was as retaliation for informing were interrupted by me and I moved to another topic. This was done to make Spears believe that I was disorganized and could not stay on course. It made him more cocky and reckless with his answers.

On September 17, 1981, the Board of Directors accepted Atkins's resignation as its Chairman and CEO. It was tantamount to Atkins's being fired. I knew Spears had gone right to Williams's home where he drank several bottles of Taittinger champagne at $125.00 a bottle, from a case given years before to McKay by Yehia Omar (the Omani official later bribed by Ashland). McKay had saved an empty bottle signed and dated September 17, 1981 by McKay, Williams, and Spears. Spears was unaware the celebration bottle had been saved as memorabilia. Consequently, I led Spears through numerous questions where I challenged his direct testimony. Then he had denied celebrating over Atkins's dismissal, and denied drinking and being happy and excited over Atkins's termination. The sequence of the impeachment follows.

Q. And is it known in Ashland that you're considered the lawyer that—throughout the '70s and '80s John Hall turns to when he wants advice?

A. I think that was the case until I left and went to the personnel department.

Q. And you were trained under Arloe Mayne, though, weren't you?

A. Yes, sir.

Q. Trained you, right. Now, Arloe was Orin Atkins' chief lawyer, right, that he'd turned to in the company?

A. They had worked together many years. Arloe was the chief lawyer for the corporation.

Q. And you were John Hall's? We just covered that.

A. I was a lawyer working for the corporation.

Q. That was close—

A. And I worked frequently with John Hall.

Q. All right. Now as of November '81 Orin Atkins is gone, right? Right?

A. Yes, sir.

Q. For whatever reason. And Arloe's on his way out the door, right?

A. Yes, sir.

Q. Now who became the head of all the law department, not general counsel, but the head of all law?

A. Me.

Q. All right. Feazell, general counsel, reports to you, right?

A. Yes.

Q. Who became chairman of the board?

A. Hall.

Q. But there was nothing to celebrate concerning Orin Atkins' departure, was there?

A. That decision hadn't been made at the time of the so-called celebration.

Q. Of course. And when you went over to Harry Williams' house that night of September 17th it was with mixed feelings, right?

A. Sure was.

Q. And I believe you said you felt bad about it?

A. Yes.

Q. Harry laughed?

A. Harry what?

Q. Harry laughed. I believe you said he laughed, and you were sad?

A. I didn't say Harry laughed.

Q. Well, were you sad?

A. I was relieved. But I certainly had mixed feeling. I had worked with Orin Atkins for many, many years, and I was uncomfortable about it. And I left very early.

Q. Now you do know, do you not, McKay and Williams say that together they worked with you and Hall to correct the problem Atkins had done wrong and to get a new leadership?

A. Yes.

Q. You disagree with that, right?

A. Yes.

Q. All right. So there would be no reason for you to be celebrating with McKay and Williams the night that Orin is out and Hall is in, would there?

A. I told you I didn't characterize it as a celebration. That's what's been alleged here.

Q. Well, you know sometimes you do memorabilia when you celebrate something, sign the baseball that won the game or something or—you've done that before as a kid, haven't you?

A. Yes.
Q. Honor that moment?
A. Yes.
Q. You signed the Yehia Omar champagne bottle that night, didn't you?
A. May have.
Q. You may have. Would you recognize your signature if you saw it?
A. I would.
Q. All right. And I'd like to tell you—I've got a champagne bottle here, Yehia Omar's fingerprints on it.
MR. ROBINSON: If we could mark—I don't know the numbers. Give us 1000. I know Williams doesn't have 1000. And we'll fix it later.

I pulled the bottle from a paper bag discarded in the trash can in front of the jury box. Spears sat as if stunned and the jury moved forward in their seats with smiles on their faces, aware that Spears was in real trouble.

BY MR. ROBINSON:
Q. Now, would you tell us why you would sign a Yehia Omar champagne bottle the night Orin Atkins is discharged or when the other two people who signed are Williams and McKay unless you were celebrating the success of the team and the victory?
A. I was relieved.
Q. You were relieved after how many drinks?
A. We didn't stay very long.
Q. You drank three or four bottles of that stuff, didn't you?
A. No, I didn't.
Q. Well, that's your signature in the middle?
A. Yes, sir.
Q. That's Dick Spears taking the prime spot on the bottle, right, right in the middle?
A. Right.
Q. And over on the one side is McKay, right?
A. Right.
Q. And Harry actually puts "loving it, Harry Williams." Do you see that?
A. Yeah.
Q. You see that? "Loving it."
A. I see that.
Q. It looks like you all were drinking and celebrating, doesn't it?
A. I didn't know we were even going to have champagne. But it certainly looks like we were drinking and celebrating.

Q. It looks like by the time you signed it you knew you had it, right? And you say this is not a celebration of a team effort to get new leadership?

A. It would—it was in my opinion—

MR. ROBINSON: Can the jury see this, your Honor?

BY MR. ROBINSON:

A. —come by the house and have a drink. Come by the house and have a drink. Harry's diary says "I was relieved." I have read that. Sure I was relieved. I was terribly tense, glad it was over. But I didn't stay very long. I was uncomfortable when I went. And I was—and I was uncomfortable today about it.

Q. Well, did you sign that before the bottle was empty or after?

A. I have no idea.

Q. You know it was after, don't you?

A. No, I don't know it was after.

Q. Well in any event, we know do we not that according to McKay and Williams there was a four-man team. Now you know John Hall—he had a lot of responsibility on the 17th. He didn't have time to go drinking, did he?

A. No. He wasn't invited, I don't think.

Q. Now is it a coincidence that three out of four on this described team are sitting in Harry's apartment drinking Yehia's champagne, signing the bottle? Is that it, if there wasn't team? Is that just a coincidence or what?

A. Well, I think just the—they invited me over. I went over to it. I had worked closely with McKay particularly. Harry had somehow gotten involved in the thing. And there you go.

Q. Okay. And do you—out of 40,000 employees, do you see it as somewhat of a coincidence the three out of four of the team were sipping Yehia's champagne the very day that's dated on the bottle and Orin's out?

A. I don't know. Hall and Dick Spears didn't say there was any team.

Q. And you don't use the term team in your vernacular frequently?

A. Sure.

Q. You do, don't you?

A. Yeah.

Q. So when Harry Williams puts in his diary that it was part of the new team, that's the description you and John Hall use all the time, isn't it.

A. Sure.

Q. Management team?

A. Football team.

Q. Team, right?

A. Yeah.

Q. Now, when Bell—Bell retired in '86, didn't he?

A. I don't remember what the date was.

Q. Well, what do you think as head of personnel. Mr. Bell—do you think?

A. Well, this is not a memory test, is it?

Q. Well, sometimes it is.

THE COURT: Don't argue with the attorney. Just answer his questions.

THE WITNESS: All right. . . .

Next, I made the jury understand that Williams was a very conservative man who, but for being assigned by Hall and Spears to the Atkins matter, would have stayed out of it.

Q. Harry's job in state government relations had nothing to do with the problem that existed in 1981 with Yehia and Ashland did it?

A. Yes, sir. Exactly right.

Q. And unless somebody put him into that he had no business being there. Is that right?

A. That's exactly rate.

Q. And you know that Harry from your knowledge coming into '81 was certainly a conservative guy who wears pin-striped suits and doesn't take unnecessary risks, right?

A. I don't know that.

Q. You don't see—you don't see Harry wearing Colonel Sanders seersucker suits, do you?

MR. ROBINSON: That was a friendly—this was a friendly—

Here I poked fun at the suit Ashland's chief counsel was wearing.

MR. JOHNSON: I want to say that's very personal, your Honor.

THE COURT: All I know is I've seen a lot of maroon ties the law few days.

MR. ROBINSON: All right.

BY MR. ROBINSON:

Q. But I mean Harry's conservative, isn't he, to your knowledge? Didn't take risks coming into '81, did he?

A. I don't know what Harry did.

Q. But there he is sitting with you and Nagel in Washington, D.C.

A. And Bill McKay, there again, three of you who they say were part of the four-man team, is that a coincidence that you all were there getting together?

A. Well, Bill McKay being there to me was a coincidence. . . .

Q. Do you feel that it's appropriate for him [Atkins] to be given the duty to oversee the conclusion of the Queenan report after he had been discharged, after he had resigned?

A. He was not given that duty.

Q. He was not?

A. That was given to Hall.

Q. Okay. Have you ever seen the board minutes excerpt of what the board designated his duty to be?

A. I haven't—I have, and it's incorrect.

Q. The board minutes are incorrect of what their intention was?

A. To the extent they create the implication that—that Mr. Atkins was in charge of the investigation they are incorrect.

Q. . . . September 17, '81, a meeting with the board of directors of Ashland Oil was held. Commencing at 8:00 a.m. All the directors of the corporation who are not employees were present. This means outside directors, right? Right?

A. Yeah, I think so.

Q. Except Grubb and Murray. Butler acted as secretary. Now you know Butler certainly has the capability of keeping accurate notes, doesn't he?

A. That don't mean he always will. He's got the capability. I agree with that.

Q. Well you have his—now, over here Mr. Butler's note:

"Hall was advised that the understanding with Mr. Atkins was that while he would continue to have the title of chairman of the board and chief executive officer to September 30 he would act in that capacity during the period only with respect to"—. . .

BY MR. ROBINSON:

Q. "Hall was advised he would act in the capacity during the period only with respect to the investigation being made by the Kirkpatrick, Lockhart firm, and Hall would be in all other respects chief executive officer."

Now this is what you say is incorrect?

A. Yes, sir.

Q. You weren't there?

A. I was in the immediate area. I remember it being discussed and somehow this glitch came out. I don't believe it for a second. I think John Hall was in charge all the way.

Q. All right. But the point is that's your word, your memory and your word, right?

A. Sure.

Q. Now, this is an actual document. This is the minutes of the meeting recorded in time, right, frozen in time?

A. Frozen in time.

Q. Typed right there?

A. Right. Typed right out.

Q. So somebody can take that document and compare it with your memory and your word, right?

A. Yes, sir.

Q. And judge which is accurate, right?

A. (Nods head affirmatively.)

Q. Do you agree that it would be inappropriate for Hall who was in total charge to allow Atkins to oversee the conclusion of the Queenan report the way the minutes show based on what he knew about what Atkins had been doing in the preceding month?

A. I agree. If you leave off that last phrase I agree under any circumstances it would have been wrong. It was wrong for John Hall to split the CEO's duties in any form or fashion . . .

A. Doesn't mean a thing to me, Mr. Robinson, because I think the board minutes are in error. I'm totally convinced of that. And I think it could be confirmed by the board of directors, including probably Mr. Butler who wrote the minutes. I think it's a simple glitch in the minutes. There's no way that could have happened, the scenario you just suggested.

Q. But, sir, I mean if somebody's on a fact-finding mission and they get the minutes, you got to admit that ordinarily it looks a little stronger than your memory of seven years ago without any notes, doesn't it, I mean just taking it for what it's worth, right?

We then broke for lunch and the next few questions and answers are astounding.

CONTINUED CROSS-EXAMINATION

BY MR. ROBINSON:

Q. Mr. Spears, although you do have a right to do that, you did discuss your testimony with your lawyers over lunch, did you not?

A. Yes, sir.

Q. Okay. And you probably discussed what I'm getting ready to show you on McClenahan, didn't you? Exhibit 365, you probably discussed that over lunch, didn't you?

A. No, sir.

Q. Did you discuss the board minutes and your answers?

A. Yes.

Q. Anybody tell you that your answers were wrong and you ought to do better?

A. Yes.

The following questions led Spears through the final days before Atkins was fired and some notes he passed to Williams on a napkin at a lunch thereafter in Washington, D.C.

Williams's diary entries were then used to confront Spears and get him to adopt, at least in part, what Williams recorded as remarks made by Spears.[3] I was wrapping up the cross-examination by trying to show that once Williams had served his purpose in 1981 for Spears and Hall, he was isolated, and once Williams saw the writing on the wall, he tried to salvage his job of 15 years with Ashland Oil by trying to get the man he believed to be his best friend, Spears, to relocate him, but save him. The excerpts are as follows.

Q. Dick, send me to New York so that I can at least leap like a frog off a lillypad and get a new job, but don't destroy my career. Do you remember that conversation?

A. I remember a conversation with Harry when he inquired about going to New York.

Q. And was it so he could save his career because of the way that you and Hall had sent a bad message out throughout the—

A. No.

Q. No? And you don't remember?

A. The reason—what I said to him about that was that it required a presentation to the financial community and that was not your strength there, it won't work.

Q. Bell recommended him. Bell was his immediate supervisor and he recommended it, didn't he?

A. I didn't know that.

Q. You don't remember that?

A. No.

Q. All right. Mr. Williams was telling you in '82 and '83 that the Queenan report should be disclosed, wasn't he?

A. I don't remember in '82. I think by '83 he was.

---

[3] Williams kept a coded 500-page diary about his actions and inner thoughts throughout the time frame at issue (1981-1983). He had referred to Spears in there under the code name, "The Prince of Darkness." I used Williams's entries in his diary to republish what Williams had previously testified to. The purpose was to get Spears to admit much of Williams's entries as accurate conversations that had occurred. Where Spears disagreed, I showed that we had his word and no contemporaneous notes to corroborate him as did Williams.

Q. Okay. Now, do you agree that the consent decree gave you and Harry Williams both an equal duty to disclose any violations of that decree to the SEC?

A. Yes. . . .

Q. Well, if Harry Williams feels there is a violation and he brings it to your attention, are you telling us if you disagree with him he then stops his belief to take it in, he follows you like you're Moses?

A. No. He's perfectly entitled to go ahead and take it in.

Q. It's all right, isn't it?

A. Once it's been determined. But if it's determined that it's not a violation he can still take it in.

Q. What if he's determined that the persons he's bringing it to, the chief lawyer, you, and the chairman of the board Hall, were involved in a coverup to prevent that from happening?

A. He never—

Q. Where does he go then?

A. Well, in the first place, he never mentioned the '75 decree in his life. Harry didn't.

Q. He never what?

A. He never mentioned the '75 decree to me in his life.

Q. We have your word on that, don't we?

A. Yes.

MR. JOHNSON: Your Honor, I'm going to object.

THE COURT: Those questions are argumentative. He's under oath.

Q. All right. You have a document to support that statement you just made?

A. I don't have any diary, no.

Q. So this Harry Williams feels that a consent decree and Orin Atkins made him sign that he will comply with the consent decree in office policy in 1975 and '77, you agree do you not that Harry Williams had an obligation first to follow the consent decree, that took priority over any policy of Ashland Oil. As a matter of law and ethics.

A. I think the policies of Ashland Oil were to comply with the consent decree. There wasn't any conflict between them.

Q. I'm saying if Harry Williams felt there was a consent decree, which there was, and he felt that you and Hall were violating it and covering it up, you agree that he should not be discharged or have his job abolished because he does in fact tell the Securities Exchange Commission, because of what his conscience tells him he must do.

A. He can tell them whatever he wants to tell them.

Q. And not be discharged or have his job abolished, right?

A. If there is a violation of law, he can do it.

Q. And any type elimination of his job as a result of that that would be to retaliation would be wrong, wouldn't it?

A. I think we're entitled to fire whistle blowers.

Here, at page 5409 of the transcript, Spears made a fatal admission and he knew it afterwards. His answer, "I think we're entitled to fire whistle blowers," rocked the jury.

Q. All right. And who was the Queenan report being suggested it should be taken to according to Williams, the SEC?

A. The SEC.

Q. All right. And who did he blow the whistle to in April of '82, '83? You know now it's the SEC, do you not?

A. I thought it was the Department of Justice.

Q. And the SEC, do you know that or not?

A. No, I didn't know it was the SEC. . . .

Q. Can you tell us how Mr. Williams got involved in '81 if it wasn't through you? How he jumped out of state government relations into this mess, if it wasn't through you?

A. I think he was just curious. He wanted to get involved, he wanted to be a player. He thought I would be his patron if somehow he hung around me. Maybe I talked to him too much. He was not involved in any way, he had nothing to do with any of the transactions. He was not, as you well point out, he was not capable of doing anything. He brought no information into the picture. I think it's simply a situation of wedging into the thing.

Q. What's that?

A. Wedging into the thing.

Q. Okay. Do you agree that as long as an employee is industrious and productively involved in the enterprises which are successful at the company, that they can reasonably anticipate they will not be discharged?

A. That's true, but they also can be discharged at will of the company.

Q. Well, I'm going to get off of this, but once a person does his job like I just read to you, and can reasonably expect what we just read to you that you agree with, and then follows what the consent decree requires him to do, which we've been through, you're saying you still have the right to discharge him?

A. He never complained about the consent decree.

Q. You weren't present when Harry Williams first talked to John Hall about getting involved in the 1981 Yehia matter, were you?

A. I don't know what you're talking about.

Q. Well, if Harry Williams says he met John Hall in April of '81 and discussed getting involved with you and McKay and Hall in this matter involving Yehia and Orin Atkins, and you weren't present, you don't know what if any promises Hall made to Williams in that room as inducement to get him to help, do you?

A. If I was not present I don't know anything about it. . . .

Q. Did you tell Harry Williams that if Bill McKay sues the company he'll never get another job?

A. No.

Q. He just made that one up too?

A. I said something similar. I said to extract the kind of settlement he wants out of this company he'll have to sue. . . .

Q. . . . This is a page of Mr. Williams' notes, date he was discharged. It's July 25. Whatever. Do you see where Mr. Williams said he was told over three months ago, which would be about the time—looks like to the day—the date that he blew the whistle. "Three months ago I've been identified by senior management as a source to the investigation and they knew my days were numbered." Did you hear that scuttlebutt during that three months, that his days are numbered?

A. No, sir.

Q. Did you hear the scuttlebutt that he was identified by senior management as the source?

A. No. I heard, I testified earlier there was speculation. But I never heard the scuttlebutt that Harry was the source.

Q. Did you hear John Hall ask Bill McKay to find out if Harry was?

A. No.

Q. You suspected he was, didn't you?

A. I suspected it was Harry or McKay or Dave Williams.

Q. And then it was narrowed down was it not to somebody who had Washington connections, right? You heard that?

A. No, I don't remember that.

Q. You never heard that either?

A. Yeah. I heard people talking about Washington connections but—but the next thing I really heard about it was when Bob McCowan said, "I asked him if he did it and he said no."

Q. Well, you wouldn't expect him to tell you the truth on that, would you?

A. Harry? I guess not.

Q. You expect him, at a time that there's a bruhaha about being an informant, to tell you that he made an anonymous tip to the government? You expect him to do that?

A. I suppose not.

Q. You would, wouldn't you? In other words, if you made an anonymous tip and your boss was upset about it you'd tell him it's me, boss?
A. I think I would leave, or if I made the tip I'd go in and tell him I was going.
Q. You would what?
A. I would either leave the company or if I were going to the government I would go in and tell them I was doing it.
Q. Then you might lose your job as a result?
A. Absolutely.
Q. You'd do that.
A. Yes, sir.
Q. He's got 15 years down there and he's gone to you, the head lawyer, Hall, the chairman of the board, tried to get you to take it in. You don't do it. What other way is there to keep your job and comply with what he thinks is required other than do it anonymously?
A. And I got to remind you, not one violation of anything has occurred as a result of that tip. After all these reviews, no determination has been made of any violation of anything.
Q. You signed a consent decree, didn't you?
A. That's right, but that's not a determination. That's a settlement.
Q. That's a legal way of bailing out without having to be blamed of being guilty, isn't it, you settle it. That's all it is.
A. It's a settlement the government didn't read from.
Q. That's what they did in '75, too, isn't it?

At page 5419 of the transcript, Spears did as I would not have expected. He actually admitted in front of the judge and jury that Williams was fired and it was called a "force reduction." It reads:

(5419)
A. That's right.
Q. It's a nice way of getting out of admitting you're guilty and agree to get on down the road, right? Isn't that what it boils down to?
A. It's exactly what it says it is. No concession was made.
Q. Why did you tell Harry, why did you tell him to stay away from Bill McKay when he came to you about being discharged? Why did you remind him that "I told you, Harry," unless he had been fired, unless he stayed in touch with McKay?
A. Well, I think the situation was that we knew McKay was headed for trouble with his open confrontations with the chairman, deliberate open confrontations with the chairman. And I felt if Harry were involved in those situations he would be, if McKay were terminated he would be terminated.

Q. And—

A. So when this discharge thing came along, it's a termination, we could easily have terminated Harry. I think Bell just decided to do the force reduction at the same time.

Q. That was just a way to do it, right?

A. Exactly.

Q. A way to conceal the real reason. He was being fired, wasn't he?

A. Wasn't a need to conceal anything.

Q. He was being fired; can't you say that?

A. Yes.

Q. All right, thank you. All these years of the litigation you've been saying his job was abolished, now you say he was fired.

A. It was abolished and we never replaced him.

Q. But he was being fired of what he had been doing with McKay.

A. He should have been fired earlier.

Q. That's your opinion, but you're admitting under oath now for the first time ever, aren't you, that he was fired because of what he had done?

A. It's a distinction without a difference.

Q. Okay. How come, you think Mr. McCowan's kind of like a cheerleader type? Is he kind of like a cheerleader type?

A. No, I've never said that to him.

Q. Well no, you haven't said it to him. But is that what you think of him? Kind of a true salesman?

A. Yes, he is. Very much so.

Q. Here's Harry Williams, 15 years, given four days notice and Mr. McCowan, what's he say here? Did you ever discuss this with anybody? That this being fired is a great opportunity to go out and start a new career. Out of adversity comes opportunity. You think that was the right thing to tell Harry after 15 years and 4 days notice?

A. Can I have a second—

Q. Go get him, kid?

A. In a different way, to tell him the same day that thing I did, get out of the building, get out of town, go find yourself a new course.

Q. How about this in here about when Harry asked him after hearing all these rah-rah, sis-boom-bah things, he says chum, I'm not at liberty to say. What he means here, is it not, not at liberty is, you're being fired the way you just admitted for the first time in five years. Isn't that right? He wasn't at liberty to say what you finally said; is that right?

A. The force reduction was there, it was do-able, it's right. The man was not replaced. But he could have been fired easily.

Q. And policy is you can't even get a letter?

Meaning a letter of recommendation for a new job.

A. That's right.

Q. Go do your best, Harry, right? I believe you sent him down to a place where he learns how to write resumes, didn't you?

A. Yes, sir.

MR. ROBINSON: And he appreciates it. That's all I have.

In conclusion, the jury found against every defendant but Mr. McGowan. They assessed $750,000 in punitive damages against Mr. Hall, the CEO, and $1,000,000 against Mr. Spears.

III. The Lesson

There are many books and articles written about cross-examination. The one I recall most is *The Art of Cross-Examination* by Francis Wellman. Every trial lawyer should read and reread it.

Cross-examination is much like music. It has its own rhythm and without a rhythm, a flow, it comes across as disjointed and lands flat, like an out-of-key note, to its listener, the judge and jury. The question is, in my opinion, more important than the answer. It is the one chance a lawyer has to do a "Pearl Harbor sneak attack" throughout the proceedings. It is when the lawyer need not allow pretrial discovery or review of documents or exhibits. In cross-examination, the ambush still is a fair attack. Again, like music, the words of the questions, the phrases used, much like lyrics to songs, the way a singer like Frank Sinatra or Willie Nelson hangs on phrases is of tremendous significance.

During cross-examination, the lawyer should control the tempo, the movement, the entire courtroom. If the lawyer does not do so, then he or she is failing. The lawyer should know his or her exhibits, how and when the lawyer will use them, and be in such command of the facts that the judge realizes it and gives the lawyer leeway, the jury hangs on the lawyer's every word with respect and anticipation, and the witness recognizes the lawyer's preparedness and thus respects and fears the examiner. It is only through the witness's fear and respect for the examiner that the witness will give you the answers you want. Truth is the first casualty in trials, criminal and civil, and witnesses back down only when cornered and in fear of how they will be perceived by the judge and jury.

There are many unwritten rules for cross-examination, such as "never ask a question to which you do not know the answer." I disagree with that. Since the questions are many times actually more important than the answers, the sequence, speed, and pattern of the questions evolve into the equivalent of a seed, for final argument, planted early in the case which will sprout and grow consistent with your theory of the case, a theory first mentioned in the opening statement.

My examples of the Ashland Oil cross-examinations should be reread. Each cross carefully tracked my theory of the case which was that certain Ashland officials, including the CEO, paid millions of dollars in bribes through a phoney chrome mine deal in order that the recipients of the bribes, high-level Omani government officials, would and did use their influence to procure favorable crude oil contracts for Ashland. The pay-offs violated a federal court and Securities and Exchange Commission consent decree and the Foreign Corrupt Practices Act. After the plaintiffs discovered the illegalities, they sought Ashland's upper managment's disclosure to the United States government. Rather than disclose, Ashland hired a powerful law firm to do a "white wash" cover-up which reported to the Board of Directors of Ashland Oil, Inc. that there were no criminal acts committed, thus killing the need to disclose. Thereafter, the plaintiffs were fired in retaliation because Williams "blew the whistle." All evidence followed this single theme. Cross-examination brought about admissions of key elements for liability, i.e., the men who were paid millions "appeared" to be government officials, the chrome pay-off "appeared" to be *linked* to getting crude oil (a bribe), and for damages, as Williams was fired and not laid off for a "job force reduction." There was a flow, a pattern in the cross-examination. Both witnesses were smarter than I, but neither was a trial lawyer and each was arrogant. I used my trial skills and knowledge of the jury to play on the witnesses' arrogance and gradually drew admissions fatal to Ashland's case.[4]

These same principles apply in all cases, civil or criminal. Be prepared, totally prepared; be confident, but not cocky; be humorous, but not flippant; know the rules of evidence and procedure and stay on track with your theme. Cross-examination, in my opinion, is the skill least possessed and the most absent in people who call themselves trial lawyers. I suggest that one read books like this one, watch actual cross-examinations, and practice cross-examinations with others and yourself until you have the confidence and the ability to do it right.

---

[4] Messrs. Tachau and McCall did likewise to witnesses Hall and Atkins respectively.

Impeaching the Professional Informant*

The following transcript is taken from a murder trial that took place in Rochester, New York. My client was accused of being the gunman in an armed robbery of a local tavern. He was charged with three other individuals with robbery in the first degree and two counts of murder in the second degree.

The incident took place at a tavern which was in the neighborhood of a local factory. It was the practice of the tavern to have large amounts of cash on hand so that the factory workers could cash their checks on payday. The bar was filled with a number of patrons who were cashing their paychecks when four individuals wearing ski masks entered the premises. At least two of the individuals were armed with shotguns and the proprietor was instructed to go in the back room and open the safe to remove the cash on hand for the paychecks.

One of the individuals accompanied the owner to the safe area. The owner had difficulty in opening the safe and refused to cooperate with the individuals. There was a scuffle between the owner and one of the individuals, and an individual alleged to be my client shot the owner. One of the other patrons rushed to the aid of the owner and was shot by the same individual. The individuals then fled the scene. My client was arrested based upon information provided to the local police by an exgirlfriend that led to the police obtaining and developing a great deal of physical evidence that linked my client to the commission of the crime. This included, among other things, the murder weapon, which was found to carry his fingerprints. There was also a firearms report that connected the spent shells at the scene to that weapon. There were however, no eyewitnesses to the incident. Despite the testimony of the exgirlfriend that implicated my client, and the physical evidence as aforementioned, the District Attorney called the witness whose transcript is included.

This individual was an inmate at the local jail. His cell was in proximity with that of my client. He was put on the witness stand by the District Attorney for the purpose of offering a so-called jailhouse confession of my client. Needless to say, this evidence, if believed by the jury, would be devastating. It was essential to convince the jury that this witness was unworthy of belief. One of the things that you will be unable to discern from the transcript is the manner in which this or any other witness testifies. The transcript of necessity does not pick up inflection and tone of voice, nor does it show the attitude of the witness or the cross-examiner. This individual was obviously cunning and street-wise. He projected an arrogant attitude. It was the basic theme of this cross-examination that his credibility be subjected to a full-scale attack on many levels.

The most important factor was establishing that the witness had a motive to lie. Quite simply, in return for his testimony in this case and in an unrelated case, he would receive favorable consideration in the disposition of criminal

---

* By Karl F. Salzer, member of the Monroe County, New York State, and American Bar Associations, and of The Association of Trial Lawyers of America. Past president of the Criminal Defense League, Inc.

charges and the sentence. As a sidelight to this, it was an important fact that in the past he had made similar arrangements to extricate himself from trouble. Both of these factors would raise a question as to the veracity of the witness in the eyes of the jury.

A third factor was establishing that the witness had an opportunity to review the police reports that my client had in his possession. It was our theory that the witness obtained all of the information necessary to fabricate his testimony from the police reports. He was able to determine from the depositions and reports enough facts to be able to come up with a story that my client supposedly gave to him that bore a resemblance to the actual occurrence of the crime as indicated by the people in the bar. In the cross-examination, not only did he admit to looking at the reports, but he also went so far as to admit on the stand that he could not differentiate between what he had read and what my client had supposedly told him. Establishing the motive and opportunity was the cornerstone of this impeachment. This information was developed through the normal discovery means as well as the use of an investigator who obtained certain information relating to the prior arrangements of the witness and the prosecution. With regard to the opportunity to lie, I was fairly confident that the witness would admit that he had reviewed the police reports, but was astounded when he admitted that some of his testimony as to the details of the murder came from the police reports and not my client. I had hoped to be able to make that implication to the jury, and he went beyond my expectations with that admission.

The third area of impeachment was the individual's criminal record. The District Attorney who is presenting a witness with a criminal record will bring out on his or her direct examination the fact that the person has a criminal record. This case was no exception. In anticipation of this, I subpoenaed not only his criminal record, but also the documents, depositions, and reports of each incident to amplify the charges.

There is no more dramatic illustration of that than the beginning of the cross-examination. At one time, this witness was charged with criminal impersonation. Since this was an offense which directly related to the witness's veracity, the more details of his actions that could be brought out on cross-examination, the more would his willingness to lie for his own benefit be illustrated. When the subpoenaed records were examined, I decided to begin my cross-examination with the criminal impersonation incident. The witness made up a phony name and told a young lady that he was a proprietor of a production company and that he was going to give her a job. He convinced her that part of the employment would involve her taking off her clothes; thereafter, he fondled her. This provided a dramatic beginning to the cross-examination and, because the incident was so disgusting, would render the remainder of his testimony unworthy of belief. It was necessary to make it apparent to the jury that this individual would place his own self-interest above anything else.

Later on in the cross-examination, we delved, at length, into the other portions of his criminal record. Normally, an individual in such a circumstance will readily admit all of the details of these incidents. However, with respect to the burglary, which led to his making a deal with the District Attorney, the witness surprisingly was reticent to make any admissions as to his complicity. This led to some rather sarcastic questions about his unwillingness to admit to being involved in the burglary when it was obvious that he was an integral part of a break-in. He was in possession of stolen property from the burglary and was actually driving the car. But, his failure to admit to his participation made him an even bigger liar.

The witness maintained that he had won the confidence of my client. This was his reason for my client making this confession. The witness admitted that he lied to my client about helping him with the case to gain that confidence. He also admitted lying on other occasions for the same purpose. It is rare that any witness admits to lying.

The approach used in the cross-examination of this witness could only be undertaken with an unsavory character such as this witness. His attitude and criminal record seemed to lend themselves to this approach. Since he was cold and calculating, it was necessary to change the topic of discussion from time to time. Sarcasm was injected throughout most of the questioning to further illustrate his lack of credibility. Although he provided several surprises as above illustrated, the whole key to this examination was in the preparation. By obtaining all of the documents relating to his prior criminal record, I was able to bring forth more detail than by simply asking him if he was convicted of a certain crime on a certain date. By the use of the discovery and investigator, I was able to establish his opportunity to lie. The easiest of all of the elements to establish was the motive to lie. However, again through preparation, I was able to establish that he had in the past made similar arrangements with the prosecution for his testimony. After obtaining all of the information, it was necessary to put that information in the proper order to try to both open and finish the cross-examination effectively and dramatically. I also tried to avoid as much as possible the details of the so-called confession. It would have been foolish to reiterate the damaging part of his testimony. There are a couple of references to that testimony and those are included only because they contradicted the other eyewitnesses. The purpose was to switch the focus from the substance of his testimony to his credibility. Preparation and strategy are the two most important elements in any cross-examination. The implementation of both allowed an effective impeachment.

Names in this transcript have been changed.

RICHARD SMITH called herein as a witness on behalf of the People of the State of New York, having first been duly sworn, was examined and testified as follows.

DIRECT EXAMINATION

BY MR. RELIN:

Q. Mr. Smith, do you have a prior criminal record?

A. Yes, I do.

Q. And were you convicted of assault in 1970?

A. Yes, I was.

Q. Were you convicted of burglary and bail jumping also in 1983?
A. Yes, I was.
Q. And relating to the assault conviction, did you serve a period of time on that conviction?
A. Yes, I did.
Q. How long was that?
A. I am not sure. I think twenty some odd months.
Q. And relating to the Burglary Third conviction and the bail jumping conviction, did you serve time as a result of those convictions?
A. Yes, twenty some odd months.
Q. Were you also convicted of disorderly conduct in 1984?
A. Yes, I was.
Q. And did you serve time as a result of that conviction?
A. No, I didn't.
Q. Relating to interstate transportation of stolen property in 1982, do you recall being convicted for that offense?
A. I was convicted, yes.
Q. Did you serve time as a result of that?
A. Yes, I did.
Q. How long would that be?
A. It was, all the State and the federal was running together so it was twenty some odd months total for both of them.
Q. Were you also convicted of Criminal Possession of Stolen Property in the Third Degree on November 29th of 1985?
A. Yes, I was.
Q. And how much time did you receive as a result of that?
A. I think I had gotten time served. I am not sure what the, I may have gotten.
Q. How long had you been in custody at the time that you had pled to the Criminal Possession of Stolen Property in the Third Degree?
A. About ten months.
Q. And it's your recollection that the sentence was time served; in other words, the time that you had served in jail resulted in the sentence?
A. I think it was something like that, yes.
Q. What had you been charged with as a result of that that had taken you to jail?
A. Well, a parole detainer held me in jail. I was charged with possession of stolen property, burglary and grand larceny.
Q. Did there come a time that you had contacted an investigator with the Rochester Police Department?

A. Yes.

Q. And was that for purposes of giving information to the investigator?

A. Yes.

Q. And did that relate to this case and another case?

A. Yes, it did.

Q. And did you in fact have conversations with the investigator and eventually representatives of the Monroe County District Attorney's Office?

A. Eventually I got in contact with the District Attorney's Office, I believe.

Q. Now, Mr. Smith, in return for your testimony in both this case and in another case was there an agreement reached that you would plead guilty to Criminal Possession of Stolen Property in the Third Degree?

A. Yes.

MR. SALZER: Object to the form.

THE COURT: Sustained as leading.

Q. What was the agreement that was made between yourself and a representative of the District Attorney's Office and your attorney concerning your pending charges, the burglary charges and criminal possession of stolen property charges?

A. Well, my case was actually beat in a suppression hearing but I had time—

MR. SALZER: Objection, that is not responsive.

THE COURT: Sustained. Strike the answer.

Q. Just tell us briefly what the agreement was, what your understanding of the agreement was between yourself, your attorney and the Monroe County District Attorney's Office.

A. That I would be released from jail. I still owed parole time in turn for my testimony at this case.

Q. And also in another case?

A. Yes.

Q. And that that release would take place—you had already served ten months by the time that that release had taken place?

A. That's correct.

MR. SALZER: Object to the form.

THE COURT: Sustained. Strike the answer.

Q. Mr. Smith, when did you go into jail, the Monroe County Jail, as a result of that offense, the burglary offense and the parole detainer?

A. March 3rd.

Q. And that would be in what year?

A. Of '84—'85, I'm sorry.

Q. 1985?

A. Yes.

Q. And where were you in the Monroe County Jail, what location, where were you kept?

A. Third Floor West High.

Q. Did there come a time that you met the defendant, Jesse Jones?

A. Yes.

Q. Could you point him out and indicate to us what he is wearing?

A. Yes. That's him there in the gray suit.

MR. RELIN: Let the record reflect that the witness has identified the defendant.

THE COURT: The record will indicate the identification of Mr. Jones.

Q. How long after you went into the jail did you meet Mr. Jones?

A. I think I had met him the first day.

Q. And where was he staying at that time?

A. Same gallery, Three West High.

Q. And could you indicate to use how many galleries there on the third floor of the jail?

A. Well, there is four different sections of the jail on the third floor.

Q. Four different sections?

A. Right.

Q. And the one that you referred to, West High, is a specific section?

A. Right.

Q. How many people are kept at that particular location, how many different inmates of the jail?

A. Thirteen.

Q. And how many cells are there for the people?

A. Thirteen cells.

Q. And what other areas are there within the jail where inmates would go out if they were outside their cells?

A. There is tables. That's where they would probably go, if anywhere.

Q. Tables?

A. Yes.

Q. What type of tables are those?

A. Tables that you sit at and eat at, whatever; four different tables, I believe.

Q. How long a period of time during the course of the day do you go outside your cell and be at a location such as the tables that you have described?

A. Anytime from seven in the morning to ten at night, so you are able to go out there anytime.

Q. Sir, from seven o'clock in the morning until ten o'clock at night you are free to move around the area of that particular location; is that correct?

A. That's true.

MR. SALZER: Object to the form.

THE COURT: Sustained as leading.

Strike the answer.

Q. What happens at ten o'clock at night?

A. You get locked in for the night.

Q. Now, during the time that you met the defendant, Jesse Jones, did there come a time that you had conversations with the defendant relating to the alleged Rick's Bar incident?

A. Yes, several.

Q. And how long after you got into the jail and you talked, about sometime in March, did you start to have conversations with him concerning that particular incident?

A. Sometime in March or April, the end of March or the beginning of April.

Q. And approximately how long had you been in there by the time these conversations started?

A. Approximately a couple of weeks, maybe two to three weeks.

THE COURT: I think it would help if you would take your hand down so the jury can hear.

Q. Now, during the time that you were in jail—when did you get out of jail, Mr. Smith?

A. November 11th.

Q. Of 1985?

A. 1985.

Q. So you were in from March and through November?

A. Right.

MR. SALZER: Object to the form.

THE COURT: Sustained as leading.

Strike the answer.

Q. How many different conversations? How many different times did you have conversations with the defendant relating to the Rick's Bar incident, if you can approximate to us?

A. Several. I couldn't—I don't even recall.

Q. Well, how many would that be? Give us an approximation. Ten, twenty, thirty?

A. I would say closer to fifty to a hundred times.

Q. Fifty to a hundred times?

A. Yes, and maybe more.

Q. And did you at any time force him to have conversations with you?

A. No.

MR. SALZER: Object to the form.

THE COURT: Sustained. Strike the answer.

Q. Did you do anything in order to provoke those conversations?

MR. SALZER: Object to the form.

A. No.

THE COURT: Sustained. Strike the answer. Mr. Smith, if there is an objection, wait for me to rule on it before you answer.

Q. Mr. Smith, were there conversations that took place relating to the planning of the robbery?

A. Yes, there was.

MR. SALZER: Object to the form.

THE COURT: Sustained, leading. Strike the answer.

Q. Could you tell us what conversations took place relating to that?

A. There were several conversations between Jesse and I about how they had planned this thing for a couple of weeks and what they were going to do.

Q. All right. Could you tell us as specifically as you recall what those conversations were?

A. Well, something about they had first—they were getting ready to plan the robbery and they went out and got some guns from a store on Monroe Avenue that they had robbed and also that Michael R. had robbed it before so they knew the layout of the place pretty well and where the safe was in reference to cash and checks, whatever.

Q. Are you talking about Rick's?

A. Yes.

Q. And were there conversations relating to who the people were who were involved in this?

A. Yes. Ace, which is Adrian J., Michael R., Thurman D., I believe, and Jesse Jones.

Q. And what other conversations do you recall relating to that aspect of the incident at Rick's?

A. Just how it went down. They went in to rob it and of course they were waiting outside, waiting for Rick to pull us; that they went inside at that point, Ace and Michael R. and Jesse, and they went inside and Michael R. went in the back room with Rick. Rick wouldn't open up the safe. He came out. There was a couple of shots fired, and that

Jesse had shot Rick. As Rick fell another fellow got off the bar and he had shot him also and that they couldn't be recognized because they had—he had a long green coat on, a mask and gloves.

Q. Did he make any indication to you as to how the transportation was obtained?

A. They had stole the car.

Q. And did he indicate to you where it was from, where it had been stolen from?

A. No, but I think he said he had parked it near a McDonald's or that he had got it from near a McDonald's. I think—that's right, they did get it from McDonald's, I believe.

Q. Did he indicate to you as to how many people were armed when they went into the premises at Rick's?

A. I believe there was just two of them armed.

Q. And who was that?

A. Michael R. and Jesse.

Q. And did Mr. Jones indicate to you what he was armed with?

A. A sawed off shotgun.

Q. And what about Mr. R., what was he armed with?

A. I think it was a .22 pistol.

Q. Did Mr. Jones indicate to you what his function was inside Rick's as to what he was supposed to do?

A. He was covering the bar.

MR. SALZER: Object to the form.

THE COURT: Sustained as leading.

I will strike the answer.

Q. What was Mr. Jones doing at the time this took place, if anything?

A. Mr. Jones was standing on a platform covering the bar.

Q. Did he indicate to you how many shots were fired during the course of this incident?

A. I am not really sure. I think four to five shots were fired.

Q. Mr. Smith, did you also have discussions with Mr. Jones as to what happened after the incident had taken place?

A. Yes. When they had left the bar I think they had an accident when they were leaving the bar and I understand he went over to his girlfriend's house or M., M., whatever the name was, and he had dropped the guns off there. He threw the coat someplace behind a business or a house, someone's house or business, I am not sure.

Q. And do you recall where his girlfriend lived?

A. Clifford Avenue or Clinton. I am not sure. I think it's Clifford.

Q. Did the defendant have conversations with you relating to either Vernessa M. or Anne M.?

A. Yes, he did.

Q. And could you describe to the Court and jury the nature of those conversations?

A. He was worried about them coming and testifying. He was trying to get them to leave Rochester and if he couldn't do that he was trying to arrange to have them bumped off or make sure that they didn't show up here to testify.

Q. Did he at any time approach you for that purpose?

A. Yes, he did.

Q. What did he say to you?

A. He just wanted to know if I could get it arranged.

Q. Get what arranged?

A. Get it arranged to have her not testify, either to get her knocked off or kicked off or whatever his expression was, but he did not want her here to testify. He had indicated once she was going to change her story and I think maybe she did, maybe she made a different testimony to the lawyer or something. At one time he wasn't sure what he wanted to have done with her.

Q. Did he express concern to you about having her testify?

A. Yes, he did.

Q. And did he give you any specific instructions as to what you were to do if you were to get out of jail?

A. Well, I was supposed to have set something up to get rid of her.

Q. Did the defendant give you any description of Rico's car?

A. It was a black car. I am not sure what type.

Q. And was there any description as to anyone entering the bar before this incident took place?

A. Yes. They watched Rick enter the bar.

Q. Did anyone else enter the bar?

A. Yes. I think it was either—I think he told me that Adrian J. went in and checked it out first and then back out to the car and let them know how many was there inside.

Q. And did he indicate to you how he had carried the gun when he entered the bar?

A. It was underneath his coat.

Q. Did he indicate to you as to whether you had indicated I think previously that they had worn stocking masks?

A. Yes.

Q. Did he indicate to you as to whether they had worn gloves as well?

A. They were all wearing gloves and stocking masks.

Q. And the defendant also indicated to you that he had shot both people; is that correct?

MR. SALZER: Object to the form.

THE COURT: Sustained as leading.

MR. RELIN: Your witness.

CROSS-EXAMINATION BY MR. SALZER:

Q. Did you ever go by the name Richard M.?

A. Yes.

Q. Ah, you did. Okay. And, as a matter of fact, at one time you held yourself out as being the proprietor of a Washington Productions, didn't you?

A. I believe so.

Q. And you talked to a young lady about being the head of Washington Productions?

A. That's correct.

Q. Now, this whole thing is not true. You are not Richard M., you are Richard Smith, correct?

A. That's correct.

Q. And you are not employed by Washington Productions?

A. No.

Q. Washington Productions is just something you made up?

A. That's correct.

Q. And this young lady, do you recall her name, by the way?

A. No, I don't.

Q. Do you recall the name Loren H.?

A. No, I don't.

Q. But you have held yourself out as being the owner of Washington Productions?

A. That's correct.

Q. And did you ever talk to a young lady about Washington Productions?

A. I may have, yes.

Q. And in fact you held yourself out to this young lady and told her that you were going to give her a job with Washington Productions, correct?

A. That's correct.

Q. And as a condition of the employment with this non-existent company you told her that she had to take her clothes off, correct?

A. That's correct.

Q. And she did take her clothes off, right?

A. I am not sure.

Q. Oh, you are not sure. You recall everything but you are not sure. I see. You recall telling her this but you don't recall whether or not she took her clothes off?

A. That's correct.

Q. Is that your testimony to these people?

A. That's my testimony to these people.

Q. Well, after you don't recall her taking her clothes off do you remember what happened after that, Mr. Smith?

A. No, I don't.

Q. Oh, you don't. You don't recall you fondling her?

A. No, I do not.

Q. And you don't recall telling her that that was part of the condition of employment?

A. No. I was under the influence of alcohol quite heavily at that time.

Q. Oh, I see, I see. So it was the alcohol that made you do this, is that what I get from yor testimony?

A. That's what you get from my testimony.

Q. Incidentally, your lawyer is here in the courtroom with you?

A. Yes, he is.

Q. Richard Goldberg?

A. Yes.

Q. When and where did this incident take place with this young lady?

A. I am not sure.

Q. And you received an adjournment in contemplation of dismissal for those charges, didn't you?

A. Yes, sir.

Q. And you were originally charged with criminal impersonation, weren't you?

A. That's correct.

Q. So you did then make up this identity and you did make up this phony corporation?

A. That's correct.

Q. Okay. Now, have you ever seen a diagram of the inside of Rick's Bar, Mr. Smith?

A. No, I haven't.

Q. Incidentally, you have talked to the District Attorney about your testimony here, haven't you?

A. Yes, I did.

Q. How many times?

A. Two or three times.

Q. Were you subpoenaed to come here to testify today?

A. Yes, I was.

Q. And when did you receive the subpoena?

A. Friday.

Q. Okay. You were supposed to be here Thursday, right?

A. That's correct.

Q. And you didn't appear Thursday, right?

A. That's right. I was working.

Q. And then they subpoenaed you Friday to be here this morning?

A. That's correct.

Q. Showing you People's Exhibit 1, which is on the blackboard, you have never seen that diagram?

A. No, I haven't.

Q. Never shown that while you were in the District Attorney's Office?

A. No, I haven't.

Q. All right. Now, if I understand your testimony correctly, you said that Mr. Jones told you that his function when he went in the bar, that what he did was he stayed on some elevated area to watch everything?

A. On some kind of a platform, yes.

Q. And, of course, you don't know on this particular diagram where there is a platform or where there isn't; is that correct?

A. I do not know.

Q. So, what did he tell you, he was on the platform so he could be up and above and see everything?

A. I don't think that was the part of the conversation. We talked about how they couldn't identify him and he stayed back on some type of stage or some type of platform away from everyone.

Q. Now, you go into the jail on the latest charge, the burglary charge, oh, in March; is that correct?

A. March 3rd.

Q. And, as I understand it, it takes you a couple of weeks and then you start having these conversations with Mr. Jones; is that correct?

A. That's correct.

Q. And you obviously need—he trusted you and he took you into his confidence; is that correct?

A. Well, we used to do law work together, yes. He used to use my law books, my forms.

Q. You are only there two weeks, you had never seen him before, correct?

A. That's correct.

Q. Incidentally, did he ever express to you any racial comments, any comments about white people in general?

A. We may have had that conversation but I am not sure.

Q. And he just starts telling you about the incident. Did you ask him about it?

A. We talked about it. We were doing casework, looking for case notes together on different cases, identity and so on and so forth.

Q. What I am getting at is how did it come up in the first instance? He just starts telling you two weeks after you were in there and he has never seen you before?

A. He started telling me bits and pieces of case notes he needed and that's when we got in the conversation about what went on.

Q. When did you go to the police?

A. I'm not sure. September, October.

Q. So it's a good six months anyway before you go to the police, correct?

A. Correct.

Q. And when you went to the police you are looking to make a deal for yourself; is that correct?

A. That's correct.

Q. And your deal with the District Attorney is not only for your testimony here but testimony for a fellow by the name of Paul M.; is that correct?

A. That's correct.

Q. Did you meet Mr. M. before or after Mr. Jones?

A. After.

Q. Now, and so Mr. Jones is already telling you about his case before you meet M.?

A. That's correct.

Q. Did you ever have a confrontation with Mr. Jones about Mr. M.?

A. I don't think so.

Q. Did you ever get in a fight with Mr. Jones in the jail, Mr. Smith?

A. No.

Q. Never?

A. No.

Q. Never got in a fight with him over your bragging that you were going to get Paul M.?

A. No, no.

Q. Incidentally, could Paul M. read or write?

A. No, he couldn't.

Q. And it's a fact, isn't it, that how you got into confidence with Mr. M. is that you used to read the legal papers to him; isn't that correct?

A. That's not correct.

Q. Oh, that's not correct. He just starts telling you also, correct?

A. Me and about thirteen, fourteen other people, that's correct.

Q. Oh, I see. Were you the first?

A. No, I don't think I was.

Q. Now, what time of the day would you have these conversations?

A. All times of the day, anytime from seven in the morning until ten at night.

Q. Anybody else around?

A. Not usually. If you are doing your law work nobody would come over and sit at your table.

Q. So it was always just you and him?

A. Jesse and me, David, a couple of other people.

Q. That's what I am asking you. Who else was there?

A. As far as when him and I were discussing the case, no one.

Q. So just you and him?

A. That's correct.

Q. Probably the same thing with Mr. M., just you and him?

A. That's correct.

Q. Incidentally, did you ever, when you were doing law work with Mr. Jones, did you ever have access to his legal papers?

A. I seen his legal papers, yes.

Q. And he has a whole file of papers, isn't that correct, very thick file?

A. He has quite a few papers, yeah.

Q. And in fact he has copies of all the police reports filed, correct?

A. I don't know what he has got copies of. I have seen some of the police reports, yes.

Q. And you have also seen that he has a copy of testimony of other proceedings; is that correct?

A. I have seen some of his papers but what I see of them I wouldn't remember.

Q. Well, did you ever see any transcripts of any testimony?

A. I seen some testimony papers, some arrest records and whatever.

Q. And you saw, didn't you, in his papers, you saw the papers about the burglary at the gun shop; you saw those?

A. I may have saw those. I am not sure.

Q. And did you see the police reports relative to the car that the police recovered?

A. I am not sure if I did or not.

Q. And did you see the witnesses' supporting depositions, the people that were inside of Rick's Bar?

A. I may have.

Q. And did you see the police reports relative to the search warrant?

A. Yes, I did.

Q. And did you see depositions and papers relative to Vernessa M.?

A. I seen something with her name on it but what it was I couldn't tell you.

Q. And you also saw papers with respect to supporting depositions of Anne M.; is that correct?

A. I am not sure what I seen of hers.

Q. Incidentally, Vernessa M. was Jesse's girlfriend, wasn't she?

A. Yes, I believe she was.

Q. And, according to you, he was going to have her bumped off through you, correct?

A. He is going to try and arrange it, yes.

Q. Did you tell him that you had the ability to do this?

A. I think I did.

Q. Did you have the ability to do that?

A. No.

Q. So that was a lie, correct?

A. Sure.

Q. Did you ever lie to him in order to take him into your confidence?

A. Sure did.

Q. And it was your intention all along to make a deal for yourself; is that correct?

A. That's correct.

Q. That was your deal as you read each and every one of these papers that we talked about that you saw, the legal papers, correct?

A. That's correct. Anything that I could read or get I was going to use for a deal, sure.

Q. Sure, that's right, and you wanted to find out from the legal papers as much as you could about the case; is that correct?

A. That's correct.

Q. Now, do you know an inmate by the name of Raymond S.?

A. I don't think so.

Q. Do you know an inmate by the name of Kenneth G.?

A. Yes.

Q. G. caught you going through Mr. Jones's papers, didn't he?
A. No, he did not.
Q. He didn't?
A. No.
Q. So that's not true?
A. That's not true.
Q. Did you ever go through Mr. Jones's papers when he wasn't around?
A. No.
Q. And in fact I suppose then it's also untrue that you have another confrontation with Mr. Jones wherein he punched you because you were going through his papers?
A. Mr. Jones never punched me.
Q. Didn't you tell—didn't you brag to some of the other inmates that you were going to do whatever it took to get out of jail?
A. I don't believe I ever said that.
Q. Didn't you brag to other inmates and isn't it a fact that you said you would do whatever necessary to get out of jail?
A. I don't think that's true.
Q. Oh, you don't think that's true?
A. I don't think that's true.
Q. Oh, okay, but you are not sure whether you ever said that?
A. I don't think I would ever say anything like that, not being in jail.
Q. Oh, I see, okay, and it's your testimony that you never went through Mr. Jones's papers when he wasn't around?
A. I never went through Mr. Jones's papers when he wasn't around, that's correct.
Q. And you never had a fight with Mr. Jones about that?
A. I never had a fight with Mr. Jones.
Q. And in fact you had a fight with Mr. Jones right in the beginning of your stay there, didn't you, because you were bragging you were going to get Paul M.?
A. No.
Q. And he took exception to that?
A. Paul M. never came up to Three West High until about October, November, so that's not correct at all.
Q. And didn't you tell us you knew an inmate by the name of P. who was staying there?
A. I may have. I was a trustee on the floor, but I—
Q. Oh, you were a trustee?
A. That's correct.

Q. Oh, I see, and you recall having a conversation with P.?
A. I don't recall—I may know him by sight but not by the name.
Q. Do you ever recall telling P. to fabricate a story that Mr. Jones told because you were going to do the same thing?
A. That's not true.
Q. Nah, that didn't happen either. Is that definitely not true or you just think that's not true?
A. That's not true.
Q. As opposed to the other thing where you think it didn't happen, correct?
A. It's not true.
Q. Now, this—well, you say then, okay, back at Rick's, you say that Mr. Jones told you that he was standing up on a platform?
A. That's correct.
Q. Didn't tell you that he was standing down at the middle or the end of the bar, correct, but he was standing up on some platform?
A. I understand he was standing up on some type of platform or stage or something like that.
Q. Did he tell you how high the stage was?
A. No, he did not.
Q. You have no idea how high he was above the others?
A. No, I don't.
Q. And he had a dark green coat on; is that correct?
A. Like an army jacket, I believe it was.
Q. Was it a long coat?
A. Yes, it was.
Q. Go to his knees?
A. I am not actually sure; just a long, dark green coat.
Q. It wasn't a light gray tweed coat?
A. I believe it was a green coat, army jacket.
Q. It wasn't light gray, he never told you that?
A. No, he didn't.
Q. Now, how long did he tell you—how long did they wait before Mr. F., Rick—did you know his name was Mr. F., by the way?
A. Yes.
Q. From reading the papers?
A. That's correct.
Q. How long did these, Mr. Jones tell you that they waited outside before they went in?

A. I don't even know if that ever got into our conversation. I know they waited outside for him to come. Somebody knew what he was driving.

Q. That's what you said on your direct examination?

A. I don't know how long they waited out there. I don't have any idea. I know they waited for him outside the bar. Somebody knew what he was driving, a black car, I believe.

Q. And you have no idea how long they waited?

A. No, I don't.

Q. What time did the incident take place?

A. I don't even have any idea of that.

Q. And you say that there was an accident, according to Mr. Jones, in the car?

A. I don't know if it was according to Mr. Jones or I read that on the papers that he had, but I know that—

Q. Now, how much of your testimony, Mr. Smith, this morning, comes from your knowledge of what you read and how much from what Mr. Jones supposedly told you?

A. I can't remember what I read and how much he told me. There was bits and pieces that we discussed in the matter and that was it.

Q. So you are telling this jury right now that some of your testimony on direct comes from your knowledge of what you read in those papers?

A. That's correct.

Q. But didn't you, in response to Mr. Relin's questions, this was everything that Mr. Jones told you, right?

A. These are things that he had told me and things that I had read.

Q. So tell me now what did you read. Tell the jury now—let's try to separate the two, Mr. Smith. What do you remember from what you read, what part of your testimony is what you read?

A. I don't remember. I remember some of the things that I read and I remember some of the things that he had told me.

Q. Oh, I see, so it's probably impossible for you now at this point in time just to remember what you read and what he told you, right?

A. I cannot remember what is which, no.

Q. It's because it's all just one big mush in your head right now?

A. It was over a period of five and six months that I put this stuff together and wrote it on paper, yes.

Q. And how long—oh, you wrote it on paper?

A. Yes.

Q. Did you turn that over to the District Attorney?

A. Yes.

MR. SALZER: Your Honor, I would like to see those before we go any further.

MR. RELIN: We gave Mr. Salzer a copy of the papers.

MR. SALZER: No, you did not.

THE COURT: Members of the jury—excuse me, gentlemen. Members of the jury, it's near time when we would take our morning recess, so we will take our short recess at this time and I admonish you not to discuss the case and we will call you back in about ten or fifteen minutes.

(The Court recessed at 11:29 a.m.; reconvened at 11:46 a.m.; Defendant present and represented by counsel; Jury present in the jury box.)

THE COURT: Mr. Salzer?

RICHARD SMITH resumes the stand.

CROSS-EXAMINATION BY MR. SALZER: (Resuming)

Q. Now, Mr. Smith, you indicated on your direct examination that Mr. Jones had told you that Michael R. was the fellow that had gone into the back with Mr. F. is that correct?

A. That's correct.

Q. And you also indicated just before we took the break that you had made notes on these conversations; is that correct?

A. Yes, that's—yes, I scratched some things down, wrote some things down, that's correct.

Q. Do you recall if your notes indicated that Ace is the guy that took the owner into the kitchen?

A. It says here that he took him into the kitchen with him, but I have changed a few notes in there, too, as you can see.

(Defendant's Exhibit J, notes, were marked for identification.)

Q. Showing you what's been marked for identification as Exhibit J, this is one of those notes; isn't that correct?

A. Yes.

Q. And these were printed in or written by you?

A. Yes, they were.

Q. And it indicates thereon that Ace went in the kitchen?

A. Ace went in the kitchen right with the owner.

Q. And you now say that that's been changed, correct?

A. I think, according to one of my conversations—

Q. No, it's now changed, correct?

A. It's changed, correct.

Q. And your direct examination indicated that it was Michael R., correct?

A. That's correct.

Q. And you also on your direct examination—correct me if I am wrong—indicated that according to Mr. Jones that Ace didn't have a gun when he went in the place?

A. I believe Michael R. and Jesse were the ones with the gun. I don't really recall any conversation with him having a gun, Ace.

Q. Didn't you say in your direct examination before—you know what direct is and cross, correct?

A. Yes.

Q. When Mr. Relin was asking the questions didn't you say that you made the statement that Mr. Jones told you, or was this something—Mr. Jones told you that Adrian J. didn't have a gun?

A. I don't know what he had and basically I thought he said he either had—maybe he had a knife or he didn't have any type of weapon. It was two or three different conversations about that with him, but I just knew that Michael R. and Jesse had a gun.

Q. So you, this is not something that you read, though, this is something that you definitely recall?

A. Yes.

Q. Oh, I see. Now, you indicated that Mr. Jones said to you that they brought the guns to Vernessa's house right after?

A. After the robbery, yes.

Q. And where did she live?

A. Clifford or Clinton. I am not sure of the address.

Q. Did you ever have written in your notes that it was Chili Avenue?

A. Yes, I did.

Q. And you also had in your notes that it was Chili Avenue that Mr. Jones lived; is that correct?

A. That's correct.

Q. And so the guns, according to Mr. Jones, the guns are brought to Vernessa's house; is that correct?

A. That's correct.

Q. And in your notes it also indicates that they had stocking hats on inside the bar; isn't that correct?

A. Some type of stocking hat or ski mask, yes.

Q. Ski mask?

A. Ski mask or stocking hat, I am not sure, to cover the face.

Q. Well, is it ski mask or stocking?

A. I am not sure which one it was.

Q. You know an Anthony B. who was in the jail?

A. Yes, I do.

Q. Is he a white guy or a black guy?

A. White.

Q. And he was—he had some connection with somebody who was in Rick's at the time of this incident; isn't that correct?

A. He was in Rick's at the time of the incident, he told me.

Q. Anthony B. was in Rick's?

A. That's what he told me, yes.

Q. And did you have a conversation with him relative to what had happened inside of Rick's?

A. I don't think we ever discussed what had happened.

Q. Is Mr. B. another source of your information besides the police reports and aside from talking to Mr. Jones?

A. No, no, he is not.

Q. That's not true either, is it?

A. I never got any information from Mr. B. I don't think we even discussed it. He told me that he was in there and I said, well, that's fine. We dropped the conversation right there.

Q. And that's when—is that one of the things that you just think didn't happen or did that definitely not happen?

A. That definitely didn't happen.

Q. Now, who is the police officer that you contacted with the Rochester Police about making a deal?

A. I don't recall his name. I wrote over to the District Attorney's office, I believe, I think I contacted a—I contacted somebody that was involved in the case, but nobody ever came over. I believe—I think the—

Q. So you don't remember the name of the police officer?

A. No, I do not.

Q. But you eventually have a conversation with the District Attorney, someone from the District Attorney's Office, right?

A. That's correct.

Q. Is that Mr. Garner?

A. Yes, it was.

Q. And your lawyer is present; isn't that correct?

A. That's correct.

Q. And, incidentally, on this deal that you got, you were charged with several felonies, correct?

A. That's correct.

Q. And you pled to a misdemeanor; isn't that correct?

A. That's correct.

Q. And you knew you were facing on the felonies, if you were convicted, three and a half to seven; isn't that correct?

A. The evidence was suppressed in my case, that's correct.

Q. Look it, just answer the question, Mr. Smith. You knew you were going to get that in, didn't you? You wanted to get that in.

A. The evidence was suppressed.

Q. You were going to get that in when he questioned you, right?

A. That's not—I just said it.

Q. Yeah, you just said it even though it wasn't responsive to the question, right, Mr. Smith?

A. I said it.

Q. You said it when he questioned you and it was objected to and sustained, right?

A. I don't recall.

Q. You were going to get that in, though, weren't you?

A. Yes.

Q. But you were facing three and a half to seven, weren't you, Mr. Smith?

A. I was facing, yeah.

Q. You were facing three and a half to seven, right?

A. That's correct.

Q. On a burglary. Did you commit the burglary, by the way?

A. I don't think I am going to answer that.

THE COURT: I direct you to answer, Mr. Smith.

A. I didn't commit a burglary but I did have possession of stolen property.

Q. Oh, how did you come into possession of the stolen property then?

A. It was through another fellow that was with me.

Q. At the time that the burglary was committed?

A. That's correct.

Q. But you didn't commit the burglary?

A. That's correct.

Q. Oh, I see. Tell me how that happened. You were with some guy. Is this the guy that steals the stuff and you didn't?

A. I ended up with two boxes of merchandise from David M. From that point in time we were arrested, we were chased.

Q. But you weren't with him when it was stolen?

A. No. I was with him when it was stolen but I wasn't involved in a burglary.

Q. I see. And did you go with him to this particular place to steal this stuff?

A. I picked him up there, yes.

Q. Was this prearranged or just happened to meet him there?
A. It was arranged.
Q. All right. So, you knew—and you knew M. was going to steal the stuff, right?
A. Yes.
Q. I see. You knew that he was going to steal this stuff and you knew he was going to break in?
A. That's correct.
Q. And your job or your role in that is that you are going to go pick him up with the stolen property, right?
A. That's correct.
Q. Incidentally, was it a house or a business?
A. It was a business.
Q. And what was taken?
A. Cigarettes, money.
Q. How much money?
A. I don't even recall, two hundred and some odd dollars, three hundred and some odd dollars.
Q. What was your cut?
A. Half.
Q. I see. What else is taken besides cigarettes and money?
A. Coffee, other things. I am not sure.
Q. What business?
A. Hank's Place.
Q. Right down here on Main Street, right around the corner?
A. That's correct.
Q. And you knew M. was going in there, right?
A. Yes.
Q. Did you drive him there in the first instance?
A. Yes.
Q. And did you wait around for him to come out?
A. Yes.
Q. Were you in the alley behind the bar or were you right on Main Street?
A. I was in the alley behind the bar, walked around to meet him.
Q. This is at what time of the day or night?
A. Twelve thirty, one o'clock.
Q. And by your definition you are not involved in the burglary?
A. Well, I didn't—you asked me if I was, if I broke into the place, and I—

Q. Were you involved in the burglary, Mr. Smith, yes or no?

A. I was involved in picking the merchandise up.

Q. I see. I see. By the way, since you offered to the jury that the evidence was suppressed in your case, you knew that it was the District Attorney's intention to appeal that ruling?

A. That's correct.

Q. And once the deal is finalized you walk out of the jail, right?

A. That's correct.

Q. And all you have got to do once you walk out of the jail is come in here like you did today and then come—then come when Mr. M. is on trial, correct?

A. That's correct.

Q. Have you testified in that proceeding yet?

A. No, I haven't.

Q. And you are already sentenced, right?

A. Yes.

Q. Now, you say on your direct examination that you were convicted of assault in 1970; is that correct?

A. I believe so, yes.

Q. Well, were you or weren't you?

A. I was convicted of assault but I don't remember the year.

Q. And who did you assault?

A. It was either a police officer or someone else. I am not sure.

Q. You are not sure who you assaulted?

A. I was arrested a couple of times for assault and I beat a couple of charges so I am not sure what I was convicted of that time or who.

Q. I see. Have you ever made any other deals to testify against anybody else?

A. Yes.

Q. When was that?

A. 1983.

Q. And were you an inmate in the Monroe County Jail at that time?

A. Erie County.

Q. Oh, I see. So what were you in the Erie County Jail for in 1983?

A. Burglary and bail jumping.

Q. And was that the same program as this charge? You take somebody in your confidence and then make a deal to help yourself out?

A. Yes.

Q. By the way, you already admitted that you lied to Mr. Jones about this whole thing, correct?

A. Lied to him about what whole thing? The situation about helping him out?

Q. Well, you take him into your confidence, that you lied to him in order to induce him to tell you things, correct?

A. That's true.

Q. And you lied to Mr. M.?

A. That's true.

Q. Did you lie to this guy in 1983 when you were in the Monroe County Jail?

A. Correct.

Q. And that's what you are doing here today; is that correct?

A. Yes.

Q. But you are telling the truth today, aren't you?

A. Yes, I am.

Q. And how many people did you testify against in 1983?

A. I testified against Mark H. It was on a murder trial.

Q. And did that, by part of that agreement did you receive less time than you would have?

A. Yes, I received a one to three.

Q. Now, this burglary in 1983, were you involved in that or is this another one where you just happened to be in the neighborhood?

A. I was involved in a burglary.

Q. Did you go into that building?

A. Went to several buildings.

Q. I see. You were only charged with one burglary?

A. I don't know how many burglaries I was charged with. It was a so many count indictment. I am not sure.

Q. Well, how many buildings did you go into?

A. Ten, twelve.

Q. And it was your intent in going into these ten to twelve buildings to steal things, right?

A. That's correct.

Q. And were these homes or—

A. Homes.

Q. Now, you also say that in 1982 you got some concurrent time on the charge of interstate transportation of stolen property; is that correct?

A. That's correct.

Q. Was that in federal court?

A. Yes, it was.

Q. Was that in this state or some other state?
A. Jacksonville, Florida.
Q. And what did you have in your possession, what kind of stolen property?
A. A hundred fifty thousand dollars worth of ivory.
Q. Worth of what?
A. Ivory, ivory figurines, statues.
Q. Where did you get this ivory?
A. From a house.
Q. In Buffalo or someplace else?
A. No, in Florida.
Q. Oh, I see. So you committed a burglary in Florida, did you?
A. Yes.
Q. I see. How many burglaries in Florida did you commit?
A. I don't know, three, four.
Q. Could have been more maybe?
A. Could have been more.
Q. Three or four, just the number that you remember?
A. Just taking offhand. I was on the run from Buffalo is what it was.
Q. So, if I understand your testimony, you are on the run from the ten to twelve burglaries in Buffalo and you commit three or four more in Florida?
A. That's correct.
Q. And that's when they arrest you?
A. Yes.
Q. And all you get out of it is one to three on the state charge, correct?
A. Correct.
Q. And you got two years on the federal charge, correct?
A. Correct, running together, yes.
Q. What is the legal term for that; do you know?
A. Running concurrent.
Q. Concurrent. And how much time did you actually serve in jail?
A. Twenty-two months.
Q. So you are out on parole when you are not involved in the burglary over in Hank's, right?
A. I was on parole.
Q. You were out of jail on parole at the time that you are not involved in that burglary in Hank's?
A. That's correct.

Q. And, incidentally, you, as part of the deal that's made with the District Attorney's Office on this case, was anything done with the parole board?

A. Yes.

Q. I see. And you then, again, as I say, walk out of jail on November 11th or whatever it was, right?

A. That's correct.

Q. Now, in 1984 you say that you were convicted of disorderly conduct; is that correct?

A. Yes.

Q. And that was a plea down from the charge of aggravated harassment; is that correct?

A. That's correct.

Q. What did you do in that case? What is aggravated harassment; do you know?

A. I was supposed to have callen somebody up and threatened them.

Q. Who was this person that you supposedly called up and threatened?

A. I cannot remember her name.

Q. Oh, it's a her?

A. Yes.

Q. What were you supposed to have threatened her about?

A. I don't know. I was never convicted of the charge because I was not guilty of the charge.

Q. I see. But you pled down, took a plea bargain and plead guilty to disorderly conduct?

A. That's correct.

Q. And of course you didn't do anything disorderly with your conduct, did you?

A. I was given fifteen days in jail, I believe.

Q. You didn't answer my question, Mr. Smith. You didn't do anything disorderly with your conduct either, did you?

A. Yes—no, I—no, I didn't.

Q. So you take fifteen days in jail for something you are not guilty of?

A. I was on parole and if I had been convicted of the other charges I would have been violated so my lawyer worked out an agreement with the District Attorney.

Q. So you did, though, you took fifteen days in jail on something that you didn't do, right?

A. That's correct.

Q. Now, the charges in Buffalo, what did you steal from those places?

A. Sterling, gold, rings, things like that.

Q. Anything you could get your hands on basically?

A. Basically, yes.

Q. Incidentally, you, prior to the time when you were Mr. M. with Washington Productions, did you ever at any time hold yourself out to be someone other than Richard Smith?

A. I have used several different names.

Q. Well, tell the jury some of those names.

A. Richard M., V.

Q. What was the other one?

A. V., T., B. I used several different names especially when I was on the run.

Q. Enlighten me.

A. Richard M., V.

Q. V.?

A. Yes.

Q. What was the other one?

A. P.

Q. All Richard, though?

A. Yes.

Q. Always use Richard?

A. Usually.

Q. What else, P., V. What are some of the other ones?

A. B. I just told you that. M. That's it.

Q. I see. Mr. Smith, in point of fact it's the truth, is it not, that everything that you told this jury about what Mr. Jones said is not the truth; isn't that correct?

A. Everything that I told this jury is the truth.

Q. Everything that you told?

A. Yes.

Q. Everything. And everything is all the same; everything is the truth?

A. Everything I have said here today is true.

Q. That's correct?

A. That's true.

Q. Including about not being involved in the burglary?

A. Including not being involved in the burglary.

Q. And everything?

A. That's correct.

Q. Have you had a chance to think, by the way, over the break about what information that you told the jury was from Mr. Jones that you may have gotten from these papers?

A. I couldn't really split. Some of it I could probably remember. It's been over a six-month period so I couldn't, you know, I am being honest. I don't know what I read and some of the stuff you told me, I know some of the stuff he did tell me.

MR. SALZER: Thanks very much for being honest. I have nothing further.

MR. RELIN: I would ask that the last comment be stricken.

THE COURT: Yes. I will strike the last comment. Anything further, Counsel?

MR. RELIN: Yes.

REDIRECT EXAMINATION BY MR. RELIN:

Q. Mr. Smith, you indicated to the jury that you had conversations with Mr. Jones; that's correct?

A. That's correct.

Q. And the information that you testified to came out as a result of those conversations?

A. Yes.

Q. Now, relating to the information that you saw relating to reports, can you estimate to us what percentage of the information that you talked to us about relating to the conversations were also contained within the reports?

MR. SALZER: Object to the form.

THE COURT: Sustained.

Q. Is there any question that the information that you have given us this morning relating to conversations with the defendant did in fact come from the defendant?

A. It came from the defendant, yes.

Q. Not the reports?

A. Not the reports.

Q. And you don't know how much information you read over relating to those reports?

MR. SALZER: Object to the form.

THE COURT: Sustained.

Q. Did the defendant say anything to you relating to the car that was stolen as to what he had planned on doing with that?

MR. SALZER: Objection. Beyond the scope of cross-examination.

THE COURT: Sustained.

Q. Relating to the search warrant, did the defendant indicate to you anything concerning the search warrant?

A. Yes. He said the judge had messed up and changed a nine or a seven or had the wrong number of the house on there or something on the search warrant.

Q. So he indicated to you that the judge had messed up and there was a wrong number on the search warrant?

A. That's correct.

Q. And relating to the circumstances as to when the defendant was arrested, did he describe those circumstances to you?

A. Yes.

MR. SALZER: Object, beyond the scope of cross-examination.

THE COURT: Sustained.

MR. RELIN: Nothing futhter.

MR. SALZER: I have no further questions.

THE COURT: All right. You may step down, Mr. Smith.

Impeachment with Prior Inconsistent Statement*

Operation Greylord was an investigation in which undercover FBI agents, posing as corrupt lawyers, offered money to various people in order to influence the outcome of misdemeanor and traffic cases in the Circuit Court of Cook County (Chicago). One of these agents was Terry Hake who, wearing a hidden body recorder, offered many functionaries in the court system money to influence judges, and then tried to talk to the judges to ascertain whether or not they received the money.

One judge whom Terry Hake sought to approach and influence was John Laurie, a young associate judge in the Chicago court system. The scenario concerning this operation was that an undercover FBI agent would go into a store and shoplift, hoping to get caught. Once he was caught, the police would book him as a defendant and, because of the rules of the court system, the case would be assigned to a particular courtroom depending on the type of crime. Once booked, he would "hire" his fellow undercover agent, Terry Hake, to represent him as his defense counsel. Hake would then approach sheriffs, bailiffs, policemen, clerks, or other persons in the court system and offer them money to talk to the judge about the case. One such person whom he approached in the case involving Judge John Laurie was Joseph Trunzo, a Chicago police officer. Hake, on tape, gave Trunzo money to give to Laurie in a shoplifting case in which the agent had been caught leaving Marshall Field's department store with some stolen items. When the case came up for trial, Hake went in to see Judge Laurie. The tape recording of that conversation was played in court. Hake testified that he asked Laurie whether he would get an NG (not guilty) if he tried the case. Laurie was alleged to have said, "Sure." This would have been very damaging testimony because it would have meant that the judge was guaranteeing a decision of not guilty before he heard the evidence.

It was our contention that what the judge said was, "Put the case on. We'll see." This would indicate indecision before he heard the evidence which would be a reasonable response from a judge who had not been corrupted. The tape recorder functioned on the day of the conversation, and immediately after that day in court, Hake wrote a report (FBI 302) in which he summarized the conversation between himself and Judge Laurie. This is before he heard the tape or even knew the recorder was functioning properly. In the report he stated that he had asked Judge Laurie if he would get a not guilty, and Judge Laurie had said he would see (consistent with the defense position). A clerk at the FBI drafted a transcript from the tape. That transcript of the taped conversation between Judge Laurie and Hake relates the conversation as follows:

---

* By Patrick A. Tuite. Patrick A. Tuite is a graduate of the University of Illinois Law School, 1961; was an Assistant State's Attorney for Cook County, 1961 to 1969, during which time he was Chief of State's Attorney's Criminal Division. Since January 1, 1969, he has been in the private practice of law. In 1984, he was voted the best criminal defense lawyer in Chicago in a poll taken of lawyers and judges in Chicago. He has been listed in all of the editions of the Best Lawyers in the area of criminal defense.

Hake: Will I get an NG?

Laurie: We'll see.

After that transcript was written up, Hake listened to the tape and compared it to the transcript, wrote another FBI 302, and confirmed that the transcript was an accurate reflection of what was on the tape.

It wasn't until the eve of trial, three years later, that Hake said he listened to the original tape recording and he heard Judge Laurie say, "Sure" in answer to the question as to whether or not he would get a not guilty. This is obviously, as I mentioned earlier, very damaging, but also it was contrary to Hake's earlier report and earlier attestation of his original transcript which contained the words "We'll see."

During the trial of Judge Laurie, in court, the answer of Judge Laurie on the tape on the crucial point was inaudible. We played it hundreds of times in our office before trial, and the Court played it at least ten times outside the presence of the jury; nobody could hear the response made by Judge Laurie. This, therefore, was a very crucial question, and, following, are parts of the transcript of my cross-examination of Terry Hake in order to impeach his change of testimony.

We first tried to show that Hake would lie and cause his "clients" to lie under oath in state court proceedings in order to obtain an acquittal in the contrived cases. Therefore, as he was not reluctant to suborn perjury, we posited that he would be willing to perjure himself on the witness stand in the federal trial. Hake tried to explain his answers that he was not committing perjury because he was working for the government and was not benefiting from the unlawful testimony.

BY MR. TUITE:

Q. Mr. Hake, what do you call someone who doesn't tell the truth?

A. A liar.

Q. What do you call someone who doesn't tell the truth under oath?

A. A perjurer.

Q. As a lawyer, do you know what it is to suborn perjury?

A. Yes I do.

Q. And suborning perjury is to tell somebody to tell a lie under oath, isn't that true?

A. Yes, or to suggest it or something like that.

Q. And during the course of this investigation, on a number of occasions you lied to people, didn't you?

A. During the course of this investigation?

Q. Yes.

A. No, I did not.

Q. Didn't you tell lies to various persons in order to get results that you were hoping to get?

A. I don't perceive them as lies, Mr. Tuite, because I did not do them for my personal benefit. I was doing them in my capacity as an undercover agent for the FBI, a Federal Law Enforcement Officer.

Q. Well, a lie is not the truth, is it?

A. No, it's not the truth.

Q. What you are saying is that you had a reason to lie, isn't that what you are really saying?

A. I'm saying I had no reason to receive a personal benefit from my role as an undercover agent. I had no personal benefit to gain from this. I was enforcing the laws of the United States. This was an undercover operation. I was doing good.

Q. Well, the point is that you were lying to do this so-called good, weren't you?

A. I don't perceive it as a lie. If you want to call it a lie, that's all right. But in my opinion, in my belief, what I did in this operation was not a lie.

Q. Well, when you told somebody to their face, with a straight face, something that wasn't true, don't you consider that a lie?

A. During the course of the Greylord investigation, no, I do not.

Q. Did you call it—do you call it the truth?

A. No, it wasn't the truth. It's just like—an undercover drug agent buying drugs from someone. He's acting in an undercover capacity.

Q. What you are saying is that—

A. He has no criminal intent.

Q. Well, we are not talking about criminal intent, Mr. Hake. We are talking about fact versus fiction. Do you understand the difference between something that's fact and something that's fiction?

A. Yes, I do, Mr. Tuite.

Q. Now, you may have—people may have various reasons to tell untruths and we are not talking about that. What I'm trying to establish is that during this investigation, and particularly in the McClain and Wilson cases, you told lies to various people.

A. I do not perceive them as lies. I don't do it for my personal benefit. I had no criminal intent. I was an undercover agent of the FBI.

Q. Well, do you believe then that you can tell untruths as long as you are doing it for the Government?

A. It's not always right when you do it for the Government. If you intend to deceive someone for personal benefit or something, and you are an agent of the Government, it's not right.

Q. Well, do you think that as you testify now, you are doing it for the Government?

A. I'm doing if for the people of the United States, I believe.

Q. And that's a good in your mind, isn't that right?

A. Yes.

Q. So that if you tell an untruth, in your mind it's not wrong, even here on the witness stand?

A. Here under oath it's wrong, yes, it is.

Q. All right. Well, didn't you have Mr. McClain, for instance, who was really FBI Agent Lane, testify under oath falsely before Judge Laurie?

A. Yes, he did.

Q. And you know that that is perjury?

A. It's not perjury because there was no—perjury requires criminal intent under the Illinois code. There was no criminal intent on my part or on Roy Lane's part to commit perjury in the McClain case.

Q. Well,—was Agent Lane telling the truth when he testified under oath before Judge Laurie, yes or no?

A. No, he was not.

After establishing the facility with which Hake could tell or have others tell untruths, I moved on to his prior inconsistent statements.

A fundamental method of impeachment occurs when a witness has made an unsworn statement inconsistent with his trial testimony. That was done here because Hake had written a report the very day of the conversation with Judge Laurie based on his memory of what Laurie had said to him face to face in the judge's chambers. This was important because it was done without the benefit of listening to the tape and was based on Hake's memory as reported the very same day.

BY MR. TUITE:

Q. You then say to the Judge, after you tell him he had a hundred thirty cash in his pocket, and then you say we will get—"Will I get an NG then?" You testify that Judge Laurie said, "Sure"?

A. Yes.

Q. Right. Did you make a report of that conversation—that day or the next day?

A. I think I made it within—I think it was four days later, on December 21.

Q. Okay. Now, this is 1-4, this is January 4th, when you had that conversation?

A. Oh, yes, I made it—I don't know exactly when I made it. I'm sure it was within a few days of that very day.

Q. Well, let me show you what's—and there would be—when you make the report, as I understand it, it's from memory and not from the tapes?

A. It's from memory, yes.

Q. I show you what's been marked as Defendant's Exhibit Number 15 for identification, and I ask you if that's the report you made, and if it is, tell us—tell the ladies and gentlemen of the FBI the jury the date you made it?

A. I made—it is the report and I made it on January 4, 1982, that very day.

Q. That very day, from your memory of discussing the matter with Judge Laurie, is that right?

A. Yes, yes.

Q. And is there a paragraph in that report about what you said to Judge Laurie, and what did he say—he said to you when you asked him if you could get a not guilty. Is that in there?

A. Yes.

Q. Would you tell—would you read that portion of that report to this jury.

A. It says, "Murphy told Laurie that he did not mind the case being reinstated if he could get a not guilty. Laurie said that he would see."

Q. And when you say Murphy, that was the name you were using for reports, Leo Murphy?

A. That was my code name, yes.

Q. That was your code name. But it was—you asked to get a not guilty and Judge Laurie said he would see, isn't that in your report?

A. Yes it is.

Q. Is there anything in that report, in any fashion whatsoever, that Judge Laurie said sure?

A. Not in that paragraph, no.

Q. Anywhere in the report. Take a look at the whole thing.

A. No. Nothing.

Q. So you weren't trying to lie to your fellow agents of the FBI, were you?

A. No, that's just a recollection of what I thought he said.

Q. Right. And that was what your recollection that day, right?

A. Yes, it was.

Later, Hake reviewed the transcript of the tape which was typed by an FBI typist while listening to the recording. Hake wrote a report which stated that the transcript was accurate. Again, that transcript said that Judge Laurie said, "We'll see" at the point where the judge was asked whether Hake would get a not guilty in a case coming up for trial.

This report impeached Hake's direct testimony that Judge Laurie said, "Sure" when asked if Hake would get an acquittal and impeached his testimony that the tape now had the word "Sure."

BY MR. TUITE:

Q. And, in fact, sometime later you reviewed a transcript of that conversation, didn't you?

A. Yes.

Q. And the transcript that you reviewed said at that point, when you said, "And then will I get a NG," the transcript said, "We'll see," didn't it?

A. Yes.

Q. And didn't you then write a report which I will mark as Defendant's Exhibit 16, that that transcript accurately reflected the conversation?

A. I wrote this report on April 5th, 1982.

Q. After listening—and you listened to the tape, is that right?

A. And compared the duplicate tape to the transcript, to the rough draft transcript, or the—or the transcript.

Q. And that rough draft transcript had the words "We'll see" after your question, "Will I then get a NG," isn't that right?

A. And what my report says is, "On April 5th, 1982, project development specialist Leo Murphy," that was me, "reviewed the entire tape recording of the FBI the conversation between Murphy and Judge John Laurie, which occurred on January 4th, 1982, and compared the recording to a transcript of the FBI the same. The reporting PDS"—that's me, project development specialist—"found the transcript to accurately reflect the pertinent information that is recorded on the tape."

Q. And the transcript reflected the words "We'll see," didn't it?

A. The transcript said "We'll see," yes.

Q. You didn't change it at that time, did you?

A. No, because I heard—I thought I heard "We'll see" on the tape.

Q. Right.

A. I put down what I thought I heard on the tape on the transcript.

Q. And that's because you remember even on January 4th, it was the Judge that said he would see, isn't that right?

A. That's what I remembered him having said, after I spoke to him.

An even stronger method of impeaching from a prior inconsistent statement occurs when the prior statement is under oath. What you then have are two statements under oath that are diametrically opposed. In fact, the federal perjury statute provides that if there are two statements, both under oath and both diametrically opposed, the government need not prove which one is false because obviously one of them is false. 18 USC §1623 (1976). The same is true under Illinois law, Ill Rev Stat ch 38, ¶32-2(b)(1981).

In fact, prior sworn inconsistent statements are not merely impeaching but can be considered by the jury as substantive evidence. Fed R Evid 801(d)(1)(A).

Some months later in the trial of a traffic court clerk who had taken the money from Hake which was then to be passed on to Judge Laurie, Hake was cross-examined by the clerk's lawyer and attested to the fact that Judge Laurie said, "We'll see" and that the transcript of the tape reflected that. My cross regarding that prior sworn testimony went as follows:

Q. And, in fact, you testified in this very building, March 8th of this year, about that conversation didn't you?

A. Yes.

Q. And do you recall at that time being asked these questions, and giving these answers—page 337 and 338 of the Conn (the traffic court clerk) testimony:

"Question: And then on the top of 188 you say, 'And then can I get an NG then.' Do you remember saying that?

Answer: Yes.

Question: And an NG means a not guilty?

Answer: Yes.

Question: And doesn't Judge Laurie say 'We'll see'?

Answer: Yes, he does."

Wasn't that your testimony in this very building just three months ago?

A. Yes, it was.

Q. That was under oath, wasn't it?

A. Yes, it was.

Q. And didn't you go further and admit that that indicated an amount of uncertainty on the part of the FBI the Judge?

A. Yes.

Q. You testified that—

A. I think so.

Q. Wasn't the following question—"And now doesn't that indicate a certain amount of uncertainty, 'We'll see'?"

"Answer: Yes."

A. I remember that, yes.

Q. Do you remember that?

A. Yes.

Q. When you left the courtroom that—when you left those chambers that day, and you went out to try the McClain case, you did not have a feeling of certainty that the Judge would find your client not guilty, did you?

A. I did, because he said sure.

Q. Well, wait a minute. You said—you made the report that day that he said "We'll see"?

A. Yes.
Q. What does "We'll see" mean to you?
A. We'll see?
Q. Yes.
A. It means we'll see, probably.
Q. It doesn't mean anything of certainty, does it?
A. No, it means—well, let's see what happens.
Q. Let's see what happens. Let's see how the testimony comes out, isn't that right? Right?
A. Yes.

It should be noted that based upon the change in Hake's testimony and the impeachment of him, the jury acquitted John Laurie which was, for a long time, the only acquittal in the Operation Greylord cases brought by the federal government in Chicago.

Cross-Examination/Impeachment*

Perry Mason was probably best known during the early 1960s for brilliant cross-examination which inevitably would force the witness to break down and compel him or her to confess his or her guilt. His legend has led to the general belief that every trial lawyer worth his or her salt is a cunning and artful cross-examiner. Consequently, the jury expects nothing less than brilliance. If you don't produce, they are disappointed. This means that they are often disappointed because cross-examination is one of the most difficult aspects of the trial and the one most likely to go wrong. When this happens, the inexperienced attorney suffers humiliation.

A few brilliant cross-examiners are gifted or intuitive. For them, the skill came naturally. Fortunately for the rest of us who are not so gifted, the art of competent cross-examination can be learned. Generally, you will learn experience from the school of mistakes appropriately called "trial and error." However, the following is an approach I have found useful which may assist the lawyer in learning more in fewer trials.

Preparation

Preparation is the key to successful litigation. This is especially true regarding the cross-examination phase of a trial. Modern discovery rules have essentially allowed complete discovery, virtually eliminating the element of surprise during trial. Therefore, Mason's famous method of surprise which occurred about three-quarters of the way into the show would not be possible today.

Discovery is proper when the information sought is not privileged and appears reasonably calculated to lead to discovery of admissible evidence. This is true even when the initial information itself is inadmissible.

If discovery has been properly completed, the case should unfold in front of the jury as you have anticipated. Nothing should be done extemporaneously. Everything that will happen in the courtroom should have been anticipated weeks before the trial. Plan ahead by establishing your goal for each witness to be cross-examined. Waiting until after the witness's direct examination is too late to prepare for the cross. Your arguments should have been formulated for the trial summation before you even get to the courthouse to select a jury. If your case varies by more than 10 per cent from these predictions, you were not prepared.

The first and most important step in preparation is developing a theory of the case. This is the most plausible explanation of "what really happened" that supports your position.

Through the discovery research process, a realistic inventory of the admissible undisputed and disputed evidence will be developed. By integrating the undisputed facts with your version of the disputed facts, a logical and plausible explanation that the jury will follow is created.

---

* By Dianne Jay Weaver, Esq.

Once this process of developing a cohesive position through consistent integration of the disputed with the undisputed facts is developed, the lawyer can determine what must be accomplished at trial to advance the theory and obtain a favorable verdict. Start by reviewing the elements of each cause of action. Next analyze how you will prove each of the required elements through the presentation of witnesses and exhibits. Well in advance of any testimony, it must be determined how each witness will be used at trial to support and illustrate the theory.

After developing your theory of the case, perform the same analysis to determine the probable theory of your opponent. This readies you to prepare the cross-examination of your opponent's anticipated witnesses and allows you to attack your opponent's theory. Establishing the goals for cross-examination of each of your opponent's witnesses should be achieved by analyzing their depositions, demeanor, and any material available on the subject about which they are to testify. The information should be well-annotated, summarized, and indexed so that impeachment is smooth and dramatic. Potential questions are organized into an outline providing a map depicting areas of weaknesses. Know that map thoroughly, because fumbling with depositions destroys the impact of cross-examination.

Cross-Examination of the Expert Witness

Every "expert" has the belief that he or she knows more about his or her particular area of expertise than anyone else in the courtroom. Prove the expert wrong.

Cross-examination of the expert witness requires additional research. A good expert witness often makes or breaks the case. Therefore, an effective cross of the expert is often necessary to break your opponent's theory of the case. This can be accomplished by challenging the expert's qualifications and questioning the adequacy of the expert's investigation, as well as his or her supporting data. Pointing out the expert's pecuniary interests in the case is also frequently an effective cross-examination technique.

However, underlying each of these techniques, the lawyer must become a partial master in the expert's subject area. Furthermore, a mastery of the relationship between the expert testimony and the facts in the case is essential. Neutralize his or her expertise by knowing more about the case, the interrelationship of the case facts with the area of expertise, and the opposing views accepted by the expert's colleagues in this particular area of his or her expertise. The expert's confidence and power will be diminished when it is evident through cross-examination questions that the lawyer refuses to permit the jury to be fooled. This leads to the appearance that the lawyer's knowledge is superior to the expert's regarding the particular subject. The discovery that he or she is not the only expert in the room tends to unsettle the expert. Your knowledge serves to gain the trust and confidence of the jury. Most importantly, it allows you to truly probe and expose the weaknesses in the expert's testimony.

If You Can't Handle the Answer, Don't Ask the Question

Make it short and sweet. Cross-examination is not the time to argue. Limit your exposure to disaster by crossing only to the extent necessary to elicit answers that support the argument you will use in summation. Don't be concerned if you feel that the jury has not followed you. Your logic will appear clairvoyant when this information is used during summation. Once you have obtained the information, sit down. Don't say another word.

The standard maxim regarding cross-examination is: "Never ask a question you don't know the answer to." This is only partially correct in that it must be taken one step further for a truly effective and successful cross-examination. Regardless of the amount of advance preparation, it is always possible that the witness on cross will offer an unexpected answer. Essentially, this will have the same impact as asking a question whose answer is unknown. Thus, it is critical to have contemplated every possible answer that a witness could offer during cross-examination. Be prepared to handle these contingent answers. Handling the answer may be accomplished by further questioning of the witness or may be achieved through questioning of other witnesses to explain or contradict the answer received. If it is determined that one of the possible answers a witness could give cannot be handled, the question should not be asked.

Furthermore, another technique known as "closing doors" can be used. This method of cross-examination is used when the answer to an important question is unknown. You ask seemingly unrelated questions, whose answers appear innocuous but are important in determining in advance the answer to the target question. The avenues of escape are cut off by asking these innocuous questions. Each door is locked until only the door representing the desired answer remains open. Then you can confidently ask the question to receive the "right" answer.

Additionally, if you have a question which is so important that it can be the turning point of a losing case, ask it. You have nothing to lose. Questions can also be asked without knowing the answer when all answers can be characterized as a win-win situation. In other words, this is acceptable where all possible answers can be argued to support your position in closing.

Control and Taking Advantage of the Witness

None of the advanced planning will be rewarding and the goals of cross-examination will not be achieved unless the witness is controlled during cross-examination. Start with control and remain in control. It is much easier than trying to re-establish command once control is lost. Control is established most effectively by taking advantage of the witness during the moments immediately after the direct examination. Even the experienced witness is apprehensive when the opposing counsel is stepping to the podium with cool confidence to commence his or her cross-examination. The witness is at his or her weakest moment; he or she does not know exactly what to expect at the moment. This anxiety must be exploited, keeping the witness off guard so the witness never becomes relaxed or confident during the cross. Of course, the best way to accomplish this is by initially asking a burst of short leading questions at a very crucial point. Additionally, this grabs the jury's attention. Moreover, the principle of primacy will help them remember the information you have obtained. This short staccato method is also effective later during the cross-examination when it is necessary to make the witness cooperate to elicit seemingly innocent admissions, important to the theory of the case. When the witness is nervous, it will be easy, through appropriately polite and deceptively friendly questioning, to give the witness a false sense of security and lower his or her defenses.

Preparation is once again one of the best preventative cures for losing control. Organize the information you wish to elicit in short leading questions designed to obtain brief answers. If the witness is intent on continuing beyond the answer you wish, and control appears to have been lost, simply say, "Stop."

Another method which can be successfully used during cross-examination of a witness who insists on continuing is to interrupt the witness by asking him or her a follow-up question. This serves to regain control without appearing rude to the witness in front of the jury.

Finally, by all means, do not argue with the witness. At that point you are losing ground and the jury may very well side with the witness.

Conclusion

Following this approach is a step towards successful, brilliant cross-examination. Preparation, control, and knowledge are merely the ingredients. Their mixture must be stirred by dedication and hands-on experience. Learning by doing can be painful, but the knowledge gained produces a trial lawyer worth his salt, just like a contemporary Perry.

Part Three
Research Work

Judicial Questionnaire

Judicial Questionnaire

Believing that judges with trial court experience could offer significant insights into the efficacy and impact of the various means of impeaching witnesses, the authors thought that the shared wisdom of the judges might provide a consensus as to the most and least effective means of impeaching witnesses available to the litigating lawyers.

Recognizing that the time available to trial judges to offer comments and observations on cross-examination in general and impeachment in particular is both limited and likely to be interrupted by the press of court business, it was determined that formulating and distributing a questionnaire would be the most unobtrusive way to seek the views and thoughts of trial judges. Realizing that what was to be elicited by the questionnaire was simply the informed opinions of experienced observers of the litigating process, which is susceptible to neither precise nor scientific quantification, it was concluded that the questionnaire should be straightforward and uncomplicated, offering the responding trial judge an opportunity to furnish his or her opinion quite briefly and easily or, if desired, in a more expansive fashion, thus providing the means of establishing and quantifying a consensus on the most and the least efficacious ways to impeach while also offering an opportunity to extrapolate on the views quantified in the questionnaire.

Since, as earlier noted, it was understood that the information and conclusions to be derived from the questionnaire would be neither precise nor scientific, and since it was possible, if not likely, that the pattern expected to be established by the responses could be influenced by the nature of the trials over which the respondents presided and the length of time in judicial service, the questionnaire requested such information. The experience of some trial judges is limited to, or greatly emphasizes, either *criminal* or *civil* matters; it was thought that this distinction might well elicit significantly differing views on the purposes and methods of cross-examination and impeachment.

Similarly considered were possible differences in experiences, and, thus, in opinions concerning impeachment of witnesses, of *state* and *federal* judges. Whether any such differing views were occasioned by the claimed substantial differences in the nature, complexity, and length of cases in state and federal courts, the often apocryphal difference in the quality of jurors, judging, and lawyering, or the sometimes markedly different rules of evidence governing impeachment of witnesses, the preparation, distribution, and collation of the completed questionnaires were purposed to capture and evaluate the anticipated differences between the opinions of the federal trial judges and of the state trial judges, and the patterns expected to be established by the responses.

Thus, underlying the preparation and distribution of the questionnaire were the hope and expectation that the responses of judges with substantial experience presiding over both civil and criminal trials in state and federal courts would offer patterns from which certain conclusions could be drawn as to the purposes and means of cross-examination and the efficacy of different methods of impeachment. For example, in Question 9, in which the responding trial judges were requested to rate the least to the most effective means of impeaching a witness, it was assumed that the answers would establish definite patterns from which lessons could be drawn, and it was hoped that those lessons would be helpful to all litigating lawyers, but, most significantly, to the young or less experienced litigating lawyers.

Questionnaire to Judges

1. How is your actual trial work divided between civil and criminal cases?
   Civil ____% Criminal ____%
2. How many years have you been a judge? ____
3. How many years have you been admitted to the Bar? ____
4. As a practicing attorney, what percentage of your trials were civil? Criminal?
   Civil ____% Criminal ____%
5. What do you view as the main goal of cross-examination?
6. In your opinion, is a good cross-examination totally prepared, totally improvised, or a mixture of both? Answer by marking the scale below.
   Totally Prepared Totally Improvised
   ____
   1 2 3 4 5 6 7 8 9 10
7. In your opinion, what is the difference between a "bad faith question" and one that is a trick question?
8. In the absence of objection, will you permit a question that you suspect may be asked in "bad faith"?
   ____ Yes No ____
9. Do you think that the credibility of a witness is more greatly affected by: [Please use a scale of 1 to 7, "1" being the most important and "7" the least important.]
   ____ Evidence of the witness's inability to perceive what he/she testified to;
   ____ Evidence of the witness's inability to understand what he/she testified to;
   ____ Evidence of the witness's inability to recall the events which he/she testified to;
   ____ Evidence that the witness made a prior statement inconsistent with what he/she testified to;
   ____ Evidence that the witness was convicted of a crime;
   ____ Evidence that the witness was convicted of a crime involving dishonesty;
   ____ Evidence of the witness's bias or prejudice in favor of one of the parties.
10. In impeaching a witness's credibility, a lawyer should:
   ____ be calm, deliberate, and unemotional
   ____ be indignant, tough, emotional

_____ vary the approach:
by being calm and deliberate with a witness who is _______ .
by being indignant, tough, and emotional with a witness who is _______.

11. What advice would you give a young trial lawyer for coping with anxiety during cross-examination?

Date:
Name:
Court:

As earlier noted, if the responses of judges with substantial trial experience offered nothing else to the litigating lawyer, it was expected that their rating of Question 9's seven bases to attack credibility would establish a pattern, evidencing a consensus as to the most effective means of impeaching a witness during cross-examination.

Indeed, since the competency of a witness is determined by the trial judge and requires that the judge be satisfied that the witness observed those events as to which he or she is expected to testify, that he or she recalls those events with sufficient specificity, and that he or she comprehends what he or she will testify to, it was reasonably concluded that deficiencies in a witness's ability to perceive, to understand, and to recall would receive the highest ratings from the responding trial judges, providing a significant lesson to the litigating lawyer and guidance as to the areas requiring preparation and emphasis in impeachment.

Sixty-one per cent (61%) of the state and federal trial judges responded to the somewhat fewer than one hundred questionnaires distributed; unexpectedly, their responses to Question 9 form no pattern whatsoever—a conclusion which may itself be instructive.

Thus, contrary to expectations, while a plurality of the federal judges who responded rated the witness's inability to have perceived what he or she will testify to as the most important factor in impeaching credibility, a bare plurality of state judges indicated that the witness's bias or prejudice was the most significant impeaching material, rating deficiencies in perception as rather less significant than other impeaching factors.

Most litigating lawyers consider the impact on a jury of a witness's prior criminal conviction as perhaps the most devastating piece of evidence for impeachment of credibility, particularly if the conviction is for a crime involving dishonesty. Interestingly, while the responding federal judges deemed the negative impact on credibility of a criminal conviction a bit more significant than their state court counterparts—due, perhaps, to experiences of each with witnesses with criminal records—few responding judges, regardless of jurisdiction, viewed a criminal conviction as a very significant factor in assessing credibility. As well, while a criminal conviction involving dishonesty was a factor a bit more substantial in impeaching credibility, both state and federal judges opined that both a prior inconsistent statement and witness bias or prejudice have greater negative impact on a witness's credibility than a criminal conviction, even one involving dishonesty.

Perhaps the lesson to be derived from the collective experience of the trial judges who responded to the questionnaire is simply that impeachment of witnesses is a very personal matter, dependent as much on the biases, prejudices, experiences, and predilections of the trier of fact as it is on the vulnerability of the particular individual witness and the litigating lawyer's preparation for and ability to mount and complete a successful attack on credibility. If, indeed, this is the lesson concerning impeachment to be extracted from the responses of trial judges to the questionnaire, it may offer guidance in conducting a jury *voir dire* that most litigating lawyers have not considered: Asking questions to elicit from each juror his or her rating of the several means of impeaching credibility, structured for those applicable to the witnesses who will be called in the particular trial.

While the opinions of the responding trial judges on the most efficacious methods for impeaching a witness's credibility offered no pattern or consensus, their views concerning cross-examination in general were patterned and predictable, though sometimes cast in different, if colorfully instructive, responses.

For example, the trial judges' responses to Question 5—the main goal of cross-examination—were rather predictable, save for one who bifurcated his answer in order to be instructive. Before opining as to the proper goals of cross-examination, that judge offered a facetious object lesson in what *not* to do on cross-examination:

> Usual goals are—Ego trip for lawyer; help client lose the case; offend the Judge; waste time; anger the jury; "shake the tree" by bringing out unhelpful facts; repeat and re-emphasize the direct testimony; allow witness to deny bias, motive, etc.; show that snitch witness is real bad and, by the way, whose friend and associate [is he]?

Another judge put it more succinctly: "[A]lthough not a goal—knowing when not to cross-examine and when to stop having begun to do so."

In positive responses to Question 5, virtually all of the responding trial judges either mentioned or expounded on one of four themes as the goals of cross-examination. One of the responding judges summarized these themes as:

(a) Undermining the substance of the witness's testimony;
(b) Undermining the witness's credibility;
(c) Contradicting the witness's testimony;
(d) Introducing evidence in support of the examiner's case if tactfully advantageous to do so through an adversary witness.

Responding to Question 6, an overwhelming majority of the judges agreed that an effective cross-examination requires a mixture of preparation and improvisation. Emphasizing a common problem experienced by some lawyers who carry pretrial preparation of cross-examination to the ultimate, one judge suggested that

> [t]he worst possible cross-examination is a totally prepared and scripted one. The lawyer who writes out all his questions in advance tends to overlook gold mines in responses that he does not hear,

while another noted that

> [n]o one who is not thoroughly prepared can conduct an effective cross-examination. But the cross-examiner must improvise skillfully to accommodate the unexpected turns in the testimony.

Or, as one judge so tersely observed,

> [T]o the extent that it is possible, it should be totally prepared. To the extent that it is necessary, it should be totally improvised.

Thus, as would be expected, experienced trial judges place a high priority on complete pretrial preparation of cross-examination. However, those experienced judges emphasize the ineffectiveness of prepared cross-examination which is not coupled with the ability to devote undivided attentiveness to the witness's answers and the willingness to venture from the prepared to take advantage of opportunities and accommodate the unforeseen.

A common theme ran through the responses to Question 11 by these experienced trial judges: "What advice would you give a young trial lawyer for coping with anxiety during cross-examination?" Virtually all of the judges showed a caring solicitude for the young and inexperienced lawyer and stressed preparation, deliberateness, self-control, and the recognition that even the legendary litigating lawyers sometimes experience anxiety during cross-examination of witnesses. Indeed, one of the responses candidly acknowledged the unspeakable in advising the young, inexperienced trial lawyer to "not be rattled or put off by . . . invalid judicial rulings."

The more felicitously phrased and instructive responses to this most significant question follow:

> Be patient and natural . . . listen to the answers . . . Have a plan . . . and a plan of defense . . . Do not be rattled or put off by interruptions, objections, or invalid judicial rulings. . . . Don't lose your sense of humor; the republic will not founder if you lose the case and if the case was any good it would have been given to your senior partner to try. . . . Know when to stop; it is a commando raid, not an invasion.
>
> Have the last five or ten questions prepared in advance so that no matter what happens you can finish strong.
>
> Prepare work in advance . . . recognize the limitations of cross-examination and do not do too much . . . have the source materials for impeachment clearly designated and at hand . . . the examiner should at all times have his emotions well under control.
>
> Breathing exercises . . . a martini at lunch.
>
> Remember that anxiety is the sign of a good lawyer.

> Recognize that he or she will probably always be anxious. The only way to [learn] to cross-examine effectively is to continue to keep trying it.
>
> Prepare carefully and thoroughly . . . slow down . . . recognize that everyone else gets nervous too—it will pass.
>
> With most people, anxiety, nervousness, tension on cross-examination are to be expected and usually improve performance; they should not be regarded as any handicap or to be eradicated or avoided.
>
> Proceed slowly—don't rush . . . think only about this witness . . . listen to what the witness is saying and how it is being said . . . remember that you are prepared . . . forget about your worries and concentrate on the next question and answer.
>
> Remember that it is the rare case that is won on cross-examination.
>
> Have a "safe" area of cross-examination to fall back on if you should get into trouble.

The responses to the questionnaire by the many state and federal judges with substantial trial experience offered no startling revelations to impart to litigating lawyers and furnished no consensus for guidance to the cross-examiner. Nonetheless, it should be recognized that they should confirm to the courtroom veteran what was long suspected, and provide comfort and courage to the raw and inexperienced litigating lawyer about to venture into the uncharted fields of cross-examination. Indeed, since law is not a science, the responses of these judges should provide lasting impressions for the lawyer interested in litigation and, perhaps, inspiration on that most creative and dangerous art of the cross-examiner—impeachment.

Cases

Federal Rules

Federal Rules of Evidence

Authorities

A

E. Arnolds, W. Carroll, M. Lewis, & M. Seng, Eyewitness Testimony: Strategies and Tactics (Shepard's/McGraw-Hill 1984) **§5.01**

R. Aron, K.T. Duffy, & J.L. Rosner, Cross-Examination of Witnesses: The Litigator's Puzzle (Shepard's/McGraw-Hill 1989) **§§5.09, 7.01, 7.13, 7.14, 7.15, 7.16**

R. Aron, J. Fast, & R. Klein, Trial Communication Skills (Shepard's/McGraw-Hill 1986) **§§3.05, 7.01, 7.04, 7.07, 7.08, 7.09, 7.10, 7.11, 7.12, 7.16**

R. Aron & J. Rosner, How to Prepare Witnesses for Trial (Shepard's/McGraw-Hill 1985) **§§7.01, 7.03, 7.06**

B

S. Baldwin, Master Advocate's Handbook (L.D. Rumsey ed 1986) **§3.03**

R.L. Birdwhistell, Introduction to Kinesics (1952) **§7.04**

W. Blackstone, Commentaries of the Law of England (1899) **§1.04**

C

R.L. Carlson, E.J. Imwinkelried, & E.J. Kionka, Materials for the Study of Evidence: Cases and Materials (2d ed 1986) **§1.05**

H.H. Cohn, The Principles of Jewish Law (Justice Menachem Elon ed 1978) **§§1.01, 1.03**

D

C. Darwin, The Expression of the Emotion in Man and Animals (1872) **§7.04**

E

Ekman, Sorenson, & Frieson, *Pan Cultural Elements in Facial Display of Emotion,* 3 Sci 37 (1970) **§7.04**

F

J. Fast, Body Language (1979) **§7.04**

G

E. Goffman, Behavior in Public Places (1969) **§7.04**

Griffith, *Body Language Politics,* Time, Feb 6, 1984, at 59 **§7.04**

H

E.T. Hall, The Hidden Dimension (1966) **§7.04**

Sir W.S. Holdsworth, A History of English Law (1927) **§1.04**

K

J. Kestler, Questioning Techniques and Tactics (Shepard's/McGraw-Hill 1982) **§5.04**

Kirshenbaum, *Prosecution and Defense in Jewish Criminal Law,* 5 (No 4) Dimension 5 (Summer 1971) **§1.01**

M

A. Mehrabian, Silent Messages (1971) **§7.04**

P

J. Pluckett, A Concise History of the Common Law (5th ed 1956) **§1.04**

S

M.J. Saks & R. Hastie, Social Psychology in Court (1978) **§3.05**

Scheflen, *Human Communications,* 13 Behavioral Sci 13 (1968) **§7.04**

T

Two Acquitted of Child Molestation in Nation's Longest Trial, NY Times, Jan 19, 1990, at Al, Col 2 **§4.03**

W

L. Wellman, The Art of Cross-Examination (4th ed 1979) **§3.04**

3A Wigmore, Evidence in Trials at Common Law (Chadbourn rev ed 1970) **§1.07**

Woocher, *Did Your Eyes Deceive You? Expert Testimony on the Unreliability of Eyewitness Identification,* 29 Stan L Rev 969 (1977) **§3.05**

Index

A

B

C

D

E

F

G

H

I

J

K

L

M

N

O

P

Q

R

S

T

U

V

W